Praise for the First Edition

Looking to go full stack? Getting MEAN will take you there.
—Matt Merkes, MyNeighbor

Fantastic explanations and up-to-date, real-world examples.
—Rambabu Posa, GL Assessment

From novice to experienced developer, all who want to use the MEAN stack will get useful advice here.
—Davide Molin, CodingShack

A ground-up explanation of MEAN stack layers.
—Andrea Tarocchi, Red Hat

Maybe the best coding book I've ever read.
—An Amazon reviewer

Just an awesome first book to learn the MEAN stack.
—An Amazon reviewer

Getting MEAN

WITH MONGO, EXPRESS, ANGULAR, AND NODE

SECOND EDITION

SIMON HOLMES
CLIVE HARBER

MANNING
SHELTER ISLAND

For online information and ordering of this and other Manning books, please visit
www.manning.com. The publisher offers discounts on this book when ordered in quantity.
For more information, please contact

>   Special Sales Department
>   Manning Publications Co.
>   20 Baldwin Road
>   PO Box 761
>   Shelter Island, NY 11964
>   Email: orders@manning.com

Manning Publications Co.
20 Baldwin Road
PO Box 761
Shelter Island, NY 11964

Acquisitions editor:	Brian Sawyer
Development editor:	Kristen Watterson
Technical development editor:	Luis Atencio
Review editor:	Ivan Martinović
Production editor:	Anthony Calcara
Copy editor:	Kathy Simpson
Proofreader:	Katie Tennant
Technical proofreader:	Tony Mullen
Typesetter:	Dottie Marsico
Cover designer:	Marija Tudor

ISBN 9781617294754
Printed in the United States of America

brief contents

contents

vii

preface

Back in 1995, I got my first taste of web development, putting together a few pages of simple HTML for a piece of university coursework. It was a small part of my course, which was a mixture of software engineering and communication studies—an unusual mixture. I learned the fundamentals of software development, database design, and programming. But I also learned about the importance of the audience and end user and how to communicate with them, both verbally and nonverbally.

In 1998, on the communication-studies side of the degree, I was required to write a publication for an organization of my choice. I decided to write a prospectus for the school where my mother was teaching at the time. But I decided to do it as a website. Again, this was all front-end work. Fortunately, I no longer have a copy of it, as I shudder at the thought of the code. We're talking HTML with frames, table layouts, inline styles, and a smattering of basic JavaScript. By today's standards, it was shocking, but back then it was quite futuristic. I was the first person at the university to submit a website as a publication. I even had to tell my instructors how to open it in their browsers from the floppy disk it was submitted on! After it was completed and marked, I sold the website to the school it featured. I figured there was probably a future in this web development thing.

During the following years, I made use of both parts of my degree working as the "web guy" in a London design agency. Because it was a design agency, user experience (before it was called UX) and the front end were crucial. But of course, there has to be a back end to support the front end. As the only web guy, I fulfilled both roles as the classic full-stack developer. There wasn't much separation of concerns in those days. The database was tightly coupled to the back end. Back-end logic, markup, and front-end logic all wove together tightly, largely because the project was thought of as a single thing: the website.

Many of the best practices from this book were borne from the pain of finding out the hard way during these years. Something that might seem harmless, most definitely easier, or sometimes even sensible at the time can come back to bite you later. Don't let this put you off from diving in and having a go. Mistakes are there to be made, and—in this arena, at least—mistakes are a great way of learning. They say that intelligence is learning from your mistakes. This is true, but you'll be a step ahead if you can also learn from others' mistakes.

The web development landscape changed over the years, but I was still heavily involved with creating—or managing the creation of—full websites and applications. I came to appreciate that there's a real art to gluing together applications made from different technologies. It's a skill in itself: knowing the technologies and what they can do is only part of the challenge.

When Node.js came onto my radar, I jumped right in and embraced the idea full on. I had done a lot of context switching between various languages, and the idea of having a single language to focus on and master was extremely compelling. I figured that when used the right way, JavaScript could streamline development by reducing the cost of context switching between languages. Playing with Node, I started to create my own MVC framework before discovering Express. Express solved a lot of the problems and challenges I faced when trying to learn Node and use it to create a website or web application. In many ways, adopting it was a no-brainer.

Naturally, behind pretty much any web application is a database. I didn't want to fall back on my previous go-to option, Microsoft SQL Server, as the cost made it prohibitive to launch small personal projects. Some research led me to the leading open source NoSQL database: MongoDB. It worked natively with JavaScript! I was possibly more excited than I should have been about a database. But MongoDB was different from all the databases I'd used before. My previous experience was with relational databases; MongoDB is a document database, which is something quite different, making the way you approach database design quite different as well. I had to retrain my brain to think in this new way, and eventually, it all made sense.

There was one piece missing. JavaScript in the browser was no longer only about enhancing functionality; it was also about *creating* the functionality and managing the application logic. Of the available options, I was already leaning toward AngularJS. When I heard Valeri Karpov of MongoDB coin the term "MEAN stack," that was it. I knew that here was a next-generation stack.

I knew that the MEAN stack would be powerful. I knew that the MEAN stack would be flexible. I knew that the MEAN stack would capture the imagination of developers. Each of the individual technologies is great, but when you put them all together, you have something exceptional on your hands. This is where *Getting MEAN* comes from. Getting the best out of the MEAN stack is about more than knowing the technologies; it's also about knowing how to get those technologies working together.

This second edition takes things to the next level. Angular moved from JavaScript to TypeScript, a superset of JavaScript that introduces typesafety. We bring the Angular component right up to date in this edition and use advances in JavaScript to make building applications easier and simpler to understand.

acknowledgments

I must start with the people who mean the world to me, who inspire me to push myself, and who ultimately make everything worthwhile. I'm talking about my daughters, Eri and Bel. Everything I do starts and ends with these two little ladies.

Thanks, of course, must go to the Manning team. I know it extends beyond the people I'm about to name, so if you were involved in any way, thank you! Here are the people I've personally dealt with: Right from the beginning, there was Robin de Jongh, who was instrumental in getting the project started and also in shaping the book. And many thanks go to Bert Bates for providing great insight and challenging me to justify my thinking and opinions from an early stage. Those were fun conversations.

Crucial to the momentum and feel of the book were my developmental editors, Toni Arritola and Kristen Watterson, and of course my technical developmental editor, Luis Atencio, and technical proofer, Tony Mullen. I'd also like to extend my thanks to Clive Harber for his important contributions to this book. Thank you all for your sharp eyes, great ideas, and positive feedback.

The next two people really impressed me with their amount of effort and attention to detail. So thank you, Kathy Simpson and Katie Tennant, for the copyediting and proofreading, and for staying on top of everything on increasingly short time frames.

Last but by no means least for the Manning team is Candace Gillhoolley, who kept up the marketing pace on the book, giving me the sales numbers to maintain my motivation.

Manning must also be congratulated for its Manning Early Access Program (MEAP) and associated online discussion forum. The comments, corrections, ideas, and feedback from early readers proved to be invaluable in improving the quality of this book. I don't have the names of everybody who contributed. You know who you are—thank you!

Special thanks for their insights and suggestions go to the following peer reviewers who read the manuscript at various stages of its development: Al Krinker, Alex Saez, Avinash Kumar, Barnaby Norman, Chris Coppenbarger, Deniz Vehbi, Douglas Duncan, Foster Haines, Frank Krul, Giuseppe Caruso, Holger Steinhauer, James Bishop, James McGinn, Jay Ordway, Jon Machtynger, Joseph Tingsanchali, Ken W. Alger, Lorenzo DeLeon, Olivier Ducatteeuw, Richard Michaels, Rick Oller, Rob Green, Rob Ruetsch, and Stefan Trost.

A couple of extra shout-outs to Tamas Piros and Marek Karwowski for putting up with me and my late-night technology discussions. Thanks, guys!

—SIMON HOLMES

Opportunities like this don't come along every day, and when Manning approached me to work on this book, how could I say no? I'd like to thank the team at Manning for giving me this particular title to work on and placing their trust in me to get it finished, especially Kristen, who has been really kind with her feedback.

I'd also like to thank Tony Mullen for stepping in on short notice as technical proofer and saying that things weren't terrible.

Special thanks go to my family for supporting me and putting up with late nights and early mornings to get this book on the shelf.

Finally, for those people who believed that I had some kind of book in me (you know who you are): here's a start. Thanks.

—CLIVE HARBER

about this book

JavaScript has come of age. Building an entire web application from front to back with one language is now possible with JavaScript (even if that JavaScript is TypeScript-flavored). The MEAN stack is comprised of the best-of-breed technologies in this arena. You've got MongoDB for the database, Express for the server-side web-application framework, Angular for the client-side framework, and Node for the server-side platform.

This book introduces these technologies and explains how to get them working well together as a stack. Throughout the book, you'll build a working application, focusing on one technology at a time, seeing how each technology fits into the overall application architecture. Therefore, this is a practical book designed to get you comfortable with all the technologies and using them together.

A common theme running through the book is "best practice." This book is a springboard to building great things with the MEAN stack, so there's a focus on creating good habits, doing things the right way, and planning.

This book doesn't teach HTML, CSS, or basic JavaScript; previous knowledge is assumed. It does include a brief primer on the Twitter Bootstrap CSS framework and an introduction to TypeScript. Also, see appendix D for a good, long discussion on JavaScript theory, best practice, tips, and gotchas; it's worth checking out early.

Roadmap

This book takes you on a journey through 12 chapters, in four parts.

In part 1, chapter 1 takes a look at the benefits of learning full-stack development and explores the components of the MEAN stack. Chapter 2 builds on this knowledge of the components and discusses options for using them together to build things.

xix

In part 2, chapter 3 gets you going with creating and setting up a MEAN project, getting you acquainted with Express. Chapter 4 provides much deeper understanding of Express. You'll build a static version of the application. Chapter 5 takes what you've learned about the application so far and works with MongoDB and Mongoose to design and build the data model you'll need. Chapter 6 covers the benefits and processes of creating a data API. You'll create a REST API by using Express, MongoDB, and Mongoose. Chapter 7 ties this REST API back into the application by consuming it from your static Express application.

In part 3, chapter 8 introduces Angular and TypeScript to the stack. You'll see how to use them to build components for an existing web page, including calling your REST API to get data. Chapter 9 covers the fundamentals of creating a single-page application (SPA) with Angular, showing how to build a modular, scalable, and maintainable application. Chapter 10 builds on the foundations of chapter 9, developing the SPA further by covering some critical concepts and increasing the complexity of the Angular application.

In part 4, chapter 11 touches every part of the MEAN stack as you add an authentication API to the application, enabling users to register and log in. Chapter 12 builds on the API, consuming it in the Angular application, creating registered-user-only functionality, and detailing additional best practices for SPAs.

About the code

All source code in listings or in the text is in a `fixed-width font like this` to separate it from ordinary text. Method and function names, properties, JSON elements, and attributes in the text are presented in this same font.

In some cases, the original source code has been reformatted to fit on the pages. In general, the original code was written with page-width limitations in mind, but sometimes, you may find a slight formatting difference between the code in the book and that provided in the source download. In a few rare cases, when we couldn't reformat long lines without changing their meaning, the book listings contain line-continuation markers (➥).

Code annotations accompany many of the listings, highlighting important concepts. In many cases, numbered bullets link to explanations that follow in the text.

The source code for the application built throughout the book is available to download at www.manning.com/books/getting-mean-with-mongo-express-angular-and-node-second-edition. It's also available on GitHub at https://github.com/clive-harber/gettingMean-2.

There's a separate folder (branch on GitHub) for each stage of the application, typically at the end of a chapter. The folders (or branches) don't include the node modules folder, as is best practice. To run the application in any of the given folders, you need to install the dependencies by using `npm install` in the command line. The book covers this instruction and shows why it's necessary.

liveBook discussion forum

The purchase of *Getting MEAN* includes free access to a private web forum run by Manning Publications, where you can make comments about the book, ask technical questions, and receive help from the author and from other users. To access the forum, go to https://livebook.manning.com/#!/book/getting-mean-with-mongo-express-angular-and-node-second-edition/discussion. You can also learn more about Manning's forums and the rules of conduct at https://livebook.manning.com/#!/discussion.

Manning's commitment to our readers is to provide a venue where a meaningful dialogue between individual readers and between readers and authors can take place. It isn't a commitment to any specific amount of participation on the part of the authors, whose contributions to the forum remain voluntary (and unpaid). We suggest you try asking them some challenging questions lest their interest stray! The forum and the archives of previous discussions will be accessible from the publisher's website as long as the book is in print.

about the authors

SIMON HOLMES is the author of the first edition of *Getting MEAN*. He's been a full-stack developer since 2000, as well as a solutions architect, trainer, team lead, and engineering manager. He also runs a training company, Full Stack Training Ltd. Simon has a wide range of experience from his past, and through his work mentoring and training, he understands where people struggle.

CLIVE HARBER has been programming computers since he was thirteen. He holds a Master's degree in Chemical Engineering from University of Wales, Swansea. Having written code in a number of programming languages and different paradigms over the years for the sports and betting industries, telecommunications, and health care and retail sectors, he's now at a point where he feels he can be useful to the programming community as a whole.

Clive has helped out on a number of other Manning titles as both a reviewer and a technical reviewer, including *Vue.js in Action*, *Testing Vue.js Applications*, *React in Action*, *Elixir in Action*, 2nd ed., *Mesos in Action*, *Usability Matters*, *Testing Microservices with Mountebank*, *Cross-Platform Desktop Applications*, and *Web Components in Action*.

about the cover illustration

The figure on the cover of this book is captioned "Habit of a Lady of Constantinople ca. 1730." The illustration is taken from Thomas Jefferys' *A Collection of the Dresses of Different Nations, Ancient and Modern* (four volumes), London, published between 1757 and 1772. The title page states that these are hand-colored copperplate engravings, heightened with gum arabic. Thomas Jefferys (1719–1771) was called "Geographer to King George III." He was an English cartographer who was the leading map supplier of his day. He engraved and printed maps for government and other official bodies; he also produced a wide range of commercial maps and atlases, especially of North America. His work as a map maker sparked an interest in local dress customs of the lands he surveyed and mapped, which are brilliantly displayed in this collection.

Fascination with faraway lands and travel for pleasure were relatively new phenomena in the late eighteenth century, and collections such as this one were popular, introducing both the tourist and the armchair traveler to the inhabitants of other countries. The diversity of the drawings in Jefferys' volumes speaks vividly of the uniqueness and individuality of the world's nations some 200 years ago. Dress codes have changed since then, and diversity by region and country, so rich at the time, has faded away. Now it's often hard to tell the inhabitants of one continent from another. Perhaps, viewing the situation optimistically, we've traded cultural and visual diversity for more varied personal lives (or more varied and interesting intellectual and technical lives).

At a time when it's hard to tell one computer book from another, Manning celebrates the inventiveness and initiative of the computer business with book covers based on the rich diversity of the regional life of two centuries ago, brought back to life by Jefferys' pictures.

Part 1

Setting the baseline

Full-stack development is rewarding when you get it right. An application has many moving parts, and it's your job to get them working in harmony. The best first steps you can take are understanding the building blocks you have to work with and looking at the ways you can put them together to achieve different results.

These steps are what part 1 is all about. In chapter 1, you'll take a look at the benefits of learning full-stack development in some detail and explore the components of the MEAN stack. Chapter 2 builds on this knowledge of the components and discusses how you can use them together to build things.

By the end of part 1, you'll have a good understanding of possible software and hardware architectures for a MEAN stack application, as well as the plan for the application you'll build throughout the book.

Introducing full-stack development

1

This chapter covers

- Evaluating full-stack development
- Getting to know the MEAN stack components
- Examining what makes the MEAN stack so compelling
- Previewing the application you'll build throughout this book

If you're like us, you're probably impatient to dive into some code and get on with building something. But let's take a moment first to clarify what we mean by *full-stack development* and look at the component parts of the stack to make sure that you understand each one.

When we talk about full-stack development, we're really talking about developing all parts of a website or application. The full stack starts with the database and web server in the back end, contains application logic and control in the middle, and goes all the way through to the user interface at the front end.

3

The MEAN stack is a pure JavaScript stack comprised of four main technologies, with a cast of supporting technologies:

- **M**ongoDB—the database
- **E**xpress—the web framework
- **A**ngular—the front-end framework
- **N**ode.js—the web server

MongoDB has been around since 2007 and is actively maintained by MongoDB, Inc., previously known as 10gen.

Express was first released in 2009 by T. J. Holowaychuk and has become the most popular framework for Node.js. It's open source, with more than 100 contributors, and is actively developed and supported.

Angular is open source and backed by Google. The first version of Angular, known as AngularJS or Angular 1, has been around since 2010. Angular 2, now known simply as Angular, was officially released in 2016 and is continually being developed and extended. The current version is Angular 7.1; Angular 2+ isn't backward-compatible with AngularJS. See the sidebar "Angular versions and release cycles" for a bit more information about the number and release cycles.

Angular versions and release cycles

The change from Angular 1.x to Angular 2 was a big deal in the developer community. It was a long time coming, different, and not backward-compatible. But now Angular is releasing versions much more frequently, aiming for every six months. The current version is Angular 7.1, with further iterations already being heavily worked on.

The frequency of change is nothing to worry about, though; the changes are nowhere near as big as the complete rewrite that happened between 1.x and 2.0. The changes are generally small, incremental changes. There may be some breaking changes between 4 and 5, or 5 and 6, and so on, but these changes are normally small, specific items that are easy to pick up—unlike the change from Angular 1.x to 2.0.

Node.js was created in 2009, and its development and maintenance are currently under the purview of the Node Foundation, of which Joyent (the organization that created Node) is a major member. Node.js uses Google's open source V8 JavaScript engine at its core.

1.1 *Why learn the full stack?*

Indeed, why learn the full stack? It sounds like an awful lot of work! Well, yes, it *is* quite a lot of work, but it's also rewarding, as you get to create fully functioning data-driven websites and applications all by yourself. And with the MEAN stack, the work isn't as hard as you might think.

1.1.1 *A brief history of web development*

Back in the early days of the web, people didn't have high expectations of websites. Not much emphasis was given to presentation; building websites was much more about what was going on behind the scenes. Typically, if you knew something like Perl and could string together a bit of HTML, you were a web developer.

As use of the internet spread, businesses started to take more of an interest in how their online presence portrayed them. In combination with increased browser support for Cascading Style Sheets (CSS) and JavaScript, this interest led to more-complicated front-end implementations. It was no longer a case of being able to string together HTML; you needed to spend time on CSS and JavaScript, making sure that it looked right and worked as expected. And all this needed to work in different browsers, which were much less compliant than they are today.

This is where the distinction between front-end developer and back-end developer came in. Figure 1.1 illustrates this separation over time.

While back-end developers focused on the mechanics behind the scenes, front-end developers focused on building a good user experience. As time went on, higher expectations were made of both camps, encouraging this trend to continue. Developers often had to choose an area of expertise and focus on it.

HELPING DEVELOPERS WITH LIBRARIES AND FRAMEWORKS

During the 2000s, libraries and frameworks started to become popular and prevalent for the most common languages on both the front and back ends. Think Dojo and

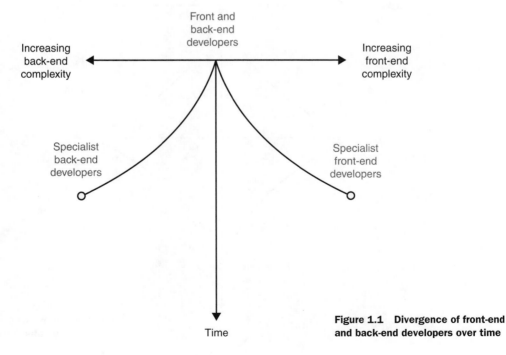

Figure 1.1 Divergence of front-end and back-end developers over time

jQuery for front-end JavaScript; think Symfony for PHP and Ruby on Rails. These frameworks were designed to make life easier for developers, lowering the barriers to entry. A good library or framework abstracts away some of the complexities of development, allowing you to code faster and requiring less in-depth expertise. This trend toward simplification has resulted in a resurgence of full-stack developers who build both the front end and the application logic behind it, as figure 1.2 shows.

Figure 1.2 illustrates a trend rather than proclaims a definitive "all web developers should be full-stack developers" maxim. There have been full-stack developers throughout the entire history of the web, and moving forward, it's most likely that some developers will choose to specialize in either front-end or back-end development. The intention is to show that through the use of frameworks and modern tools, you no longer have to choose one end or the other to be a good web developer.

A huge advantage in embracing the framework approach is that you can be incredibly productive, because you'll have an all-encompassing vision of the application and how it ties together.

MOVING THE APPLICATION CODE FORWARD IN THE STACK

Continuing with the trend toward frameworks, the past few years have seen an increasing effort to move the application logic away from the server and into the front end.

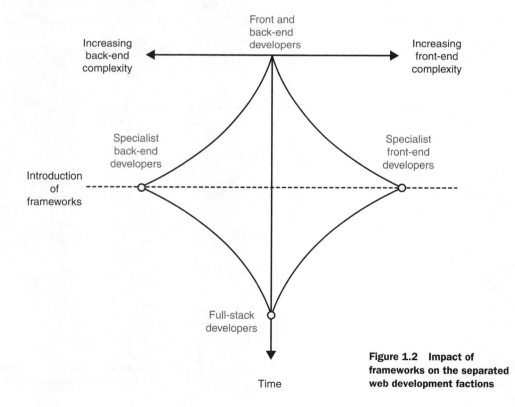

Figure 1.2 Impact of frameworks on the separated web development factions

Think of this as coding the back end in the front end. Some of the most popular JavaScript frameworks doing this are Angular, React, and Vue.js.

Tightly coupling the application code to the front end this way tends to blur the lines between traditional front-end and back-end developers. One of the reasons why people like to use this approach is that it reduces the load on the servers, thus reducing cost. What you're doing in effect is crowdsourcing the computational power required for the application by pushing that load into users' browsers.

We'll discuss the pros and cons of this approach in section 1.5 and explain when it may (or may not) be appropriate to use one of these technologies.

1.1.2 *The trend toward full-stack developing*

As discussed, the paths of front-end and back-end developers are merging; it's entirely possible to be fully proficient in both disciplines. If you're a freelancer, consultant, or part of a small team, being multiskilled is extremely useful, increasing the value that you can provide for your clients. Being able to develop the full scope of a website or application gives you better overall control and can help the parts work seamlessly together, because they haven't been built in isolation by separate teams.

If you work as part of a large team, chances are that you'll need to specialize in (or at least focus on) one area. But it's generally advisable to understand how your component fits with other components, giving you a greater appreciation of the requirements and goals of other teams and the overall project.

In the end, building on the full stack yourself is rewarding. Each part comes with its own challenges and problems to solve, keeping things interesting. The technology and tools available today enhance this experience and empower you to build great web applications relatively quickly and easily.

1.1.3 *Benefits of full-stack development*

There are many benefits to learning full-stack development. For starters, there's the enjoyment of learning new things and playing with new technologies, of course. Then you have the satisfaction of mastering something different and the thrill of being able to build and launch a full database-driven application all by yourself.

The benefits of working in a team include the following:

- You're more likely to have a better view of the bigger picture by understanding the different areas and how they fit together.
- You'll form an appreciation of what other parts of the team are doing and what they need to be successful.
- Like other team members, you can move around more freely.

The additional benefits of working by yourself include

- You can build applications end-to-end by yourself without depending on other people.
- You develop more skills, services, and capabilities to offer customers.

All in all, there's a lot to be said for full-stack development. Most of the accomplished developers we've met have been full-stack developers. Their overall understanding and ability to see the bigger picture is a tremendous bonus.

1.1.4   Why the MEAN stack specifically?

The MEAN stack pulls together some of the "best-of-breed" modern web technologies into a powerful, flexible stack. One great thing about the MEAN stack is that it not only uses JavaScript in the browser, but also uses JavaScript throughout. Using the MEAN stack, you can code the front end and back end in the same language. That being said, it's more common to build the Angular part of the stack in TypeScript. We'll discuss this reasoning in chapter 8.

Figure 1.3 demonstrates the principal technologies of the MEAN stack and shows where each one is commonly used.

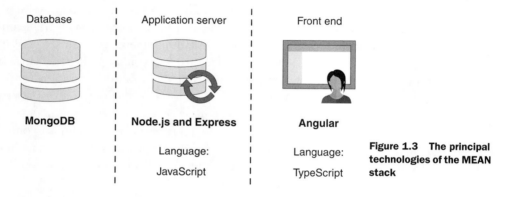

Database	Application server	Front end
MongoDB	**Node.js and Express**	**Angular**
	Language:	Language:
	JavaScript	TypeScript

Figure 1.3   The principal technologies of the MEAN stack

The principal technology allowing full-stack JavaScript to happen is Node.js, bringing JavaScript to the back end.

1.2   Introducing Node.js: The web server/platform

Node.js is the *N* in *MEAN*. Being last doesn't mean that it's the least important: it's the foundation of the stack!

In a nutshell, Node.js is a software platform that allows you to create your own web server and build web applications on top of it. Node.js isn't itself a web server; neither is it a language. It contains a built-in HTTP server library, meaning that you don't need to run a separate web server program such as NGINX, Apache, or Internet Information Services (IIS). This gives you greater control of how your web server works but also increases the complexity of getting it up and running, particularly in a live environment.

With PHP, for example, you can easily find a shared-server web host running Apache and send some files over FTP, and—all being well—your site is running. This works because the web host has already configured Apache for you and others to use. With Node.js, this isn't the case, because you configure the Node.js server when you create your application. Many of the traditional web hosts are behind the curve on

Node.js support, but several new Platform as a Service (PaaS) hosts are springing up to address this need, including Heroku, Nodejitsu, and DigitalOcean. The approach to deploying live sites on these PaaS hosts is different from the old FTP model but easy when you get the hang of it. You'll be deploying a site live to Heroku as you go through the book.

An alternative approach to hosting a Node.js application is doing it yourself on a dedicated server or virtual server from a cloud provider like AWS or Azure, on which you can install anything you need. But production server administration is a topic for another book! And although you could independently swap out any of the other components with an alternative technology, if you take Node.js out, everything that sits on top of it changes.

1.2.1 *JavaScript: The single language through the stack*

One of the main reasons why Node.js is gaining broad popularity is that you code it in a language that most web developers are already familiar with: JavaScript. Until Node was released, if you wanted to be a full-stack developer, you had to be proficient in at least two languages: JavaScript on the front end and something like PHP or Ruby on the back end.

> **Microsoft's foray into server-side JavaScript**
>
> In the late 1990s, Microsoft released Active Server Pages (now known as Classic ASP). ASP could be written in VBScript or JavaScript, but the JavaScript version didn't take off, largely because at the time, a lot of people were familiar with Visual Basic, which VBScript looks like. Many books and online resources were for VBScript, so it snowballed into becoming the standard language for Classic ASP.

With the release of Node.js, you can use what you already know and put it to use on the server. One of the hardest parts of learning a new technology like this is learning the language, but if you already know some JavaScript, you're one step ahead!

There's a learning curve when you're taking on Node.js, even if you're an experienced front-end JavaScript developer. The challenges and obstacles in server-side programming are different from those on the front end, but you'll face those challenges no matter what technology you use. On the front end, you may be concerned about making sure that everything works in a variety of browsers on different devices. On the server, you're more likely to be aware of the flow of the code to ensure that nothing gets held up and that you don't waste system resources.

1.2.2 *Fast, efficient, and scalable*

Another reason for the popularity of Node.js is that, when coded correctly, it's extremely fast and makes efficient use of system resources. These features enable a Node.js application to serve more users on fewer server resources than most of the other mainstream server technologies. Business owners also like the idea of Node.js because it can reduce their running costs, even at large scale.

How does Node.js do this? Node.js is light on system resources because it's single-threaded, whereas traditional web servers are multithreaded. In the following sections, we'll look at what those terms mean, starting with the traditional multithreaded approach.

TRADITIONAL MULTITHREADED WEB SERVER

Most of the current mainstream web servers are multithreaded, including Apache and IIS. What this means is that every new visitor (or session) is given a separate thread and associated amount of RAM, often around 8 MB.

Thinking of a real-world analogy, imagine two people going into a bank wanting to do separate things. In a multithreaded model, they'd each go to a separate bank teller who would deal with their requests, as shown in figure 1.4.

You can see in figure 1.4 that Simon goes to bank teller 1, and Sally goes to bank teller 2. Neither side is aware of or affected by the other. Bank teller 1 deals with Simon, and nobody else, throughout the entirety of the transaction; the same goes for bank teller 2 and Sally.

This approach works perfectly well as long as you have enough tellers to service the customers. When the bank gets busy and the customers outnumber the tellers, the service starts to slow and the customers have to wait to be seen. Although banks don't always worry about this situation too much and seem happy to make you stand in line, the same isn't true of websites. If a website is slow to respond, users are likely to leave and never come back.

This is one of the reasons why web servers are often overpowered and have so much RAM, even though they don't need it 90% of the time. The hardware is set up in such a way as to be prepared for a huge spike in traffic. This setup is like the bank hiring an additional 50 full-time tellers and moving to a bigger building because it gets busy at lunchtime.

Surely there's a better way—a way that's a bit more scalable. Here's where the single-threaded approach comes in.

SINGLE-THREADED WEB SERVER

A Node.js server is single-threaded and works differently from a multithreaded server. Rather than giving each visitor a unique thread and a separate silo of resources, the server has every visitor join the same thread. A visitor and thread interact only when necessary—when the visitor is requesting something or the thread is responding to a request.

Returning to the bank-teller analogy, there'd be only one teller who deals with all the customers. But rather than taking on and managing all requests end to end, the teller delegates any time-consuming tasks to back-office staff and deals with the next request. Figure 1.5 illustrates how this process might work, using the two requests from the multithreaded example.

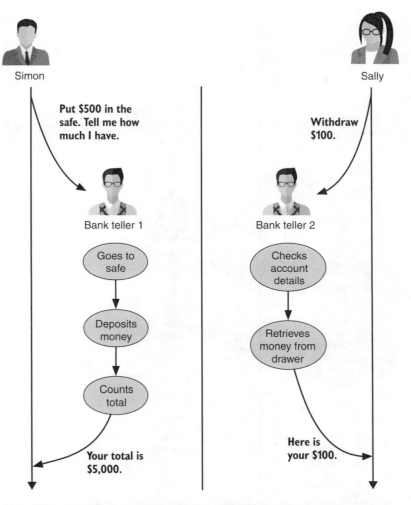

Figure 1.4 Example of a multithreaded approach: Visitors use separate resources. Visitors and their dedicated resources have no awareness of or contact with other visitors and their resources.

In the single-threaded approach shown in figure 1.5, Sally and Simon give their requests to the same bank teller. But instead of dealing with one of them exclusively before the next, the teller takes the first request and passes it to the best person to deal with it before taking the next request and doing the same thing. When the teller is told that a requested task is complete, the teller passes the result back to the visitor who made the request.

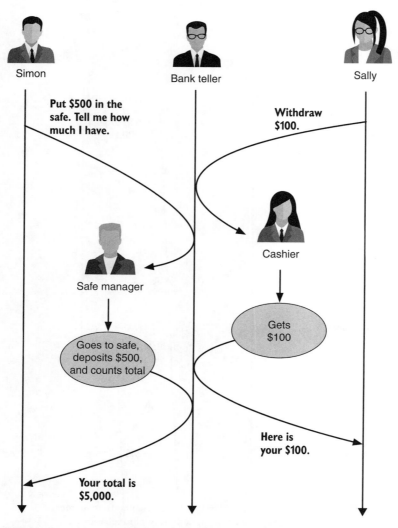

Figure 1.5   Example of a single-threaded approach: Visitors use the same central resource. The central resource must be well disciplined to prevent one visitor from affecting others.

Blocking vs. nonblocking code

With the single-threaded model, it's important to remember that all of your users use the same central process. To keep the flow smooth, you need to make sure that nothing in your code causes a delay, blocking another operation. An example would be if the bank teller has to go to the safe to deposit the money for Simon, in which case Sally would have to wait to make her request.

Similarly, if your central process is responsible for reading each static file (such as CSS, JavaScript, or images), it won't be able to process any other request, thus blocking the flow. Another common task that's potentially blocking is interacting with a database. If your process is going to the database each time it's asked, be it searching for data or saving data, it won't be able to do anything else.

For the single-threaded approach to work, you must make sure that your code is non-blocking. The way to achieve this is to make any blocking operations run asynchronously, preventing them from blocking the flow of your main process.

Despite there being a single teller, neither of the visitors is aware of the other, and neither is affected by the requests of the other. This approach means that the bank doesn't need several tellers always on hand. This model isn't infinitely scalable, of course, but it's more efficient. You can do more with fewer resources. It doesn't mean, however, that you'll never need to add more resources.

This particular approach is possible in Node.js due to the asynchronous capabilities of JavaScript, as you'll see in action throughout the book. But if you're not sure about the theory, check out appendix D (available online or in the e-book), particularly the section on callbacks.

1.2.3 Using prebuilt packages via npm

A package manager, npm, gets installed when you install Node.js. npm gives you the ability to download Node.js modules or *packages* to extend the functionality of your application. Currently, more than 350,000 packages are available through npm, an indication of how much depth of knowledge and experience you can bring to an application. This figure is up from 46,000, when the first edition of *Getting MEAN* was written four years ago!

Packages in npm vary widely in what they give you. You'll use some npm packages throughout this book to bring in an application framework and a database driver with schema support. Other examples include helper libraries such as Underscore, testing frameworks like Mocha, and utilities like Colors, which adds color support to Node.js console logs. You'll look more closely at npm and how it works when you start building an application in chapter 3.

As you've seen, Node.js is extremely powerful and flexible, but it doesn't give you much help when you're trying to create a website or application. Express can give you a hand here. You install Express by using npm.

1.3 Introducing Express: The framework

Express is the *E* in *MEAN*. Because Node.js is a platform, it doesn't prescribe how it should be set up or used, which is one of its great strengths. But every time you create websites and web applications, quite a few common tasks need doing. Express is a web application framework for Node.js that's designed to perform these tasks in a well-tested, repeatable way.

1.3.1   *Easing your server setup*

As already noted, Node.js is a platform, not a server, which allows you to get creative with your server setup and do things that you can't do with other web servers. It also makes getting a basic website up and running harder.

Express abstracts away this difficulty by setting up a web server to listen to incoming requests and return relevant responses. In addition, it defines a directory structure. One folder is set up to serve static files in a nonblocking way; the last thing you want is for your application to have to wait when someone requests a CSS file! You could configure this yourself directly in Node.js, but Express does it for you.

1.3.2   *Routing URLs to responses*

One of the great features of Express is that it provides a simple interface for directing an incoming URL to a certain piece of code. Whether this interface will serve a static HTML page, read from a database, or write to a database doesn't matter. The interface is simple and consistent.

Express abstracts away some of the complexity of creating a web server in native Node.js to make code quicker to write and easier to maintain.

1.3.3   *Views: HTML responses*

It's likely that you'll want to respond to many of the requests to your application by sending some HTML to the browser. By now, it will come as no surprise to you that Express makes this task easier than it is in native Node.js.

Express provides support for many templating engines that make it easier to build HTML pages in an intelligent way, using reusable components as well as data from your application. Express compiles these together and serves them to the browser as HTML.

1.3.4   *Remembering visitors with session support*

Being single-threaded, Node.js doesn't remember a visitor from one request to the next. It doesn't have a silo of RAM set aside for you; it sees only a series of HTTP requests. HTTP is a stateless protocol, so there's no concept of storing a session state. As it stands, it's difficult to create a personalized experience in Node.js or have a secure area where a user has to log in; it's not much use if the site forgets who you are on every page. You can do it, of course, but you have to code it yourself.

You'll never guess what: Express has an answer to this problem too! Express can use *sessions* so that you can identify individual visitors through multiple requests and pages. Thank you, Express!

Sitting on top of Node.js, Express gives you a great helping hand and a sound starting point for building web applications. It abstracts away many complexities and repeatable tasks that most of us don't need—or want—to worry about. We only want to build web applications.

1.4 Introducing MongoDB: The database

The ability to store and use data is vital for most applications. In the MEAN stack, the database of choice is MongoDB, the *M* in *MEAN*. MongoDB fits into the stack incredibly well. Like Node.js, it's renowned for being fast and scalable.

1.4.1 Relational databases vs. document stores

If you've used a relational database before, or even a spreadsheet, you'll be used to the concepts of columns and rows. Typically, a column defines the name and data type, and each row is a different entry. See table 1.1 for an example.

Table 1.1   An example of rows and columns in a relational database table

firstName	middleName	lastName	maidenName	nickname
Simon	David	Holmes		Si
Sally	June	Panayiotou		
Rebecca		Norman	Holmes	Bec

MongoDB is *not* like that! MongoDB is a document store. The concept of rows still exists, but columns are removed from the picture. Rather than a column defining what should be in the row, each row is a document, and this document both defines and holds the data itself. Table 1.2 shows how a collection of documents might be listed. (The indented layout is for readability, not a visualization of columns.)

Table 1.2   Each document in a document database defines and holds the data, in no particular order.

firstName: "Simon"	middleName: "David"	lastName: "Holmes"	nickname: "Si"
lastName: "Panayiotou"	middleName: "June"	firstName: "Sally"	
maidenName: "Holmes"	firstName: "Rebecca"	lastName: "Norman"	nickname: "Bec"

This less-structured approach means that a collection of documents could have a wide variety of data inside. In the next section, you'll look at a sample document to get a better idea of what we're talking about.

1.4.2 MongoDB documents: JavaScript data store

MongoDB stores documents as BSON, which is binary JSON (JavaScript Serialized Object Notation). Don't worry for now if you're not fully familiar with JSON; check out the relevant section in appendix D. In short, JSON is a JavaScript way of holding data, which is why MongoDB fits so well into the JavaScript-centric MEAN stack!

The following code snippet shows a simple example MongoDB document:

```
{
  "firstName" : "Simon",
  "lastName" : "Holmes",
  _id : ObjectId("52279effc62ca8b0c1000007")
}
```

Even if you don't know JSON well, you can probably see that this document stores the first and last names of Simon Holmes. Rather than a document holding a data set that corresponds to a set of columns, a document holds name/value pairs, which makes a document useful in its own right because it both describes and defines the data.

A quick word about _id: You most likely noticed the _id entry alongside the names in the preceding example MongoDB document. The _id entity is a unique identifier that MongoDB assigns to any new document when it's created.

You'll look at MongoDB documents in more detail in chapter 5, when you start to add data to your application.

1.4.3 *More than just a document database*

MongoDB sets itself apart from many other document databases with its support for secondary indexing and rich queries. You can create indexes on more than the unique identifier field, and querying indexed fields is much faster. You can also create some fairly complex queries against a MongoDB database—not to the level of huge SQL commands with joins all over the place, but powerful enough for most use cases.

As you build an application through the course of this book, you'll get to have some fun with MongoDB and start to appreciate exactly what it can do.

1.4.4 *What is MongoDB not good for?*

As of version 4, there's little that a traditional RDBMS can do that MongoDB can't, beyond the obvious differences we've already discussed. One of the biggest issues in earlier versions of MongoDB was lack of transaction support. MongoDB 4, the version used in this book, has the capability to perform multidocument transactions with ACID (atomicity, consistency, isolation, durability) guarantees.

1.4.5 *Mongoose for data modeling and more*

MongoDB's flexibility in what it stores in documents is a great thing for the database. But most applications need some structure to their data. Note that the *application* needs structure, not the database. So where does it make most sense to define the structure of your application data? In the application itself!

To this end, the company behind MongoDB created Mongoose. In the company's words, Mongoose provides "elegant MongoDB object modeling for Node.js" (https://mongoosejs.com).

WHAT IS DATA MODELING?

Data modeling, in the context of Mongoose and MongoDB, defines what data *can* be in a document and what data *must* be in a document. When storing user information, you may want to be able to save the first name, last name, email address, and phone number. But you *need* only the first name and email address, and the email address must be unique. This information is defined in a *schema*, which is used as the basis for the data model.

WHAT ELSE DOES MONGOOSE OFFER?

As well as modeling data, Mongoose adds an entire layer of features on top of MongoDB that are useful for building web applications. Mongoose makes it easier to manage the connections to your MongoDB database and to save and read data. You'll use all of these features later. Also later in the book, we'll discuss how Mongoose enables you to add data validation at the schema level, making sure that you allow only valid data to be saved in the database.

MongoDB is a great choice of database for most web applications, because it provides a balance between the speed of pure document databases and the power of relational databases. The data is effectively stored in JSON, which makes it the perfect data store for the MEAN stack.

Figure 1.6 shows some of the highlights of Mongoose and how it fits between the database and the application.

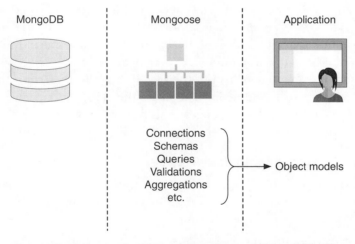

Figure 1.6 Mongoose fits between the database and the application, providing an easy-to-use interface (object models) and access to other functionality, such as validation.

1.5   Introducing Angular: The front-end framework

Angular is the *A* in *MEAN*. In simple terms, Angular is a JavaScript framework for creating the interface for your website or application. In this book, you'll be working with
Angular 7, which is the most recently available version. All previous versions have
been deprecated, and the online documentation no longer applies.

You could use Node.js, Express, and MongoDB to build a fully functioning, data-
driven web application, and you'll do that in this book. But you can put some icing on
the cake by adding Angular to the stack.

The traditional way of doing things is to have all data processing and application
logic on the server, which then passes HTML to the browser. Angular enables you to
move some or all of this processing and logic to the browser, often leaving the server
passing data from the database. We'll take a look at this process in a moment when we
discuss data binding, but first, we need to address the question of whether Angular is
like jQuery, the leading front-end JavaScript library.

1.5.1   jQuery vs. Angular

If you're familiar with jQuery, you may be wondering whether Angular works the same
way. The short answer is no, not really. jQuery is generally added to a page to provide
interactivity after the HTML has been sent to the browser and the Document Object
Model (DOM) has completely loaded. Angular comes in a step earlier, building the
HTML from templates, based on the data provided.

Also, jQuery is a library and as such has a collection of features that you can use as
you wish. Angular is known as an *opinionated framework*, which means that it forces its
opinion on you as to how it needs to be used. It also abstracts away some of the underlying complexity, simplifying the development experience.

As mentioned earlier, Angular helps put the HTML together based on the data
provided, but it does more: it also immediately updates the HTML if the data changes
and can update the data if the HTML changes. This feature is known as *two-way data
binding*, which we'll take a quick look at in the next section.

1.5.2   Two-way data binding: Working with data in a page

To understand two-way data binding, consider a simple example. Compare this
approach with traditional one-way data binding. Imagine that you have a web page
and some data, and you want to do the following:

1   Display that data as a list to the user
2   Allow the user to filter that list by inputting text into a form field

In both approaches—one-way and two-way binding—step 1 is similar. You use the data
to generate some HTML markup for the end user to see. Step 2 is where things get a
bit different.

In step 2, you want to let the user enter some text in a form field to filter the list of
data being displayed. With one-way data binding, you have to add event listeners to

the form input field manually to capture the data and update the data model (to ultimately change what's displayed to the user).

With two-way data binding, any updates to the form can be captured automatically, updating the model and changing what's displayed to the user. This capability may not sound like a big deal, but to understand its power, it's good to know that with Angular, you can achieve everything in steps 1 and 2 without writing a single line of JavaScript code! That's right—it's all done with Angular's two-way data binding ... and a bit of help from some other Angular features.

As you go through part 3 of the book, you'll get to see—and use—this in action. Seeing is believing with this feature, and you won't be disappointed.

1.5.3 *Using Angular to load new pages*

One thing that Angular was specifically designed for is *single-page application* (SPA) functionality. In real terms, an SPA runs everything inside the browser and never does a full page reload. All application logic, data processing, user flow, and template delivery can be managed in the browser.

Think Gmail. That's an SPA. Different views get shown in the page, along with a variety of data sets, but the page itself never fully reloads.

This approach can reduce the amount of resources you need on your server, because you're essentially crowdsourcing the computational power. Each person's browser is doing the hard work; your server is serving up static files and data on request.

The user experience can also be better under this approach. After the application is loaded, fewer calls are made to the server, reducing the potential of latency.

All this sounds great, but surely there's a price to pay. Why isn't everything built into Angular?

1.5.4 *Are there any downsides?*

Despite its many benefits, Angular isn't appropriate for every website. Front-end libraries like jQuery are best used for progressive enhancement. The idea is that your site will function perfectly well without JavaScript, and the JavaScript you use makes the experience better. That isn't the case with Angular or indeed with any other SPA framework. Angular uses JavaScript to build the rendered HTML from templates and data, so if your browser doesn't support JavaScript or there's a bug in the code, the site won't run.

This reliance on JavaScript to build the page also causes problems with search engines. When a search engine crawls your site, it won't run all JavaScript; with Angular, the only thing you get before JavaScript takes over is the base template from the server. If you want to be 100% certain that your content and data are indexed by search engines rather than only your templates, you need to think about whether Angular is right for that project.

You have ways to combat this issue: in short, you need your server to output compiled content as well as Angular. But, if you don't *need* to fight this battle, we recommend against doing so.

One thing you can do is use Angular for some things and not others. There's nothing wrong with using Angular selectively in your project. You might have a data-rich interactive application or section of your site that's ideal for building in Angular, for example. Or you might have a blog or some marketing pages around your application. These elements don't need to be built in Angular and arguably would be better served from the server in the traditional way. So part of your site is served by Node.js, Express, and MongoDB, and another part also has Angular doing its thing.

This flexible approach is one of the most powerful aspects of the MEAN stack. With one stack, you can achieve a great many things so long as you remember to be flexible in your thinking and don't think of the MEAN stack as being a single architecture stack.

Things are improving, though. Web-crawling technologies, particularly those employed by Google, are becoming ever more capable, and this issue is quickly becoming part of the past.

1.5.5   Developing in TypeScript

Angular applications can be written in many flavors of JavaScript, including ES5, ES2015+, and Dart. But the most popular by far is TypeScript.

TypeScript is a superset of JavaScript, meaning that it *is* JavaScript, but with added features. In this book, you'll use TypeScript to build the Angular part of your application. But don't worry: we'll start from the ground up in part 3 and cover the parts of TypeScript you need to know.

1.6   Supporting cast

The MEAN stack gives you everything you need to create data-rich interactive web applications, but you may want to use a few extra technologies to help you along the way. You can use Twitter Bootstrap to create a good user interface, Git to help manage your code, and Heroku to help by hosting the application on a live URL, for example. In later chapters, we'll look at incorporating these technologies into the MEAN stack. In this section, we'll cover briefly what each one can do for you.

1.6.1   Twitter Bootstrap for user interface

In this book, you're going to use Twitter Bootstrap to create a responsive design with minimal effort. It's not essential for the stack, and if you're building an application from existing HTML or a specific design, you probably won't want to add it. But in this book, you'll build an application in a *rapid prototype* style, going from idea to application with no external influences.

Bootstrap is a front-end framework that provides a wealth of help for creating a great user interface. Among its features, Bootstrap provides a responsive grid system, default styles for many interface components, and the ability to change the visual appearance with themes.

RESPONSIVE GRID LAYOUT

In a responsive layout, you serve up a single HTML page that arranges itself differently on different devices by detecting the screen resolution rather than trying to sniff out the actual device. Bootstrap targets four different pixel-width breakpoints for their layouts, loosely aimed at phones, tablets, laptops, and external monitors. If you give a bit of thought to how you set up your HTML and CSS classes, you can use one HTML file to offer the same content in different layouts suited to screen size.

CSS CLASSES AND HTML COMPONENTS

Bootstrap comes with a set of predefined CSS classes that can create useful visual components, such as page headers, alert-message containers, labels and badges, and stylized lists. The creators of Bootstrap put a lot of thought into the framework. Bootstrap helps you build an application quickly without having to spend too much time on the HTML layout and CSS styling.

Teaching Bootstrap isn't an aim of this book, but we'll point out various features as you use them.

ADDING THEMES FOR A DIFFERENT FEEL

Bootstrap has a default look and feel that provides a neat baseline, and it's so commonly used that your site could end up looking like anybody else's. Fortunately, you can download themes for Bootstrap to give your application a different twist. Downloading a theme is often as simple as replacing the Bootstrap CSS file with a new one. You'll use a free theme in this book to build your application, but it's also possible to buy premium themes from several websites to give an application a unique feel.

1.6.2 *Git for source control*

Saving code on your computer or a network drive is all very well and good, but a computer or network drive holds only the current version and lets only you (or other users on your network) access it.

Git is a distributed revision control and source code management system that allows several people to work on the same codebase at the same time on different computers and networks. These can be pushed together, with all changes stored and recorded. It's also possible to roll back to an earlier state if necessary.

HOW TO USE GIT

Git is typically used from the command line, although GUIs are available for Windows, Linux, and Mac. Throughout this book, you'll use command-line statements to issue the commands that you need. Git is powerful, and we'll scratch the surface of it in this book, but everything we do will be provided as part of the examples.

In a typical Git setup, you have a local repository on your machine and a remote centralized master repository hosted somewhere like GitHub or Bitbucket. You can pull from the remote repository into your local one or push from local to remote. All these tasks are easy to perform from the command line, and GitHub and Bitbucket have web interfaces so that you can visually keep track of everything you've committed.

WHAT IS GIT USED FOR HERE?

In this book, you'll use Git for two reasons:

- The source code of the sample application in this book will be stored on GitHub, with different branches for various milestones. You'll be able to clone the master or the separate branches to use the code.
- You'll use Git as the method of deploying your application to a live web server for the world to see. For hosting, you'll use Heroku.

1.6.3 Hosting with Heroku

Hosting Node.js applications can be complicated, but it doesn't have to be. Many traditional shared hosting providers haven't kept up with the interest in Node.js. Some providers install it for you so that you can run applications, but the servers generally aren't set up to meet the unique needs of Node.js. To run a Node.js application successfully, you need a server that has been configured with it in mind, or you can use a PaaS provider that's specifically designed for hosting Node.js.

In this book, you'll take the latter approach. You'll use Heroku (https://www .heroku.com) as your hosting provider. Heroku is one of the leading hosts of Node.js applications and it has an excellent free tier that you'll make use of.

Applications on Heroku are essentially Git repositories, making the publishing process incredibly simple. After everything is set up, you can publish your application to a live environment by using a single command:

```
$ git push heroku master
```

1.7 Putting it together with a practical example

As we've already mentioned a few times, throughout the course of this book, you'll build a working application on the MEAN stack. This process will give you a good grounding in each of the technologies and show you how they fit together.

1.7.1 Introducing the example application

So what are you going to be building as you go through the book? You'll be building an application called Loc8r. Loc8r lists nearby places with Wi-Fi where people can go to get some work done. It also displays facilities, opening times, a rating, and a location map for each place. Users will be able to log in and submit ratings and reviews.

This application has some grounding in the real world. Location-based applications themselves aren't particularly new and come in a few guises. Swarm and Facebook Check In list everything nearby that they can and crowdsource data for new places and information updates. Urbanspoon helps people find nearby places to eat, allowing a user to search on price bracket and type of cuisine. Even companies like Starbucks and McDonald's have sections of their applications that help users find the nearest one.

REAL OR FAKE DATA?

Okay, we're going to fake the data for Loc8r in this book, but you could collate the data, crowdsource it, or use an external source if you wanted to. For a rapid prototype approach, you'll often find that faking data for the first private version of your application speeds the process.

END PRODUCT

You'll use all layers of the MEAN stack to create Loc8r, including Twitter Bootstrap to help you create a responsive layout. Figure 1.7 shows some screenshots of what you'll build throughout the book.

Figure 1.7 Loc8r is the application you'll build throughout this book. It displays differently on different devices, showing a list of places and details about each place, and allows visitors to log in and leave reviews.

1.7.2 How the MEAN stack components work together

By the time you've been through this book, you'll have an application running on the MEAN stack, using JavaScript all the way through. MongoDB stores data in binary JSON, which, through Mongoose, is exposed as JSON. The Express framework sits on top of Node.js, where the code is written in JavaScript. In the front end is Angular, which is TypeScript. Figure 1.8 illustrates this flow and connection.

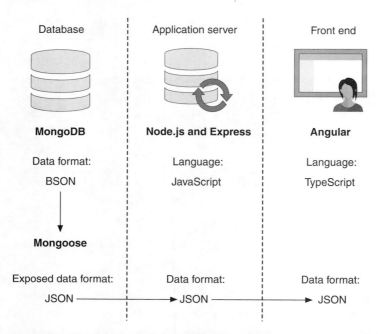

Figure 1.8   JavaScript (partly as TypeScript) is the common language throughout the MEAN stack, and JSON is the common data format.

We'll explore various ways that you can architect the MEAN stack and how you'll build Loc8r in chapter 2.

Because JavaScript plays such a pivotal role in the stack, please take a look at appendix D (available online and in the e-book), which has a refresher on JavaScript pitfalls and best practices.

Summary

In this chapter, you learned

- Which technologies make up the MEAN stack and how they work together
- Where MongoDB fits as the data layer
- How Node.js and Express work together to provide an application server layer
- How Angular provides an amazing front-end, data-binding layer
- A few ways to extend the MEAN stack with additional technologies

Designing a MEAN stack architecture

In chapter 1, we took a look at the component parts of the MEAN stack and how they fit together. In this chapter, we're going to look in more detail at how they fit together.

We'll start off by looking at what some people think of as *the* MEAN stack architecture, especially when they first encounter the stack. Using some examples, we'll explore why you might use a different architecture and then switch things up a bit and move things around. MEAN is a powerful stack that can be used to solve a diverse range of problems ... if you get creative with how you design your solutions.

2.1   *A common MEAN stack architecture*

A common way to architect a MEAN stack application is to have a representational state transfer (REST) API feeding a single-page application (SPA). The API is typically built with MongoDB, Express, and Node.js, with the SPA being built in Angular. This approach is particularly popular with those who come to the MEAN stack from an Angular background and are looking for a stack that provides a fast, responsive API. Figure 2.1 illustrates the basic setup and data flow.

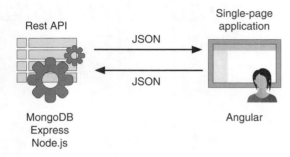

Figure 2.1   A common approach to MEAN stack architecture, using MongoDB, Express, and Node.js to build a REST API that feeds JSON data to an Angular SPA run in the browser

What is a REST API?

REST stands for *REpresentational State Transfer*, which is an architectural style rather than a strict protocol. REST is stateless; it has no idea of any current user state or history.

API is an abbreviation for *application program interface*, which enables applications to talk to one another. In the case of the web, an API is normally a set of URLs that respond with data when called in the correct manner with the correct information.

A *REST API* is a stateless interface to your application. In the case of the MEAN stack, the REST API is used to create a stateless interface to your database, enabling a way for other applications, such as an Angular SPA, to work with the data. In other words, you create a collection of structured URLs that return specific data when called.

Figure 2.1 is a great setup, ideal if you have or intend to build an SPA as your user-facing side. Angular is designed with a focus on building SPAs, pulling in data from a REST API as well as pushing it back. MongoDB, Express, and Node.js are also extremely capable when it comes to building an API, using JSON all the way through the stack, including the database itself.

This is where many people start with the MEAN stack, looking for an answer to the question, "I've built an application in Angular; now where do I get the data?"

Having an architecture like this is great if you have an SPA, but what if you have differing requirements? The MEAN stack is far more flexible than the current design suggests. All four components are individually powerful and have a lot to offer.

2.2   *Looking beyond SPAs*

Coding an SPA in Angular is like driving a Porsche along a coastal road with the roof down. Both are amazing. They're fun, fast, sexy, agile, and exceedingly capable. If, historically, you've not done either thing before, it's most likely that both are a vast improvement.

But sometimes, they're not appropriate. If you want to pack up the surfboards and take your family away for the week, you're going to struggle with the sports car. As amazing as your car may be, in this case you're going to want to use something different. It's the same story with SPAs. Yes, building them in Angular is amazing, but sometimes an SPA isn't the best solution to your problem. Let's take a brief look at some things to bear in mind about SPAs when designing a solution and deciding whether a full SPA is right for your project.

SPAs generally offer a fantastic user experience while reducing the load on your servers and therefore also your hosting costs. In sections 2.3.1 and 2.3.2, you'll look at a good use case for an SPA and a bad one, and you'll have built a full SPA by the end of this book.

2.2.1   *Hard to crawl*

JavaScript applications are hard for search engines to crawl and index. Most search engines look at the HTML content on a page but don't execute or even download much JavaScript. For those that do, the actual crawling of JavaScript-created content is nowhere near as good as content delivered by the server. If all your content is served via a JavaScript application, you can't be sure how much of it will be indexed.

A related downside is that automatic previews from social-sharing sites like Facebook, LinkedIn, and Pinterest don't work well, also because they look at the HTML of the page you're linking to and try to extract some relevant text and images. Like search engines, they don't run JavaScript on the page, so content served by JavaScript won't be seen.

All this is slowly improving. We hope that future editions of this book won't need to have this section!

MAKING AN SPA CRAWLABLE

You can use a couple of workarounds to make your site look crawlable. Both involve creating separate HTML pages that mirror the content of your SPA. You can have your server create an HTML-based version of your site and deliver that to crawlers, or you can use a headless browser such as PhantomJS to run your JavaScript application and output the resulting HTML.

Each method requires quite a bit of effort and can end up being a maintenance headache if you have a large, complex site. You also have potential search engine optimization (SEO) pitfalls. If your server-generated HTML is deemed to be too different from the SPA content, your site will be penalized. Running PhantomJS to output the HTML can slow the response speed of your pages, which is something for which search engines—Google in particular—downgrade you.

DOES IT MATTER?

Whether this matters depends on what you want to build. If the main growth plan for whatever you're building is through search engine traffic or social sharing, you want to give these concerns a great deal of thought. If you're creating something small that will stay small, managing the workarounds is achievable, whereas at a larger scale, you'll struggle.

On the other hand, if you're building an application that doesn't need much SEO—or indeed, if you *want* your site to be harder to scrape—you don't need to be concerned about this issue. It could even be an advantage.

2.2.2   *Analytics and browser history*

Analytics tools like Google Analytics rely heavily on entire new pages loading in the browser, initiated by a URL change. SPAs don't work this way. There's a reason why they're called *single-page* applications!

After the first page load, all subsequent page and content changes are handled internally by the application. The browser never triggers a new page load; nothing gets added to the browser history; and your analytics package has no idea who's doing what on your site.

ADDING PAGE LOADS TO AN SPA

You can add page load events to an SPA by using the HTML5 history API, which will help you integrate analytics. The difficulty comes in managing this and ensuring that everything is being tracked accurately, which involves checking for missing reports and double entries.

The good news is that you don't have to build everything from the ground up. Several open source analytics integrations for Angular are available online, addressing most of the major analytics providers. You still have to integrate them into your application and make sure that everything is working correctly, but you don't have to do everything from scratch.

IS IT A MAJOR PROBLEM?

The extent to which this is a problem depends on your need for undeniably accurate analytics. If you want to monitor trends in visitor flows and actions, you're probably going to find analytics easy to integrate. The more detail and definite accuracy you need, the more work it is to develop and test. Although it's arguably much easier to include your analytics code on every page of a server-generated site, analytics integration isn't likely to be the sole reason to choose a non-SPA route.

2.2.3   *Speed of initial load*

SPAs have a slower first page load than server-based applications, because the first load has to bring down the framework and the application code before rendering the required view as HTML in the browser. A server-based application only has to push out the required HTML to the browser, reducing latency and download time.

SPEEDING THE PAGE LOAD

You have some ways of speeding up the initial load of an SPA, such as a heavy approach to caching and lazy-loading modules when you need them. But you'll never get away from the fact that the SPA needs to download the framework (at least, some of the application code) and will most likely hit an API for data before displaying something in the browser.

SHOULD YOU CARE ABOUT SPEED?

The answer to whether you should care about the speed of the initial page load is, once again, "It depends." It depends on what you're building and how people are going to interact with it.

Think about Gmail. Gmail is an SPA and takes quite a while to load. Granted, this load time is normally only a couple of seconds, but everyone online is impatient these days and expects immediacy. But people don't mind waiting for Gmail to load because it's snappy and responsive once you're in. And when you're in, you often stay in for a while.

But if you have a blog pulling in traffic from search engines and other external links, you don't want the first page load to take a few seconds. People will assume that your site is down or running slowly and will click the Back button before you've had the chance to show them content.

2.2.4 To SPA or not to SPA?

Just a reminder that the preceding sections aren't an exercise in SPA-bashing; we're just taking a moment to think about some things that often get pushed to the side until it's too late. The three points about crawlability, analytics integration, and page load speed aren't designed to give clear-cut definitions about when to create an SPA and when to do something else. They're there to give a framework for consideration.

It may be the case that none of those things is an issue for your project and that an SPA is definitely the right way to go. If you find that each point makes you pause and think, and it looks as though you need to add workarounds for all three, an SPA probably isn't the way to go.

If you're somewhere in between, it's a judgment call about what's most important and, crucially, what's the best solution for the project. As a rule of thumb, if your solution includes a load of workarounds at the outset, you probably need to rethink it.

Even if you decide that an SPA isn't right for you, that doesn't mean that you can't use the MEAN stack. In the next section, we'll take a look at how you can design a different architecture.

2.3 Designing a flexible MEAN architecture

If Angular is like having a Porsche, the rest of the stack is like also having an Audi RS6 in the garage. A lot of people may be focusing on your sports car out front and not give a second glance to the estate car in your garage. But if you do go into the garage and have a poke around, you'll find that there's a Lamborghini V10 engine under the hood. There's a lot more to that estate car than some people think!

Only ever using MongoDB, Express, and Node.js together to build a REST API is like only ever using the Audi RS6 to do the school drop-off runs. They're all extremely capable and will do the job very well, but they have a lot more to offer.

We talked a little about what the technologies can do in chapter 1, but here are a few starting points:

- MongoDB can store and stream binary information.
- Node.js is particularly good for real-time connections using web sockets.
- Express is a web application framework with templating, routing, and session management built in.

There's also a lot more, and we're certainly not going to be able to address the full capabilities of all the technologies in this book. We'd need several books to do that! What we can do here is give you a simple example and show you how you can fit together the pieces of the MEAN stack to design the best solution.

2.3.1 Requirements for a blog engine

In this section, you'll take a look at the familiar idea of a blog engine and see how you can best architect the MEAN stack to build one.

A blog engine typically has two sides: a public-facing side serving up articles to readers and (we hope) being syndicated and shared across the internet, and an administrator interface where blog owners log in to write new articles and manage their blogs. Figure 2.2 shows some of the key characteristics of these two sides.

Looking at the lists in figure 2.2, you can easily see a high level of conflict between the characteristics of the two sides. You've got content-rich, low interaction for the blog articles but a feature-rich, highly interactive environment for the admin interface. The blog articles should be quick to load to reduce bounce rates, whereas the

Blog entries   Admin interface

Characteristics   Characteristics
☒ Content-rich   ☒ Feature-rich
☒ Low interaction   ☒ High interaction
☒ Fast first load   ☒ Fast response to actions
☒ Short user duration   ☒ Long user duration
☒ Public and shareable   ☒ Private

Figure 2.2 Conflicting characteristics of the two sides of a blog engine: the public-facing blog entries and the private admin interface

admin area should be quick to respond to user input and actions. Finally, users typically stay on a blog entry for a short time but may share it with others, whereas the admin interface is private, and an individual user could be logged in for a long time.

Taking what we've discussed about potential issues with SPAs and looking at the characteristics of blog entries, you'll see quite a lot of overlap. Bearing this in mind, it's likely that you wouldn't choose to use an SPA to deliver your blog articles to readers. On the other hand, the admin interface is a perfect fit for an SPA.

So what do you do? Arguably the most important thing is to keep the blog readers coming. If they get a bad experience, they won't come back; neither will they share. If a blog doesn't get readers, the writer will stop writing or move to another platform. Then again, a slow and unresponsive admin interface will also see your blog owners jumping ship. So what *do* you do? How do you keep everybody happy and keep the blog engine in business?

2.3.2 *A blog engine architecture*

The answer lies in not looking for a one-size-fits-all solution. You effectively have two applications: public-facing content that should be delivered direct from the server and an interactive private admin interface that you want to build as an SPA. To start, look at the two applications separately, starting with the admin interface.

ADMIN INTERFACE: AN ANGULAR SPA

We've already stated that this interface would be an ideal fit for an SPA built in Angular. The architecture for this part of the engine should look familiar: a REST API built with MongoDB, Express, and Node.js, with an Angular SPA up front. Figure 2.3 shows how this looks.

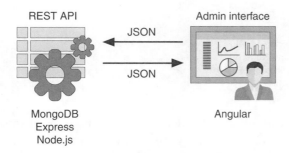

Figure 2.3 **A familiar sight: the admin interface is an Angular SPA making use of a REST API built with MongoDB, Express, and Node.js.**

There's nothing particularly new shown in figure 2.3. The entire application is built in Angular and runs in the browser, with JSON data being passed back and forth between the Angular application and the REST API.

BLOG ENTRIES: WHAT TO DO?

Looking at the blog entries, you can see that things get a little more difficult.

If you think of the MEAN stack only as an Angular SPA calling a REST API, you're going to get a bit stuck. You could build the public-facing site as an SPA anyway, because you want to use JavaScript and the MEAN stack. But it's not the best solution. You could decide that the MEAN stack isn't appropriate in this case and choose a different technology stack. But you don't want to do that! You want end-to-end JavaScript.

Take another look at the MEAN stack, and think about all the components. You know that Express is a web application framework. You know that Express can use template engines to build HTML on the server. You know that Express can use URL routing and MVC patterns. You should start to think that perhaps Express has the answer!

BLOG ENTRIES: MAKING GOOD USE OF EXPRESS

In this blog scenario, delivering the HTML and content directly from the server is exactly what you want to do. Express does this particularly well, even offering a choice of template engines right from the get-go. The HTML content will require data from the database, so you'll use a REST API again. (For more on why it's best to take this approach, see section 2.3.3.) Figure 2.4 lays out the basis for this architecture.

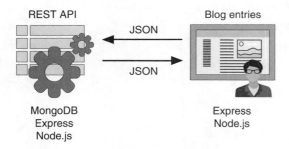

Figure 2.4   An architecture for delivering HTML directly from the server: an Express and Node.js application at the front, interacting with a REST API built in MongoDB, Express, and Node.js

This approach enables you to use the MEAN stack (or part of it, at least) to deliver database-driven content directly from the server to the browser. But it doesn't have to stop there. The MEAN stack is even more flexible.

BLOG ENTRIES: USING MORE OF THE STACK

You're looking at an Express application delivering blog content to visitors. If you want visitors to be able to log in, perhaps to add comments to articles, you need to track user sessions. You could use MongoDB with your Express application to do just this.

You might also have some dynamic data in the sidebar of your posts, such as related posts or a search box with type-ahead autocompletion. You could implement these in Angular. Remember, Angular isn't only for SPAs; it can also be used to create individual

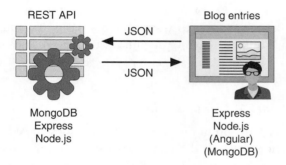

Figure 2.5   Adding the options of using Angular and MongoDB as part of the public-facing aspect of the blog engine, serving the blog entries to visitors

components that add some rich data interactivity to an otherwise static page. Figure 2.5 shows these optional parts of MEAN added to the blog entry architecture.

Now you have the possibility of a full MEAN application delivering content to visitors who interact with your REST API.

BLOG ENGINE: A HYBRID ARCHITECTURE

At this point, you have two separate applications, each using a REST API. With a little bit of planning, you can have a common REST API used by both sides of the application. Figure 2.6 shows what this looks like as a single architecture, with the single REST API interacting with the two front-end applications.

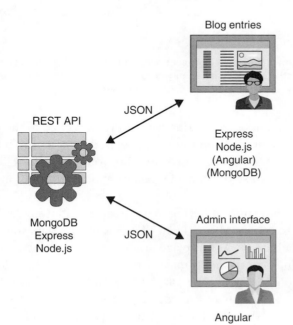

Figure 2.6   A hybrid MEAN stack architecture: a single REST API feeding two separate user-facing applications, built using different parts of the MEAN stack to provide the most appropriate solution

This figure is a simple example to show how you can piece together the various parts of the MEAN stack into different architectures to answer the questions that your projects ask of you. Your options are limited only by your understanding of the components and your creativity in putting them together. There's no one correct architecture for the MEAN stack.

2.3.3 *Best practice: Building an internal API for a data layer*

You've probably noticed that every version of the architecture includes an API to surface the data and allow interaction between the main application and the database. There's a good reason for this.

If you were to start by building your application in Node.js and Express, serving HTML directly from the server, it would be easy to talk to the database directly from the Node.js application code. With a short-term view, this way is the easy way. But with a long-term view, it becomes the difficult way, because it tightly couples your data to your application code in such a way that nothing else can use it.

The other option is to build your own API that can talk to the database directly and output the data you need. Then your Node.js application can talk with this API instead of directly with the database. Figure 2.7 shows a comparison of the two setups.

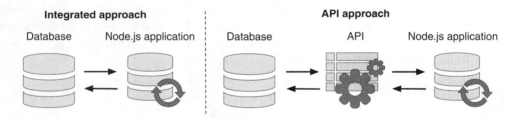

Figure 2.7   The short-term view of integrating data into your Node.js application. You can set up your Node.js application to talk directly to your database, or you can create an API that interacts with the database, and have your Node.js application talk only with the API.

Looking at figure 2.7, you could well be wondering why you'd want to go to the effort of creating an API just to sit between your application and your database. Isn't it creating more work? At this stage, yes, it's creating more work, but you want to look farther down the road. What if you want to use your data in a native mobile application or in an Angular front end later?

You certainly don't want to find yourself having to write separate but similar interfaces for each. If you've built your own API up front that outputs the data you need, you can avoid this work. If you have an API in place, when you want to integrate the data layer into your application, you can simply make it reference your API. It doesn't matter whether your application is Node.js, Angular, iOS, or Android. It doesn't have to be a public API that anyone can use so long as you can access it. Figure 2.8 shows a comparison of the two approaches when you have Node.js, Angular, and iOS/Android applications all using the same data source.

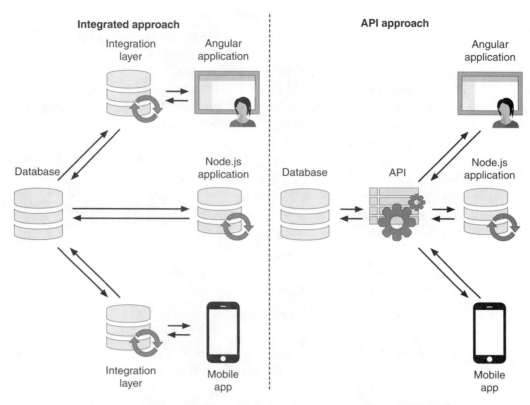

Figure 2.8   The long-term view of integrating data into your Node.js application and additional Angular and iOS applications. The integrated approach has become fragmented, whereas the API approach is simple and maintainable.

As figure 2.8 shows, the previously simple integrated approach is becoming fragmented and complex. You'll have three data integrations to manage and maintain, so any changes will have to be made in multiple places to maintain consistency. If you have a single API, you don't have any of these worries. With a little bit of extra work at the beginning, you can make life much easier for your future self. We'll look at creating internal APIs in chapter 6.

2.4   *Planning a real application*

As we talked about in chapter 1, throughout the course of this book you'll build a working application on the MEAN stack, called Loc8r. Loc8r lists nearby places with Wi-Fi where people can go to get some work done. It also displays facilities, opening times, a rating, and a location map for each place. Visitors will be able to submit ratings and reviews.

For the sake of the demo application, you'll create fake data so that you can test it quickly and easily. In the next section, we'll walk you through the application planning.

2.4.1 *Planning the application at a high level*

The first step is thinking about what screens you'll need in your application. Focus on the separate page views and the user journeys. You can do this at a high level, not really concerning yourself with the details of what's on each page. It's a good idea to sketch out this stage on a piece of paper or a whiteboard, which helps you visualize the application as a whole. It also helps with organizing the screens into collections and flows while serving as a good reference point when you're ready to build. As no data is attached to the pages or application logic behind them, it's easy to add and remove parts, change what's displayed where, and even change how many pages you want. Chances are that you won't get it right the first time; the key is to start, and then iterate and improve until you're happy with the separate pages and overall user flow.

PLANNING THE SCREENS

Think about Loc8r. As stated earlier, your aim is as follows:

> *Loc8r lists nearby places with Wi-Fi where people can go to get some work done. It also displays facilities, opening times, a rating, and a location map for each place. Visitors will be able to submit ratings and reviews.*

From this description, you can get an idea about some of the screens you're going to need:

- A screen that lists nearby places
- A screen that shows details about an individual place
- A screen for adding a review about a place

You'll probably also want to tell visitors what Loc8r is for and why it exists, so you should add another screen to the list:

- A screen for "about us" information

DIVIDING THE SCREENS INTO COLLECTIONS

Next, take the list of screens and collate them where they logically belong together. The first three screens in the list, for example, deal with locations. The About page doesn't belong anywhere, so it can go in a miscellaneous Others collection. A sketch of this arrangement looks something like figure 2.9.

Making a quick sketch like figure 2.9 is the first stage in planning, and you need to go through this stage before you can start thinking about architecture. This stage gives you a chance to look at the basic pages and think about the flow. Figure 2.9, for example, also shows a basic user journey in the Locations

Figure 2.9 Collate the separate screens for your application into logical collections.

collection, going from the List page to a Details page and then to the form to add a review.

2.4.2   *Architecting the application*

On the face of it, Loc8r is a fairly simple application, with a few screens. But you still need to think about how to architect it, because you're going to be transferring data from a database to a browser, letting users interact with the data, and allowing data to be sent back to the database.

STARTING WITH THE API

Because the application will use a database and pass data around, start building the architecture with the piece you're definitely going to need. Figure 2.10 shows the starting point: a REST API built with Express and Node.js to enable interactions with the MongoDB database.

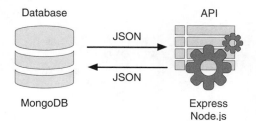

Figure 2.10   Start with the standard MEAN REST API, using MongoDB, Express, and Node.js.

Building an API to interface with your data is a bit of a given and the base point of the architecture. The more interesting question is how you architect the application itself.

APPLICATION ARCHITECTURE OPTIONS

At this point, you need to take a look at the specific requirements of your application and how to put together the pieces of the MEAN stack to build the best solution. Do you need something special from MongoDB, Express, Angular, or Node.js that will swing the decision a certain way? Do you want HTML to be served directly from the server, or is an SPA a better option?

For Loc8r, you have no unusual or specific requirements, and whether it should be easily crawlable by search engines depends on the business growth plan. If the aim is to bring in organic traffic from search engines, yes, it needs to be crawlable. If the aim is to promote the application as an application and drive use that way, search engine visibility is a lesser concern.

Thinking back to the blog example, you can immediately envisage three possible application architectures, as shown in figure 2.11:

- A Node.js and Express application
- A Node.js and Express application with Angular additions for interactivity
- An Angular SPA

With these three options in mind, which is the best for Loc8r?

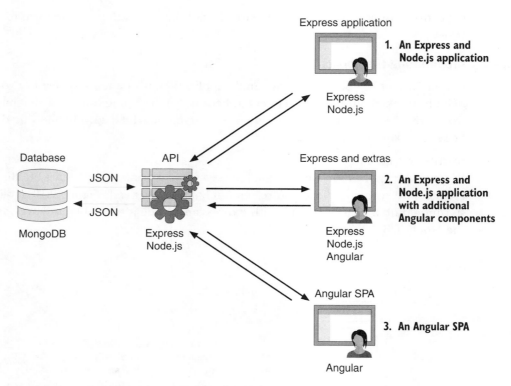

Figure 2.11   Three options for building the Loc8r application, ranging from a server-side Express and Node.js application to a full client-side Angular SPA

CHOOSING AN APPLICATION ARCHITECTURE

No specific business requirements are pushing you to favor one particular architecture over another. It doesn't matter, because you're going to do all three in this book. Building all three of the architectures allows you to explore how each approach works and enables you to take a look at each of the technologies in turn, building up the application layer by layer.

You'll be building the architectures in the order in which they're shown in figure 2.11, starting with a Node.js and Express application, and then adding some Angular before refactoring to an Angular SPA. Although this isn't necessarily how you might build a site normally, it gives you a great opportunity to learn all aspects of the MEAN stack. In section 2.5, we'll talk about this approach and walk through the plan in a bit more detail.

2.4.3   *Wrapping everything in an Express project*

The architecture diagrams that you've been looking at so far imply that you'll have separate Express applications for the API and the application logic. This is perfectly possible and a good way to go for a large project. If you're expecting large amounts of traffic, you may even want your main application and your API on different servers. An additional benefit of this approach is that you can have more specific settings for each of the servers and applications that are best suited to particular needs.

Another way is to keep things simple and contained by having everything inside a single Express project. With this approach, you have only one application to worry about hosting and deploying and one set of source code to manage. This is what do with Loc8r: creating one Express project that contains a few subapplications. Figure 2.12 illustrates this approach.

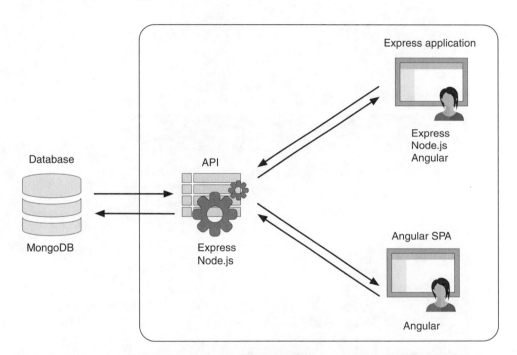

Figure 2.12 The architecture of the application with the API and application logic wrapped inside the same Express project

When you're putting together an application in this way, it's important to organize your code well so that the distinct parts of the application are kept separate. As well as making code easier to maintain, this makes it easier to split the code into separate projects if a future you decides that doing so is the right route. We'll keep coming back to this key theme throughout the book.

2.4.4 *The end product*

As you can see, you use all layers of the MEAN stack to create Loc8r. You also include Twitter Bootstrap to create a responsive layout. Figure 2.13 shows some screenshots of what you'll build throughout the book.

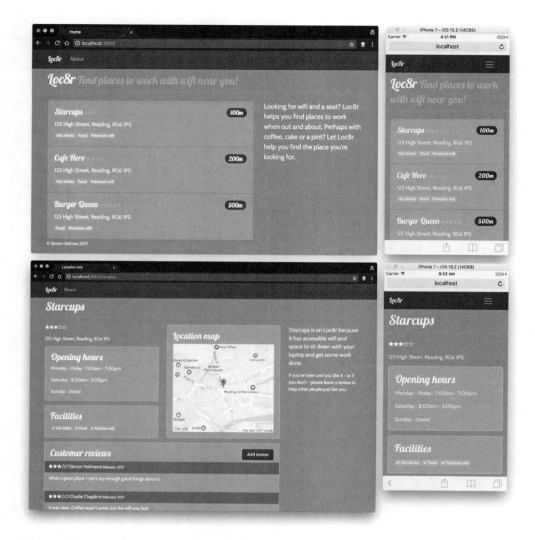

Figure 2.13   Loc8r is the application you'll build throughout this book. It displays differently on different devices, showing a list of places and details about each place, and enables visitors to log in and leave reviews.

2.5   *Breaking the development into stages*

In this book, you have two aims:

- Build an application on the MEAN stack.
- Learn about the different layers of the stack as you go.

You'll approach the project in the way that you'd go about building a rapid prototype, but with a few tweaks to give you the best coverage of the whole stack. Start by looking at the five stages of rapid prototype development, and then see how to use this approach to build up Loc8r layer by layer, focusing on the different technologies as you go.

2.5.1 *Rapid prototype development stages*

The following sections break the process into stages, which lets you concentrate on one thing at a time, increasing your chances of success. We find that this approach works well for making an idea a reality.

STAGE 1: BUILD A STATIC SITE

The first stage is building a static version of the application, which is essentially several HTML screens. The aims of this stage are

- To quickly figure out the layout
- To ensure that the user flow makes sense

At this point, you're not concerned with a database or flashy effects on the user interface; all you want to do is create a working mockup of the main screens and journeys that a user will take through the application.

STAGE 2: DESIGN THE DATA MODEL AND CREATE THE DATABASE

When you have a working static prototype that you're happy with, the next thing to do is look at any hardcoded data in the static application, and put it in a database. The aims of this stage are

- To define a data model that reflects the requirements of the application
- To create a database to work with the model

The first part is defining the data model. Stepping back to a bird's-eye view, what are the objects you need data about, how are the objects connected, and what data is held in them?

When you try to do this stage before building the static prototype, you're dealing with abstract concepts and ideas. When you have a prototype, you can see what's happening on different pages and what data is needed where. Suddenly, this stage becomes much easier. Almost unknown to you, you've done the hard thinking while building the static prototype.

STAGE 3: BUILD YOUR DATA API

After stages 1 and 2, you have a static site on one hand and a database on the other. This stage and the next take the natural steps of linking them. The aim of stage 3 is

- To create a RESTful API that allows your application to interact with the database

STAGE 4: HOOK THE DATABASE INTO THE APPLICATION

When you get to this stage, you have a static application and an API exposing an interface to your database. The aim of this stage is

- To get your application to talk to your API

When this stage is complete, the application will look pretty much the same as it did before, but the data will be coming from the database. When it's done, you'll have a data-driven application!

STAGE 5: AUGMENT THE APPLICATION

This stage is all about embellishing the application with additional functionality. You might add authentication systems, data validation, or methods for displaying error messages to users. This stage could include adding more interactivity to the front end or tightening the business logic in the application.

The aims of this stage are

- To add finishing touches to your application
- To get the application ready for people to use

These five stages of development provide a great methodology for approaching a new build project. In the next section, you'll take a look at how you'll follow these steps to build Loc8r.

2.5.2 *The steps to build Loc8r*

In building Loc8r throughout this book, you have two aims. First, of course, you want to build a working application on the MEAN stack. Second, you want to learn about the different technologies, how to use them, and how to put them together in different ways.

Throughout the book, you'll follow the five stages of development, but with a couple of twists so that you get to see the whole stack in action. Before looking at the steps in detail, quickly remind yourself of the proposed architecture shown in figure 2.14.

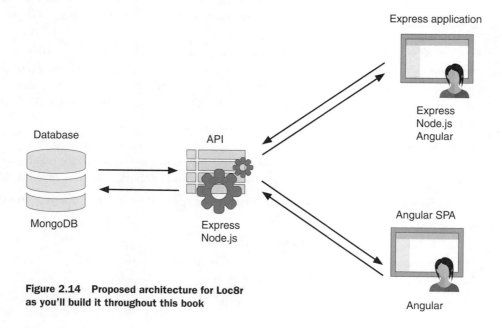

Figure 2.14 Proposed architecture for Loc8r as you'll build it throughout this book

Step 1: Build a static site

You'll start by following stage 1 and building a static site. We recommend doing this for any application or site, because you can learn a lot with relatively little effort. When building the static site, it's good to keep one eye on the future, keeping in mind what the final architecture will be. The architecture for Loc8r is already defined, as shown in figure 2.14.

Based on this architecture, you'll build the static application in Node and Express, using that as your starting point into the MEAN stack. Figure 2.15 highlights this step in the process as the first part of developing the proposed architecture. This step is covered in chapters 3 and 4.

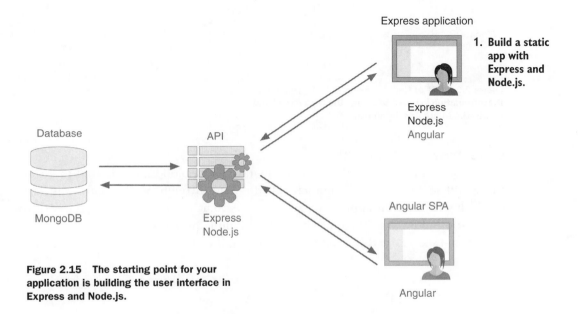

Figure 2.15   The starting point for your application is building the user interface in Express and Node.js.

Step 2: Design the data model and create the database

Still following the stages of development, you'll continue to stage 2 by creating the database and designing the data model. Again, any application is likely to need this step, and you'll get much more out of it if you've been through step 1 first.

Figure 2.16 illustrates how this step adds to the overall picture of building up the application architecture.

In the MEAN stack, you'll use MongoDB for this step, relying heavily on Mongoose for the data modeling. The data models are actually defined inside the Express application. This step is covered in chapter 5.

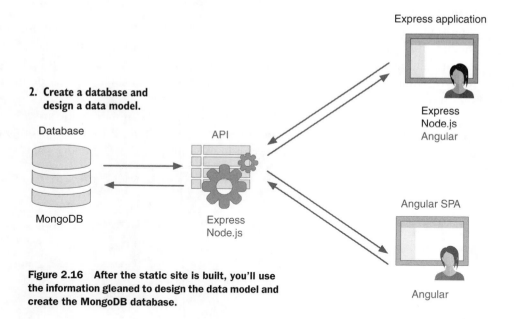

**2. Create a database and
design a data model.**

**Figure 2.16   After the static site is built, you'll use
the information gleaned to design the data model and
create the MongoDB database.**

STEP 3: BUILD YOUR REST API

When you've built the database and defined the data models, you'll want to create a
REST API so that you can interact with the data through making web calls. Pretty
much any data-driven application will benefit from having an API interface, so this
step is another one you'll want to have in most build projects.

You can see where this step fits into building the overall project in figure 2.17.

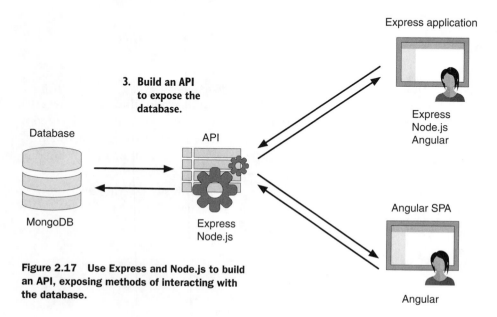

**3. Build an API
to expose the
database.**

**Figure 2.17   Use Express and Node.js to build
an API, exposing methods of interacting with
the database.**

In the MEAN stack, this step is done mainly in Node.js and Express, with quite a bit of help from Mongoose. You'll use Mongoose to interface with MongoDB rather than deal with MongoDB directly. This step is covered in chapter 6.

STEP 4: USE THE API FROM YOUR APPLICATION

This step matches stage 4 of the development process and is where Loc8r starts to come to life. The static application from step 1 will be updated to use the REST API from step 3 to interact with the database created in step 2.

To learn about all parts of the stack and the different ways in which you can use them, you'll use Express and Node.js to make calls to the API. If, in a real-world scenario, you planned to build the bulk of an application in Angular, you'd hook your API into Angular instead. That approach is covered in chapters 8, 9, and 10.

At the end of this step, you'll have an application running on the first of the three architectures: an Express and Node.js application. Figure 2.18 shows how this step glues together the two sides of the architecture.

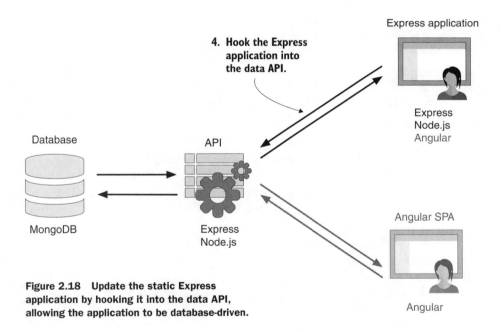

Figure 2.18   Update the static Express application by hooking it into the data API, allowing the application to be database-driven.

In this build, you'll do the majority of this step in Node.js and Express. This step is covered in chapter 7.

STEP 5: EMBELLISH THE APPLICATION

Step 5 relates to stage 5 in the development process, where you get to add extra touches to the application. You'll use this step to take a look at Angular and see how you can integrate Angular components into an Express application. This addition to the project architecture is highlighted in figure 2.19.

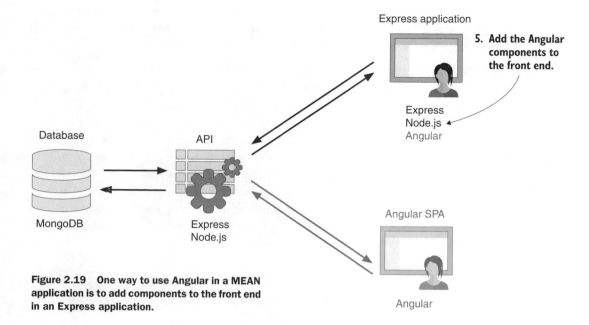

Figure 2.19   One way to use Angular in a MEAN application is to add components to the front end in an Express application.

This step is all about introducing and using Angular. To support this step, you'll most likely also change some of your Node.js and Express setup. This step is covered in chapter 8.

STEP 6: REFACTOR THE CODE INTO AN ANGULAR SPA

In step 6, you'll radically change the architecture by replacing the Express application and moving all the logic into an SPA, using Angular. Unlike the previous steps, this step replaces some of what came before it rather than building on it.

This step would be an unusual one in a normal build process—to develop an application in Express and redo it in Angular—but it suits the learning approach in this book particularly well. You'll be able to focus on Angular, as you already know what the application should do, and a data API is ready for you to use.

Figure 2.20 shows how this change affects the overall architecture. This step once again focuses on Angular and is covered in chapters 9 and 10.

STEP 7: ADD AUTHENTICATION

In step 7, you'll add functionality to the application by enabling users to register and log in. You'll also see how to make use of users' data while they're using the application. You'll build on everything you've done so far and add authentication to the Angular SPA. As part of this step, you'll save user information in the database and secure certain API endpoints so that they can be used only by authenticated users.

Figure 2.21 shows what you'll be working with in the architecture. In this step, you'll work with all the MEAN technologies. This step is covered in chapters 11 and 12.

That's the planned software architecture. In the next section, we'll have a quick chat about hardware.

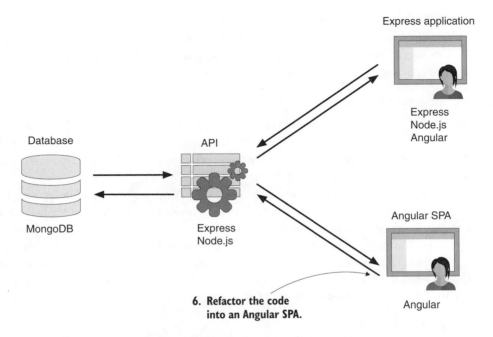

Figure 2.20 Effectively rewriting the application as an Angular SPA

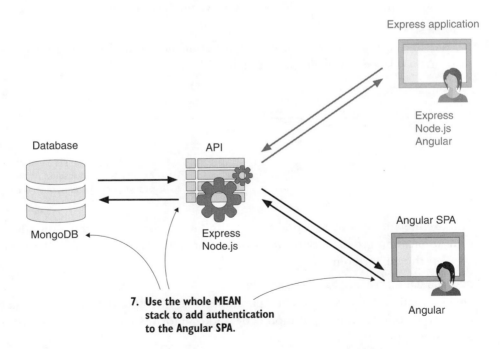

Figure 2.21 Using all the MEAN stack to add authentication to the Angular SPA

2.6   *Hardware architecture*

No discussion of architecture would be complete without a section on hardware. You've seen how the software and code components can be put together, but what type of hardware do you need to run it all?

2.6.1   *Development hardware*

The good news is that you don't need anything particularly special to run a development stack. A single laptop or even a virtual machine (VM) is enough to develop a MEAN application. All components of the stack can be installed on Windows, macOS, and most Linux distributions.

We've successfully developed applications on Windows and macOS laptops, as well as on Ubuntu VMs. Our preference is native development on macOS, but we know others who swear by Linux VMs.

If you have a local network and several servers, you can run different parts of your application across them. It's possible to have one machine as a database server, another for the REST API, and a third for the main application code itself, for example. So long as the servers can talk to one another, this setup isn't a problem.

2.6.2   *Production hardware*

The approach to production hardware architecture isn't all that different from development hardware. The main difference is that production hardware is normally higher-spec and open to the internet to receive public requests.

STARTER SIZE

It's possible to have all parts of your application hosted and running on the same server. You can see a basic diagram in figure 2.22.

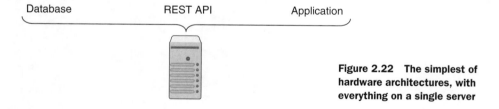

Figure 2.22   The simplest of hardware architectures, with everything on a single server

This architecture is okay for applications with low traffic but isn't generally advised as your application grows, because you don't want your application and database fighting over the same resources.

GROWING UP: A SEPARATE DATABASE SERVER

One of the first things moved to a separate server is often the database. Now you have two servers: one for the application code and one for the database. Figure 2.23 illustrates this approach.

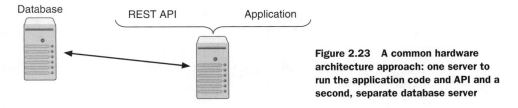

Figure 2.23 A common hardware architecture approach: one server to run the application code and API and a second, separate database server

This model is common, particularly if you choose to use a Platform as a Service (PaaS) provider for your hosting. You'll use that approach in this book.

GOING FOR SCALE

Much as we talked about in the section on development hardware, you can have a different server for the different parts of your application: a database server, an API server, and an application server. This setup allows you to deal with more traffic as the load is spread across three servers, as illustrated in figure 2.24.

Figure 2.24 A decoupled architecture using three servers: one for the database, one for the API, and one for the application code

But it doesn't stop there. If your traffic starts to overload your three servers, you can have multiple instances (or clusters) of these servers, as shown in figure 2.25.

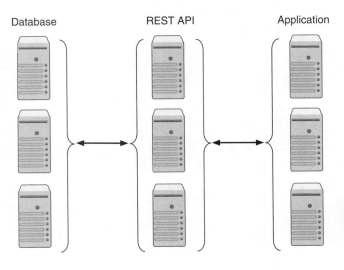

Figure 2.25 You can scale MEAN applications by having clusters of servers for each part of your entire application.

Setting up this approach is a little more involved than the previous methods, because you need to ensure that your database remains accurate and that the load is balanced across servers. Once again, PaaS providers offer a convenient route into this type of architecture.

You'll get started on the journey in chapter 3 by creating the Express project that will hold everything together.

Summary

In this chapter, you learned

- How to design a common MEAN stack architecture with an Angular SPA, using a REST API built in Node.js, Express, and MongoDB
- How to assess the factors in your project to determine whether an SPA fits well
- How to design a flexible architecture in the MEAN stack
- The best practice of building an API to expose a data layer
- Development and production hardware architectures

Part 2

Building a
Node web application

Node.js underpins any MEAN application, so that's where you'll start. Throughout part 2, you'll build a data-driven web application by using Node.js, Express, and MongoDB. You'll learn the individual technologies as you go, steadily building up the application to a point where you have a fully functioning Node web application.

In chapter 3, you'll get going by creating and setting up a MEAN project, getting acquainted with Express before getting a much deeper understanding of Express by building out a static version of the application in chapter 4. Taking what you've learned about the application so far, in chapter 5 you'll work with MongoDB and Mongoose to design and build the data model you'll need.

Good application architecture should include a data API rather than tightly couple database interactions with application logic. In chapter 6, you'll create a REST API by using Express, MongoDB, and Mongoose before tying it back into the application in chapter 7 by consuming the REST API from your static application. As you get to the end of part 2, you'll have a data-driven website using Node.js, MongoDB, and Express, as well as a fully functioning REST API.

Creating and setting up a MEAN project

3

This chapter covers

- Managing dependencies by using npm and package.json
- Creating and configuring Express projects
- Setting up an MVC environment
- Adding Twitter Bootstrap for layout
- Publishing to a live URL, and using Git and Heroku

In this chapter, you'll start building your application. Remember from chapters 1 and 2 that, throughout this book, you're going to build an application called Loc8r—a location-aware web application that displays listings near users and invites people to log in and leave reviews.

> **Getting the source code**
>
> The source code for this application is on GitHub at https://github.com/cliveharber/
> gettingMean-2. Each chapter with a significant update will have its own branch. We
> encourage you to build it up from scratch through the course of the book, but if you
> want to, you can get the code that you'll be building throughout this chapter from the
> chapter-03 branch on GitHub. In a fresh folder in terminal, if you already have Git
> installed, the following two commands will clone it:
>
> ```
> $ git clone -b chapter-03 https://github.com/cliveharber/
> gettingMean-2.git
> ```
>
> This gives you a copy of the code that's stored on GitHub. To run the application, you
> need to install some dependencies with the following commands:
>
> ```
> $ cd gettingMean-2
> $ npm install
> ```
>
> Don't worry if some of this doesn't make sense yet or if some of the commands
> aren't working. During this chapter, you'll install these technologies as you go.

In the MEAN stack, Express is the Node web application framework. Together,
Node.js and Express underpin the entire stack, so you'll start there. In terms of building up the application architecture, figure 3.1 shows where this chapter focuses. You'll
do two things:

1 Create the project and the encapsulating Express application that will house
   everything except the database.
2 Set up the main Express application.

You'll start with a bit of groundwork by looking at Express and seeing how you can
manage dependencies and modules by using npm and a package.json file. You'll need
this background knowledge to get going and set up an Express project.

Before you do anything, make sure that you have everything you need installed on
your machine. When that's done, look at creating new Express projects from the command line and the various options you can specify at this point.

Express is great, but you can make it better—and get to know it better—by tinker-
ing a little and changing some things around. This involves a quick look at model-
view-controller (MVC) architecture. Here is where you get under the hood of Express
a little and see what it's doing by modifying it to have a clear MVC setup.

When the framework of Express is set up as you want it, you'll then include Twitter's Bootstrap framework and make the site responsive by updating the Pug templates. In the final step of this chapter, you'll push the modified, responsive, MVC
Express application to a live URL using Heroku and Git.

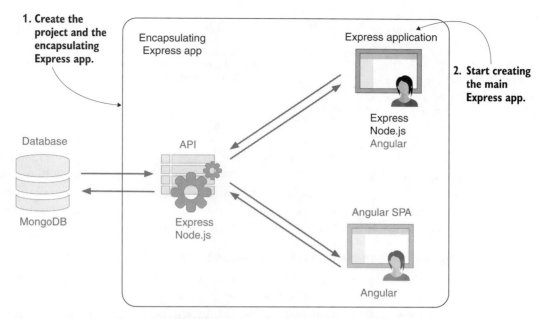

Figure 3.1 Creating the encapsulating Express application and starting to set up the main Express application

3.1 A brief look at Express, Node, and npm

As previously mentioned, Express is a web application framework for Node. In basic terms, an Express application is a Node application that happens to use Express as the framework. Remember from chapter 1 that npm is a package manager that gets installed when you install Node, which enables you to download Node modules or packages to extend the functionality of your application.

But how do these things work together, and how do you use them? A key piece of this puzzle is the package.json file.

3.1.1 Defining packages with package.json

In every Node application, you should have a file in the root folder of the application called package.json. This file can contain various metadata about a project, including the packages that it depends on to run. The following listing shows an example package.json file that you might find in the root of an Express project.

Listing 3.1 Example package.json file in a new Express project

```
{
  "name": "application-name",
  "version": "0.0.0",
  "private": true,
  "scripts": {
    "start": "node ./bin/www"
  },
```

Various metadata defining the application

```
"dependencies":
  "body-parser": "~1.18.3",
  "cookie-parser": "~1.4.3",
  "debug": "~4.1.0",
  "express": "^4.16.4",
  "morgan": "^1.9.1",
  "pug": "^2.0.3",
  "serve-favicon": "~2.5.0"
}
}
```

Package dependencies
needed for the
application to run

This listing is the file in its entirety, so it's not particularly complex. Various metadata at the top of the file is followed by the dependencies section. In this default installation of an Express project, quite a few dependencies are required for Express to run, but you don't need to worry about what each one does. Express itself is modular so that you can add components or upgrade them individually.

3.1.2   *Working with dependency versions in package.json*

Alongside the name of each dependency is the version number that the application will use. Notice that they're prefixed with either a tilde (~) or a caret (^).

Take a look at the dependency definition for Express 4.16.3, which specifies a particular version at three levels:

- Major version (4)
- Minor version (16)
- Patch version (3)

Prefixing the whole version number with a ~ is like replacing the patch version with a wildcard, which means that the application will use the latest patch version available. Similarly, prefixing the version with a caret (^) is like replacing the minor version with a wildcard. This has become best practice, because patches and minor versions should contain only fixes that won't have any effect on the application. But new major versions are released when a breaking change is made, so you want to avoid automatically using later versions of these in case the breaking change affects your application. If you find a module that breaks these rules, it's easy to specify an exact version to use by removing any prefixes. Note that it's good practice to always specify the full version and not use wildcards for this reason: you always have a reference for a specific version that you *know* works.

3.1.3   *Installing Node dependencies with npm*

Any Node application or module can have dependencies defined in a package.json file. Installing them is easy and is done the same way regardless of the application or module.

Using a terminal prompt in the same folder as the package.json file, run the following command:

```
$ npm install
```

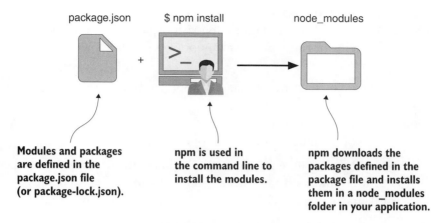

package.json $ npm install   node_modules

Modules and packages are defined in the package.json file (or package-lock.json).

npm is used in the command line to install the modules.

npm downloads the packages defined in the package file and installs them in a node_modules folder in your application.

Figure 3.2   The npm modules defined in a package.json file are downloaded and installed in the application's node_modules folder when you run the `npm install` terminal command.

This command tells npm to install all the dependencies listed in the package.json file. When you run it, npm downloads all the packages listed as dependencies and installs them in a specific folder in the application, called node_modules. Figure 3.2 illustrates the three key parts.

npm installs each package into its own subfolder because each one is effectively a Node package in its own right. As such, each package also has its own package.json file defining the metadata, including the specific dependencies. It's quite common for a package to have its own node_modules folder. You don't need to worry about manually installing all the nested dependencies, though, because this task is handled by the original `npm install` command.

ADDING MORE PACKAGES TO AN EXISTING PROJECT

You're unlikely to have the full list of dependencies for a project right from the outset. It's far more likely that you'll start with a few key ones that you know you'll need and perhaps some that you always use in your workflow.

Using npm, it's easy to add more packages to the application whenever you want. Find the name of the package you want to install, open a command prompt in the same folder as the package.json file, and then run a simple command like this:

```
$ npm install --save package-name
```

With this command, npm downloads and installs the new package in the node_modules folder. The `--save` flag tells npm to add this package to the list of dependencies in the package.json file. As of npm version 5, the `--save` flag is no longer required, as NPM saves changes to the package.json file automatically. We've added it here for completeness. When this command is run, npm generates a package-lock.json file to maintain versions of dependencies between environments, which is helpful when you're deploying from development to a live server.

UPDATING PACKAGES TO LATER VERSIONS

The only time npm downloads and reinstalls existing packages is when you upgrade to a new version. When you run `npm install`, npm goes through all the dependencies and checks the following:

- The version defined in the package-lock.json file (if it exists) or package.json (if it doesn't)
- The latest matching version on npm (which may be different if you used ~ or ^)
- The version of the module (if there is one) in the node_modules folder

If your installed version is different from the definition in the package.json (or package-lock.json) file, npm downloads and installs the defined version. Similarly, if you're using a wildcard, and a later matching version is available, npm downloads and installs it in place of the previous version.

With that knowledge under your belt, you can start creating your first Express project.

3.2 *Creating an Express project*

All journeys must have a starting point, which for building a MEAN application is creating a new Express project. To create an Express project, you'll need to have five key things installed on your development machine:

- Node and npm
- The Express generator installed globally
- Git
- Heroku
- Suitable command-line interface (CLI) or terminal

3.2.1 *Installing the pieces*

If you don't have Node, npm, or the Express generator installed yet, see appendix A for instructions and pointers to online resources. All can be installed on Windows, macOS, and all mainstream Linux distributions.

By the end of this chapter, you'll also have used Git to manage the source control of your Loc8r application and pushed it to a live URL hosted by Heroku. Please take a look through appendix B, which guides you through setting up Git and Heroku.

Depending on your operating system, you may need to install a new CLI or terminal. See appendix B to find out whether this requirement applies to you.

> **NOTE** Throughout this book, we'll often refer to the CLI as *terminal*. When we say "Run this command in terminal," we mean run it in whichever CLI you're using. When terminal commands are included as code snippets throughout this book, they start with a $. You shouldn't type this symbol in terminal; it's simply there to denote a command-line statement. If you're entering the echo command $ `echo 'Welcome to Getting MEAN'`, for example, type `echo 'Welcome to Getting MEAN'`.

3.2.2 *Verifying the installations*

To create a new Express project, you must have Node and npm installed, and you must also have the Express generator installed globally. You can verify by checking for the version numbers in terminal, using the following commands:

```
$ node --version
$ npm --version
$ express --version
```

Each of these commands should output a version number to terminal. If one of them fails, head to appendix A for details on how to install it again.

3.2.3 *Creating a project folder*

Assuming that all is good, start by creating a new folder on your machine called loc8r. This folder can be on your desktop, in your documents, or in a Dropbox folder; the location doesn't matter as long as you have full read and write access rights to the folder.

Simon personally does a lot of his MEAN development in Dropbox folders so that his work is immediately backed up and accessible on any of his machines. If you're in a corporate environment, however, this approach may not be suitable for you, so create the folder wherever you think is best.

3.2.4 *Configuring an Express installation*

An Express project is installed from the command line, and the configuration is passed in with parameters of the command you use. If you're not familiar with using the command line, don't worry; none of what we'll go through in the book is particularly complex, and it's all easy to remember. Once you've started using it, you'll probably love how it makes some operations so fast.

You can install Express in a folder with a simple command (but don't do this yet):

```
$ express
```

This command installs the framework with default settings in your current folder. This step probably is a good start, but take a look at some configuration options first.

CONFIGURATION OPTIONS WHEN CREATING AN EXPRESS PROJECT

What can you configure when creating an Express project this way? You can specify the following:

- Which HTML template engine to use
- Which CSS preprocessor to use
- Whether to create a .gitignore file

A default installation uses the Jade template engine, but it has no CSS preprocessing or session support. You can specify a few options, as laid out in table 3.1.

Table 3.1   Command-line configuration options for creating a new Express project

Configuration command	Effect
`--css=less|stylus`	Adds a CSS preprocessor to your project, either Less or Stylus, depending on which you type in the command
`--view=ejs|hbs|pug`	Changes the HTML template engine from Jade to EJS, Handlebars, or Pug, depending on which you type
`--git`	Adds a .gitignore file to the directory

You aren't going to do that here, but if you want to create a project that uses the Less CSS preprocessor and the Handlebars template engine and includes a .gitignore file, you'd run the following command in terminal:

```
$ express --css=less --view=hbs --git
```

To keep things simple in your project, you won't use CSS preprocessing, so you can stick with the default of plain CSS. But you do need to use a template engine, so in the next section, you'll take a quick look at the options.

DIFFERENT TEMPLATE ENGINES

When you're using Express in this way, a few template options are available, including Jade, EJS, Handlebars, and Pug. The basic workflow of a template engine is creating the HTML template, including placeholders for data, and then passing it some data. Then the engine compiles the template and data together to create the final HTML markup that the browser will receive.

All engines have their own merits and quirks, and if you already have a preferred one, that's fine. In this book, you'll use Pug. Pug is powerful and provides all the functionality you're going to need. Pug is the next evolution of Jade; due to trademark issues, the creators of Jade had to rename it, and they chose Pug. Jade still exists, so existing projects won't break, but all new releases are under the name Pug. Jade was (and still is) the default template engine in Express, so you'll find that most examples and projects online use it, which means that it's helpful to be familiar with the syntax. Finally, the minimal style of Jade and Pug make them ideal for code samples in a book.

A QUICK LOOK AT PUG

Pug is unusual compared with the other template engines, in that it doesn't contain HTML tags in the templates. Instead, Pug takes a rather minimalist approach, using tag names, indentation, and a CSS-inspired reference method to define the structure of the HTML. The exception is the `<div>` tag. Because it's so common, if the tag name is omitted from the template, Pug assumes that you want a `<div>`.

> **TIP** Pug templates must be indented with spaces, not tabs.

The following code snippet shows a simple example of a Pug template:

```
#banner.page-header
  h1 My page
  p.lead Welcome to my page
```
Pug template contains no HTML tags

This snippet shows the compiled output:

```
<div id="banner" class="page-header">
  <h1>My page</h1>
  <p class="lead">Welcome to my page</p>
</div>
```
Compiled output is recognizable HTML

From the first lines of the input and output, you should be able to see that

- With no tag name specified, a <div> is created.
- #banner in Pug becomes id="banner" in HTML.
- .page-header in Pug becomes class="page-header" in HTML.

Note also that the indentation in Pug is important, as it defines the nesting of the HTML output. Remember that the indentation must be done with spaces, not tabs!

To recap, you don't need a CSS preprocessor, but you do want the Pug template engine. How about the .gitignore file?

A QUICK INTRO TO .GITIGNORE FILES

A .gitignore file is a simple configuration file that sits in the root of your project folder. This file specifies which files and folders Git commands should ignore. In essence, it says, "Pretend these files don't exist, and don't track them," meaning that they won't end up in source control.

Common examples include log files and the node_modules folder. Log files don't need to be up on GitHub for everyone to see, and your Node dependencies should be installed from npm whenever your application is downloaded. You'll be using Git in section 3.5, so ask the Express generator to create a file for you.

With that starting knowledge behind you, it's time to create a project.

3.2.5 *Creating an Express project and trying it out*

You know the basic command for creating an Express project and have decided to use the Pug template engine. You'll also let it generate a .gitignore file for you. Now create a new project. In section 3.2.3, you should have created a new folder called loc8r. Navigate to this folder in terminal, and run the following command:

```
$ express --view=pug --git
```

This command creates a bunch of folders and files inside the loc8r folder that form the basis of your Loc8r application. But you're not quite ready yet. Next, you need to install the dependencies. As you may remember, you do this by running the following command from a terminal prompt in the same folder as the package.json file:

```
$ npm install
```

As soon as you run it, your terminal window lights up with all the things it's download-ing. When it finishes, the application is ready for a test drive.

TRYING IT OUT

Make sure that everything works as expected. In section 3.2.6, we'll show you a better way of running the project.

In terminal, in the loc8r folder, run the following command (but if your applica-tion is in a folder with a different name, swap out `loc8r` accordingly):

```
$ DEBUG=loc8r:* npm start
```

You should see a confirmation similar to this:

```
loc8r:server Listening on port 3000 +0ms
```

This confirmation means that the Express application is running. You can see it in action by opening a browser and heading over to localhost:3000. We hope that you'll see something like the screenshot in figure 3.3.

Figure 3.3   Landing page for a bare-bones Express project

Admittedly, this isn't exactly ground-breaking stuff, but getting the Express applica-tion up and running to the point of working in a browser was easy, right?

If you head back to terminal now, you should see a couple of log statements con-firming that the page has been requested and that a stylesheet has been requested. To get to know Express a little better, take a look at what's going on here.

HOW EXPRESS HANDLES THE REQUESTS

The default Express landing page is simple. The page contains a small amount of HTML, of which some of the text content is pushed as data by the Express route. There's also a CSS file. The logs in terminal should confirm that this is what Express requested and has returned to the browser. But how?

About Express middleware

The app.js file contains a bunch of lines that start with `app.use` somewhere in the middle. These lines are known as *middleware*. When a request comes in to the application, it passes through each piece of middleware in turn. Each piece of middleware may or may not do something with the request, but it's always passed on to the next one until it reaches the application logic itself, which returns a response.

Take `app.use(express.cookieParser());`, for example. This line takes an incoming request, parses out any of the cookie information, and attaches the data to the request in a way that makes it easy to reference in the controller code.

You don't need to know what each piece of middleware does right now, but you may well find yourself adding to this list as you build out applications.

All requests to the Express server run through the middleware defined in the app.js file (see the sidebar "About Express middleware"). As well as doing other things, a default piece of middleware looks for paths to static files. When the middleware matches the path against a file, Express returns this asynchronously, ensuring that the Node.js process isn't tied up with this operation and therefore blocking other operations. When a request runs through all the middleware, Express attempts to match the path of the request against a defined route. We'll get into this topic in a bit more detail in section 3.3.3.

Figure 3.4 illustrates this flow, using the example of the default Express homepage from figure 3.3. The flow in figure 3.4 shows the separate requests made and how Express handles them differently. Both requests run through the middleware as a first action, but the outcomes are different.

3.2.6   *Restarting the application*

A Node application compiles before running, so if you make changes to the application code while it's running, they won't be picked up until the Node process is stopped and restarted. Note that this is true only for application code; Jade templates, CSS files, and client-side JavaScript can all be updated on the fly.

Restarting the Node process is a two-step procedure. First, you have to stop the running process in terminal by pressing Ctrl-C. Then, you have to start the process again in terminal, using the same command as before: `DEBUG=loc8r:* npm start`.

This process doesn't sound problematic, but when you're actively developing and testing an application, having to do these two steps every time you want to check an update becomes quite frustrating. Fortunately, there's a better way.

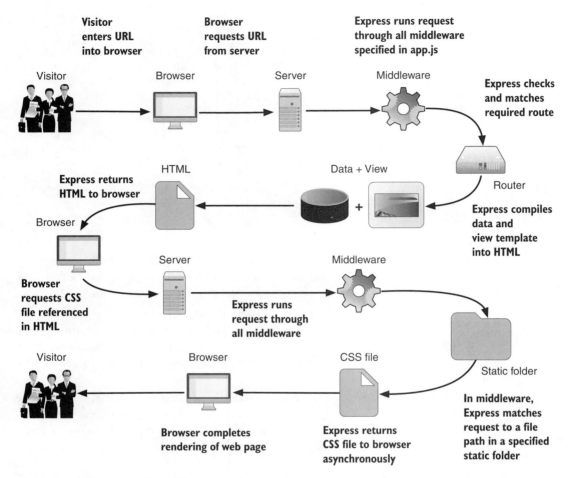

Figure 3.4 The key interactions and processes that Express goes through when responding to the request for the default landing page. The HTML page is processed by Node to compile data and a view template, and the CSS file is served asynchronously from a static folder.

AUTOMATICALLY RESTARTING THE APPLICATION WITH NODEMON

Some services have been developed to monitor application code and restart the process when they detect that changes have been made. One such service, and the one you'll use in this book, is nodemon. nodemon wraps the Node application and, other than monitoring for changes, causes no interference.

To use nodemon, start by installing it globally, much as you did with Express. Use npm in terminal:

```
$ npm install -g nodemon
```

When the installation is finished, you'll be able to use nodemon wherever you want. Using it is simple. Instead of typing node to start the application, you type nodemon. So, making sure that you're in the loc8r folder in terminal and that you've stopped the Node process, if it's still running, enter the following command:

```
$ nodemon
```

You should see a few extra lines output to terminal, confirming that nodemon is running and that it has started node ./bin/www. If you head back over to your browser and refresh, you should see that the application is still there.

> **NOTE** nodemon is intended only for easing the development process in your development environment and shouldn't be used in a live production environment. Projects like pm2 or foreman are designed for production use.

USING THE SUPPLIED DOCKER ENVIRONMENT

Each chapter comes with a Dockerfile set up. Head over to appendix B to see how to install and use the Docker containers. You don't have to use Docker to benefit from this book; it's been added as a convenience.

3.3 Modifying Express for MVC

Firstly, what is MVC architecture? MVC architecture separates the data (model), the display (view) and the application logic (controller). This separation aims to remove any tight coupling between the components, theoretically making code more maintainable and reusable. A bonus is that these components fit nicely into your rapid prototype development approach and allow you to concentrate on one aspect at a time as we discuss each part of the MEAN stack.

Whole books are dedicated to the nuances of MVC, but we won't go to that depth here. We'll keep the discussion of MVC at a high level and show you how to use it with Express to build your Loc8r application.

3.3.1 A bird's-eye view of MVC

Most applications or sites that you build are designed to take an incoming request, do something with it, and return a response. At a simple level, this loop in an MVC architecture works like this:

1 A request comes into the application.
2 The request gets routed to a controller.
3 The controller, if necessary, makes a request to the model.
4 The model responds to the controller.
5 The controller merges the view and the data to form a response.
6 The controller sends the generated response to the original requester.

In reality, depending on your setup, the controller may compile the view before sending the response to the visitor. The effect is the same, though, so keep this simple flow in mind as a visual for what will happen in your Loc8r application. See figure 3.5 for an illustration of this loop.

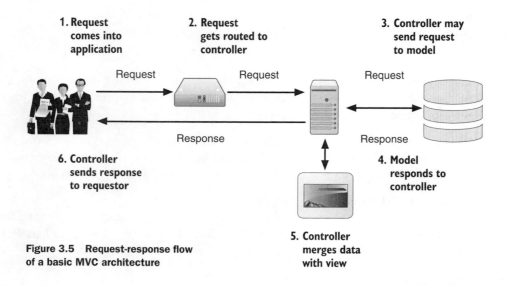

1. Request comes into application

2. Request gets routed to controller

3. Controller may send request to model

Request   Request   Request

Response   Response

6. Controller sends response to requestor

4. Model responds to controller

5. Controller merges data with view

Figure 3.5   Request-response flow of a basic MVC architecture

Figure 3.5 highlights the parts of the MVC architecture and shows how they link together. It also illustrates the need for a routing mechanism along with the model, view, and controller components.

Now that you've seen how you want the basic flow of your Loc8r application to work, it's time to modify the Express setup to make this happen.

3.3.2   *Changing the folder structure*

If you look inside the newly created Express project in the loc8r folder, you should see a file structure including a views folder and even a routes folder, but no mention of models or controllers. Rather than cluttering the root level of the application with some new folders, keep things tidy by creating one new folder for all your MVC architecture. Follow these three quick steps:

1   Create a new folder called app_server.
2   In app_server, create two new folders called models and controllers.
3   Move the views and routes folders from the root of the application into the app_server folder.

Figure 3.6 illustrates these changes and shows the folder structures before and after modification.

Now you have an obvious MVC setup in the application, which makes it easier to separate your concerns. But if you try to run the application now, it won't work, as you've just broken it. So fix it. Express doesn't know that you've added some new folders or have any idea what you want to use them for, so you need to tell it.

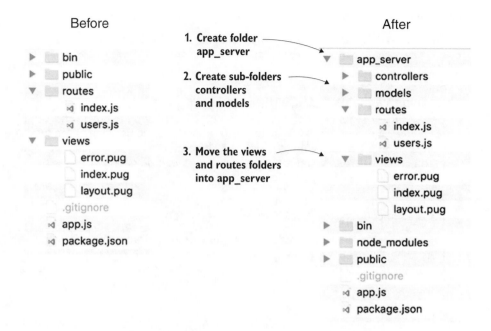

Figure 3.6   Changing the folder structure of an Express project into an MVC architecture

3.3.3 *Using the views and routes relocated folders*

The first thing you need to do is tell Express that you've moved the views and routes folders, because Express will be looking for them in their old location.

USING THE NEW VIEWS FOLDER LOCATION

Express will be looking for /views, but it needs to look for /app_server/views. Changing the path is simple. In app.js, find the following line:

```
app.set('views', path.join(__dirname, 'views'));
```

Change it to the following (modifications in bold):

```
app.set('views', path.join(__dirname, 'app_server', 'views'));
```

Your application still won't work, because you've moved the routes, so tell Express about them too.

USING THE NEW ROUTES FOLDER LOCATION

Express will be looking for /routes, but it needs to look for /app_server/routes. Changing this path is also simple. In app.js, find the following lines:

```
const indexRouter = require('./routes/index');
const usersRouter = require('./routes/users');
```

Change these lines to the following (modifications in bold):

```
const indexRouter = require('./app_server/routes/index');
const usersRouter = require('./app_server/routes/users');
```

Defining variables in ES2015

One of the most fundamental changes in ES2015 is deprecation of the `var` keyword to define variables. It still works, but instead, you should use one of the two new keywords: `const` and `let`. Variables defined with `const` *can't* be changed at a later point in the code, whereas variables defined with `let` *can* be changed.

Best practice is to define variables with `const` unless their values are going to change. All instances of `var` in app.js can be changed to `const`. We've done this in the source code for this book; feel free to do it too.

One other thing to bear in mind is that `const` and `let` are block-level variable initializers, whereas `var` is a context-level variable initializer. If these terms mean nothing to you, read appendix D, available with the e-book or online from manning.com.

Note that you also changed `var` to `const` to upgrade to ES2015. Check out the sidebar "Defining variables in ES2015" if this concept is new to you. If you save your changes and run the application again, you'll find that it works once more!

3.3.4 *Splitting controllers from routes*

In a default Express setup, controllers are part of the routes, but you want to separate them out. Controllers should manage the application logic, and routing should map URL requests to controllers.

UNDERSTANDING ROUTE DEFINITION

To understand how routes work, take a look at the route already set up for delivering the default Express homepage. Inside index.js in app_server/routes, you should see the following code snippet:

```
/* GET homepage. */
router.get('/', function(req, res) {        ① Where the
  res.render('index', { title: 'Express' });    router looks
});                                             for the URL
                                             ② Controller content, albeit
                                                very basic right now
```

In the code at ① you can see `router.get('/')`. The router checks internally for GET requests that map to the homepage URL path, which is `'/'`. The anonymous function that runs the code ① is the controller. This basic example has no application code to speak of. So ① and ② are the pieces you want to separate here.

Rather than dive straight in and put the controller code in the controllers folder, test the approach in the same file first. To do this, you can define the anonymous function from the route definition as a named function. Then pass the name of this function through as the callback in the route definition. Both of these steps are in the following listing, which you can put in place inside app_server/routes/index.js.

> **Listing 3.2   Taking the controller code out of the route: step 1**

```
const homepageController = (req, res) => {
  res.render('index', { title: 'Express' });
};
/* GET homepage. */
router.get('/', homepageController);
```

Gives a name to the arrow function

Passes the name of the function through as a callback in the route definition

If you refresh your homepage now, it should still work as before. You haven't changed anything in how the site works—only moved a step toward separating concerns.

Understanding res.render

You'll look at this topic more in chapter 4, but render is the Express function for compiling a view template to send as the HTML response that the browser will receive. The render method takes the name of the view template and a JavaScript data object in the following construct:

```
                      JavaScript object containing
                      data for template to use

res.render('index',   {title: 'express'});

       Name of template to use,
       in this case referencing index.pug
```

Note that the template file doesn't need to have the file extension suffix, so index.pug can be referenced as index. You also don't need to specify the path to the view folder, because you've already done this in the main Express setup.

Now that you're clear about how route definition works, it's time to put the controller code in its proper place.

MOVING THE CONTROLLER OUT OF THE ROUTES FILE

In Node, to reference code in an external file, you create a module in your new file, and then require it in the original file. See the sidebar "Creating and using Node modules" for some overarching principles behind this process.

Creating and using Node modules

Taking some code out of a Node file to create an external module is, fortunately, simple. In essence, you create a new file for your code, choose which bits of it you want to expose to the original file, and then require your new file in your original file.

(continued)

In your new module file, you expose the parts of the code that you want to by using the `module.exports` method, like so:

```
module.exports = function () {
  console.log("This is exposed to the requester");
};
```

Then you `require` this in your main file, like so:

```
require('./yourModule');
```

If you want your module to have separate named methods exposed, you can do so by defining them in your new file in the following way:

```
module.exports.logThis = function (message){
  console.log(message);
};
```

Even better is to define a named function and export it at the end of the file. This lets you expose all the functions you need to in one place, creating a handy list for your future self (or subsequent developers).

```
const logThis = function (message) {
  console.log(message);
};
module.exports = {
 logThis
};
```

To reference this in your original file, you need to assign your module to a variable name, and then invoke the method. You might enter this in your main file:

```
const yourModule = require('./yourModule');
yourModule.logThis("Hooray, it works!");
```

This code assigns your new module to the variable `yourModule`. The exported function `logThis` is now available as a method of `yourModule`.

Note that, when using the `require` function, you don't need to specify a file extension. The `require` function looks for a couple of things: an npm module, a JavaScript file of the same name, or an index.js file inside a folder of the given name.

The first thing you need to do is create a file to hold the controller code. Create a new file called main.js in app_server/controllers. In this file, create and export a method called index, and use it to house the `res.render` code, as shown in the following listing.

Listing 3.3   Setting up the homepage controller in app_server/controllers/main.js

```
/* GET homepage */
const index = (req, res) => {          Creates an index function
  res.render('index', { title: 'Express' });   Includes controller code for the homepage
};
```

```
module.exports = {
  index
};
```
**Exposes the index
function as a method**

That's all there is to exporting the controller. The next step is to require this controller module in the routes file so that you can use the exposed method in the route definition. The following listing shows how the index.js file in app_server/routes should look.

Listing 3.4   Updating the routes file to use external controllers

```
const express = require('express');
const router = express.Router();
const ctrlMain = require('../controllers/main');
/* GET homepage. */
router.get('/', ctrlMain.index);
module.exports = router;
```
① **Requires the main
controllers file**

② **References the index method of the
controllers in the route definition**

This code links the route to the new controller by "requiring" the controller file **①** and referencing the controller function in the second parameter of the router.get function **②**.

Now you have the routing and controller architecture, as illustrated in figure 3.7, where app.js requires routes/index.js, which in turn requires controllers/main.js. If you test this now in your browser, you should see that the default Express homepage displays correctly once again.

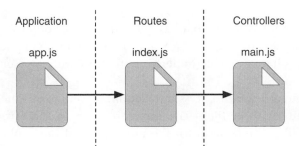

Application   Routes   Controllers

app.js   index.js   main.js

**Figure 3.7   Separating the controller
logic from the route definitions**

Everything is set up with Express for now, so it's almost time to start the building process. But you need to do a couple more things. The first is adding Twitter Bootstrap to the application.

3.4   *Importing Bootstrap for quick, responsive layouts*

As discussed in chapter 1, your Loc8r application uses Twitter's Bootstrap framework to speed the development of a responsive design. You'll also make the application stand out by adding some font icons and custom styles. The aim is to help you keep moving forward quickly with building the application and not get sidetracked with the semantics of developing a responsive interface.

3.4.1   Downloading Bootstrap and adding it to the application

Instructions for downloading Bootstrap, downloading the font icons (by Font Awesome), creating a custom style, and adding the files to the project folder are in appendix B. Note that you use Bootstrap 4.1. A key point is that the downloaded files are all static files to be sent directly to the browser; they don't need any processing by the Node engine. Your Express application already has a folder for this purpose: the public folder. When you have it ready, the public folder should look something like figure 3.8.

Bootstrap also requires jQuery and Popper.js for some of the interactive components to work. Because they aren't core to your application, you'll reference them from a content delivery network (CDN) in the next step.

Figure 3.8   Structure of the public folder in the Express application after adding Bootstrap

3.4.2   Using Bootstrap in the application

Now that all of the Bootstrap pieces are sitting in the application, it's time to hook it up to the front end, which means taking a look at the Pug templates.

WORKING WITH PUG TEMPLATES

Pug templates often have a main layout file that has defined areas for other Pug files to extend. This makes a great deal of sense when you're building a web application, because many screens or pages have the same underlying structure with different content on top.

This is how Pug appears in a default Express installation: If you look in the views folder in the application, you see three files—layout.pug, index.pug, and error.pug. The index.pug file is controlling the content for the index page of the application. Open it, and you see that not much is in there. The entire contents are shown in the following listing.

Listing 3.5   The complete index.pug file

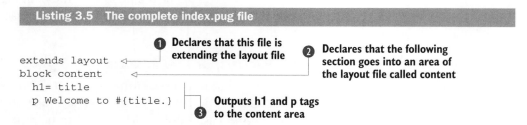

There's more going on here than meets the eye. Right at the top of the file is a statement declaring that this file is an extension of another file ❶—in this case, the layout file. Following is a statement defining a block of code ❷ that belongs to a specific area of the layout file: an area called content. Finally, there's the minimal content displayed on the Express index page: a single <h1> tag and a single <p> tag ❸.

There are no references to <head> or <body> tags here, or any stylesheet references. These are handled in the layout file, so that's where you want to go to add global scripts and stylesheets to the application. Open layout.pug, and you should see something similar to the following listing.

Listing 3.6   Default layout.pug file

```
doctype html
html
  head
    title= title
    link(rel='stylesheet', href='/stylesheets/style.css')       Empty named block
  body                                                           can be used by other
    block content        ◁─────────────────────────────────┘    templates
```

This shows the layout file being used for the basic index page in the default Express installation. There's a head section and a body section, and within the body section, there's a block content line with nothing inside it. This named block can be referenced by other Pug templates, such as the index.pug file in listing 3.5. The block content from the index file gets pushed into the block content area of the layout file when the views are compiled.

ADDING BOOTSTRAP TO THE ENTIRE APPLICATION

If you want to add some external reference files to the entire application, using the layout file makes sense in the current setup. In layout.pug, you need to accomplish four things:

- Reference the Bootstrap and Font Awesome CSS files.
- Reference the Bootstrap JavaScript file.
- Reference jQuery and Popper.js, which Bootstrap requires.
- Add viewport metadata so that the page scales nicely on mobile devices.

The CSS file and the viewport metadata should both be in the head of the document, and the two script files should be at the end of the body section. The following listing shows all this in place in layout.pug, with the new lines in bold.

Listing 3.7   Updated layout.pug including Bootstrap references

```
doctype html              Sets the viewport metadata for
html                      better display on mobile devices
  head                                                              Includes
    meta(name='viewport', content='width=device-width,             Bootstrap
      ↪initial-scale=1.0')       ◁───────────                      and Font
    title= title                                                   Awesome CSS
    link(rel='stylesheet', href='/stylesheets/bootstrap.min.css')
    link(rel='stylesheet', href='/stylesheets/all.min.css')
```

```
    link(rel='stylesheet', href='/stylesheets/style.css')
body
    block content
    script(src='https://code.jquery.com/jquery-3.3.1.slim.min.js',
    ➥integrity='sha384-
    ➥q8i/X+965DzO0rT7abK41JStQIAqVgRVzpbzo5smXKp4YfRvH+8abtTE1Pi6jizo',
    ➥crossorigin='anonymous')
    script(src='https://cdnjs.cloudflare.com/ajax/libs/
    ➥popper.js/1.14.3/umd/popper.min.js',integrity='sha384-
    ➥ZMP7rVo3mIykV+2+9J3UJ46jBk0WLaUAdn689aCwoqbBJiSnjAK/l8WvCWPIPm49',
    crossorigin='anonymous')
    script(src='/javascripts/bootstrap.min.js')
```

Brings in the Bootstrap JavaScript file

Brings in jQuery and Popper, needed by Bootstrap. Make sure that the script tags are all at the same indentation.

With that done, any new template that you create automatically has Bootstrap included and will scale on mobile devices—as long as your new templates extend the layout template, of course. Should you have any problems or unexpected results at this stage, remember that Pug is sensitive to indentation, spacing, and newlines. All indentation must be done with spaces to get the correct nesting in the HTML output.

TIP If you followed along in appendix B, you'll also have some custom styles in the style.css file in /public/stylesheets to prevent the default Express styles from overriding the Bootstrap files and help you get the look you want.

Now you're ready to test.

VERIFYING THAT IT WORKS
If the application isn't already running with nodemon, start it, and view it in your browser. The content hasn't changed, but the appearance should have. You should have something that looks like figure 3.9.

Figure 3.9 Bootstrap and your styles having an effect on the default Express index page

If yours doesn't look like this, make sure that you've added the custom styles as outlined in appendix B. Remember that you can get the source code of the application so far from the chapter-03 branch on GitHub. In a fresh folder in terminal, use the following command to clone it:

```
$ git clone -b chapter-03 https://github.com/cliveharber/
    ⇒gettingMean-2.git
```

Now you've got something working locally. In the next section, you'll see how you can get it running on a live production server.

3.5 *Making it live on Heroku*

A common perceived headache with Node applications is deploying them to a live production server. You're going to get rid of that headache early and push your Loc8r application to a live URL right away. As you iterate and build it up, you can keep pushing out the updates. For prototyping, this approach is great, because it makes showing your progress to others easy.

As mentioned in chapter 1, there are a few PaaS providers such as Google Cloud Platform, Nodejitsu, OpenShift, and Heroku. You'll use Heroku here, but there's nothing to stop you from trying other options. Next, you'll get Heroku up and running, and walk through a few basic Git commands to deploy your application to a live server.

3.5.1 *Getting Heroku set up*

Before you can use Heroku, you need to sign up for a free account and install the Heroku CLI on your development machine. Appendix B has more detailed information on how to do this. You also need a bash-compatible terminal; the default terminal for Mac users is fine, but the default CLI for Windows users won't do. If you're on Windows, you need to download something like the GitHub terminal, which comes as part of the GitHub desktop application. When you have everything set up, you can continue getting the application ready to push live.

UPDATING PACKAGE.JSON

Heroku can run applications on various types of codebases, so you need to tell it what your application is running. Besides telling it that you're running a Node application using npm as the package manager, you also need to tell it which version you're running to ensure that the production setup is the same as the development setup.

If you're not sure which versions of Node and npm you're running, you can find out with a couple of terminal commands:

```
$ node --version
$ npm --version
```

Currently, these commands return v11.0.0 and 6.4.1, respectively. Using the ~ syntax to add a wildcard for a minor version, as you've seen previously, you need to add these to a new engines section in the package.json file. The complete updated package.json file is shown in the following listing, with the added section in bold.

Listing 3.8   Adding an engines section to package.json

```
{
  "name": "Loc8r",
  "version": "0.0.1",
  "private": true,
  "scripts": {
    "start": "node ./bin/www"
  },
  "engines": {                          Adds an engines section to
    "node": ">=11.0.0",                 package.json to tell Heroku
    "npm": ">=6.4.0"                    which platform your application
  },                                    is on and which version to use
  "dependencies": {
    "body-parser": "~1.18.3",
    "cookie-parser": "~1.4.3",
    "debug": "~3.1.0",
    "express": "~4.16.3",
    "morgan": "~1.9.0",
    "pug": "~2.0.0-beta11",
    "serve-favicon": "~2.5.0"
  }
}
```

When pushed up to Heroku, this code tells Heroku that your application uses the latest minor version of Node 11 and the latest minor version of npm 6.

CREATING A PROCFILE

The package.json file tells Heroku that the application is a Node application but doesn't tell it how to start it. For this task, you need a Procfile, which is used to declare the process types used by your application and the commands used to start them.

For Loc8r, you want a web process, and you want it to run the Node application. In the root folder of the application, create a file called Procfile. (The name is case sensitive and has no file extension.) Enter the following line in the Procfile:

```
web: npm start
```

When pushed up to Heroku, this file tells Heroku that the application needs a web process and that it should run `npm start`.

TESTING IT LOCALLY WITH HEROKU LOCAL

The Heroku CLI comes with a utility called Heroku Local. You can use this utility to verify your setup and run your application locally before pushing the application up to Heroku. If the application is currently running, stop it by pressing Ctrl-C in the terminal window that's running the process. Then, in the terminal window, make sure you're in your application folder, and enter the following command:

```
$ heroku local
```

If all is well with the setup, this command starts the application running on localhost again, but this time on a different port: 5000. The confirmation you get in terminal should be along these lines:

```
16:09:02 web.1  | > loc8r@0.0.1 start /path/to/your/application/folder
16:09:02 web.1  | > node ./bin/www
```

You'll probably also see the warning `No ENV file found`. This message is nothing to worry about at this stage. If you fire up a browser and head over to localhost:5000 (note that the port is 5000 instead of 3000), you should see the application up and running again.

Now that you know the setup is working, it's time to push your application up to Heroku.

3.5.2 *Pushing the site live using Git*

Heroku uses Git as the deployment method. If you already use Git, you'll love this approach; if you haven't, you may feel a bit apprehensive about it, because the world of Git can be complex. But it doesn't need to be, and when you get going, you'll love this approach too!

STORING THE APPLICATION IN GIT

The first action is storing the application in Git on your local machine. This process involves the following three steps:

1 Initialize the application folder as a Git repository.
2 Tell Git which files you want to add to the repository.
3 Commit these changes to the repository.

This process may sound complex but isn't. You need a single, short terminal command for each step. If the application is running locally, stop it in terminal (Ctrl-C). Then, ensuring you're still in the root folder of the application, stay in terminal, and run the following commands:

These three things together create a local Git repository containing the entire code-base for the application. When you update the application later and want to push some changes live, you'll use the second two commands, with a different message, to update the repository. Your local repository is ready. It's time to create the Heroku application.

CREATING THE HEROKU APPLICATION

This next step creates an application on Heroku as a remote Git repository of your local repository. You do all this with a single terminal command:

```
$ heroku create
```

You'll see a confirmation in terminal of the URL that the application is on, the Git repository address, and the name of the remote repository, as in this example:

```
https://pure-temple-67771.herokuapp.com/ | git@heroku.com:pure-temple-
   67771.git
Git remote heroku added
```

If you log in to your Heroku account in a browser, you'll also see that the application exists there. Now that you have a place on Heroku for the application, the next step is pushing the application code up.

DEPLOYING THE APPLICATION TO HEROKU

You have the application stored in a local Git repository, and you've created a new remote repository on Heroku. The remote repository is empty, so you need to push the contents of your local repository to the `heroku` remote repository.

If you don't know Git, there's a single command for this purpose, which has the following construct:

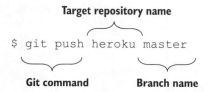

Target repository name

```
$ git push heroku master
```

Git command   **Branch name**

This command pushes the contents of your local Git repository to the `heroku` remote repository. Currently, you only have a single branch in your repository—the master branch—so that's what you'll push to Heroku. See the sidebar "What are Git branches?" for more information on Git branches.

When you run this command, terminal displays a load of log messages as it goes through the process, eventually showing (about five lines from the end) a confirmation that the application has been deployed to Heroku. This confirmation is something like the following except that, of course, you'll have a different URL:

```
http://pure-temple-67771.herokuapp.com deployed to Heroku
```

What are Git branches?

If you work on the same version of the code and push it up to a remote repository like Heroku or GitHub periodically, you're working on the *master* branch. This process is absolutely fine for linear development with one developer. If you have multiple developers, however, or your application is already published, you don't want to be doing your development on the master branch. Instead, you start a new branch from the master code in which you can continue development, add fixes, or build a new feature. When work on a branch is complete, it can be merged back into the master branch.

ABOUT WEB DYNOS ON HEROKU

Heroku uses the concept of *dynos* for running and scaling an application. The more dynos you have, the more system resources and processes you have available to your application. Adding more dynos when your application gets bigger and more popular is easy.

Heroku also has a great free tier, which is perfect for application prototyping and building a proof of concept. You get one web dyno free with each application, which is more than adequate for your purposes here. If you have an application that needs more resources, you can always log in to your account and pay for more.

In the following section, you'll check out the live URL.

VIEWING THE APPLICATION ON A LIVE URL

Everything is in place, and the application is live on the internet! You can see it by typing the URL given to you in the confirmation, via your account on the Heroku website, or by using the following terminal command:

```
$ heroku open
```

This command launches the application in your default browser, and you should see something like figure 3.10.

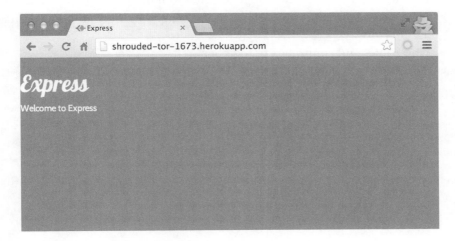

Figure 3.10 MVC Express application running on a live URL

Your URL will be different, of course, and within Heroku, you can change it to use your domain name instead of the address it gave you. In the application settings on the Heroku website, you can change it to the more meaningful subdomain herokuapp.com.

Having your prototype on an accessible URL is handy for cross-browser and cross-device testing, as well as for sending it to colleagues and partners.

A SIMPLE UPDATE PROCESS

Now that the Heroku application is set up, updating it is easy. Every time you want to push some new changes through, you need three terminal commands:

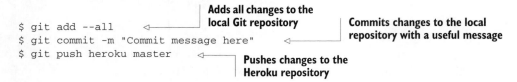

```
$ git add --all
$ git commit -m "Commit message here"
$ git push heroku master
```

Adds all changes to the local Git repository

Commits changes to the local repository with a useful message

Pushes changes to the Heroku repository

That's all there is to it, for now at least. Things may get a bit more complex if you have multiple developers and branches to deal with, but the process of pushing the code to Heroku using Git remains the same.

In chapter 4, you'll get to know Express even more when you build out a prototype of the Loc8r application.

Summary

In this chapter, you learned

- How to create a new Express application
- How to manage application dependencies with npm and the package.json file
- How a standard Express project can be changed to meet an MVC approach to architecture
- How routes and controllers fit together
- The simplest way to publish an Express application live to Heroku using Git

Building a static site with Node and Express

This chapter covers

- Prototyping an application by building a static version
- Defining routes for application URLs
- Creating views in Express by using Pug and Bootstrap
- Using controllers in Express to tie routes to views
- Passing data from controllers to views

By the end of chapter 3, you should have had an Express application running, set up in an MVC way, with Bootstrap included to help with building page layouts. Your next step is building on this base, creating a static site that you can click through. This step is critical in putting together any site or application. Even if you've been given a design or some wireframes to work from, there's no substitute for rapidly creating a realistic prototype that you can use in the browser. Something always comes to light in terms of layout or usability that you hadn't noticed before. From this static prototype, you'll take the data out from the views and put it into the controllers. By the end of this chapter, you'll have intelligent views that can display data passed to them and controllers passing hardcoded data to the views.

Getting the source code

If you haven't yet built the application from chapter 3, you can get the code from the chapter-03 branch on GitHub at https://github.com/cliveharber/gettingMean-2. In a fresh folder in terminal, enter the following commands to clone it and install the npm module dependencies:

```
$ git clone -b chapter-03 https://github.com/cliveharber/
➥gettingMean-2.git
$ cd gettingMean-2
$ npm install
```

In terms of building up the application architecture, this chapter focuses on the Express application as shown in figure 4.1.

Two main steps are accomplished in this chapter, so two versions of the source code are available. The first version contains all the data in the views and represents the application as it stands at the end of section 4.4. This code is available from the chapter-04-views branch on GitHub.

The second version has the data in the controllers, in the state in which the application will be at the end of this chapter. This code is available from the chapter-04 branch on GitHub.

To get one of these versions, use the following commands in a fresh folder in terminal, remembering to specify the branch that you want:

```
$ git clone -b chapter-04 https://github.com/cliveharber/gettingMean-2.git
$ cd gettingMean2
$ npm install
```

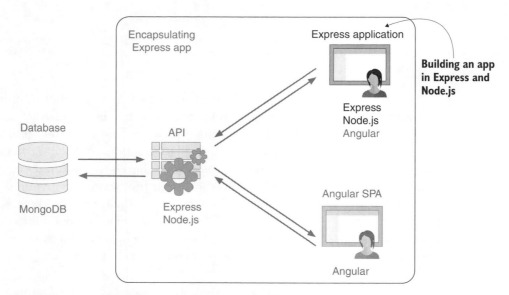

Figure 4.1   **Using Express and Node to build a static site for testing views**

If you want to run the Docker environment, see appendix B. Now you're ready to get back to Express.

4.1 Defining the routes in Express

In chapter 2 you planned the application and decided on the four pages you're going to build. You have a collection of Locations pages and a page in the Others collection, as shown in figure 4.2.

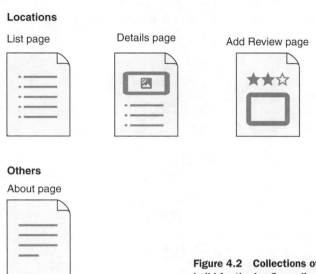

Locations

List page   Details page   Add Review page

Others

About page

Figure 4.2   Collections of screens you'll build for the Loc8r application

Having a set of screens is great, but these screens need to relate to incoming URLs. Before you do any coding, it's a good idea to map out the links between screens and URLs and to get a good standard in place. Take a look at table 4.1, which shows a simple mapping of the screens against URLs. These mappings will form the basis of the routing for your application.

Table 4.1   Defining a URL path, or route, for each of the screens in the prototype

Collection	Screen	URL path
Locations	List of locations (the homepage)	`/`
Locations	Location detail	`/location`
Locations	Location review form	`/location/review/new`
Others	About Loc8r	`/about`

When somebody visits the homepage, for example, you want to show them a list of places, but when somebody visits the /about URL path, you want to show them information about Loc8r.

4.1.1   *Different controller files for different collections*

In chapter 3, you moved any sense of controller logic out of the route definitions and into an external file. Looking to the future, you know that your application will grow, and you don't want to have all the controllers in one file. A logical starting point for splitting them up is dividing them by collections.

Looking at the collections you've decided on, you decide to split the controllers into Locations and Others. To see how this approach might work from a file-architecture point of view, you can sketch something like figure 4.3. Here, the application includes the routes file, which in turn includes multiple controller files, each named according to the relevant collection.

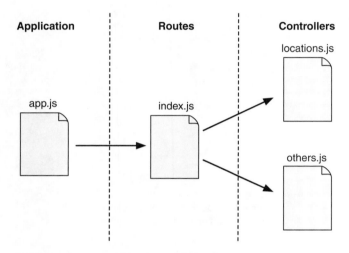

Figure 4.3   Proposed file architecture for routes and controllers in your application

You have a single route file, as well as one controller file for each logical collection of screens. This setup is designed to help you organize your code in line with how your application is organized. You'll look at the controllers shortly, but first, you'll deal with the routes.

The time for planning is over; now it's time for action! Head back to your development environment and open the application. You'll start by working in the routes file index.js.

REQUIRING THE CONTROLLER FILES

As shown in figure 4.3, you want to reference two controller files in this routes file. You haven't created these controller files yet; you'll do that shortly.

These files will be called locations.js and others.js. They will be saved in app_server/controllers. In index.js you'll `require` both of these files and assign each to a relevant variable name, as shown in the following listing.

Listing 4.1   Requiring the controller files in app_server/routes/index.js

```
const express = require('express');
const router = express.Router();
const ctrlLocations = require('../controllers/locations');
const ctrlOthers = require('../controllers/others');
```

Replaces existing ctrlMain reference with two new requires

Now you have two variables that you can reference in the route definitions, containing different collections of routes.

SETTING UP THE ROUTES

In index.js, you need to have the routes for the three screens in the Locations collection and the About page in the Others collection. Each route will also need a reference to a controller. Remember that routes serve as a mapping service, taking the URL of an incoming request and mapping it to a specific piece of application functionality.

From table 4.1, you already know which paths you want to map, so you need to put everything together into the routes/index.js file. What you need to have in the file is shown in entirety in the following listing.

Listing 4.2   Defining the routes and mapping them to controllers

```
const express = require('express');
const router = express.Router();
const ctrlLocations =
    require('../controllers/locations');
const ctrlOthers = require('../controllers/others');

/* Locations pages */
router.get('/', ctrlLocations.homelist);
router.get('/location', ctrlLocations.locationInfo);
router.get('/location/review/new', ctrlLocations.addReview);

/* Other pages */
router.get('/about', ctrlOthers.about);

module.exports = router;
```

Requires controller files

Defines location routes and maps them to controller functions

Defines other routes

This routing file maps the defined URLs to some specific controllers, although you haven't created those yet. You'll take care of that task in the following section.

4.2   *Building basic controllers*

At this point, you'll keep the controllers basic so that your application will run, and you can test the URLs and routing.

4.2.1   *Setting up controllers*

You currently have one file: the main.js file in the controllers folder (in the app_server folder), which has a single function that's controlling the homepage. This function is shown in the following code snippet:

```
/* GET 'home' page */
const index = (req, res) => {
  res.render('index', { title: 'Express' });
};
```

You don't want a "main" controller file anymore, but you can use this one as a template. Start by renaming this file others.js.

ADDING THE OTHERS CONTROLLERS

Recall from listing 4.2 that you want one controller in others.js called `about`. Rename the existing `index` controller `about`; keep the same view template for now; and update the `title` property to something relevant. This approach makes it easy to test whether the route is working as expected. The following listing shows the full content of the others.js controller file after these little changes.

Listing 4.3   Others controller file

```
/* GET 'about' page */
const about = (req, res) => {                      Defines the route, using the
  res.render('index', { title: 'About' });         same view template but
};                                                 changing the title to About
module.exports = {
  about        ⟵——————    Updates the export to
};                                      reflect the name change
```

That's the first controller done, but the application still won't work, as there aren't any controllers for the Locations routes yet.

ADDING THE LOCATIONS CONTROLLERS

Adding the controllers for the Locations routes is going to be pretty much the same process. In the routes file, you specified the name of the controller file to look for and the name of the three controller functions.

In the controllers folder, create a file called locations.js, and create and export three basic controller functions: `homelist`, `locationInfo`, and `addReview`. The following listing shows how this file should look.

Listing 4.4   Locations controller file

```
/* GET 'home' page */
const homelist = (req, res) => {
  res.render('index', { title: 'Home' });
};

/* GET 'Location info' page */
const locationInfo = (req, res) => {
  res.render('index', { title: 'Location info' });
};

/* GET 'Add review' page */
const addReview = (req, res) => {
  res.render('index', { title: 'Add review' });
};
```

```
module.exports = {
  homelist,
  locationInfo,
  addReview
};
```

Everything is in place, so you're ready to test it.

4.2.2 Testing the controllers and routes

Now that the routes and basic controllers are in place, you should be able to start and run the application. If you don't already have it running with nodemon, head to the root folder of the application in the terminal and start it:

```
$ nodemon
```

> **Troubleshooting**
>
> If you're having problems restarting the application at this point, the main thing to check is that all the files, functions, and references are named correctly. Look at the error messages you're getting in the terminal window to see whether they give you any clues. Some messages are more helpful than others. Take a look at the following possible error and pick out the parts that are interesting to you:
>
> ```
> module.js:340
>       throw err;
>       ^
> Error: Cannot find module '../controllers/other'        ❶ Clue 1: A module
>     at Function.Module._resolveFilename (module.js:338:15)   can't be found.
>     at Function.Module._load (module.js:280:25)
>     at Module.require (module.js:364:17)
>     at require (module.js:380:17)
>     at module.exports (/Users/sholmes/Dropbox/
>       Manning/GettingMEAN/Code/Loc8r/        ❷ Clue 2: A file-throwing
>       BookCode/routes/index.js:2:3)            error occurred.
>     at Object.<anonymous> (/Users/sholmes/Dropbox/
>       Manning/GettingMEAN/Code/Loc8r/
>       BookCode/app.js:26:20)
>     at Module._compile (module.js:456:26)
>     at Object.Module._extensions..js (module.js:474:10)
>     at Module.load (module.js:356:32)
>     at Function.Module._load (module.js:312:12)
> ```
>
> First, you see that a module called `other` can't be found ❶. Farther down the stack trace, you see the file where the error originated ❷. Open the routes/index.js file, and you'll discover that you wrote `require('../controllers/other')`, when the file you want to require is others.js. To fix the problem, correct the reference by changing it to `require('../controllers/others')`.

All being well, this run should give you no errors, meaning that the routes are pointing to controllers. At this point, you can head over to your browser and check each of the four routes you've created, such as localhost:3000 for the homepage and localhost:3000/location for the location information page. Because you changed the data being sent to the view template by each of the controllers, you can easily see that each one is running correctly—the title and heading should be different on each page. Figure 4.4 shows a collection of screenshots of the newly created routes and controllers. You can see that each route is getting unique content, so you know that the routing and controller setup has worked.

Figure 4.4   Screenshots of the four routes created so far, with different heading text coming through from the specific controllers associated with each route

The next stage in this prototyping process is putting some HTML, layout, and content on each screen. You'll do this by using views.

4.3   *Creating some views*

When you have your empty pages, paths, and routes sorted out, it's time to get some content and layout into your application. This step is where you bring the application to life and start to see your idea become reality. For this step, the technologies that you'll use are Pug and Bootstrap. Pug is the template engine you're using in Express (although you can use others if you prefer), and Bootstrap is a front-end layout framework that makes it easy to build a responsive website that looks different on desktop and mobile devices.

4.3.1   *A look at Bootstrap*

Before getting started, let's take a quick look at Bootstrap. We won't go into all the details about Bootstrap and everything it can do, but it's useful for you to see some of the key concepts before you try to throw it into a template file.

Bootstrap uses a 12-column grid. No matter the size of the display you're using, there will always be these 12 columns. On a phone, each column is narrow, and on a large external monitor, each column is wide. The fundamental concept of Bootstrap is that you can define how many columns an element uses, and this number can be different for different screen sizes.

Bootstrap has various CSS references that let you target up to five different pixel-width breakpoints for your layouts. These breakpoints are noted in table 4.2, along with the example device that each size targets.

Table 4.2   Breakpoints that Bootstrap sets to target different types of devices

Breakpoint name	CSS reference	Example device	Width
Extra-small devices	(none)	Small phones	Fewer than 576
Small devices	sm	Smartphones	576 or more
Medium devices	md	Tablets	768 or more
Large devices	lg	Laptops	992 or more
Extra-large devices	xl	External monitors	1,200 or more

To define the width of an element, you combine a CSS reference from table 4.2 with the number of columns you want it to span. A class denoting a column is constructed like this:

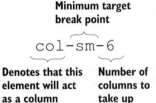

This class of col-sm-6 makes the element it's applied to take up six columns on screens of size sm and larger. On tablets, laptops, and monitors, this column will take up half the available width.

To get the responsive side of things to work, you can apply multiple classes to a single element. If you wanted a div to span the entire width or the screen on phones but only half the width on tablets and larger devices, you could use the following code snippet:

```
<div class="col-12 col-md-6"></div>
```

The col-12 class tells the layout to use 12 columns on extra-small devices, and the col-md-6 class tells the layout to use 6 columns for medium devices and larger. Figure 4.5 illustrates the effect of this class on different devices if you have two of them on the page, one after another, like this:

```
<div class="col-12 col-md-6">DIV ONE</div>
<div class="col-12 col-md-6">DIV TWO</div>
```

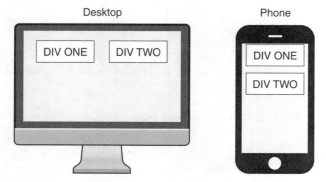

Figure 4.5 **Bootstrap's responsive column system on a desktop and mobile device. CSS classes are used to determine the number of columns (out of 12) that each element should take up at different screen resolutions.**

This approach allows for a semantic way of putting together responsive templates, and you'll rely heavily on it for the Loc8r pages. Speaking of which, you'll make a start in the next section.

4.3.2 Setting up the HTML framework with Pug templates and Bootstrap

The pages you'll have in the application have some common requirements. At the top of each page, you'll want a navigation bar and logo; at the bottom of the page, you'll have a copyright notice in the footer; and you'll have a content area in the middle. What you're aiming for is something like figure 4.6. This framework for a layout is simple, but it suits your needs. It provides a consistent look and feel while allowing for different layouts to go in the middle.

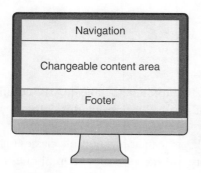

Figure 4.6 **Basic structure of the reusable layout, comprising a standard navigation bar and footer with an extendable, changeable content area in between**

As you saw in chapter 3, Pug templates use the concept of extendable layouts, enabling you to define this type of repeatable structure once in a layout file. In the layout file, you can specify which parts can be extended; when you have this layout file set up, you can extend it as many times as you want. Creating the framework in a layout file means that you only have to do it once, and you can maintain it in only one place.

LOOKING AT THE LAYOUT

To build the common framework, you'll work mainly with the layout.pug file in the app_server/views folder. This file is minimal and looks like this code snippet:

```
doctype html
html
  head
    meta(name='viewport', content='width=device-width, initial-scale=1.0')
    title= title
    link(rel='stylesheet', href='/stylesheets/bootstrap.min.css')
    link(rel='stylesheet', href='/stylesheets/all.min.css')
    link(rel='stylesheet', href='/stylesheets/style.css')
  body
    block content
    script(src='https://code.jquery.com/jquery-3.3.1.slim.min.js',
      ➡integrity='sha384
      ➡q8i/X+965DzO0rT7abK41JStQIAqVgRVzpbzo5smXKp4YfRvH+8abtTE1Pi6jizo',
      ➡crossorigin=anonymous)
    script(src=https://cdnjs.cloudflare.com/ajax/libs/popper.js/1.14.3/
      ➡umd/popper.min.js,
      ➡integrity='sha384
      ➡ZMP7rVo3mIykV+2+9J3UJ46jBk0WLaUAdn689aCwoqbBJiSnjAK/l8WvCWPIPm49',
      ➡crossorigin='anonymous')
    script(src='/javascripts/bootstrap.min.js')
```

There isn't any HTML content in the body area yet—only a single extendable block called `content` and a couple of script references. You want to keep all this but add a navigation section above the `content` block and a footer below it.

BUILDING THE NAVIGATION

Bootstrap offers a collection of elements and classes that you can use to create a sticky navigation bar that's fixed to the top and collapses the options into a drop-down menu on mobile devices. We won't explore the details of Bootstrap's CSS classes here. All you need to do is grab the example code from the Bootstrap website, tweak it a little, and update it with the correct links.

In the navigation, you want to have

- The Loc8r logo linking to the homepage
- An About link on the left, pointing to the /about URL page

The code that does these things is in the following snippet and can be placed in the layout.pug file above the `block content` line:

```
nav.navbar.fixed-top.navbar-expand-md.navbar-light        ◁──  Sets up a Bootstrap navigation bar
  .container                                                    fixed to the top of the window
    a.navbar-brand(href='/') Loc8r
      button.navbar-toggler(type='button', data-toggle='collapse',
      ➡data-target='#navbarMain')                         ◁──
        span.navbar-toggler-icon                                Sets up collapsing navigation for
    #navbarMain.navbar-collapse.collapse                        smaller screen resolutions
    ul.navbar-nav.mr-auto
      li.nav-item
        a.nav-link(href='/about/') About                  ◁──  Adds an About link to
                                                               the left side of the bar
```

Adds a brand-styled link to the homepage

If you pop that code in and run it, you'll notice that the navigation now overlays the page heading. You'll fix this problem when you build the layouts for the content area in sections 4.3.3 and 4.4, so it's nothing to worry about.

> **TIP**   Remember that Pug doesn't include any HTML tags and that correct indentation is critical for providing the expected outcome.

That's it for the navigation bar, which is all you need for a while. If Pug and Bootstrap are new to you, it may take a little while to get used to the approach and the syntax, but as you can see, you can achieve a lot with little code.

WRAPPING THE CONTENT

Working down the page from top to bottom, the next area is the `content` block. You don't have much to do with this block, as other Pug files decide the contents. As it stands, though, the `content` block is anchored to the left margin and is unconstrained, meaning that it stretches the full width of any device.

Addressing this situation is easy with Bootstrap. Still in layout.pug, wrap the `content` block in a container `div` like so, remembering to ensure that the indentation is correct:

```
.container
  block content
```

The `div` with a class of `container` is centered in the window and constrained to sensible maximum widths on large displays. The contents of a container `div` remains aligned to the left as normal, though.

ADDING THE FOOTER

At the bottom of the page, you want to add a standard footer. You could add a bunch of links in here, or terms and conditions, or a privacy policy. For now, to keep things simple, you'll add a copyright notice. As this change is going in the layout file, it'll be easy to update this notice across all the pages should you need to at a later date.

The following code snippet shows all the code needed for your simple footer in layout.pug:

```
footer
  .row
    .col-12
      small &copy; Getting Mean - Simon Holmes/Clive Harber 2018
```

This code is placed inside the container `div` that holds the `content` block, so when you add it, make sure that the `footer` line is at the same level of indentation as the `block content` line.

ALL TOGETHER NOW

Now that the navigation bar, content area, and footer have been dealt with, you have the complete layout file. The full code for layout.pug is shown in the following listing.

```
doctype html
html
  head
    meta(name='viewport', content='width=device-width, initial-scale=1.0')
    title= title
    link(rel='stylesheet', href='/stylesheets/bootstrap.min.css')
    link(rel='stylesheet', href='/stylesheets/all.min.css')
    link(rel='stylesheet', href='/stylesheets/style.css')
  body
    nav.navbar.fixed-top.navbar-expand-md.navbar-light
      .container
        a.navbar-brand(href='/') Loc8r
          button.navbar-toggler(type='button', data-toggle='collapse',
          ➥data-target='#navbarMain')
            span.navbar-toggler-icon
          #navbarMain.navbar-collapse.collapse
            ul.navbar-nav.mr-auto
              li.nav-item
                a.nav-link(href='/about/') About

    .container.content
      block content

      footer
        .row
          .col-12
            small &copy; Getting MEAN - Simon Holmes/Clive Harber 2018
    script(src='https://code.jquery.com/jquery-3.3.1.slim.min.js',
    ➥integrity='sha384-
    ➥q8i/X+965DzO0rT7abK41JStQIAqVgRVzpbzo5smXKp4YfRvH+8abtTE1Pi6jizo',
    ➥crossorigin='anonymous')
    script(src='https://cdnjs.cloudflare.com/ajax/libs/
    ➥popper.js/1.14.3/umd/popper.min.js' integrity='sha384- ZMP7rVo
    ➥]3mIykV+2+9J3UJ46jBk0WLaUAdn689a CwoqbBJiSnjAK/l8WvCWPIPm49',
    ➥crossorigin='anonymous')
    script(src='/javascripts/bootstrap.min.js')
```

Annotations: Starting layout with a fixed navigation bar. Extendable content block is now wrapped in a container div. Simple copyright footer in the same container as the content block.

That's all it takes to create a responsive layout framework with Bootstrap, Pug, and Express. If you've got everything in place, when you run the application, you should see something like the screenshots in figure 4.7, depending on your device.

You see that the navigation still overlays the content, but you'll address that problem when you start looking at the content layouts. It's a good indication that the navigation is working as you want it to, though: you want the navigation to be ever present, fixed to the top of the window. Also notice that Bootstrap has collapsed the navigation into a drop-down menu on the smaller screen of the phone—a nice result for little effort on your part.

TIP If you can't access your development site on a phone, you can always try resizing your browser window. All major web browsers allow you to emulate various mobile devices and screen sizes through their built-in developer tools.

Figure 4.7   The homepage after the layout template has been set up. Bootstrap automatically collapsed the navigation on the small screen size of the phone. The navigation bar overlaps the content, but that problem will be fixed when the content layouts are created.

Now that the generic layout template is complete, it's time to start building the actual pages of your application.

4.3.3   *Building a template*

When you're building templates, start with whichever one makes the most sense to you. This template may be the most complicated or the simplest, or the first in the main user journey. For Loc8r, a good place to start is the homepage, which is the example we'll go through in the most detail.

DEFINING A LAYOUT

The primary aim for the homepage is to display a list of locations. Each location needs to have a name, an address, the distance away from the user, user ratings, and a facilities list. You also want to add a header to the page and some text to put the list in context, so that users know what they're looking at when they visit.

You may find it useful, as we do, to sketch a layout or two on a piece of paper or a whiteboard. We find this sketch helpful for creating a starting point for the layout, making sure that we've got all the pieces we need on a page without getting bogged down in the technicalities of code. Figure 4.8 shows what you might sketch for the homepage of Loc8r.

You'll see that there are two layouts: one for a desktop and one for a phone. It's worth making the distinction at this point, with your understanding of what Bootstrap can do and how it works. This is the beginning of starting to think about response design.

At this stage, the layouts are by no means final, and you may well tweak and change them as you build the code. But any journey is easier if you have a destination and a map, which the sketch gives you. You can start your code off in the right direction. The few minutes it takes to create a sketch can save you hours, if you find that you

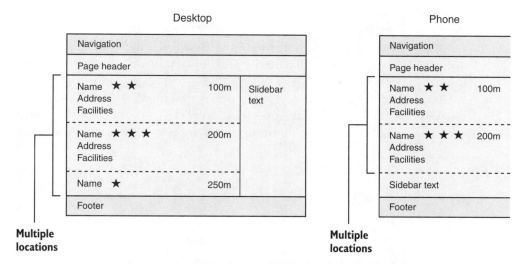

Figure 4.8 Desktop and mobile layout sketches for the homepage. Sketching the layouts for a page can give you a quick idea of what you're going to build without getting distracted by the intricacies of Adobe Photoshop or the technicalities of code.

need to move parts around or even throw them out and start again. The process is much easier with a sketch than with a load of code.

Now that you have an idea of the layout and the pieces of content required, it's time to put everything together in a new template.

SETTING UP THE VIEW AND THE CONTROLLER

The first step is creating a new view file and linking it to the controller. In the app_server/views folder, make a copy of the index.pug view, and save it in the same folder as locations-list.pug. It's best not to call the file homepage or something similar, as at some point, you may change your mind about what should be displayed on the homepage. This way, the name of the view clearly identifies it, and it can be used anywhere without confusion.

The second step is telling the controller for the homepage that you want to use this new view. The controller for the homepage is in the locations.js file in app_server/controllers. Update this file to change the view called by the `homelist` controller, as shown in the following code snippet (modifications in bold):

```
const homelist = (req, res) => {
  res.render('locations-list', { title: 'Home' });
};
```

Now you're ready to build the view template.

CODING THE TEMPLATE: PAGE LAYOUT

When we write the code for layouts, we prefer to start with the big pieces and then move toward the detail. As you extend the layout file, the navigation bar and footer are already done, but you still have the page header, the main area for the list, and the sidebar to consider.

At this point, you need to take a first stab at how many of the 12 Bootstrap columns you want each element to take up on different devices. The following code snippet shows the layout of the three distinct areas of the Loc8r List page in locations-list.pug:

```
.row.banner
  .col-12
    h1 Loc8r
      small  Find places to work with wifi near you!
.row
  .col-12.col-md-8
    p List area.
  .col-12.col-md-4
    p.lead Loc8r helps you find places to work when out and about.
```

Page header that fills the entire width of the screen

Container for the list of locations, spanning all 12 columns on extra-small and small devices, and 8 columns on medium devices and larger

Container for secondary or sidebar information, spanning all 12 columns on extra-small and small devices, and 4 columns on medium devices and larger

You might go back and forth a bit, testing the columns at various resolutions until you're happy with them. Having device simulators can make this process easier, but a simple method is to change the width of your browser window to force the different Bootstrap breakpoints. When you've got something that you think is probably okay, you can push it up to Heroku and test it for real on your phone or tablet.

CODING THE TEMPLATE: LOCATIONS LIST

Now that the containers for the homepage are defined, it's time for the main area. You have an idea of what you want here from the sketches you drew for the page layout. Each place should show the name, address, rating, distance from the user, and key facilities.

Because you're creating a clickable prototype, all the data will be hardcoded into the template for now. This approach is the quickest way of putting a template together and ensuring that you have the information you want displayed the way you want. You'll worry about the data side later. If you're working from an existing data source or have constraints on what data you can use, naturally you'll have to bear those facts in mind when creating the layouts.

Again, getting a layout you're happy with may take a bit of testing, but Pug and Bootstrap working together make the process considerably easier than it might be. The following code snippet shows what you might come up with for a single location to replace the p List area placeholder in locations-list.pug:

```
.card
  .card-block
```

Creates a new Bootstrap card and card block to wrap the content

```
h4
   a(href="/location") Starcups
   small  
      i.fas.fa-star
      i.fas.fa-star
      i.fas.fa-star
      i.far.fa-star
      i.far.fa-star
   span.badge.badge-pill.badge-default.float-right 100m
   p.address 125 High Street, Reading, RG6 1PS
   .facilities
      span.badge.badge-warning Hot drinks
      span.badge.badge-warning Food
      span.badge.badge-warning Premium wifi
```

Name of the listing and a link to the location

Uses Font Awesome icons to output a star rating

Uses Bootstrap's badge helper class to display the distance away

Address of the location

Facilities of the location, output using Bootstrap's badge classes

Once again, you can see how much you can achieve with relatively little effort and code, all thanks to the combination of Pug and Bootstrap. Remember that some custom classes to help with styling are in the styles.css file in public/stylesheets, available in the GitHub repo. Without these classes, your visuals will look much different. To get an idea of what the preceding code snippet does, take a look at figure 4.9.

Figure 4.9 Onscreen rendering of a single location on the List page

This section is set to go across the full width of the available area: 12 columns on all devices. Remember, though, that this section is nested inside a responsive column, so "full width" is the full width of the containing column, not necessarily that of the browser viewport. This explanation will make more sense when you put everything together and see the application in action.

CODING THE TEMPLATE: PUTTING IT TOGETHER

You have the layout of page elements, the structure of the list area, and some hard-coded data, so it's time to see what everything looks like. To get a better feel for the layout in the browser, it's a good idea to duplicate and modify the List page so that several locations show up. The code, including a single location for brevity, is shown in the following listing.

Listing 4.6 Complete template for app_server/views/locations-list.pug

```
extends layout

block content
   .row.banner
      .col-12
         h1 Loc8r
            small  Find places to work with wifi near you!
```

Starts header area

```
.row
  .col-12.col-md-8   ◁─────────────        Starts responsive main
    .card                                   listing column section
      .card-block
        h4
          a(href="/location") Starcups
          small                                An individual listing;
            i.fas.fa-star                          duplicates this section
            i.fas.fa-star                           to create a list of
            i.fas.fa-star                            multiple items
            i.far.fa-star
            i.far.fa-star
          span.badge.badge-pill.badge-default.float-right 100m
        p.address 125 High Street, Reading, RG6 1PS
        p.facilities
          span.badge.badge-warning Hot drinks
          span.badge.badge-warning Food
          span.badge.badge-warning Premium wifi
  .col-12.col-md-4
    p.lead Looking for wifi and a seat? Loc8r helps you find places to
    ➥work when out and about. Perhaps with coffee, cake or a pint?
    ➥Let Loc8r help you find the place you're looking for.
```

Sets up sidebar
area and
populates it
with some
content

When you've got this code in place, you've got the homepage listing template done. If
you run the application and head to localhost:3000, you should see something like figure 4.10.

See how the layout changes between a desktop view and a mobile view? That
change is thanks to Bootstrap's responsive framework and your choice of CSS classes.
Scrolling down in the mobile view, you see the sidebar text content between the main
list and the footer. On the smaller screen, it's more important to display the list in the
available space than the text.

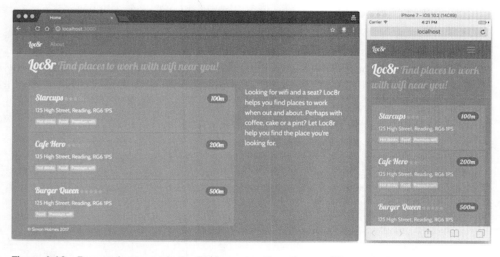

Figure 4.10   Responsive template for the homepage in action on different devices

Great; you created got a responsive layout for the homepage by using Pug and Bootstrap in Express and Node. Next, you'll add the other views.

4.4 Adding the rest of the views

The Locations List page is built, so you need to create the other pages to give users a site that they can click through. In this section, we'll cover adding these pages:

- Details
- Add Review
- About

We won't go through the process in much detail for all of them, though—only a bit of explanation, the code, and the output. You can always download the source code from GitHub if you prefer.

4.4.1 Details page

The logical step, and arguably the next-most-important page to look at, is the Details page for an individual location.

This page needs to display all the information about a location, including

- Name
- Address
- Rating
- Opening hours
- Facilities
- Location map
- Reviews, each with
    - Rating
    - Reviewer name
    - Review date
    - Review text
    - Button to add a new review
    - Text to set the context of the page

That's quite a lot of information! This template is the single most complicated one in your application.

PREPARATION

The first step is updating the controller for this page to use a different view. Look for the `locationInfo` controller in the locations.js file in app_server/controllers. Change the name of the view to `location-info`, as shown in the following code snippet:

```
const locationInfo = (req, res) => {
  res.render('location-info', { title: 'Location info' });
};
```

The next step is obtaining a key to access the Google Maps API. To get your keys, you need to sign up for an account, if you don't already have one, at the following address:

```
https://developers.google.com/maps/documentation/javascript/
    get-api-key?utm_source=geoblog&utm_medium=social&utm_campaign=
    2016-geo-na-website-gmedia-blogs-us-blogPost&utm_content=TBC
```

Make sure that you keep your API key safe; you'll need it for the next listing.

Remember, if you run the application at this point, it won't work, because Express can't find the view template—not surprising, as you haven't created it yet. That's the next part.

THE VIEW

Create a new file in app_server/views and save it as location-info.pug. The content of this file is shown in listing 4.7, which is the largest listing in this book. Remember that for the purposes of this stage in the prototype development, you're generating clickable pages with the data hardcoded directly into them.

Listing 4.7   View for the Details page, app_server/views/location-info.pug

```
extends layout

block content
  .row.banner
    .col-12                          Starts with page header
      h1 Starcups
  .row
    .col-12.col-lg-9        ◁──      Sets up nested responsive
      .row                           columns needed for the
        .col-12.col-md-6    ◁──      template
          p.rating
            i.fas.fa-star
            i.fas.fa-star
            i.fas.fa-star
            i.far.fa-star
            i.far.fa-star
          p 125 High Street, Reading, RG6 1PS
          .card.card-primary                      One of several
            .card-block                           Bootstrap card
              h2.card-title Opening hours          components used to
              p.card-text Monday - Friday : 7:00am - 7:00pm  define information
              p.card-text Saturday : 8:00am - 5:00pm   areas—in this case,
              p.card-text Sunday : closed           opening hours
          .card.card-primary
            .card-block
              h2.card-title Facilities
              span.badge.badge-warning          The   entity is being
                i.fa.fa-check                    used because Pug doesn't
                |  Hot drinks               always understand
              |                             whitespace and has a habit
              span.badge.badge-warning          of trimming it away.
                i.fa.fa-check
                |  Food
```

```
                        |  
                    span.badge.badge-warning
                      i.fa.fa-check
                        |  Premium wifi
                    |  
            .col-12.col-md-6.location-map
              .card.card-primary
                .card-block
                  h2.card-title Location map
                  img.img-fluid.rounded(src=
➥'http://maps.googleapis.com/maps/api/..............
➥staticmap?center=51.455041,-0.9690884&zoom=17&size=400x350
➥&sensor=false&markers=51.455041,-0.9690884&scale=2&key=<API Key>')
        .row
          .col-12
            .card.card-primary.review-card
              .card-block
                a.btn.btn-primary.float-right(href='/location/review/new')
                  ➥Add review
                h2.card-title Customer reviews
                .row.review
                  .col-12.no-gutters.review-header
                    span.rating
                      i.fas.fa-star
                      i.fas.fa-star
                      i.fas.fa-star
                      i.far.fa-star
                      i.far.fa-star
                    span.review Author Simon Holmes
                    small.review Timestamp 16 February 2017
                  .col-12
                    p What a great place.
                .row.review
                  .col-12.no-gutters.review-header
                    span.rating
                      i.fas.fa-star
                      i.fas.fa-star
                      i.fas.fa-star
                      i.far.fa-star
                      i.far.fa-star
                    span.reviewAuthor Charlie Chaplin
                    small.reviewTimestamp 14 February 2017
                  .col-12
                    p It was okay. Coffee wasn't great.
        .col-12.col-lg-3
          p.lead
            | Starcups is on Loc8r because it has accessible wifi and space to
              ➥sit down with your laptop and get some work done.
          p
            | If you've been and you like it - or if you don't - please leave
              ➥a review to help other people just like you.
```

Uses a static Google Maps image, including coordinates in the query string 51.455041,-0.9690884. Remember to replace the <APIKey> with the Google API Key that you obtained earlier.

Creates a link to the Add Review page, using Bootstrap's button helper class

Final responsive column for sidebar contextual information

That's a long template, and you'll look at how to shorten it soon. But the page itself is complex, containing a lot of information and a few nested responsive columns. Imagine how much longer it would be if it were written in full HTML!

Make sure that you have the full version of style.css from GitHub included, as you're using it to add a bit of life to the standard Bootstrap theme.

With that all done, the Details page layout is complete; you can head over to localhost:3000/location to check it out. Figure 4.11 shows how this layout looks in a browser and on a mobile device.

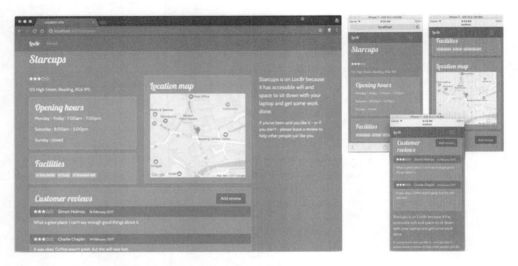

Figure 4.11   Details page layout on desktop and mobile devices

The next step in this user journey is the Add Review page, which has much simpler requirements.

4.4.2   Adding the Review page

This page is straightforward, holding a form that contains the user's name and a couple of input fields for the rating and review.

The first step is updating the controller to reference a new view. In app_server/controllers/locations.js, change the `addReview` controller to use the new view `location-review-form`, as in the following code snippet:

```
const addReview = (req, res) => {
  res.render('location-review-form', { title: 'Add review' });
};
```

The second step is creating the view itself. In the views folder app_server/views, create a new file called location-review-form.pug. Because this page is designed to be a clickable prototype, you're not going to be posting the form data anywhere, so the aim is to get the action to redirect to the Details page that displays the review data. In the form, then, set the action to `/location` and the method to `get`. Later, you'll change this to a `post` method, but this form will give you the functionality you need for now. The entire code for the review form page is shown in the following listing.

Listing 4.8   View for the Add Review page, app_server/views/location-review-form.pug

```
extends layout

block content
  .row.banner
    .col-12
      h1 Review Starcups
  .row
    .col-12.col-md-8
      form(action="/location", method="get", role="form")
        .form-group.row
          label.col-10.col-sm-2.col-form-label(for="name") Name
          .col-12.col-sm-10
            input#name.form-control(name="name")
        .form-group.row
          label.col-10.col-sm-2.col-form-label(for="rating") Rating
          .col-12.col-sm-2
            select#rating.form-control.input-sm(name="rating")
              option 5
              option 4
              option 3
              option 2
              option 1
        .form-group.row
          label.col-sm-2.col-form-label(for="review") Review
          .col-sm-10
            textarea#review.form-control(name="review", rows="5")
        button.btn.btn-primary.float-right Add my review
    .col-12.col-md-4
```

Sets the form action to /location, and the method to get

Input field for reviewer to leave their name

Drop-down select box for rating 1 to 5

Text area for the text content of the review

Submit button for the form

Bootstrap has a lot of helper classes for dealing with forms, which are evident in listing 4.8. But the page is simple, and when you run it, it should look like figure 4.12.

The Add Review page marks the end of the user's journey through the Locations collection of screens. There's only the About page left to do.

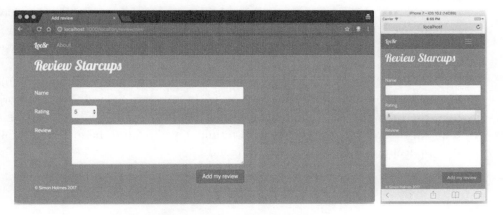

Figure 4.12   Complete Add Review page in desktop and mobile view

4.4.3   *Adding the About page*

The final page of the static prototype is the About page, which has a header and some content—nothing complicated. The layout may be useful for other pages farther down the line, such as a privacy policy, or a terms and conditions page, so you're best off creating a generic, reusable view.

The controller for the About page is in the others.js file in app_server/controllers. You're looking for the controller called about, and you want to change the name of the view to generic-text, as in the following code snippet:

```
const about = (req, res) => {
  res.render('generic-text', { title: 'About' });
};
```

Next, create the view generic-text.pug in app_server/views. This template is small and should look like the following listing.

> **Listing 4.9   View for text-only pages: app_server/views/generic-text.pug**

```
extends layout
block content
  .row.banner
    .col-12
      h1= title
  .row
    .col-12.col-lg-8
      p
        | Loc8r was created to help people find places to sit down and
        ⮡get a bit of work done.
        | <br /><br />
        | Lorem ipsum dolor sit amet, consectetur adipiscing elit. Nunc
        ⮡sed lorem ac nisi dignissim accumsan.
```

Use | to create lines of plain text within a <p> tag.

This is a simple layout. Don't worry about including page-specific content in a generic view at this point; you'll take that task on soon and make the page reusable. For the purposes of finishing the clickable static prototype, it's okay.

You'll probably want some additional lines so that the page appears to have real content. Notice that the lines starting with the pipe character (|) can contain HTML tags if you want them to. Figure 4.13 shows how the page might look in a browser with a bit more content.

That's the last of the four pages you need for the static site. You can push this page up to Heroku and have people visit the URL and click around. If you've forgotten how, the following code snippet shows the terminal commands you need, assuming that you've already set up Heroku. In terminal, you need to be in the root folder of the application. Then issue these commands:

```
$ git add --all
$ git commit -m "Adding the view templates"
$ git push heroku master
```

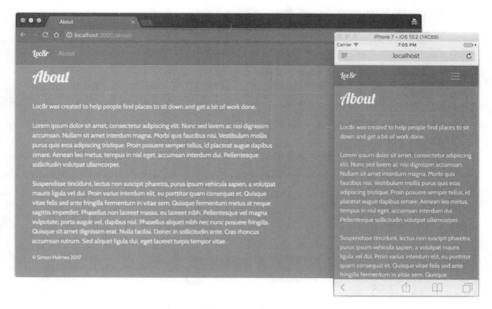

Figure 4.13   Generic text template rendering the About page

Get the source code
The source code for the application as it stands at this point is available in the chapter-04-views branch on GitHub. In a fresh folder in terminal, enter the following commands to clone it and install the npm module dependencies:

```
$ git clone -b chapter-04-views
    ➥https://github.com/cliveharber/gettingMean-2.git
$ cd gettingMean-2
$ npm install
```

What's next? The routes, views, and controllers are set up for a static site that you can click through, and you've pushed it up to Heroku so that others can also try it. In some ways, you've reached the goal for this stage; you can stop here while you play with the journeys and get feedback. This stage is definitely the easiest point in the process to make large, sweeping changes.

If you definitely plan to build an Angular SPA, and assuming that you're happy with what you've done to this point, you probably wouldn't go any further with creating a static prototype. Instead, you'd start to create an application in Angular.

But the next step you'll take now continues down the road of creating the Express application. So while keeping with the static site, you'll remove the data from the views and put it in the controllers.

4.5 *Taking the data out of the views and making them smarter*

At the moment, all the content and data are held in the views. This arrangement is perfect for testing stuff and moving things around, but you need to move forward. A goal of the MVC architecture is to have views without content or data. The views should be fed data that they present to the end user while being agnostic about the data they're fed. The views need a data structure, but what's inside the data doesn't matter to the view itself.

Consider the MVC architecture: the model holds the data; the controller processes the data; and, finally, the view renders the processed data. You're not dealing with the model yet; you'll do that starting in chapter 5. For now, you're working with the views and controllers.

To make the views smarter and do what they're intended to do, you need to take the data and content out of the views and put it in the controllers. Figure 4.14 illustrates the data flow in an MVC architecture and the changes you want to make.

Making these changes now allows you to finalize the views so that you're ready for the next step. As a bonus, you'll start thinking about how the processed data should look in the controllers. Rather than starting with a data structure, start with the ideal front end and slowly reverse-engineer the data back through the MVC steps as your understanding of the requirements solidifies.

How are you going to do these things? Starting with the homepage, you'll take every piece of content out of the Pug view. You'll update the Pug file to contain variables in

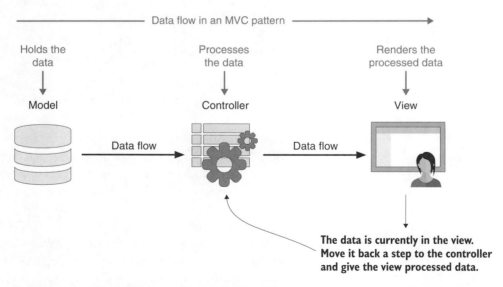

Figure 4.14 How the data should flow in an MVC pattern, from the model through the controller to the view. At this point in the prototype, your data is in the view, but you want to move it a step back into the controller.

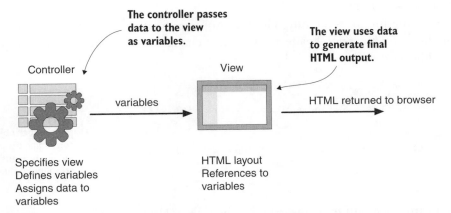

Figure 4.15 When the controller specifies the data, it passes the data to the view as variables; the view uses that data to generate the final HTML that's delivered to the user.

place of the content and put the content as variables in the controller. Then the controller can pass these values into the view. The result should look the same in the browser, and users shouldn't be able to spot a difference. The roles of the various parts and the movement and use of data are shown in figure 4.15.

At the end of this stage, the data is still hardcoded, but in the controllers instead of the views. The views are now smarter and able to accept and display whatever data is sent to them (provided that the data is in the correct format, of course).

4.5.1 *Moving data from the view to the controller*

You'll start with the homepage and move the data out of the `locations-list.pug` view into the `homelist` function in the locations.js controllers file. Start at the top with something simple: the page header. The following code snippet shows the page header section of the `locations-list.pug` view, which has two pieces of content:

```
.row.banner                    Large-font
  .col-12                      page title
    h1 Loc8r                                       Smaller-font
      small  Find places to work with wifi near you!   strapline for page
```

These two pieces of content are the first that you'll move into the controller. The homepage controller currently looks like the following:

```
const homelist = (req, res) => {
  res.render('locations-list', { title: 'Home' });
};
```

This controller is already sending one piece of data to the view. Remember that the second parameter in the `render` function is a JavaScript object containing the data to send to the view. Here, the `homelist` controller sends the data object { title: 'Home' } to the view. This object is being used by the layout file to put the string Home in the HTML `<title>`, which isn't necessarily the best choice of text.

UPDATING THE CONTROLLER

Change the title to something more appropriate for the page, and also add the two data items for the page header. Make these changes to the controller first, as follows (modifications in bold):

```
const homelist =  (req, res) => {
  res.render('locations-list', {
    title: 'Loc8r - find a place to work with wifi',
    pageHeader: {
      title: 'Loc8r',
      strapline: 'Find places to work with wifi near you!'
    }
  });
};
```

> New nested pageHeader object containing properties for the title and the strapline of the page

For neatness and future manageability, the title and the strapline are grouped within a pageHeader object. This approach is a good habit to get into and will make the controllers easier to update and maintain.

UPDATING THE VIEW

Now that the controller is passing these pieces of data to the view, you can update the view to reference them in place of the hardcoded content. Nested data items like these are referenced using dot syntax, as you do when getting data out of objects in JavaScript. To reference the page header strapline in the locations-list.pug view, use pageHeader.strapline. The following code snippet shows the page header section of the view (modifications in bold):

```
.row.banner
  .col-12
    h1= pageHeader.title
    small
       #{pageHeader.strapline}
```

> = signifies that the following content is buffered code—in this case, a JavaScript object.

> #{} delimiters are used to insert data into a specific place, such as part of a piece of text.

The code outputs pageHeader.title and pageHeader.strapline in the relevant places in the view. See the sidebar "Referencing data in Pug templates" for more details.

Referencing data in Pug templates

There are two key syntaxes for referencing data in Pug templates. The first syntax is called *interpolation,* and it's typically used to insert data into the middle of some other content. Interpolated data is defined by the opening delimiter #{ and the end delimiter }. You normally use it like this:

```
h1 Welcome to #{pageHeader.title}
```

If your data contains HTML, this is escaped for security reasons; end users won't see any HTML tags displayed as text, and the browser won't interpret them as HTML. If you want the browser to render any HTML contained in the data, you can use the following syntax:

```
h1 Welcome to !{pageHeader.title}
```

This syntax poses potential security risks, however, and should be done only for data sources that you trust. You shouldn't allow user inputs to display like this without some additional security checks.

The second method of outputting the data is with *buffered code*. Instead of inserting the data into a string, you build the string with JavaScript, using the = sign directly after the tag declaration, like this:

```
h1= "Welcome to " + pageHeader.title
```

Again, this escapes any HTML for security reasons. If you want to have unescaped HTML in your output, you can use slightly different syntax:

```
h1!= "Welcome to " + pageHeader.title
```

Once again, be careful. Whenever possible, you should use one of the escaped methods to be on the safe side.

For this buffered code approach, you can also use JavaScript template strings, like this:

```
h1= `Welcome to ${pageHeader.title}`
```

If you run the application now and head back to the homepage, the only change you should notice is that the `<title>` has been updated. Everything else still looks the same, but some of the data is now coming from the controller.

This section serves as a simple example of what you're doing at this point and how you're doing it. The complicated part of the homepage is the listing section, so in the next section, you'll look at how you can approach that task.

4.5.2 *Dealing with complex, repeating data patterns*

The first thing to bear in mind about the listing section is that it has multiple entries, all following the same data pattern and layout pattern. Like you've just done with the page header, start with the data, taking it from the view to the controller.

In terms of JavaScript data, a repeatable pattern lends itself nicely to the idea of an array of objects. You want one array to hold multiple objects, with each object containing all the relevant information for an individual listing.

ANALYZING THE DATA IN THE VIEW

Take a look at a listing to see what information you need the controller to send. Figure 4.16 reminds you how a listing looks in the homepage view.

Figure 4.16   An individual listing, showing the data that you need

From this screenshot, you can see that an individual listing on the homepage has the following data requirements:

- Name
- Rating
- Distance away
- Address
- List of facilities

Taking the data from the screenshot in figure 4.16 and creating a JavaScript object from it, you could come up with something simple, like the following code snippet:

```
{
  name: 'Starcups',
  address: '125 High Street, Reading, RG6 1PS',
  rating: 3,
  facilities: ['Hot drinks', 'Food', 'Premium wifi'],
  distance: '100m'
}
```

List of facilities is sent as an array of string values

That's all you need to represent a single location as an object. For multiple locations, you need an array of these objects.

ADDING THE REPEATING DATA ARRAY TO THE CONTROLLER

You need to create an array of the single-location objects—using the data that you currently have in the view, if you want—and add it to the data object passed to the `render` function in the controller. The following code snippet shows the updated `homelist` controller, including the array of locations:

```
const homelist = (req, res) => {
  res.render('locations-list', {
    title: 'Loc8r - find a place to work with wifi',
    pageHeader: {
      title: 'Loc8r',
      strapline: 'Find places to work with wifi near you!'
    },
    locations: [{
      name: 'Starcups',
      address: '125 High Street, Reading, RG6 1PS',
      rating: 3,
      facilities: ['Hot drinks', 'Food', 'Premium wifi'],
      distance: '100m'
    }, {
      name: 'Cafe Hero',
      address: '125 High Street, Reading, RG6 1PS',
      rating: 4,
      facilities: ['Hot drinks', 'Food', 'Premium wifi'],
      distance: '200m'
    }, {
      name: 'Burger Queen',
      address: '125 High Street, Reading, RG6 1PS',
      rating: 2,
      facilities: ['Food', 'Premium wifi'],
```

Array of locations being passed as locations to the view for rendering

```
        distance: '250m'
      }]
    });
};
```

Here, you've got the details for three locations being sent in the array. You can add many more, of course, but this code is as good a start as any. Now you need to get the view to render this information instead of the data currently hardcoded inside it.

LOOPING THROUGH ARRAYS IN A PUG VIEW

The controller is sending an array to Pug as the variable `locations`. Pug offers a simple syntax for looping through an array. In one line, you specify which array to use and what variable name you want to use as the key. The key is a named reference to the current item in the array, so its contents change as the loop iterates through the array. The construct of a Pug loop is like so:

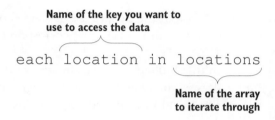

Name of the key you want to use to access the data

```
each location in locations
```

Name of the array to iterate through

Anything nested inside this line in Pug is iterated through for each item in the array. Take a look at an example using the locations data and part of the view you want. In the view file, locations-list.pug, each location starts with the code in the following snippet, with a different name each time:

```
.card
  .card-block
    h4
      a(href="/location") Starcups
```

You can use Pug's `each/in` syntax to loop through all the locations in the `locations` array and output the name of each location. How this works is shown in the next code snippet:

```
each location in locations
  .card
    .card-block
      h4
        a(href="/location")= location.name
```

Sets up a loop, defining a variable location as key

Nested items are all looped through.

Outputs the name of each location, accessing the name property of each location

Given the controller data you've got, with three locations in it, using that data with the preceding code would result in the following HTML:

```
<div class="card">
  <div class="card-block">
    <h4>
```

```
      <a href="/location">Starcups</a>
    </h4>
  </div>
</div>
<div class="card">
  <div class="card-block">
    <h4>
      <a href="/location">Cafe Hero</a>
    </h4>
  </div>
</div>
<div class="card">
  <div class="card-block">
    <h4>
      <a href="/location">Burger Queen</a>
    </h4>
  </div>
</div>
```

As you can see, the HTML construct—the divs and the h4 and a tags—are repeated three times. But the name of the location is different in each one, corresponding to the data in the controller.

Looping through arrays is easy, and with that little test, you've already got the first few lines of the updated view text you need. Now you need to follow through with the rest of the data used in the listings. You can't deal with the rating stars this way, so you'll ignore them for now and deal with them soon.

Dealing with the rest of the data, you can produce the following code snippet, which outputs all the data for each listing. As the facilities are being passed as an array, you need to loop through that array for each listing:

```
each location in locations
  .card
    .card-block
      h4
        a(href="/location")= location.name
        small  
          i.fas.fa-star
          i.fas.fa-star
          i.fas.fa-star
          i.far.fa-star
          i.far.fa-star
        span.badge.badge-pill.badge-default.float-right= location.distance
      p.address= location.address
      .facilities                                    ┌ Looping through a nested array to
        span.badge.badge-warning= facility  ◁─────┘ output facilities for each location
```

Looping through the facilities array is no problem, and Pug handles this with ease. Pulling out the rest of the data, the distance and the address, is straightforward, using the techniques you've already used.

The only part left to deal with is the rating stars. For that task, you'll need a bit of inline JavaScript code.

4.5.3 *Manipulating the data and view with code*

For the star ratings, the view is outputting spans with different classes, using Font Awesome's icon system. The rating system has a total of five stars, which are either solid or empty depending on the rating. A rating of five, for example, shows five solid stars; a rating of three shows three solid stars and two empty stars, as shown in figure 4.17; and a rating of zero shows five empty stars.

Figure 4.17   The Font Awesome star-rating system in action, showing a rating of three out of five stars

To generate this type of output, you'll use some code inside the Pug template. The code is essentially JavaScript, with some Pug-specific conventions thrown in. To add a line of inline code to a Pug template, prefix the line with a dash (hyphen). This prefix tells Pug to run the JavaScript code rather than pass it through to the browser.

To generate the output for the stars, you'll use a couple of for loops. The first loop outputs the correct number of solid stars, and the second loop outputs any remaining empty stars. The following code snippet shows how these loops look and work in Pug:

```
small  
  - for (let i = 1; i <= location.rating; i++)
    i.fas.fa-star
  - for (let i = location.rating; i < 5; i++)
    i.far.fa-star
```

Notice that the syntax is familiar JavaScript, but with no curly brackets defining the block of code to run. Instead, the block of code is defined by indentation, like the rest of Pug. Also notice the mixture of code and Pug. The lines of code are saying, "Every time I evaluate as true, render the indented Pug content." This design is nice, as you don't have to try to construct your HTML with JavaScript.

That's all the content and layout for the homepage sorted, so you can move on. You can do one more thing to improve what you've got and make some of the code reusable.

4.5.4 *Using includes and mixins to create reusable layout components*

The star-rating code will be useful in other layouts. You're going to want it on the Details page, for example, and maybe in more places in the future. You don't want to have to add it to every page manually. What if you decide that you don't like the Font Awesome icons anymore and want to change the markup? You certainly don't want to have to make changes on every single page that shows a rating—not if you can help it.

Fortunately, Pug enables you to create reusable components by using mixins and includes.

DEFINING PUG MIXINS

A *mixin* in Pug is essentially a function. You can define a mixin at the top of your file and use it in multiple places. A mixin definition is straightforward: you define the name of the mixin, and then nest the content of it with indentation. The following code snippet shows a basic mixin definition:

```
mixin welcome
  p Welcome
```

This definition outputs the Welcome text inside a <p> tag wherever it's invoked.

Mixins can also accept parameters, as JavaScript functions do. This feature will be useful for creating the mixin you need to display the rating, as the HTML output will be different depending on the actual rating. The following code snippet shows how this process can work, defining the mixin you want to use on the homepage to output the rating stars:

```
mixin outputRating(rating)        ◁————————  Defines mixin outputRating, expecting
  - for (let i = 1; i <= rating; i++)  ◁——    a single parameter rating
    i.fas.fa-star                          Uses the rating parameter inside for
  - for (let i = rating; i < 5; i++)  ◁—┘   loops to output correct HTML
    i.far.fa-star
```

In a sense, this mixin works like a JavaScript function. When you define the mixin, you can specify the parameters that it expects. You can use these parameters in the mixin. You can take the preceding code snippet and pop it into the top of the locations-list.pug file, between the extends layout and block content lines.

CALLING PUG MIXINS

After defining the mixin, you'll want to use it, of course. The syntax for calling a mixin is to place a + before its name. If you have no parameters, such as the welcome mixin, this syntax looks like the following:

```
+welcome
```

This syntax calls the welcome mixin and outputs the text Welcome inside a <p> tag.

Calling a mixin with parameters is equally easy. You send the values of the parameters inside parentheses, as you do when calling a JavaScript function. In the locations-list.pug file, at the point where you're outputting the ratings, the value of the rating is held in the variable location.rating, as shown here:

```
small  
  - for (let i = 1; i <= location.rating; i++)
    i.fas.fa-star
  - for (let i = location.rating; i < 5; i++)
    i.far.fa-star
```

You can replace this code with a call to your new mixin outputRating, sending the location.rating variable as the parameter. This call looks like the following code snippet:

```
h4
  a(href='/location')= location.name
+outputRating(location.rating)
```

This code outputs exactly the same HTML as before, but you've taken part of the code outside the contents of the layout. Right now, this code is reusable only within the same file, but next, you'll use includes to make it accessible to other files.

USING INCLUDES IN PUG

To allow your new mixin to be called from other Pug templates, you need to make it an include file, which is easy.

Within the app_server/views folder, create a subfolder called _includes. (The _ prefix is a convention that we find useful for keeping folders like this one at the top.) Within this folder, create a new file called sharedHTMLfunctions.pug, and paste the outputRating mixin definition into it, as follows:

```
mixin outputRating(rating)
  - for (let i = 1; i <= rating; i++)
    i.fas.fa-star
  - for (let i = rating; i < 5; i++)
    i.far.fa-star
```

Save the file, and you've created the include. Pug provides a simple syntax for using include files in layouts: use the keyword include, followed by the relative path to the include file. The following code snippet shows how you might do this. This line should go immediately after the extends layout line at the top of locations-list.pug:

```
include _includes/sharedHTMLfunctions
```

Now, rather than having the mixin code inline in the template, you're calling it in from an include file. Notice that you can omit the .pug file extension when calling the include. From now on, when you create a new template that needs to have rating stars, you can easily reference this include file and call the outputRatings mixin.

Now you're done with the homepage!

4.5.5 *Viewing the finished homepage*

You made quite a lot of changes to the homepage template throughout this chapter. Now, take a look at what you've ended up with. First, look at the updated controller. The following listing shows the final homelist controller, incorporating the hard-coded data for the title, page header, sidebar, and locations list.

> **Listing 4.10 The homelist controller, passing hardcoded data to the view**

```
const homelist = (req, res) => {
  res.render('locations-list', {
    title: 'Loc8r - find a place to work with wifi',    ⟵
    pageHeader: {
      title: 'Loc8r',
      strapline: 'Find places to work with wifi near you!'
    },
```

Updates text for the HTML <title>

Adds text for the page header as two items inside an object

Adds text for the sidebar

```
      sidebar: "Looking for wifi and a seat? Loc8r helps you find places
  to work when out and about. Perhaps with coffee, cake or a pint?
  Let Loc8r help you find the place you're looking for.",
      locations: [{                                    ◁
        name: 'Starcups',
        address: '125 High Street, Reading, RG6 1PS',
        rating: 3,
        facilities: ['Hot drinks', 'Food', 'Premium wifi'],
        distance: '100m'
      },{
        name: 'Cafe Hero',
        address: '125 High Street, Reading, RG6 1PS',
        rating: 4,
        facilities: ['Hot drinks', 'Food', 'Premium wifi'],
        distance: '200m'
      },{
        name: 'Burger Queen',
        address: '125 High Street, Reading, RG6 1PS',
        rating: 2,
        facilities: ['Food', 'Premium wifi'],
        distance: '250m'
      }]
  });
};
```

Creates an array of one object for each location in the list

Seeing all this code together, you can start to appreciate where you're going with this approach. You've got a clear picture of all the data required for the homepage of Loc8r, which will come in handy in chapter 5. This controller contains the text for the sidebar. We didn't talk about this step, but taking this text from the view to the controller is as simple as creating a new variable for it in the controller and referencing it in the view.

Something important that you achieved through this process is removing data from the view. Building the view with data was great as a first step, as it allowed you to focus on the end-user experience without getting distracted by technicalities. Now that you've moved the data from the view into the controller, you have a much smarter, dynamic view. The view knows what pieces of data it needs, but it doesn't care what's in those pieces of data. The following listing shows the final view for the homepage.

Listing 4.11   Final view for the homepage: app_server/views/locations-list.pug

```
extends layout
include _includes/sharedHTMLfunctions      ◁
block content
  .row.banner
    .col-12
      h1= pageHeader.title
        small  #{pageHeader.strapline}
  .row
    .col-12.col-md-8
      each location in locations           ◁
        .card
          .card-block
```

Brings in the external include file containing outputRating mixin

Outputs the page header text using different methods

Loops through the array of locations

```
h4
  a(href="/location")= location.name
  +outputRating(location.rating)        ◁─────────────────┐
    span.badge.badge-pill.badge-default.float-right=      │
location.distance                               Calls the outputRating
    p.address= location.address                 mixin for each location,
    .facilities                                 passing the value of the
      each facility in location.facilities      current location's rating
        span.badge.badge-warning= facility
```

```
.col-12.col-md-4          References the sidebar
  p.lead= sidebar   ◁───┘ content from the controller
```

That's a small template, especially considering everything it's doing. This is a testament to the power of Pug and Bootstrap working together, combined with removing all the content.

You're one step closer to the MVC—and general development—goal of separation of concerns, with the homepage at least.

4.5.6 *Updating the rest of the views and controllers*

We walked you through the process for the homepage in some detail, but we won't spend so much time on the other pages. Before you can move to the next stage of development—building the data model—you need to go through the process on all the pages. The goal is to have no data in any of the views; instead, the views will be smarter, and the data will be hardcoded into the relevant controllers.

The process for each page is this:

1. Look at the data in the view.
2. Create a structure for that data in the controller.
3. Replace the data in the view with references to the controller data.
4. Look for opportunities to reuse code.

Appendix C goes through the process for each of the three remaining pages, showing what the controller and view code should look like for each one. When you've finished, none of your views should contain any hardcoded data; the controller for each page should be passing the required data. Figure 4.18 shows a collection of screenshots of the final pages you should have at the end of this stage.

You've reached the end of the first phase of your rapid prototype development and are primed to start the next phase.

Get the source code

The source code of the application so far is available on the chapter-04 branch of GitHub's gettingMean-2 repository. In a fresh folder in terminal, enter the following commands to clone it and install the dependencies:

```
$ git clone -b chapter-04 https://github.com/cliveharber/gettingMean-2.git
$ cd gettingMean-2
$ npm install
```

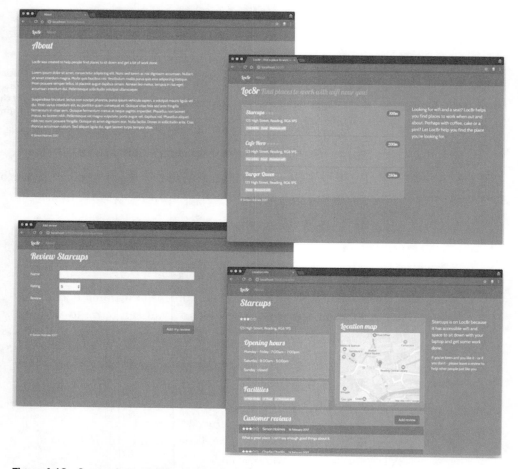

Figure 4.18   Screenshots of all four pages in the static prototype, using smart views and data hardcoded into the controllers

In chapter 5, you'll continue the journey of moving the data back up through the MVC architecture by using MongoDB and Mongoose to create a data model. That's right; it's database time!

Summary

In this chapter, you learned

- Simple ways of defining and organizing routes in Express
- How to use Node modules to hold the controllers
- The best ways to set up multiple sets of controllers by proper definition of the routes
- Prototyping views with Pug and Bootstrap
- Making reusable Pug components and mixins
- Displaying dynamic data in Pug templates
- Passing data from controllers to views

Building a data model with MongoDB and Mongoose

In chapter 4, you moved your data out of the views and back the MVC path into the controllers. Ultimately, the controllers will pass data to the views, but they shouldn't store it. Figure 5.1 recaps the data flow in an MVC pattern.

For storing the data, you'll need a database—specifically, MongoDB. This step is the next one in the process: creating a database and a data model.

> **NOTE** If you haven't yet built the application from chapter 4, you can get the code on the chapter-04 branch at https://github.com/cliveharber/gettingMean-2. In a fresh folder in terminal, enter the following command to clone it:

```
$ git clone -b chapter-04 https://github.com/cliveharber/gettingMean-2.git
```

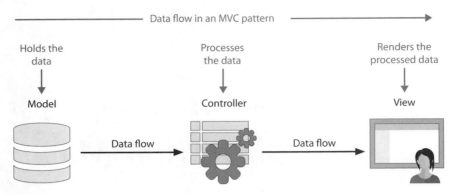

Figure 5.1   **In an MVC pattern, data is held in the model, processed by a controller, and then rendered by a view.**

You'll start by connecting your application to a database before using Mongoose to define schemas and models. When you're happy with the structure, you can add some test data directly to the MongoDB database. The final step is making sure that access to the data store also works when pushed up to Heroku. Figure 5.2 shows the flow of these four steps.

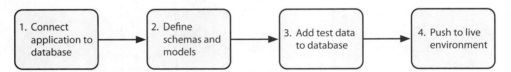

Figure 5.2   **Four main steps in this chapter, from connecting your application to a database to pushing the whole thing into a live environment**

For those of you who are worried that you've missed a section or two, don't worry; you haven't created a database yet. And you don't need to. In various other technology stacks, this situation can present an issue and throw errors. But with MongoDB, you don't need to create a database before connecting to it. MongoDB creates a database when you first try to use it. Figure 5.3 shows where this chapter focuses in terms of overall architecture.

You'll be working with a MongoDB database, but most of the work will be in Express and Node. In chapter 2, we discussed the benefits of decoupling the data integration by creating an API rather than tightly integrating data into the main Express app. Although you'll be working in Express and Node and still within the same encapsulating application, you'll be starting the foundations of your API layer.

NOTE   To follow through this chapter, you need to have MongoDB installed. If you haven't done so already, you can find the instructions in appendix A. The source code of the application as it will be at the end of this chapter is available on the chapter-05 branch on GitHub. In a fresh folder in terminal,

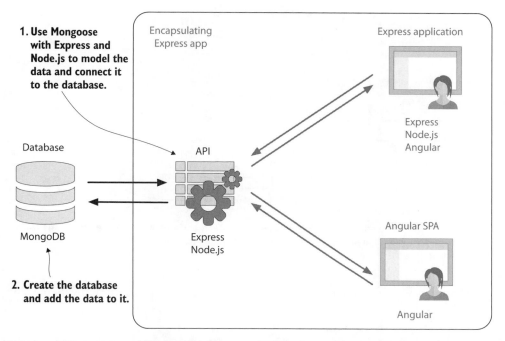

Figure 5.3 Viewing the MongoDB database and using Mongoose inside Express to model the data and manage the connection to the database

enter the following commands to clone it and install the npm module dependencies:

```
$ git clone -b chapter-05 https://github.com/cliveharber/gettingMean-2.git
$ cd gettingMean-2
$ npm install
```

5.1 Connecting the Express application to MongoDB by using Mongoose

You could connect your application directly to MongoDB and have the two interact by using the native driver. Although the native MongoDB driver is powerful, it isn't particularly easy to work with. It also doesn't offer a built-in way of defining and maintaining data structures. Mongoose exposes most of the functionality of the native driver, but in a more convenient way, designed to fit into the flow of application development.

Where Mongoose really excels is in the way it enables you to define data structures and models, maintain them, and use them to interact with your database, all from the comfort of your application code. As part of this approach, Mongoose includes the ability to add validation to your data definitions, meaning that you don't have to write validation code in every place in your application where you send data back to the database.

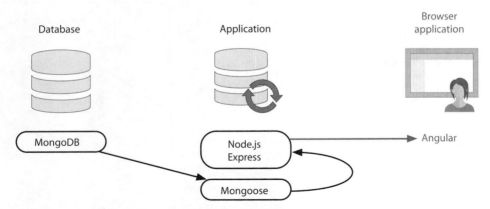

Figure 5.4   The data interactions in the MEAN stack and where Mongoose fits in. The Node/ Express application interacts with MongoDB through Mongoose; Node and Express can also talk to Angular.

Mongoose fits into the stack inside the Express application by being the liaison between the application and the database, as shown in figure 5.4.

MongoDB talks only to Mongoose, and Mongoose in turn talks to Node and Express. Angular won't talk directly to MongoDB or Mongoose—only to the Express application.

You should already have MongoDB installed on your system (covered in appendix A), but not Mongoose. Mongoose isn't installed globally but is instead added directly to your application. You'll do that in the next section.

5.1.1   Adding Mongoose to your application

Mongoose is available as an npm module. As you saw in chapter 3, the quickest and easiest way to install an npm module is through the command line. You can install Mongoose and add it to your list of dependencies in package.json with one command.

Head over to terminal, and make sure that the prompt is at the root folder of the application, where the package.json file is. Then run the following command:

```
$ npm i mongoose
```

Here, we're using an alternative version; this version saves typing. When that command has finished running, you'll see a new mongoose folder inside the node_ modules folder of the application, and the dependencies section of the package.json file should look like the following code snippet:

```
"dependencies": {
  "body-parser": "~1.18.3",
  "cookie-parser": "~1.4.3",
  "debug": "~4.1.0",
  "express": "~4.16.4",
  "mongoose": "^5.3.11",
  "morgan": "~1.9.1",
```

```
  "pug": "~2.0.3",
  "serve-favicon": "~2.5.0"
}
```

You may have slightly different version numbers, of course, but currently, the latest stable version of Mongoose is 5.3.11. Now that Mongoose is installed, you're ready to get it connected.

5.1.2 *Adding a Mongoose connection to your application*

At this stage, you'll connect your application to a database. You haven't created a database yet, but that doesn't matter, because MongoDB creates a database when you first try to use it. This can seem a little odd, but for putting an application together, it's a great advantage: you don't need to leave your application code to mess around in a different environment.

MONGODB AND MONGOOSE CONNECTION

Mongoose opens a pool of five reusable connections when it connects to a MongoDB database. This pool of connections is shared among all requests. Five is the default number; you can increase or decrease the connection options if you need to.

> **BEST PRACTICE TIP**   Opening and closing connections to databases can take a little bit of time, especially if your database is on a separate server or service. It's best to run these operations only when you need to. The best practice is to open the connection when your application starts and to leave it open until your application restarts or shuts down. This approach is the one you're going to take.

SETTING UP THE CONNECTION FILE

When you first sorted out the file structure for the application, you created three folders inside the app_server folder: models, views, and controllers. For working with data and models, you'll be predominantly located in the app_server/models folder. Setting up the connection file is a two-part process—creating the file and requiring it into the application so that it can be used:

- Step 1: Create a file called db.js in app_server/models, and save it. For now, you'll `require` Mongoose in this file with the following single command line:

  ```
  const mongoose = require('mongoose');
  ```

- Step 2: Bring this file into the application by requiring it in app.js. As the actual process of creating a connection between the application and the database can take a little while, you want to do this early in the setup. Amend the top part of app.js to look like the following code snippet (modifications in bold):

  ```
  const express = require('express');
  const path = require('path');
  const cookieParser = require('cookie-parser');
  const logger = require('morgan');
  const favicon = require('serve-favicon');
  require('./app_server/models/db');
  ```

You're not going to export any functions from db.js, so you don't need to assign it to a variable when you `require` it. You need it to be there in the application, but you won't need to hook into any of its methods from within app.js.

If you restart the application, it should run as before, but now you have Mongoose in the application. If you get an error, check that the path in the `require` statement matches the path to the new file, that your package.json includes the Mongoose dependency, and that you've run `npm install` from terminal in the root folder of the application.

CREATING THE MONGOOSE CONNECTION

Creating a Mongoose connection can be as simple as declaring the URI for your database and passing it to Mongoose's `connect` method. A database URI is a string following this construct:

The username, password, and port are optional. On your local machine, your database URI will be simple. For now, assuming that you have MongoDB installed on your local machine, adding the following code snippet to db.js is all you need to create a connection:

```
const dbURI = 'mongodb://localhost/Loc8r';
mongoose.connect(dbURI, {useNewUrlParser: true});
```

The second argument to `connect()` tells Mongoose to use its new internal URL parser, which avoids deprecation warnings due to MongoDB deprecating but leaves available the older connection string parser. If you run the application with this addition to db.js, it should start and function as before. So how do you know that your connection is working correctly? The answer lies in connection events.

MONITORING THE CONNECTION WITH MONGOOSE CONNECTION EVENTS

Mongoose publishes events based on the status of the connection, and these events are easy to hook into so that you can see what's going on. You'll use events to see when the connection is made, when there's an error, and when the connection is disconnected. When any one of these events occurs, you'll log a message to the console. The following code snippet shows the required code:

```
mongoose.connection.on('connected', () => {              Monitors for a successful
  console.log(`Mongoose connected to ${dbURI}`);         connection through Mongoose
});
mongoose.connection.on('error', err => {                 Checks for a connection error
  console.log('Mongoose connection error:', err);
});
```

```
mongoose.connection.on('disconnected', () => {
  console.log('Mongoose disconnected');
});
```

Checks for a
disconnection event

With this code added to db.js, when you restart the application, you should see the following confirmations logged to the terminal window:

```
Express server listening on port 3000
Mongoose connected to mongodb://localhost/Loc8r
```

If you restart the application again, however, you'll notice that you don't get any disconnection messages, because the Mongoose connection doesn't automatically close when the application stops or restarts. You need to listen for changes in the Node process to deal with this situation.

CLOSING A MONGOOSE CONNECTION

Closingthe Mongoose connection when the application stops is as much a part of best practices as opening the connection when it starts. The connection has two ends: one in your application and one in MongoDB. MongoDB needs to know when you want to close the connection so that it doesn't keep redundant connections open.

To monitor when the application stops, you need to listen to the Node.js process for an event called SIGINT.

Listening for SIGINT on Windows

SIGINT is an operating system–level signal that fires on UNIX-based systems such as Linux and macOS. It also fires on some later versions of Windows. If you're running on Windows and the disconnection events don't fire, you can emulate them. If you need to emulate this behavior on Windows, first add a new npm package, `readline`, to your application. As before, use the `npm install` command in the command line like this:

```
$ npm install --save readline
```

When that's done, in the db.js file, above the event listener code, add the following:

```
const readLine = require ('readline');
if (process.platform === 'win32'){
  const rl = readLine.createInterface ({
    input: process.stdin,
    output: process.stdout
  });
  rl.on ('SIGINT', () => {
    process.emit ("SIGINT");
  });
}
```

This code emits the SIGINT signal on Windows machines, allowing you to capture it and gracefully close down anything else you need to before the process ends.

If you're using nodemon to automatically restart the application, you'll also have to listen to a second event on the Node process: SIGUSR2. Heroku uses a different event, SIGTERM, so you need to listen for that event as well.

CAPTURING THE PROCESS TERMINATION EVENTS

Capturing these events prevents the default behavior from happening. You need to make sure that you manually restart the behavior required (after closing the Mongoose connection, of course).

To do this, you need three event listeners and one function to close the database connection. Closing the database is an asynchronous activity, so you need to pass through whatever function is required to restart or end the Node process as a callback. While you're at it, you can output a message to the console confirming that the connection is closed and the reason why. You can wrap all this in a function called gracefulShutdown in db.js:

```
const gracefulShutdown = (msg, callback) => {         ◁── Defines a function to accept a message and a callback function
  mongoose.connection.close( () => {
    console.log(`Mongoose disconnected through ${msg}`);
    callback();                                         Outputs a message and calls a callback when the Mongoose connection is closed
  });
};
```

Closes the Mongoose connection, passing through an anonymous function to run when it's closed

You need to call this function when the application terminates or when nodemon restarts it. The following code snippet shows the two event listeners you need to add to db.js for this to happen:

```
process.once('SIGUSR2', () => {         ◁── Listens for SIGUSR2, which is what nodemon uses
  gracefulShutdown('nodemon restart', () => {         Sends a message to graceful-Shutdown and a callback to kill the process, emitting SIGUSR2 again
    process.kill(process.pid, 'SIGUSR2');
  });
});
process.on('SIGINT', () => {         ◁── Listens for SIGINT to be emitted upon application termination
  gracefulShutdown('app termination', () => {
    process.exit(0);
  });
});
process.on('SIGTERM', () => {         Sends a message to gracefulShutdown and a callback to exit the Node process
  gracefulShutdown('Heroku app shutdown', () => {
    process.exit(0);
  });
});
```

Listens for SIGTERM to be emitted when Heroku shuts down the process

Sends a message to gracefulShutdown and a callback to exit the Node process

Now when the application terminates, it gracefully closes the Mongoose connection before it ends. Similarly, when nodemon restarts the application due to changes in the source files, the application closes the current Mongoose connection first. The nodemon listener is using `process.once` as opposed to `process.on`, as you want to listen for the SIGUSR2 event only once. nodemon also listens for the same event, and you don't want to capture it each time, preventing nodemon from working.

> **TIP** It's important to manage opening and closing your database connections properly in every application you create. If you use an environment with different process termination signals, you should ensure that you listen to them all.

COMPLETE CONNECTION FILE

That's quite a lot of stuff you've added to the db.js file, so take a moment to recap. So far, you've

- Defined a database connection string
- Opened a Mongoose connection at application startup
- Monitored the Mongoose connection events
- Monitored some Node process events so that you can close the Mongoose connection when the application ends

Altogether, the db.js file should look like the following listing. Note that it includes the extra code required by Windows to emit the SIGINT event.

> **Listing 5.1   Complete database connection file db.js in app_server/models**

```
const mongoose = require('mongoose');
const dbURI = 'mongodb://localhost/Loc8r';
mongoose.connect(dbURI, {useNewUrlParser: true});
mongoose.connection.on('connected', () => {
  console.log(`Mongoose connected to ${dbURI}`);
});
mongoose.connection.on('error', err => {
  console.log(`Mongoose connection error: ${err}`);
});
mongoose.connection.on('disconnected', () => {
  console.log('Mongoose disconnected');
});
const gracefulShutdown = (msg, callback) => {
  mongoose.connection.close( () => {
    console.log(`Mongoose disconnected through ${msg}`);
    callback();
  });
};
// For nodemon restarts
process.once('SIGUSR2', () => {
  gracefulShutdown('nodemon restart', () => {
    process.kill(process.pid, 'SIGUSR2');
  });
```

Defines a database connection string and uses it to open a Mongoose connection

Listens for Mongoose connection events and outputs statuses to the console

Reusable function to close the Mongoose connection

Listens to Node processes for termination or restart signals and calls the gracefulShutdown function when appropriate, passing a continuation callback

```
});
// For app termination
process.on('SIGINT', () => {
  gracefulShutdown('app termination', () => {
    process.exit(0);
  });
});
// For Heroku app termination
process.on('SIGTERM', () => {
  gracefulShutdown('Heroku app shutdown', () => {
    process.exit(0);
  });
});
```

Listens to Node processes for termination or restart signals and calls the gracefulShutdown function when appropriate, passing a continuation callback

When you have a file like this one, you can easily copy it from application to application, because the events you're listening for are always the same. All you have to do each time is change the database connection string. Remember that you also required this file into app.js, right near the top, so that the connection opens up early in the application's life.

Using multiple databases

What you've seen so far is known as the default connection and is well suited to keeping a single connection open throughout the uptime of an application. But if you want to connect to a second database, perhaps for logging or managing user sessions, you can use a named connection. In place of the `mongoose.connect` method, you'd use a method called `mongoose.createConnection` and assign it to a variable. You can see this in the following code snippet:

```
const dbURIlog = 'mongodb://localhost/Loc8rLog';
const logDB = mongoose.createConnection(dbURIlog);
```

This snippet creates a new Mongoose connection object called `logDB`. You can interact with it in the same way as you would with `mongoose.connection` for the default connection. Here are a couple of examples:

```
logDB.on('connected', () => {
  console.log(`Mongoose connected to ${dbURIlog}`);
});
logDB.close( () => {
  console.log('Mongoose log disconnected');
});
```

Monitoring a connection event for a named connection

Closing a named connection

5.2   *Why model the data?*

In chapter 1, we talked about how MongoDB is a document store rather than a traditional table-based database using rows and columns. This fact gives MongoDB great freedom and flexibility, but sometimes you want—or *need*—structure to your data.

Take the Loc8r homepage, for example. The listing section shown in figure 5.5 contains a specific dataset that's common to all locations.

Figure 5.5 Listing section of the homepage has defined data requirements and structure

The page needs these data items for all locations, and the data record for each location must have a consistent naming structure. Without this structure, the application wouldn't be able to find the data and use it. At this point in development, the data is held in the controller and passed into the view. In terms of MVC architecture, you started with the data in the *view* and then moved it back a step to the *controller.* Now what you need to do is move it back one final step to where it should belong: in the *model.* Figure 5.6 illustrates your current position, highlighting the goal.

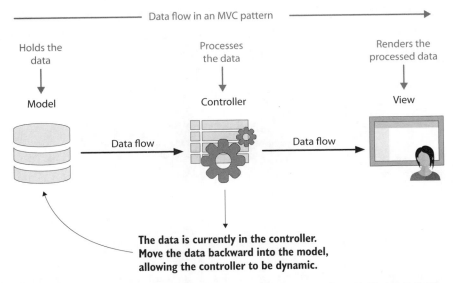

Figure 5.6 How data should flow in an MVC pattern, from the model through the controller and into the view. At this point in your prototype, your data is in the controller, so you want to move it a step back into the model.

One outcome of moving the data back through the MVC flow step by step as you've done so far is that it helps solidify the requirements of the data structure, ensuring that the data structure accurately reflects the needs of your application. If you try to define your model first, you end up second-guessing what the application will look like and how it will work.

When you talk about modeling data, you're describing how you want the data to be structured. In your application, you could create and manage the definitions manually and do the heavy lifting yourself, or you could use Mongoose and let it do the hard work.

5.2.1 *What is Mongoose and how does it work?*

Mongoose was built specifically as a MongoDB Object Document Modeler (ODM) for Node applications. One key principle is that you can manage your data model from within your application. You don't have to mess around directly with databases or external frameworks or relational mappers; you can define your data model in the comfort of your application.

First, we'll get some naming conventions out of the way:

- In MongoDB, each entry in a database is called a *document.*
- In MongoDB, a group of documents is called a *collection.* (Think *table* if you're used to relational databases.)
- In Mongoose, the definition of a document is called a *schema.*
- Each individual data entity defined in a schema is called a *path.*

Using the example of a stack of business cards, figure 5.7 illustrates these naming conventions and how each is related to the others.

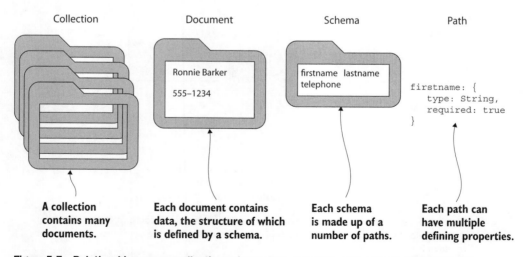

Figure 5.7   Relationships among collections, documents, schemas, and paths in MongoDB and Mongoose, using a business card metaphor

One final definition is for models. A *model* is the compiled version of a schema. All data interactions using Mongoose go through the model. You'll work with models more in chapter 6, but for now, you're focusing on building them.

5.2.2 How does Mongoose model data?

If you're defining your data in the application, how are you going to do it? In Java-Script, of course—JavaScript objects, to be precise. You've already had a sneak peek in figure 5.7, but now take a look at a simple MongoDB document to see what the Mongoose schema for it might look like. The following code snippet shows a MongoDB document, followed by the Mongoose schema:

```
{
  "firstname" : "Simon",         Example
  "surname" : "Holmes",          MongoDB
  _id : ObjectId("52279effc62ca8b0c1000007")   document
}
{
  firstname : String,      Corresponding
  surname : String         Mongoose
                           schema
}
```

As you can see, the schema has a strong resemblance to the data itself. The schema defines the name for each data path and the data type it will contain. In this example, you've simply declared the paths `firstname` and `surname` as strings.

About the _id path

You may have noticed that you haven't declared the id path in the schema. `_id` is the unique identifier—the primary key, if you like—for each document. MongoDB automatically creates this path when each document is created and assigns it a unique `ObjectId` value. The value is designed to always be unique by combining the time since the UNIX epoch with machine and process identifiers and a counter.

It's possible to use your own unique key system if you prefer (if you have a preexisting database, for example). In this book and the Loc8r application, you'll stick with the default `ObjectId`.

5.2.3 Breaking down a schema path

The basic construct for an individual path definition is the pathname followed by a properties object. In the previous example, you looked at a Mongoose schema, which demonstrates a kind of shorthand for defining a data path and its data type. A schema path is constructed of the pathname and the properties object, like so:

```
firstname: { type: String }
```
Pathname   **Properties object**

Allowed schema types

The schema type is the property that defines the data type for a given path. It's required for all paths. If the only property of a path is the type, you can use the shorthand definition. There are eight schema types that you can use:

- `String`—Any string, UTF-8 encoded.
- `Number`—Mongoose doesn't support long or double numbers, but it can be extended using Mongoose plugins; the default support is enough in most cases.
- `Date`—Typically returned from MongoDB as an `ISODate` object.
- `Boolean`—True or false.
- `Buffer`—For binary information such as images.
- `Mixed`—Any data type.
- `Array`—Can be an array of the same data type or an array of nested subdocuments.
- `ObjectId`—For a unique ID in a path other than `_id`; typically used to reference `_id` paths in other documents.

If you need to use a different schema type, it's possible to write your own custom schema types or to use an existing Mongoose plugin from http://plugins.mongoosejs.io.

The pathname follows JavaScript object definition conventions and requirements. There are no spaces or special characters, and you should try to avoid reserved words. Our convention is to use camelCase for pathnames. If you're using an existing database, use the names of the paths already in the documents. If you're creating a new database, the pathnames in the schema will be used in the documents, so think carefully.

The properties object is essentially another JavaScript object. This one defines the characteristics of the data held in the path. At a minimum, this object contains the data type, but it can include validation characteristics, boundaries, default values, and more. You'll explore and use some of these options over the next few chapters as you turn Loc8r into a data-driven application.

In the next section, you'll get moving and start defining the schemas you want in the application.

5.3   *Defining simple Mongoose schemas*

We've discussed the fact that a Mongoose schema is essentially a JavaScript object, which you define from within the application. Start by setting up and including the file so that it's done and out of the way, leaving you free to concentrate on the schema.

As you'd expect, you'll define the schema in the model folder alongside db.js. In fact, you're going to `require` it into db.js to expose it to the application. Inside the models folder in app_server, create a new empty file called locations.js. You need Mongoose to define a Mongoose schema, naturally, so enter the following line to locations.js:

```
const mongoose = require('mongoose');
```

You'll bring this file into the application by adding a require in db.js for it. At the end of db.js, add the following line:

```
require('./locations');
```

And with that, you're set up and ready to go.

5.3.1　The basics of setting up a schema

Mongoose gives you a constructor function for defining new schemas, which you typically assign to a variable so that you can access it later. This function looks like the following line:

```
const locationSchema = new mongoose.Schema({ });
```

In fact, that's exactly the construct you're going to use. Add it to the locations.js model, below the line requiring Mongoose. The empty object inside the mongoose-Schema({ }) brackets is where you'll define the schema.

DEFINING A SCHEMA FROM CONTROLLER DATA

One of the outcomes of moving the data back from the view to the controller is that the controller can give you a good idea of the data structure you need. Start simple by taking a look at the homelist controller in app_server/controllers/locations.js. The homelist controller passes the data to be shown on the homepage into the view. Figure 5.8 shows how one of the locations looks on the homepage.

Figure 5.8　A single location as displayed in the homepage list

The following code snippet shows the data for this location, as found in the controller:

```
locations: [{                                    name is a string.
  name: 'Starcups',
  address: '125 High Street, Reading, RG6 1PS',   address is another string.
  rating: 3,                                       rating is a number.
  facilities: ['Hot drinks', 'Food', 'Premium wifi'],
  distance: '100m'                                 facilities is an
}]                                                 array of strings.
```

You'll come back to the distance a bit later, as that needs to be calculated. The other four data items are fairly straightforward: two strings, one number, and one array of strings. Taking what you know so far, you can use this information to define a basic schema like the following:

```
const locationSchema = new mongoose.Schema({
  name: String,
  address: String,                  ❶ Declares an array of the same
  rating: Number,                      schema type by declaring that
  facilities: [String]                 type inside square brackets
});
```

Note the simple approach to declaring facilities as an array ❶. If your array will contain only one schema type, such as `String`, you can define it by wrapping the schema type in square brackets.

ASSIGNING DEFAULT VALUES

In some cases, it's useful to set a default value when a new MongoDB document is created based on your schema. In the `locationSchema`, the `rating` path is a good candidate. When a new location is added to the database, it won't have had any reviews, so it won't have a rating. But your view expects a rating between zero and five stars, which is what the controller needs to pass through.

What you'd like to do is set a default value of `0` for the rating on each new document. Mongoose lets you do this from within the schema. Remember that `rating: Number` is shorthand for `rating: {type: Number}`? Well, you can add other options to the definition object, including a default value. This means that you can update the rating path in the schema as follows:

```
rating: {
  type: Number,
  'default': 0
}
```

The word `default` doesn't *have* to be in quotes, but it's a reserved word in JavaScript; therefore, it's a good idea to use them.

ADDING SOME BASIC VALIDATION: REQUIRED FIELDS

Through Mongoose, you can quickly add some basic validation at the schema level. This practice helps maintain data integrity and can protect your database from missing or malformed data. Mongoose's helpers make it easy to add some of the most common validation tasks, meaning that you don't have to write or import the code each time.

The first example of this type of validation ensures that required fields aren't empty before saving the document to the database. Rather than writing the checks for each required field in code, you can add a `required: true` flag to the definition objects of each path that you decide should be mandatory. In the `locationSchema`, you certainly want to ensure that each location has a name, so you can update the name path like this:

```
name: {
  type: String,
  required: true
}
```

If you try to save a location without a name, Mongoose returns a validation error that you can capture immediately in your code without making a round trip to the database.

ADDING SOME BASIC VALIDATION: NUMBER BOUNDARIES

You can use a similar technique to define the maximum and minimum values you want for a number path. These validators are called `max` and `min`. Each location you have has a rating assigned to it, which you've given a default value of 0. The value should never be less than 0 or greater than 5. Update the `rating` path as follows:

```
rating: {
  type: Number,
  'default': 0,
  min: 0,
  max: 5
}
```

With this update, Mongoose won't let you save a rating value less than 0 or greater than 5. If you try, it returns a validation error that you can handle in your code. One great thing about this approach is that the application doesn't have to make a round trip to the database to check the boundaries. Another bonus is that you don't have to write validation code in every place in the application where you might add, update, or calculate a rating value.

5.3.2 Using geographic data in MongoDB and Mongoose

When you started to map your application's data from the controller into a Mongoose schema, you left the question of distance until later. Now it's time to discuss how you're going to handle geographic information.

MongoDB can store geographic data as longitude and latitude coordinates and can even create and manage an index based on this data. This ability enables users to do fast searches of places that are near one another or near a specific longitude and latitude—helpful indeed for building a location-based application!

> **About MongoDB indexes**
>
> Indexes in any database system enable faster and more efficient query, and MongoDB is no different. When a path is indexed, MongoDB can use this index to quickly grab subsets of data without having to scan through all documents in a collection.
>
> Think of a filing system you might have at home. Suppose that you need to find a particular credit card statement. You might keep all your paperwork in one drawer or cabinet. If everything is thrown in there randomly, you'll have to sort through all types of irrelevant documents until you find what you're looking for. If you've indexed your paperwork into folders, however, you can quickly find your credit card folder. When you've picked out this folder, you look through this one set of documents, making your search much more efficient.
>
> This scenario is akin to how indexing works in a database. In a database, though, you can have more than one index for each document, enabling you to search efficiently on different queries.

(continued)

Indexes do take maintenance and database resources, though, as it takes time to file your paperwork correctly. For best overall performance, try to limit your database indexes to the paths that most need indexing and are used for most queries.

The data for a single geographical location is stored according to the GeoJSON format specification, which you'll see in action shortly. Mongoose supports this data type, allowing you to define a geospatial path inside a schema. As Mongoose is an abstraction layer on top of MongoDB, it strives to make things easier for you. All you have to do to add a GeoJSON path in your schema:

1 Define the path as an array of the Number type.
2 Define the path as having a 2dsphere index.

To put this into action, you can add a coords path to your location schema. If you follow the two preceding steps, your schema should look like this:

```
const locationSchema = new mongoose.Schema({
  name: {
    type: String,
    required: true
  },
  address: String,
  rating: {
    type: Number,
    'default': 0,
    min: 0,
    max: 5
  },
  facilities: [String],
  coords: {
    type: { type: String },
    coordinates: [Number]
  }
});
locationSchema.index({coords: '2dsphere'});
```

The 2dsphere here is the critical part because it enables MongoDB to do the correct calculations when running queries and returning results. It allows MongoDB to calculate geometries based on a spherical object. You'll work more with this feature in chapter 6 when you build your API and start to interact with the data.

> **TIP** To meet the GeoJSON specification, a coordinate pair must be entered into the array in the correct order: longitude, then latitude. Valid longitude values range from -180 to 180, whereas valid latitude values range from -90 to 90. Getting your coordinates in the wrong order is an easy mistake to make, so keep this in mind when saving location data to the collection.

You've got the basics covered, and your schema for Loc8r currently holds everything needed to satisfy the homepage requirements. Next, it's time to take a look at the Details page. This page has more complex data requirements, and you'll see how to handle them with Mongoose schemas.

5.3.3 Creating more complex schemas with subdocuments

The data you've used up until now has been simple and can be held in a fairly flat schema. You've used a couple of arrays for the facilities and location coordinates, but again, those arrays are simple, containing only a single data type each. Now you'll look at what happens when you have a slightly more complicated dataset to work with.

Start by reacquainting yourself with the Details page and the data that it shows. Figure 5.9 shows a screenshot of the page with all the different areas of information. The name, rating, and address are right at the top; a little farther down are the facilities. On the right side is a map, based on the geographic coordinates. You've already covered

Figure 5.9   The information displayed for a single location on the Details page

these elements with the basic schema. The two areas that you don't have anything for are opening hours and customer reviews.

The data powering this view is currently held in the `locationInfo` controller in app_server/controllers/locations.js. The following listing shows the relevant portion of the data in this controller.

Listing 5.2   Data in the controller powering the Details page

```
location: {
  name: 'Starcups',
  address: '125 High Street, Reading, RG6 1PS',
  rating: 3,
  facilities: ['Hot drinks', 'Food', 'Premium wifi'],
  coords: {lat: 51.455041, lng: -0.9690884},

    days: 'Monday - Friday',
    opening: '7:00am',
    closing: '7:00pm',
    closed: false
  },{
    days: 'Saturday',
    opening: '8:00am',
    closing: '5:00pm',
    closed: false
  },{
    days: 'Sunday',
    closed: true
  }],
  reviews: [{
    author: 'Simon Holmes',
    rating: 5,
    timestamp: '16 July 2013',
    reviewText: 'What a great place.
I can\'t say enough good things about it.'
  },{
    author: 'Charlie Chaplin',
    rating: 3,
    timestamp: '16 June 2013',
    reviewText: 'It was okay. Coffee wasn\'t great,
but the wifi was fast.'
  }]
}
```

Already covered with the existing schema

Data for opening hours is held as an array of objects.

Reviews are also passed to the view as an array of objects.

Here, you have arrays of objects for the opening hours and for the reviews. In a relational database, you'd create these as separate tables and `join` them in a query when you need the information. But that's not how document databases work, including MongoDB. In a document database, anything that belongs specifically to a parent document should be contained *within* that document. Figure 5.10 illustrates the conceptual difference between the two approaches.

MongoDB offers the concept of *subdocuments* to store this repeating, nested data. Subdocuments are much like documents in that they have their own schema; each is

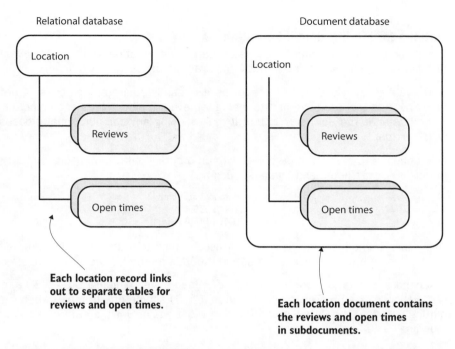

Relational database   Document database

**Each location record links
out to separate tables for
reviews and open times.**

**Each location document contains
the reviews and open times
in subdocuments.**

**Figure 5.10   Difference between how a relational database and a document database
store repeating information relating to a parent element**

given a unique _id by MongoDB when created. But subdocuments are nested inside a
document, and they can be accessed only as a path of that parent document.

USING NESTED SCHEMAS IN MONGOOSE TO DEFINE SUBDOCUMENTS

Subdocuments are defined in Mongoose by nested schemas—one schema nested
inside another. In this section, you'll create one to see how it works in code. The first
step is defining a new schema for a subdocument. Start with the opening times,
and create the following schema. Note that this schema needs to be in the same file as
the locationSchema definition and (important) must be *before* the locationSchema
definition:

```
const openingTimeSchema = new mongoose.Schema({
  days: {
    type: String,
    required: true
  },
  opening: String,
  closing: String,
  closed: {
    type: Boolean,
    required: true
  }
});
```

Options for storing time information

In the opening-time schema, you have an interesting situation: you want to save time information, such as 7:30 a.m., but without a date associated with it.

Here, you're using a `String` method, as it doesn't require any processing before being put into the database or after being retrieved. It also makes each record easy to understand. The downside is that it makes doing any computational processing with it harder.

One option is to create a date object with an arbitrary data value assigned to it and manually set the hours and minutes, such as

```
const d = new Date();
d.setHours(15);
d.setMinutes(30);
```

d is now Sun Mar 12 2017 15:30:40 GMT+0000 (GMT).

Using this method, you could easily extract the time from the data. The downsides are that you store unnecessary data, and that this method is technically incorrect.

A second option is to store the number of minutes since midnight. So 7:30 a.m. is $(7 \times 60) + 30 = 450$. This computation is a fairly simple one to make when you're putting data into the database and pulling it out again. But the data at a glance is meaningless.

This second option, however, would be our preference for making the dates smarter and could be a good extension if you want to try something new. For the sake of readability and avoiding distractions, you'll keep using the `String` method through the book.

This schema definition is simple and maps over from the data in the controller. You have two required fields: the `closed` Boolean flag and the `days` each subdocument is referring to.

Nesting this schema inside the location schema is another straightforward task. You need to add a new path to the parent schema and define it as an array of your subdocument schema. The following code snippet shows how to nest the `openingTime-Schema` inside the `locationSchema`:

```
const locationSchema = new mongoose.Schema({
  name: {
    type: String,
    required: true
  },
  address: String,
  rating: {
    type: Number,
    'default': 0,
    min: 0,
    max: 5
  },
  facilities: [String],
```

```
coords: {
  type: {type: String},
  coordinates: [Number]
},
openingTimes: [openingTimeSchema]
});
```

Adds nested schema by referencing another schema object as an array

With this in place, you can add multiple opening-time subdocuments to a given location, and these subdocuments are stored within that location document. An example document from MongoDB based on this schema is shown in the following code snippet, with the subdocuments for the opening times in bold:

```
{
  "_id": ObjectId("52ef3a9f79c44a86710fe7f5"),
  "name": "Starcups",
  "address": "125 High Street, Reading, RG6 1PS",
  "rating": 3,
  "facilities": ["Hot drinks", "Food", "Premium wifi"],
  "coords": [-0.9690884, 51.455041],
  "openingTimes": [{
    "_id": ObjectId("52ef3a9f79c44a86710fe7f6"),
    "days": "Monday - Friday",
    "opening": "7:00am",
    "closing": "7:00pm",
    "closed": false
  }, {
    "_id": ObjectId("52ef3a9f79c44a86710fe7f7"),
    "days": "Saturday",
    "opening": "8:00am",
    "closing": "5:00pm",
    "closed": false
  }, {
    "_id": ObjectId("52ef3a9f79c44a86710fe7f8"),
    "days": "Sunday",
    "closed": true
  }]
}
```

In a MongoDB document, nested opening-times subdocuments live inside the location document.

With the schema for the opening times taken care of, next you'll look at adding a schema for the review subdocuments.

ADDING A SECOND SET OF SUBDOCUMENTS

Neither MongoDB nor Mongoose limits the number of subdocument paths in a document, so you're free to use what you've done for the opening times and replicate the process for the reviews:

- Step 1: Look at the data used in a review:

```
{
  author: 'Simon Holmes',
  rating: 5,
  timestamp: '16 July 2013',
  reviewText: 'What a great place. I can\'t say enough good things
about it.'
}
```

- Step 2: Map this code into a new `reviewSchema` in app_server/models/location.js:

```
const reviewSchema = new mongoose.Schema({
  author: String,
  rating: {
    type: Number,
    required: true,
    min: 0,
    max: 5
  },
  reviewText: String,
  createdOn: {
    type: Date,
    'default': Date.now
  }
});
```

- Step 3: Add this `reviewSchema` as a new path to `locationSchema`:

```
const locationSchema = new mongoose.Schema({
  name: {type: String, required: true},
  address: String,
  rating: {type: Number, "default": 0, min: 0, max: 5},
  facilities: [String],
  coords: {type: { type: String }, coordinates: [Number]},
  openingTimes: [openingTimeSchema],
  reviews: [reviewSchema]
});
```

When you've defined the schema for reviews and added it to your main location schema, you have everything you need to hold the data for all locations in a structured way.

5.3.4   Final schema

Throughout this section, you've done quite a bit in the file, so take a look at it all together to see what's what. The following listing shows the contents of the locations.js file in app_server/models, defining the schema for the location data.

Listing 5.3   Final location schema definition, including nested schemas

```
const mongoose = require( 'mongoose' );          ◁──── Requires Mongoose so that
const openingTimeSchema = new                             you can use its methods
    mongoose.Schema({
  days: {type: String, required: true},
  opening: String,
  closing: String,                          Defines a schema
  closed: {                                 for opening times
    type: Boolean,
    required: true
  }
});
const reviewSchema = new mongoose.Schema({        Defines a schema
  author: String,                                 for reviews
  rating: {
```

```
    type: Number,
    required: true,
    min: 0,
    max: 5
  },
  reviewText: String,
  createdOn: {type: Date, default: Date.now}
});
const locationSchema = new mongoose.Schema({
  name: {
    type: String,
    required: true
  },
  address: String,
  rating: {
    type: Number,
    'default': 0,
    min: 0,
    max: 5
  },
  facilities: [String],
  coords: {
    type: {type: String },
    coordinates:[Number]
  },
  openingTimes: [openingTimeSchema],
  reviews: [reviewSchema]
});
locationSchema.index({coords: '2dsphere'});
```

Defines a schema for reviews

Starts the main location schema definition

Uses 2dsphere to add support for GeoJSON longitude and latitude coordinate pairs

References the opening times and reviews schemas to add nested subdocuments

Documents and subdocuments all have a schema defining their structure, and you've also added some default values and basic validation. To make this scenario a bit more real, the following listing shows an example MongoDB document based on this schema.

Listing 5.4 Example MongoDB document based on the location schema

```
{
  "_id": ObjectId("52ef3a9f79c44a86710fe7f5"),
  "name": "Starcups",
  "address": "125 High Street, Reading, RG6 1PS",
  "rating": 3,
  "facilities": ["Hot drinks", "Food", "Premium wifi"],
  "coords": [-0.9690884, 51.455041],
  "openingTimes": [{
    "_id": ObjectId("52ef3a9f79c44a86710fe7f6"),
    "days": "Monday - Friday",
    "opening": "7:00am",
    "closing": "7:00pm",
    "closed": false
  }, {
    "_id": ObjectId("52ef3a9f79c44a86710fe7f7"),
    "days": "Saturday",
    "opening": "8:00am",
```

Coordinates are stored as a GeoJSON pair [longitude, latitude].

Opening times are stored as nested array of objects (subdocuments).

```
      "closing": "5:00pm",
      "closed": false
    }, {
      "_id": ObjectId("52ef3a9f79c44a86710fe7f8"),
      "days": "Sunday",
      "closed": true
    }],
    "reviews": [{
      "_id": ObjectId("52ef3a9f79c44a86710fe7f9"),
      "author": "Simon Holmes",
      "rating": 5,
      "createdOn": ISODate("2013-07-15T23:00:00Z"),
      "reviewText": "What a great place. I can't say enough good
things about it."
    }, {
      "_id": ObjectId("52ef3a9f79c44a86710fe7fa"),
      "author": "Charlie Chaplin",
      "rating": 3,
      "createdOn": ISODate("2013-06-15T23:00:00Z"),
      "reviewText": "It was okay. Coffee wasn't great, but the wifi was fast."
    }]
}
```

Opening times are stored as nested array of objects (subdocuments).

Reviews are also arrays of subdocuments.

That listing should give you an idea of what a MongoDB document looks like, including subdocuments, when based on a known schema. In readable form like this, it's a JSON object, although technically, MongoDB stores it as BSON, which is Binary JSON.

5.3.5   *Compiling Mongoose schemas into models*

An application doesn't interact with the schema directly when working with data; data interaction is done through models.

In Mongoose, a model is a compiled version of the schema. When it's compiled, a single instance of the model maps directly to a single document in your database. It's through this direct one-to-one relationship that the model can create, read, save, and delete data. Figure 5.11 illustrates this arrangement.

This approach makes Mongoose a breeze to work with, and you'll get your teeth into it in chapter 6 when you build the internal API for the application.

COMPILING A MODEL FROM A SCHEMA

Anything with the word *compiling* in it tends to sound a bit complicated. In reality, compiling a Mongoose model from a schema is a simple one-line task. You need to ensure that the schema is complete before you invoke the `model` command. The `model` command follows this construct:

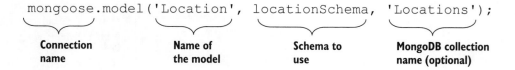

```
mongoose.model('Location', locationSchema, 'Locations');
```

Connection name   **Name of the model**   **Schema to use**   **MongoDB collection name (optional)**

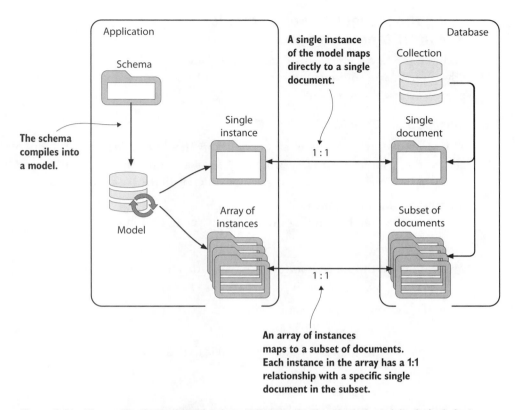

Figure 5.11　**The application and the database talk to each other through models. A single instance of a model has a one-to-one relationship with a single document in the database. It's through this relationship that the creating, reading, updating ,and deleting of data are managed.**

TIP　The MongoDB collection name is optional. If you exclude it, Mongoose uses a lowercase pluralized version of the model name. A model name of `Location`, for example, would look for a collection name of locations unless you specify something different.

As you're creating a database and not hooking into an existing data source, you can use a default collection name, so you don't need to include that parameter in the `model` command. To build a model of your location schema, you can add the following line to the code below the `locationSchema` definition:

```
mongoose.model('Location', locationSchema);
```

That's all there is to it. You've defined a data schema for the locations and compiled the schema into a model that you can use in the application. What you need now is some data.

5.4   Using the MongoDB shell to create a MongoDB database and add data

To build the Loc8r app, you'll create a new database and manually add some test data. You get to create your own personal version of Loc8r for testing and at the same time play directly with MongoDB.

5.4.1   MongoDB shell basics

The MongoDB shell is a command-line utility that gets installed with MongoDB and allows you to interact with any MongoDB databases on your system. It's powerful and can do a lot. You're only going to get acquainted with the basics to get up and running.

STARTING THE MONGODB SHELL

Drop into the shell by running the following line in terminal:

```
$ mongo
```

This command should respond in terminal with a few lines confirming

- The shell version
- The server and port that it's connecting to
- The server version it has connected to

These confirmation lines should look similar to this, so long as the version is equal to or later than 4:

```
MongoDB shell version 4.0.0
connecting to: mongodb://127.0.0.1:27017
MongoDB server version: 4.0.0
```

If you're using an older version of MongoDB, you may see different messages, but it's normally obvious if the command has worked or failed. You might also see a few lines starting with `Server has startup warnings` going on to state `Access control is not enabled for the database`. This isn't anything to worry about on your local development machine.

> **TIP**   When you're in the shell, newlines start with a > to differentiate from the standard command-line entry point. The shell commands printed in this section start with > instead of $ to make it clear that you're using the shell, but like $, you don't need to type it.

LISTING ALL LOCAL DATABASES

Next is a simple command that shows a list of all the local MongoDB databases. Enter the following line in the shell:

```
> show dbs
```

This line returns a list of the local MongoDB database names and their sizes. If you haven't created any databases at this point, you still see the two default ones, which look something like this:

```
admin    0.000GB
local    0.000GB
```

USING A SPECIFIC DATABASE

If you want to use a specific database, such as the default one called local, you can use the use command, like this:

```
> use local
```

The shell responds with a message along these lines:

```
switched to db local
```

This message confirms the name of the database the shell has connected to.

LISTING THE COLLECTIONS IN A DATABASE

When you're using a particular database, it's easy to output a list of its collections by using the following command:

```
> show collections
```

If you're using the local database, you'll probably see a single collection name output to terminal: startup_log.

SEEING THE CONTENTS OF A COLLECTION

The MongoDB shell also lets you query the collections in a database. The construct for a query or find operation is as follows:

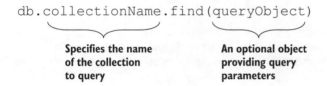

The query object is used to specify what you're trying to find in the collection, and you'll look at examples of this query object later in chapter 6. (Mongoose also uses the query object.) The simplest query is an empty query, which returns all the documents in a collection. Don't worry if your collection is large, as MongoDB returns a subset of documents that you can page through. Using the startup_log collection as an example, you can run the following command:

```
> db.startup_log.find()
```

This command returns several documents from the MongoDB startup log, the content of which isn't interesting enough to show here. This command is useful when you're getting your database up and running and making sure that things are being saved as you expect.

5.4.2 Creating a MongoDB database

You don't have to *create* a MongoDB database; you only need to start using it. For the Loc8r application, it makes sense to have a database called Loc8r. In the shell, you use it with the following command:

```
> use Loc8r
```

If you run the `show collections` command, it won't return anything yet, and you won't even see it if you run `show dbs`. But you'll be able to see it after saving some data to it.

CREATING A COLLECTION AND DOCUMENTS

Similarly, you don't have to explicitly create a collection, as MongoDB creates it for you when you first save data to it.

> **Location data more personal to you**
>
> Loc8r is all about location-based data, and the examples are all fictitious places, geographically close to where Simon lives in the United Kingdom. You can make your version more personal to you by changing the names, addresses, and coordinates.
>
> To get your current coordinates, visit https://whatsmylatlng.com. There's a button on the page to find your location by using JavaScript, which gives you a much more accurate location than the first attempt. Note that the coordinates are shown to you in latitude–longitude order, and you need to flip them around for the database so that longitude is first.
>
> To get the coordinates of any address, you can use http://mygeoposition.com. This site lets you enter an address or drag and drop a pointer to give you the geographic coordinates. Again, remember that the pairs in MongoDB must be longitude and then latitude.

To match the `Location` model, you'll want a `locations` collection. Remember that the default collection name is a lowercase pluralized version of the model name. You can create and save a new document by passing a data object into the `save` command of a collection, as in the following code snippet:

```
> db.locations.save({                    ◁————————————   Note collection name
    name: 'Starcups',                                     specified as part of the
    address: '125 High Street, Reading, RG6 1PS',         save command
    rating: 3,
    facilities: ['Hot drinks', 'Food', 'Premium wifi'],
    coords: [-0.9690884, 51.455041],
    openingTimes: [{
      days: 'Monday - Friday',
      opening: '7:00am',
      closing: '7:00pm',
      closed: false
    }, {
```

```
      days: 'Saturday',
      opening: '8:00am',
      closing: '5:00pm',
      closed: false
  }, {
      days: 'Sunday',
      closed: true
  }]
})
```

In one step, you've created the Loc8r database and a new locations collection, and added the first document to the collection. If you run show dbs in the MongoDB shell now, you should see the new Loc8r database being returned alongside the other databases, like so:

```
> show dbs
Loc8r     0.000GB
admin     0.000GB
local     0.000GB
```

Now when you run show collections in the MongoDB shell, you should see the new locations collection being returned:

```
> show collections
locations
```

You can query the collection to find the documents. Only one document is there currently, so the returned information is small. You can use the find command on the collection as well:

```
> db.locations.find()                    ◁——————————————————      Remember to run
{                                                                  the find
  "_id": ObjectId("530efe98d382e7fa4345f173"),    ◁——————         operation on the
  "address": "125 High Street, Reading, RG6 1PS",                  collection itself.
  "coords": [-0.9690884, 51.455041],
  "facilities": ["Hot drinks", "Food", "Premium wifi"],
  "name": "Starcups",
  "openingTimes": [{
    "days": "Monday - Friday",                       MongoDB has
    "opening": "7:00am",                       automatically added a
    "closing": "7:00pm",                        unique identifier for
    "closed": false                               this document.
  }, {
    "days": "Saturday",
    "opening": "8:00am",
    "closing": "5:00pm",
    "closed": false
  }, {
    "days": "Sunday",
    "closed": true
  }],
  "rating": 3,
}
```

This code snippet has been formatted for readability; the document that MongoDB returns to the shell won't have the line breaks and indentation. But the MongoDB shell can prettify it for you if you add `.pretty()` to the end of the command, like this:

```
> db.locations.find().pretty()
```

Notice that the order of the data in the returned document doesn't match the order of the data in the object you supplied. As the data structure isn't column-based, it doesn't matter how MongoDB stores the individual paths within a document. The data is always still there in the correct paths, and data held inside arrays always maintains the same order.

ADDING SUBDOCUMENTS

You've probably noticed that your first document doesn't have the full dataset; there are no review subdocuments. You can add them to the initial `save` command as you've done with the opening times, or you can update an existing document and push them in.

MongoDB has an `update` command that accepts two arguments: a query so that it knows which document to update, and the instructions on what to do when it finds the document. At this point, you can do a simple query and look for the location by name (Starcups), as you know that there aren't any duplicates. For the instruction object, you can use a `$push` command to add a new object to the reviews path. It doesn't matter if the reviews path doesn't exist yet; MongoDB adds it as part of the push operation.

Putting it all together shows something like the following code snippet:

```
> db.locations.update({            Starts with a query object
  name: 'Starcups'                 to find correct document
}, {
  $push: {
    reviews: {                     When the document is found, pushes a
      author: 'Simon Holmes',      subdocument into the reviews path
      _id: ObjectId(),
      rating: 5,                   Subdocument
      timestamp: new Date("Mar 12, 2017"),   contains this data
      reviewText: "What a great place."
    }
  }
})
```

If you run that command in the MongoDB shell while using the Loc8r database, you add a review to the document. You can repeat the command as often as you like, changing the data to add multiple reviews.

You may have noticed that here, you specify the `_id` property and assign it the value of `ObjectId()`. MongoDB doesn't automatically add `_id` to subdocuments as it does for documents, but this feature will be useful for you later. Giving the review subdocument the value of `ObjectId()` tells MongoDB to create a new unique identifier for this subdocument.

Note the `new Date()` function call for setting the timestamp of the review. Using this timestamp ensures that MongoDB stores the date as an ISO date object, not a string—which is what your schema expects, and which allows greater manipulation of dates data.

REPEAT THE PROCESS

These few commands have given you one location to test the application with, but ideally, you need a couple more. Add some more locations to your database.

When you're done with that and your data is set, you're almost at the point where you can start using it from the application. In this case, you'll be building an API. But before you jump into that task in chapter 6, there's one more piece of housekeeping. You want to keep pushing regular updates to Heroku, and now that you've added a database connection and data models to your application, you need to make sure that these updates are supported in Heroku.

5.5 Getting your database live

If you've got your application out in the wild, it's no good having your database on your local host. Your database also needs to be externally accessible. In this section, you'll push your database into a live environment and update your Loc8r application so that it uses the published database from the published site, and the local host database from the development site. You'll start by using the free tier of a service called mLab, which can be used as an add-on to Heroku. If you have a different preferred provider or your own database server, that's no problem. The first part of this section runs through setting up on mLab, but the following parts—migrating the data and setting the connection strings in the Node application—aren't platform specific.

5.5.1 Setting up mLab and getting the database URI

The first goal is getting an externally accessible database URI so that you can push data to it and add it to the application. You'll use mLab for this purpose, as it has a good free tier, excellent online documentation, and a responsive support team.

You have a couple of ways to set up a database on mLab. The quickest and easiest way is to use an add-on via Heroku. This method is what you'll use here, but it does require you to register a valid credit card with Heroku. Heroku makes you do this when you use add-ons through its ecosystem to protect itself from abusive behavior. Using the free sandbox tier of mLab won't incur any charges. If you're not comfortable using a credit card to set up your mLab database directly through Heroku, check out the sidebar "Setting up mLab manually" for details on setting up an mLab database and connecting it to your Heroku application manually. If you opt to set up your database manually, don't follow the instructions for Heroku add-on installation; otherwise, you'll end up with multiple databases associated with your application.

Setting up mLab manually

You don't have to use the Heroku add-on system if you don't want to. What you want to do is to set up a MongoDB database in the cloud and get a connection string for it.

The mLab documentation can guide you through this process; see https://docs .mlab.com.

In short, the steps are

1 Sign up for a free account.
2 Create a new database (select Single Node, Sandbox for the free tier).
3 Add a user.
4 Get the database URI (connection string).

The connection string looks something like this:

```
mongodb://dbuser:dbpassword@ds059957.mlab.com:59957/loc8r-dev
```

All the parts will be different for you, of course, and you'll have to swap out the user-name and password with what you specified in step 3.

When you have your full connection string, you should save it as part of your Heroku configuration. With a terminal prompt in the root folder of your application, you can do this with the following command:

```
$ heroku config:set MLAB_URI=your_db_uri
```

Replace `your_db_uri` with your full connection string, including the `mongodb://` protocol. The quick and easy way automatically creates the `MLAB_URI` setting in your Heroku configuration. These manual steps bring you to the same point as the quick way, and you can jump back to the main text.

ADDING THE MLAB ADD-ON TO THE HEROKU APPLICATION

The quickest way to add mLab as a Heroku add-on is through terminal. Make sure that you're in the root folder of your application, and run the following command (using mLab's old name, MongoLab):

```
$ heroku addons:create mongolab
```

Unbelievably, that's it! You have a MongoDB database ready and waiting for you in the cloud. You can prove this to yourself and open a web interface to this new database by using the following command:

```
$ heroku addons:open mongolab
```

To use the database, you'll need to know its URI.

GETTING THE DATABASE URI

You can get the full database URI by using the command line. This method gives you the full connection string that you can use in the application and also shows you the various components that you'll need to push data up to the database.

The command to get the database URI is

```
$ heroku config:get MONGODB_URI
```

This command outputs the full connection string, which looks something like this:

```
mongodb://heroku_t0zs37gc:1k3t3pgo8sb5enovqd9sk314gj@ds159330.mlab.com:59330/
    heroku_t0zs37gc
```

Keep your version handy, as you'll use it in the application soon. First, you need to break it down into its components.

BREAKING DOWN THE URI INTO ITS COMPONENTS

The URI looks like a random mess of characters, but you can break it down to make sense of it. From section 5.1.2, you know that this is how a database URI is constructed:

Taking the URI that mLab has given you, you can break it down into something like the following:

- *Username*—heroku_t0zs37gc
- *Password*—1k3t3pgo8sb5enovqd9sk314gj
- *Server address*—ds159330.mlab.com
- *Port*—59330
- *Database name*—heroku_t0zs37gc

These examples are from the example URI. Yours will be different, of course, but make note of them; they'll be useful.

5.5.2 *Pushing up the data*

Now that you have an externally accessible database set up and know all the details for connecting to it, you can push data up to it. The steps are as follows:

1 Navigate to a directory on your machine that's suitable to hold a data dump.
2 Dump the data from your development Loc8r database.
3 Restore the data to your live database.
4 Test the live database.

All these steps can be achieved quickly through terminal, so that's what you'll do. It saves jumping around between environments.

NAVIGATE TO A SUITABLE DIRECTORY

When you run the data dump command from the command line, it creates a folder called /dump in the current directory and places the data dump inside it. The first step, then, is navigating in terminal to a suitable location on your hard drive. Your home directory or documents folder will do, or you can create a specific folder if you prefer.

DUMPING THE DATA FROM THE DEVELOPMENT DATABASE

Dumping the data sounds like you're deleting everything from your local development version, but this isn't the case. The process is more an export than a trashing.

The command used is `mongodump`, which can accept many parameters, of which you need these two:

- -h—The host server (and port)
- -d—The database name

Putting it all together and using the default MongoDB port of 27017, you should end up with a command like the following:

```
$ mongodump -h localhost:27017 -d Loc8r
```

Run that command, and you have a temporary dump of the data.

RESTORING THE DATA TO YOUR LIVE DATABASE

The process of pushing up the data to your live database is similar, this time using the `mongorestore` command. This command expects the following parameters:

- -h—Live host and port
- -d—Live database name
- -u—Username for the live database
- -p—Password for the live database
- Path to the dump directory and database name (comes at the end of the command and doesn't have a corresponding flag like the other parameters)

Putting all this together, using the information you have about the database URI, you should have a command like the following:

```
$ mongorestore -h ds159330.mlab.com:59330 -d heroku_t0zs37gc
    -u heroku_t0zs37gc -p 1k3t3pgo8sb5enovqd9sk314gj dump/
```

Your command will look a bit different, of course, because you'll have a different host, live database name, username, and password. When you run your `mongorestore` command, it pushes the data up from the data dump into your live database.

TESTING THE LIVE DATABASE

The MongoDB shell isn't restricted to accessing databases on your local machine. You can also use the shell to connect to external databases (if you have the right credentials, of course).

To connect the MongoDB shell to an external database, you use the same `mongo` command but add information about the database you want to connect to. You need to include the hostname, port, and database names, and you can supply a username and password if required. Use the following construct:

```
$ mongo hostname:port/database_name -u username -p password
```

Using the setup you've been looking at in this section would give you this command:

```
$ mongo ds159330.mlab.com:59330/heroku_t0zs37gc -u heroku_t0zs37gc -p
➥ 1k3t3pgo8sb5enovqd9sk314gj
```

This command connects you to the database through the MongoDB shell. When the connection is established, you can use the commands you've already been using to interrogate it, such as

```
> show collections
> db.locations.find()
```

Now you've got two databases and two connection strings. It's important to use the right one at the right time.

5.5.3   *Making the application use the right database*

You have your original development database on your local machine plus your new live database up on mLab (or elsewhere). You want to keep using the development database while you're developing your application, and you want the live version of your application to use the live database. Yet both use the same source code. Figure 5.12 shows the issue.

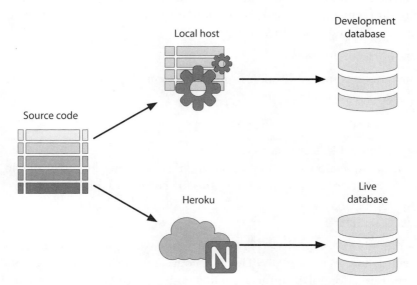

Figure 5.12   The source code runs in two locations, each of which needs to connect to a different database.

You now have one set of source code running in two environments, each of which should use a different database. The way to handle this problem is through using a Node environment variable, NODE_ENV.

THE NODE_ENV ENVIRONMENT VARIABLE

Environment variables affect the way the core process runs, and the one you'll look at and use here is NODE_ENV. The application already uses NODE_ENV; you don't see it exposed anywhere. By default, Heroku should set NODE_ENV to production so that the application will run in production mode on its server.

Ensuring Heroku is using production mode

In certain instances, depending on how the application was set up, the Heroku application may not be running in production mode. You can ensure that the Heroku environment variable is set correctly with the following terminal command:

```
$ heroku config:set NODE_ENV=production
```

You can validate this setting by using a get version of this command, like so:

```
$ heroku config:get NODE_ENV
```

You can read NODE_ENV from anywhere in the application by using the following statement:

```
process.env.NODE_ENV
```

Unless specified in your environment, this statement comes back as undefined. You can specify different environment variables when starting the Node application by prepending the assignment to the launch command, as in this example:

```
$ NODE_ENV=production nodemon
```

This command starts the application in production mode, and the value of process.env.NODE_ENV is set to production.

> **TIP**   Don't set NODE_ENV from inside the application; only read it.

SETTING THE DATABASE URI BASED ON THE ENVIRONMENT

The database connection for your application is held in the db.js file in app_server/models. The connection portion of this file currently looks like this:

```
const dbURI = 'mongodb://localhost/Loc8r';
mongoose.connect(dbURI);
```

Changing the value of dbURI based on the current environment is as simple as using an if statement to check NODE_ENV. The next code snippet shows how you can do this to pass in your live MongoDB connection. Remember to use your own MongoDB connection string rather than the one in this example:

```
let dbURI = 'mongodb://localhost/Loc8r';
if (process.env.NODE_ENV === 'production') {
  dbURI =
    'mongodb://heroku_t0zs37gc:1k3t3pgo8sb5enosk314gj@ds159330.mlab.com:5933
    ➥0/ heroku_t0zs37gc';
}
mongoose.connect(dbURI);
```

If the source code is going to be in a public repository, you probably don't want to give everybody the login credentials to your database. A way around this situation is to use an environment variable. With mLab on Heroku, you automatically have one set up; it's how you originally got access to the connection string. (If you set up your mLab account manually, this variable is the Heroku configuration variable that you set.) If you're using a different provider that hasn't added anything to the Heroku configuration, you can add your URI with the `heroku config:set` command that you used to ensure that Heroku is running in production mode.

The following code snippet shows how you can use the connection string set in the environment variables:

```
let dbURI = 'mongodb://localhost/Loc8r';
if (process.env.NODE_ENV === 'production') {
  dbURI = process.env.MONGODB_URI;
}
mongoose.connect(dbURI, { useNewUrlParser: true });
```

Now you can share your code, but only you retain access to your database credentials.

TESTING BEFORE LAUNCHING

You can test this update to the code locally before pushing the code to Heroku by setting the environment variable as you start the application from terminal. The Mongoose connection events you set up earlier output a log to the console when the database connection is made, verifying the URI used.

To do this, you need to add both the NODE_ENV and MJONGODB_URI environment variables in front of the nodemon command, like this (note that all of the following should be entered as one line):

```
$ NODE_ENV=production
    MONGODB_URI=mongodb://<username>:<password>@<hostname>:<port>/<database>
    nodemon
```

Now your console log on startup should look like this:

```
Mongoose connected to
    mongodb://heroku_t0zs37gc:1k3t3pgo8sb5enosk314gj@ds159330.mlab.com:59330
    ➥/ heroku_t0zs37gc
```

When running this command, you'll probably notice that the Mongoose connection confirmation takes longer to appear in the production environment, due to the latency of using a separate database server. This is why it's a good idea to open the database connection at application startup and leave it open.

TESTING ON HEROKU

If your local tests are successful, and you can connect to your remote database by temporarily starting the application in production mode, you're ready to push it up to Heroku. Use the same commands as normal to push the latest version of the code up:

```
$ git add --all
$ git commit -m "Commit message here"
$ git push heroku master
```

Heroku lets you look at the latest 100 lines of logs by running a terminal command. You can check those logs to see the output of your console log messages, one of which will be your `Mongoose connected to` logs. To view the logs, run the following command in terminal:

```
$ heroku logs
```

This command outputs the latest 100 rows to the terminal window, with the latest messages at the bottom. Scroll up until you find the `Mongoose connected to` message that looks something like this:

```
2017-04-14T07:01:22.066997+00:00 app[web.1]: Mongoose connected to
    mongodb://heroku_t0zs37gc:1k3t3pgo8sb5enosk314gj@ds159330.mlab.com:59330/
    heroku_t0zs37gc
```

When you see this message, you know that the live application on Heroku is connecting to your live database.

So that's the data defined and modeled, and your Loc8r application is connected to the database. But you're not interacting with the database at all yet. That comes next!

Get the source code

The source code of the application so far is available from GitHub on the chapter-05 branch of the gettingMean-2 repository. In a fresh folder in terminal, enter the following commands to clone it and install the npm module dependencies:

```
$ git clone -b chapter-05 https://github.com/cliveharber/
            gettingMean-2.git
$ cd gettingMean-2
$ npm install
```

In chapter 6, you'll use Express to create a REST API so that you can access the database through web services.

Summary

In this chapter, you learned

- Some ways of connecting a MongoDB database to an Express application using Mongoose
- Best practices for managing Mongoose connections
- How to model data using Mongoose schemas
- How schemas compile into models
- Using the MongoDB shell to work directly with the database
- Pushing your database to a live URI
- Connecting to different databases from different environments

Writing a REST API: Exposing the MongoDB database to the application

This chapter covers

- Examining the rules of REST APIs
- Evaluating API patterns
- Handling typical CRUD functions (create, read, update, delete)
- Using Express and Mongoose to interact with MongoDB
- Testing API endpoints

As you come into this chapter, you have a MongoDB database set up, but you can interact with it only through the MongoDB shell. During the course of this chapter, you'll build a REST API so that you can interact with your database through HTTP calls and perform the common CRUD functions: create, read, update, and delete.

You'll work mainly with Node and Express, using Mongoose to help with interactions. Figure 6.1 shows where this chapter fits into the overall architecture.

You'll start by looking at the rules of a REST API. We'll discuss the importance of defining the URL structure properly, the different request methods (GET, POST,

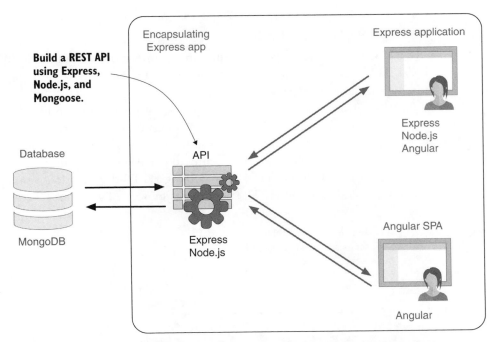

Figure 6.1 This chapter focuses on building the API that interacts with the database, exposing an interface for the applications to talk to.

PUT, and DELETE) that should be used for different actions, and how an API should respond with data and an appropriate HTTP status code. When you have that knowledge under your belt, you'll move on to building your API for Loc8r, covering all the typical CRUD operations. We'll discuss Mongoose along the way and get into some Node programming and more Express routing.

> **NOTE** If you haven't yet built the application from chapter 5, you can get the code from GitHub on the chapter-05 branch at https://github.com/ cliveharber/ gettingMean-2. In a fresh folder in terminal, enter the following commands to clone it and install the npm module dependencies:

```
$ git clone -b chapter-05 https://github.com/cliveharber/
  gettingMean-2.git
$ cd gettingMean-2
$ npm install
```

6.1 The rules of a REST API

We'll start with a recap of what makes a REST API. From chapter 2, you may remember that

- *REST* stands for *REpresentational State Transfer*, which is an architectural style rather than a strict protocol. REST is stateless; it has no idea of any current user state or history.

- *API* is an abbreviation for *application program interface*, which enables applications to talk to one another.

A REST API is a stateless interface to your application. In the case of the MEAN stack, the REST API is used to create a stateless interface to your database, enabling a way for other applications to work with the data.

REST APIs have an associated set of standards. Although you don't have to stick to these standards for your own API, it's generally best to, as it means that any API you create will follow the same approach. It also means that you're used to doing things the "right" way if you decide that you're going to make your API public.

In basic terms, a REST API takes an incoming HTTP request, does some processing, and always sends back an HTTP response, as shown in figure 6.2.

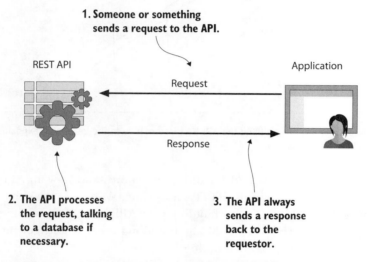

1. Someone or something sends a request to the API.

REST API

Request

Application

Response

2. The API processes the request, talking to a database if necessary.

3. The API always sends a response back to the requestor.

Figure 6.2   A REST API takes incoming HTTP requests, does some processing, and returns HTTP responses.

The standards that you'll follow for Loc8r revolve around the requests and the responses.

6.1.1   Request URLs

Request URLs for a REST API have a simple standard. Following this standard makes your API easy to pick up, use, and maintain.

The way to approach this task is to start thinking about the collections in your database, as you'll typically have a set of API URLs for each collection. You may also have a set of URLs for each set of subdocuments. Each URL in a set has the same basic path, and some may have additional parameters.

Within a set of URLs, you need to cover several actions, generally based on the standard CRUD operations. The common actions you'll likely want are

- Create a new item
- Read a list of several items
- Read a specific item
- Update a specific item
- Delete a specific item

Using Loc8r as an example, the database has a Locations collection that you want to interact with. Table 6.1 shows how the URL paths might look for this collection. Note that all URLs have the same base path and, where used, have the same location ID parameter.

Table 6.1   URL paths and parameters for an API to the Locations collection

Action	URL path	Example
Create new location	`/locations`	http://loc8r.com/api/locations
Read list of locations	`/locations`	http://loc8r.com/api/locations
Read a specific location	`/locations/:locationid`	http://loc8r.com/api/locations/123
Update a specific location	`/locations/:locationid`	http://loc8r.com/api/locations/123
Delete a specific location	`/locations/:locationid`	http://loc8r.com/api/locations/123

As you can see from table 6.1, each action has the same URL path, and three of them expect the same parameter to specify a location. This situation poses an obvious question: how do you use the same URL to initiate different actions? The answer lies in request methods.

6.1.2   Request methods

HTTP requests can have different methods that essentially tell the server what type of action to take. The most common type of request is a GET request—the method used when you enter a URL in the address bar of your browser. Another common method is POST, often used for submitting form data.

Table 6.2 shows the methods you'll be using in your API, their typical use cases, and what you'd expect to be returned.

Table 6.2   Four request methods used in a REST API

Request method	Use	Response
POST	Create new data in the database	New data object as seen in the database
GET	Read data from the database	Data object answering the request
PUT	Update a document in the database	Updated data object as seen in the database
DELETE	Delete an object from the database	Null

The four HTTP methods that you'll use are POST, GET, PUT, and DELETE. If you look at the corresponding entries in the Use column, you'll notice that each method performs a different CRUD operation.

The method is important, because a well-designed REST API often has the same URL for different actions. In these cases, the method tells the server which type of operation to perform. We'll discuss how to build and organize the routes for methods in Express later in this chapter.

If you take the paths and parameters and map across the appropriate request method, you can put together a plan for your API, as shown in table 6.3.

Table 6.3 Request methods that link URLs to the desired actions, enabling the API to use the same URL for different actions

Action	Method	URL path	Example
Create new location	POST	/locations	http://loc8r.com/api/locations
Read list of locations	GET	/locations	http://loc8r.com/api/locations
Read a specific location	GET	/locations/:locationid	http://loc8r.com/api/locations/123
Update a specific location	PUT	/locations/:locationid	http://loc8r.com/api/locations/123
Delete a specific location	DELETE	/locations/:locationid	http://loc8r.com/api/locations/123

Table 6.3 shows the paths and methods you'll use for the requests to interact with the location data. There are five actions but only two URL patterns, so you can use the request methods to get the desired results.

Loc8r only has one collection right now, so this is your starting point. But the documents in the Locations collection do have reviews as subdocuments, so you'll quickly map them out too.

Subdocuments are treated in a similar way but require an additional parameter. Each request needs to specify the ID of the location, and some requests also need to specify the ID of a review. Table 6.4 shows the list of actions and their associated methods, URL paths, and parameters.

Table 6.4 URL specifications for interacting with subdocuments; each base URL path must contain the ID of the parent document

Action	Method	URL path	Example
Create new review	POST	/locations/:locationid/reviews	http://loc8r.com/api/locations/123/reviews
Read a specific review	GET	/locations/:locationid/reviews/:reviewid	http://loc8r.com/api/locations/123/reviews/abc
Update a specific review	PUT	/locations/:locationid/reviews/:reviewid	http://loc8r.com/api/locations/123/reviews/abc

Table 6.4 URL specifications for interacting with subdocuments; each base URL path must contain the ID of the parent document *(continued)*

Action	Method	URL path	Example
Delete a specific review	`DELETE`	`/locations/:locationid/reviews/` `:reviewid`	http://loc8r.com/api/ locations/123/reviews/abc

You may have noticed that for the subdocuments, you don't have a "read a list of reviews" action, because you'll be retrieving the list of reviews as part of the main document. The preceding tables should give you an idea of how to create basic API request specifications. The URLs, parameters, and actions will be different from one application to the next, but the approach should remain consistent.

That's the story on requests. The other half of the flow, before you get stuck in some code, is responses.

6.1.3 Responses and status codes

A good API is like a good friend. If you go for a high five, a good friend won't leave you hanging. The same goes for a good API. If you make a request, a good API always responds and doesn't leave you hanging. Every single API request should return a response. The contrast between a good API and a bad one is shown in figure 6.3.

For a successful REST API, standardizing the responses is as important as standardizing the request format. There are two key components to a response:

- The returned data
- The HTTP status code

Combining the returned data with the appropriate status code should give the requester all the information required to continue.

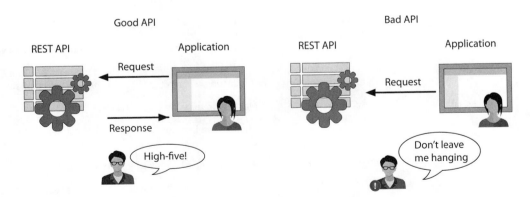

Figure 6.3 A good API always returns a response and shouldn't leave you hanging.

RETURNING DATA FROM AN API

Your API should return a consistent data format. Typical formats for a REST API are XML and/or JSON. You'll use JSON for your API, because it's the natural fit for the MEAN stack. MongoDB outputs JSON, which Node and Angular can both natively understand. JSON is, after all, the JavaScript way of transporting data. JSON is also more compact than XML, so it can help speed the response times and efficiency of an API by reducing the bandwidth required.

Your API will return one of three things for each request:

- A JSON object containing data answering the request query
- A JSON object containing error data
- A null response

During this chapter, we'll discuss how to do all these things as you build the Loc8r API. As well as responding with data, a REST API should return the correct HTTP status code.

USING HTTP STATUS CODES

A good REST API should return the correct HTTP status code. The status code most people are familiar with is 404, which is what a web server returns when a user requests a page that can't be found. This error code is probably the most prevalent one on the internet, but there are dozens of other codes, relating to client errors, server errors, redirections, and successful requests. Table 6.5 shows the 10 most popular HTTP status codes and where they might be useful for building an API.

Table 6.5   Most popular HTTP status codes and how they might be used to send responses to an API request

Status code	Name	Use case
200	OK	A successful GET or PUT request
201	Created	A successful POST request
204	No content	A successful DELETE request
400	Bad request	An unsuccessful GET, POST, or PUT request due to invalid content
401	Unauthorized	Requesting a restricted URL with incorrect credentials
403	Forbidden	Making a request that isn't allowed
404	Not found	Unsuccessful request due to an incorrect parameter in the URL
405	Method not allowed	Request method not allowed for the given URL
409	Conflict	Unsuccessful POST request when another object with the same data already exists
500	Internal server error	Problem with your server or the database server

As you go through this chapter and build the Loc8r API, you'll use several of these status codes while returning the appropriate data.

6.2 *Setting up the API in Express*

You've already got a good idea about the actions you want your API to perform and the URL paths needed to do so. As you know from chapter 4, to get Express to do something based on an incoming URL request, you need to set up controllers and routes. The controllers do the action, and the routes map the incoming requests to the appropriate controllers.

You have files for routes and controllers already set up in the application, so you could use those. A better option, though, is to keep the API code separate so that you don't run the risk of confusion and complication in your application. In fact, this is one of the reasons for creating an API in the first place. Also, keeping the API code separate makes it easier to strip it out and put it into a separate application at a future point, should you choose to do so. You do want easy decoupling here.

The first thing you want to do is create a separate area inside the application for the files that will create the API. At the top level of the application, create a new folder called app_api. If you've been following along and building up the application as you go, this folder sits alongside the app_server folder.

This folder holds everything specific to the API: routes, controllers, and models. When you've got everything set up, take a look at some ways to test these API placeholders.

6.2.1 *Creating the routes*

As you did with the routes for the main Express application, you'll have an index.js file in the app_api/routes folder that will hold all the routes you'll use in the API. Start by referencing this file in the main application file app.js.

INCLUDING THE ROUTES IN THE APPLICATION

The first step is telling your application that you're adding more routes to look out for and when it should use them. You can duplicate a line in app.js to `require` the server application routes, and set the path to the API routes as follows:

```
const indexRouter = require('./app_server/routes/index');
const apiRouter = require('./app_api/routes/index');
```

You may also have a line in app.js that still brings the example `user` routes. You can delete this now, if so, because you don't need it. Next, you need to tell the application when to use the routes. You currently have the following line in app.js telling the application to check the server application routes for all incoming requests:

```
app.use('/', indexRouter);
```

Notice the `'/'` as the first parameter. This parameter enables you to specify a subset of URLs for which the routes will apply. You'll define all your API routes starting with

/api/. By adding the line shown in the following code snippet, you can tell the application to use the API routes only when the route starts with /api:

```
app.use('/', indexRouter);
app.use('/api', apiRouter);
```

As before, you can delete the similar line for user routes if it's there. Now it's time to set up these URLs.

SPECIFYING THE REQUEST METHODS IN THE ROUTES

Up to now, you've used only the GET method in the routes, as in the following code snippet from your main application routes:

```
router.get('/location', ctrlLocations.locationInfo);
```

Using the other methods—POST, PUT, and DELETE—is as simple as switching the get with the respective keywords post, put, and delete. The following code snippet shows an example using the POST method which creates a new location:

```
router.post('/locations', ctrlLocations.locationsCreate);
```

Note that you don't specify /api at the front of the path. You specify in app.js that these routes should be used only if the path starts with /api, so it's assumed that all routes specified in this file are prefixed with /api.

SPECIFYING REQUIRED URL PARAMETERS

It's common for API URLs to contain parameters for identifying specific documents or subdocuments—locations and reviews, in the case of Loc8r. Specifying these parameters in routes is simple; you prefix the name of the parameter with a colon when defining each route.

Suppose that you're trying to access a review with the ID abc that belongs to a location with the ID 123. You'd have a URL path like this:

```
/api/locations/123/reviews/abc
```

Swapping out the IDs for the parameter names (with a colon prefix) gives you a path like this:

```
/api/locations/:locationid/reviews/:reviewid
```

With a path like this, Express matches only URLs that match that pattern. So a location ID must be specified and must be in the URL between locations/ and /reviews. Also, a review ID must be specified at the end of the URL. When a path like this is assigned to a controller, the parameters will be available to use in the code, with the names specified in the path (locationid and reviewid, in this case).

We'll review exactly how you get to them in a moment, but first, you need to set up the routes for your Loc8r API.

DEFINING THE LOC8R API ROUTES

Now you know how to set up routes to accept parameters, and you also know what actions, methods, and paths you want to have in your API. You can combine all this knowledge to create the route definitions for the Loc8r API.

If you haven't done so yet, you should create an index.js file in the app_api/routes folder. To keep the sizes of individual files under control, separate the locations and reviews controllers into different files.

You'll also use a slightly different way of defining routes in Express, which is ideal for managing multiple methods on a single route. With this approach, you define the route first and then chain on the different HTTP methods. This process streamlines route definitions, making them much easier to read.

The following listing shows how the defined routes should look.

Listing 6.1   Routes defined in app_api/routes/index.js

```
const express = require('express');
const router = express.Router();
const ctrlLocations = require('../controllers/locations');    Includes controller
const ctrlReviews = require('../controllers/reviews');         files. (You'll create
                                                               these next.)
// locations
router
  .route('/locations')
  .get(ctrlLocations.locationsListByDistance)
  .post(ctrlLocations.locationsCreate);
                                                    Defines routes
router                                              for locations
  .route('/locations/:locationid')
  .get(ctrlLocations.locationsReadOne)
  .put(ctrlLocations.locationsUpdateOne)
  .delete(ctrlLocations.locationsDeleteOne);

// reviews
router
  .route('/locations/:locationid/reviews')
  .post(ctrlReviews.reviewsCreate);

router                                              Defines routes
  .route('/locations/:locationid/reviews/:reviewid')   for reviews
  .get(ctrlReviews.reviewsReadOne)
  .put(ctrlReviews.reviewsUpdateOne)
  .delete(ctrlReviews.reviewsDeleteOne);

module.exports = router;    ⊲——— Exports routes
```

In this router file, you need to require the related controller files. You haven't created these controller files yet and will do so in a moment. This method is a good way to approach it, because by defining all the routes and declaring the associated controller functions here, you develop a high-level view of what controllers are needed.

The application now has two sets of routes: the main Express application routes and the new API routes. The application won't start at the moment, though, because none of the controllers referenced by the API routes exists.

6.2.2 *Creating the controller placeholders*

To enable the application to start, you can create placeholder functions for the controllers. These functions won't do anything, but they stop the application from falling over while you're building the API functionality.

The first step, of course, is creating the controller files. You know where these files should be and what they should be called because you've already declared them in the app_api/routes folder. You need two new files called locations.js and reviews.js in the app_api/controllers folder.

You can create a placeholder for each of the controller functions as an empty function, as in the following code snippet:

```
const locationsCreate = (req, res) => { };
```

Remember to put each controller in the correct file, depending on whether it's for a location or a review, and export them at the bottom of the files, as in this example:

```
module.exports = {
  locationsListByDistance,
  locationsCreate,
  locationsReadOne,
  locationsUpdateOne,
  locationsDeleteOne
};
```

To test the routing and the functions, though, you need to return a response.

6.2.3 *Returning JSON from an Express request*

When building the Express application, you rendered a view template to send HTML to the browser, but with an API, you instead want to send a status code and some JSON data. Express makes this task easy with the following lines:

```
res                          Uses the Express response object
  .status(status)            Sends response status code, such as 200
  .json(content);            Sends response data, such as {"status" : "success"}
```

You can use these two commands in the placeholder functions to test the success, as shown in the following code snippet:

```
const locationsCreate = (req, res) => {
  res
    .status(200)
    .json({"status" : "success"});
};
```

As you build up your API, you'll use this method a lot to send different status codes and data as the response.

6.2.4 *Including the model*

It's vitally important that the API can talk to the database; without it, the API isn't going to be of much use! To do this with Mongoose, you first need to `require` Mongoose into the controller files and then bring in the `Location` model. Right at the top of the controller files, above all the placeholder functions, add the following two lines:

```
const mongoose = require('mongoose');
const Loc = mongoose.model('Location');
```

The first line gives the controllers access to the database connection, and the second brings in the `Location` model so that you can interact with the Locations collection.

If you take a look at the file structure of your application, you see the /models folder containing the database connection, and the Mongoose setup is inside the app_server folder. But it's the API that's dealing with the database, not the main Express application. If the two applications were separate, the model would be kept part of the API, so that's where it should live.

Move the /models folder from the app_server folder into the app_api folder, creating a folder structure like that shown in figure 6.4.

Figure 6.4   Folder structure of the application at this point. app_api has models, controllers, and routes, and app_server has views, controllers, and routes.

You need to tell the application that you've moved the app_api/models folder, of course, so you need to update the line in app.js that requires the model to point to the correct place:

```
require('./app_api/models/db');
```

With that done, the application should start again and still connect to your database. The next question is how to test the API.

6.2.5 *Testing the API*

You can test the `GET` routes in your browser quickly by heading to the appropriate URL, such as http://localhost:3000/api/locations/1234. You should see the success response being delivered to the browser, as shown in figure 6.5.

This is okay for testing `GET` requests, but it doesn't get you far with the `POST`, `PUT`, and `DELETE` methods. A few tools can help you test API calls like this, but our current favorite is a free application called Postman REST Client, available as a standalone application or browser extension.

Figure 6.5   Testing a GET request of the API in the browser

Postman enables you to test API URLs with several request methods, allowing you to specify additional query string parameters or form data. After you click the Send button, Postman makes a request to the URL you specified and displays the response data and status code.

Figure 6.6 shows a screenshot of Postman making a PUT request to the same URL as before.

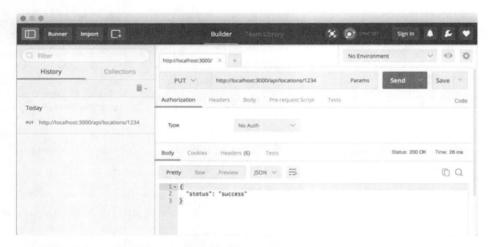

Figure 6.6   Using the Postman REST Client to test a PUT request to the API

It's a good idea to get Postman or another REST client up and running now. You'll need to use one a lot during this chapter as you build up a REST API. In the next section, you'll start on the workings of the API by using GET requests to read data from MongoDB.

6.3   GET methods: Reading data from MongoDB

GET methods are all about querying the database and returning some data. In your routes for Loc8r, you have three GET requests doing different things, as listed in table 6.6.

Table 6.6   Three GET requests of the Loc8r API

Action	Method	URL path	Example
Read a list of locations	GET	`/locations`	http://loc8r.com/api/locations
Read a specific location	GET	`/locations/:locationid`	http://loc8r.com/api/locations/123
Read a specific review	GET	`/locations/:locationid/reviews/:reviewid`	http://loc8r.com/api/locations/123/reviews/abc

You'll look at how to find a single location first, because it provides a good introduction to the way Mongoose works. Next, you'll locate a single document by using an ID, and then you'll expand into searching for multiple documents.

6.3.1   Finding a single document in MongoDB using Mongoose

Mongoose interacts with the database through its models, which is why you imported the `Location` model as `Loc` at the top of the controller files. A Mongoose model has several associated methods to help manage the interactions, as noted in the sidebar "Mongoose query methods."

Mongoose query methods

Mongoose models have several methods available to help with querying the database. Here are some of the key ones:

- `find`—General search based on a supplied query object
- `findById`—Looks for a specific ID
- `findOne`—Gets the first document to match the supplied query
- `geoNear`—Finds places geographically close to the provided latitude and longitude
- `geoSearch`—Adds query functionality to a `geoNear` operation

You'll use some but not all of these methods in this book.

For finding a single database document with a known ID in MongoDB, Mongoose has the `findById()` method.

APPLYING THE FINDBYID METHOD TO THE MODEL

The `findById()` method is relatively straightforward, accepting a single parameter: the ID to look for. As it's a model method, it's applied to the model like this:

```
Loc.findById(locationid)
```

This method won't start the database query operation; it tells the model what the query will be. To start the database query, Mongoose models have an `exec` method.

RUNNING THE QUERY WITH THE EXEC METHOD

The `exec` method executes the query and passes a callback function that will run when the operation is complete. The callback function should accept two parameters: an error object and the instance of the found document. As it's a callback function, the names of these parameters can be whatever you like.

The methods can be chained as follows:

```
Loc
  .findById(locationid)  ⊲──────  Applies the findById method to
  .exec((err, location) => {      the Location model, using Loc
    console.log("findById complete");  ⊲──── Executes the query
  });                                  Logs the message
                                       when complete
```

This approach ensures that the database interaction is asynchronous and, therefore, doesn't block the main Node process.

USING THE FINDBYID METHOD IN A CONTROLLER

The controller you're working with to find a single location by ID is `locations-ReadOne()`, in the locations.js file in app_api/controllers.

You know the basic construct of the operation: apply the `findById()` and `exec` methods to the `Location` model. To get this working in the context of the controller, you need to do two things:

- Get the `locationid` parameter from the URL, and pass it to the `findById()` method.
- Provide an output function to the `exec` method.

Express makes it easy to get the URL parameters you defined in the routes. The parameters are held inside a `params` object attached to the request object. With your route being defined like so

```
router
  .route('/api/locations/:locationid')
```

you can access the `locationid` parameter from inside the controller like this:

```
req.params.locationid
```

For the output function, you can use a simple callback that sends the found locations as a JSON response. Putting all this together gives you the following:

```
const locationsReadOne = (req, res) => {
  Loc
    .findById(req.params.locationid)
    .exec((err, location) => {
      res
        .status(200)
        .json(location);
    });
};
```

Gets a locationid from the URL parameters, and gives it to the findById method

Defines callback to accept possible parameters

Sends the document found as a JSON response with an HTTP status of 200

Now you have a basic API controller. You can try it out by getting the ID of one of the locations in MongoDB and going to the URL in your browser or by calling it in Postman. To get one of the ID values, you can run the command `db.locations.find ()` in the Mongo shell, and the command lists all the locations you have, each of which includes the `_id` value. When you've put the URL together, the output should be a full location object as stored in MongoDB; you should see something like figure 6.7.

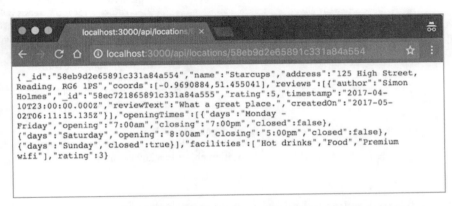

Figure 6.7   A basic controller for finding a single location by ID returns a JSON object to the browser if the ID is found.

Did you try out the basic controller? Did you put an invalid location ID in the URL? If you did, you'll have seen that you got nothing back—no warning, no message; a 200 status telling you that everything is okay, but no data returned.

CATCHING ERRORS

The problem with that basic controller is that it outputs only a success response, regardless of whether it was successful. This behavior isn't good for an API. A good API should respond with an error code when something goes wrong.

To respond with error messages, the controller needs to be set up to trap potential errors and send an appropriate response. Error trapping in this fashion typically involves `if` statements. Every `if` statement must have a corresponding `else` statement or include a `return` statement.

TIP   Your API code must never leave a request unanswered.

With your basic controller, you need to trap three errors:

- The request parameters don't include locationid.
- The findById() method doesn't return a location.
- The findById() method returns an error.

The status code for an unsuccessful GET request is 404. Bearing this fact in mind, the final code for the controller to find and return a single location looks like the following listing.

Listing 6.2   locationsReadOne controller

```
const locationsReadOne = (req, res) => {
    Loc
      .findById(req.params.locationid)
      .exec((err, location) => {
        if (!location) {
          return res
            .status(404)
            .json({
              "message": "location not found"
            });
        } else if (err) {
          return res
            .status(404)
            .json(err);
        }
        res
          .status(200)
          .json(location);
      });
};
```

❶ **Error trap 1: If Mongoose doesn't return a location, sends a 404 message and exits the function scope, using a return statement**

❷ **Error trap 2: If Mongoose returns an error, sends it as a 404 response and exits the controller, using a return statement**

❸ **If Mongoose doesn't error, continues as before, and sends a location object in a 200 response**

Listing 6.2 uses both methods of trapping with if statements. Error trap 1 ❶ and error trap 2 ❷ use an if to check for an error returned by Mongoose. Each if includes a return statement, which prevents any following code in the callback scope from running. If no error was found, the return statement is ignored, and the code moves on to send the successful response ❸.

Each of these traps provides a response for success and failure, leaving no room for the API to leave a requester hanging. If you want to, you can also throw in a few console.log() statements so that it's easier to track what's going on in terminal; the source code in GitHub has some.

Figure 6.8 shows the difference between a successful request and a failed request, using the Postman extension in Chrome.

That's one complete API route dealt with. Now it's time to look at the second GET request to return a single review.

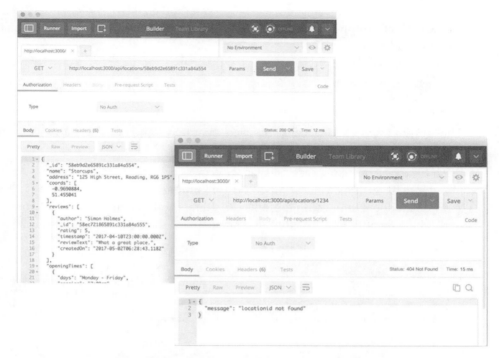

Figure 6.8 Testing successful (left) and failed (right) API responses using Postman

6.3.2 Finding a single subdocument based on IDs

To find a subdocument, you first have to find the parent document, and then pin-
point the required location using its ID. When you've found the document, you can
look for a specific subdocument. You can take the `locationsReadOne()` controller as
the starting point, and add a few modifications to create the `reviewsReadOne()` controller. These modifications are

- Accept and use an additional `reviewid` URL parameter.
- Select only the name and reviews from the document rather than have
  MongoDB return the entire document.
- Look for a review with a matching ID.
- Return the appropriate JSON response.

To do these things, you can use a couple of new Mongoose methods.

LIMITING THE PATHS RETURNED FROM MONGODB
When you retrieve a document from MongoDB, you don't always need the full document; sometimes, you want some specific data. Limiting the data being passed around
is also better for bandwidth consumption and speed.

Mongoose does this through a `select()` method chained to the model query. The following code snippet tells MongoDB that you want to get only the name and the reviews of a location:

```
Loc
  .findById(req.params.locationid)
  .select('name reviews')
  .exec();
```

The `select()` method accepts a space-separated string of the paths you want to retrieve.

USING MONGOOSE TO FIND A SPECIFIC SUBDOCUMENT

Mongoose also offers a helper method for finding a subdocument by ID. Given an array of subdocuments, Mongoose has an `id` method that accepts the ID you want to find. The `id` method returns the single matching subdocument, and it can be used as follows:

```
Loc
  .findById(req.params.locationid)                          Passes reviewid
  .select('name reviews')                                 from the parameters
  .exec((err, location) => {                                 into the id method
    const review = location.reviews.id(req.params.reviewid);    ◁────┘
  }
);
```

In this code snippet, a single review is returned to the `review` variable in the callback.

ADDING SOME ERROR TRAPPING AND PUTTING IT ALL TOGETHER

Now you've got the ingredients needed to make the `reviewsReadOne()` controller. Starting with a copy of the `locationsReadOne()` controller, you can make the modifications required to return a single review.

The following listing shows the `reviewsReadOne()` controller in review.js (modifications in bold).

> **Listing 6.3   Controller for finding a single review**

```
const reviewsReadOne = (req, res) => {
  Loc
    .findById(req.params.locationid)
    .select('name reviews')                  ◁────  Adds the Mongoose select method
    .exec((err, location) => {                       to the model query, stating that
      if (!location) {                               you want to get the name of a
        return res                                   location and its reviews
          .status(404)
          .json({
            "message": "location not found"
          });
      } else if (err) {
        return res                                       Checks that the
          .status(400)                                   returned location
          .json(err);                                    has reviews
      }
      if (location.reviews && location.reviews.length > 0) {    ◁────
```

```
const review = location.reviews.id(req.params.reviewid);
if (!review) {
  return res
    .status(400)
    .json({
      "message": "review not found"
    });
} else {
  response = {
    location : {
      name : location.name,
      id : req.params.locationid
    },
    review
  };
  return res
    .status(200)
    .json(response);
  }
} else {
  return res
    .status(404)
    .json({
      "message": "No reviews found"
    });
}
}
}
);
};
```

Uses the Mongoose subdocument .id method as a helper for searching for a matching ID → `const review = location.reviews.id(req.params.reviewid);`

If a review isn't found, returns an appropriate response

If a review is found, builds a response object returning the review and location name and ID

If no reviews are found, returns an appropriate error message

When this code is saved and ready, you can test it with Postman again. You need to have correct ID values, which you can get from the Postman query you made to check for a single location or directly from MongoDB via the Mongo shell. The Mongo command `db.locations.find()` return all the locations and their reviews. Remember that the URL is in the structure /locations/:locationid/reviews/:reviewid.

You can also test what happens if you put in a false ID for a location or a review or try a review ID from a different location.

6.3.3 *Finding multiple documents with geospatial queries*

The homepage of Loc8r should display a list of locations based on the user's current geographical location. MongoDB and Mongoose have some special geospatial aggregation methods to help find nearby places.

Here, you'll use the Mongoose aggregate `$geoNear` to find a list of locations close to a specified point, up to a specified maximum distance. `$geoNear` is an aggregation method that accepts multiple configuration options, of which of the following are required:

- `near` as a `geoJSON` geographical point
- A `distanceField` object option
- A `maxDistance` object option

The following code snippet shows the basic construct:

```
Loc.aggregate([{$geoNear: {near: {}, distanceField: "distance",
  maxDistance: 100}}]);
```

Like the `findById` method, the `$geoNear` aggregate returns a Promise, and its value can be obtained by using a callback, its `exec` method, or async/await.

CONSTRUCTING A GEOJSON POINT

The first parameter of `$geoNear` is a `geoJSON` point: a simple JSON object containing a latitude and a longitude in an array. The construct for a `geoJSON` point is shown in the following code snippet:

```
const point = {              ◁─────── Declares object
  type: "Point",             ◁─────── Defines it as type "Point"
  coordinates: [lng, lat]    ◁─── Sets longitude and latitude coordinates
};                                   in an array, longitude first
```

The route set up here to get a list of locations doesn't have the coordinates in the URL parameters, meaning that they'll have to be specified in a different way. A query string is ideal for this data type, so the request URL will look more like this:

```
api/locations?lng=-0.7992599&lat=51.378091
```

Express, of course, gives you access to the values in a query string, putting them in a query object attached to the request object, such as `req.query.lng`. The longitude and latitude values will be strings when retrieved, but they need to be added to the point object as numbers. JavaScript's `parseFloat()` function can see to this. The following code snippet shows how to get the coordinates from the query string and create the `geoJSON` point required by the `$geoNear` aggregation:

```
const locationsListByDistance = async (req, res) => {
  const lng = parseFloat(req.query.lng);        Gets coordinates
  const lat = parseFloat(req.query.lat);        from the query string
  const near = {                       Creates  and converts from
    type: "Point",                     geoJSON  strings to numbers
    coordinates: [lng, lat]            point
  };
  const geoOptions = {
    distanceField: "distance.calculated",
    spherical: true,        ◁───── You're using spherical: true here because it causes
    maxDistance: 20000,            MongoDB to use $nearSphere semantics, which
    limit: 10                      calculates distances using spherical geometry.
  };                               If this were false, it would use 2D geometry.
  try {
    const results = await Loc.aggregate([     ◁──────── The aggregation
      {
        $geoNear: {
          near,
          ...geoOptions     ◁──────── The spread operator
        }                             (see the nearby sidebar)
      }
```

```
    ]);
  } catch (err) {
    console.log(err);
  }
};
```

Trying to execute this controller code won't result in a response, as processing of the data has not been started. Remember that this code is returning a Promise object.

Spread operator

New in ES2015 is the spread operator. This operator takes an iterable (an array, string, or object) and allows it to be expanded into places where zero or more arguments (when used in a function call) or elements (for array literals) are expected.

In the case of the aggregate function in the preceding code block, it injects the object properties in `geoOptions` into the `$geoNear` object. The spread operator has many uses; details are available at http://mng.bz/wEya.

THE SPHERICAL OPTION IN THE AGGREGATION SPECIFICATION

The `geoOptions` object contains a spherical key. This value is required to be set to `true`, as you've already specified the search index in the MongoDB data store as `2dsphere`. If you try to set it to `false`, the application throws an exception:

```
const geoOptions = {
  distanceField: "distance.calculated",
  spherical: true
};
```

LIMITING GEONEAR RESULTS BY NUMBER

You'll often want to look after the API server—and the responsiveness seen by end users—by limiting the number of results when returning a list. In the `$geoNear` aggregate, adding the option `num` or `limit` does this. You specify the maximum number of results you want to have returned. You can specify both, but `num` is given priority over `limit`.

The following code snippet shows `limit` added to the previous `geoOptions` object, limiting the size of the returned dataset to 10 objects:

```
const geoOptions = {
  distanceField: "distance.calculated",
  spherical: true,
  limit: 10
};
```

Now the search brings back no more than the 10 closest results.

LIMITING GEONEAR RESULTS BY DISTANCE

When returning location-based data, another way to keep the processing of the API under control is to limit the list of results by distance from the central point. This is a case of adding another option called `maxDistance`. When you use the spherical option, MongoDB does the calculations in meters for you, making life simple. This wasn't always the case. Older versions of MongoDB used radians, which made things much more complicated.

If you want to output in miles, you'll need to do a little calculation, but you'll stick to meters and kilometers. You'll impose a limit of 20 km, which is 20,000 m. Now you can add the `maxDistance` value to the options and add these options to the controller as follows:

```
const locationsListByDistance = (req, res) => {
  const lng = parseFloat(req.query.lng);
  const lat = parseFloat(req.query.lat);
  const near = {
    type: "Point",
    coordinates: [lng, lat]
  };
  const geoOptions = {
    distanceField: "distance.calculated",
    spherical: true,
    maxDistance: 20000,
    num: 10
  };
  ...
};
```

Creates an options object, including setting the maximum distance to 20 km

The rest of the definition object

Extra credit

Try taking the maximum distance from a query string value instead of hardcoding it into the function. The code on GitHub for this chapter has the answer.

That's the last of the options you need for your $geoNear database search, so it's time to start working with the output.

LOOKING AT THE $GEONEAR AGGREGATE OUTPUT

The result object for the $geoNear aggregate method is a list of the matched items from the database or an error object. If you were using the callback function, it would have the following signature: `callback(err, result)`. As you're using `async/await`, you use `try/catch` to perform the operation or catch the error.

With a successful query, the error object is undefined; the results object is a list of items, as previously stated. You'll start by working with the successful query response before adding error trapping.

Following a successful $geoNear aggregation, MongoDB returns an array of objects. Each object contains a distance value (at the path specified by the `distance-Field`) and a returned document from the database. In other words, MongoDB includes the distance in the data. The following code snippet shows an example of the returned data, truncated for brevity:

```
[ { _id: 5b2c166f5caddf7cd8cea46b,
    name: 'Starcups',
```

```
    address: '125 High Street, Reading, RG6 1PS',
    rating: 3,
    facilities: [ 'Hot drinks', 'Food', 'Premium wifi' ],
    coords: { type: 'Point', coordinates: [Array] },
    openingTimes: [ [Object], [Object], [Object] ],
    distance: { calculated: 5005.183015553589 } } ]
```

This array has only one object, but a successful query is likely to have several objects
returned at once. The $geoNear aggregate returns the entire document contained in
the data store, but the API shouldn't return more data than is requested. So rather
than send the returned data back as the response, you have some processing to do first.

PROCESSING THE $GEONEAR OUTPUT

Before the API can send a response, you need to make sure that it's sending the right
thing and only what's needed. You know what data the homepage listing needs; you've
already built the homepage controller in app_server/controllers/location.js. The
homelist() function sends several location objects, similar to the following example:

```
{
  id: 111,
  name: 'Starcups',
  address: '125 High Street, Reading, RG6 1PS',
  rating: 3,
  facilities: ['Hot drinks', 'Food', 'Premium wifi'],
  distance: '100m'
}
```

To create an object along these lines from the results, you need to iterate through the
results and map the relevant data into a new array. Then this processed data can be
returned with a status 200 response. The following code snippet shows how this result
might look:

```
try {
    const results = await Loc.aggregate([
      {
        $geoNear: {
          near,
          ...geoOptions
        }
      }
    ]);
    const locations = results.map(result => {      ◁──────  Creates a new array to
      return {                        ◁─────┐              hold mapped results data
        id: result._id,                     │   Returns the result
        name: result.name,                  │   of the mapping
        address: result.address,
        rating: result.rating,                 Gets the distance and fixes
        facilities: result.facilities,         to the nearest integer
        distance: `${result.distance.calculated.toFixed()}m`  ◁───┘
      }
    });
    return res                         ◁─────  Sends the processed data
      .status(200)                             back as a JSON response
```

```
      .json(locations);
} catch (err) {
  ...
```

If you test this API route with Postman—remembering to add longitude and latitude coordinates to the query string—you'll see something like figure 6.9.

> ### Extra credit
> Try passing the results to an external named function to build the list of locations. This function should return the processed list, which can then be passed into the JSON response.

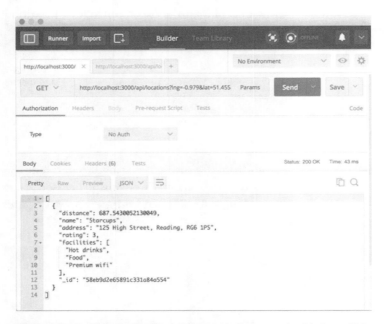

Figure 6.9   Testing the locations list route in Postman should give a 200 status and a list of results, depending on the geographical coordinates sent in the query string.

If you test this by sending coordinates too far away from the test data, you should still get a 200 status, but the returned array will be empty.

ADDING THE ERROR TRAPPING

Once again, you've started by building the success functionality. Now you need to add some error traps to make sure that the API always sends the appropriate response.

The traps you need to set should check that

- All the parameters have been sent correctly.
- The $geoNear aggregate hasn't returned an error condition.

The following listing shows the final controller, including these error traps.

Listing 6.4 Locations list controller `locationsListByDistance`

```
const locationsListByDistance = async(req, res) => {
  const lng = parseFloat(req.query.lng);
  const lat = parseFloat(req.query.lat);
  const near = {
    type: "Point",
    coordinates: [lng, lat]
  };
  const geoOptions = {
    distanceField: "distance.calculated",
    key: 'coords',
    spherical: true,
    maxDistance: 20000,
    limit: 10
  };
  if (!lng || !lat) {
    return res
      .status(404)
      .json({
      "message": "lng and lat query parameters are required"
    });
  }

  try {
    const results = await Loc.aggregate([
      {
        $geoNear: {
          near,
          ...geoOptions
        }
      }
    ]);
    const locations = results.map(result => {
      return {
        id: result._id
        name: result.name,
        address: result.address,
        rating: result.rating,
        facilities: result.facilities,
        distance: `${result.distance.calculated.toFixed()}m`
      }
    });
    res
      .status(200)
      .json(locations);
  } catch (err) {
    res
      .status(404)
      .json(err);
  }
};
```

> **Checks whether lng and lat query parameters exist in the right format; returns a 404 error and message if not**

> **If $geoNear aggregation query returns error, sends this as a response with a 404 status**

This listing completes the GET requests that your API needs to service, so it's time to tackle the POST requests.

6.4   POST methods: Adding data to MongoDB

POST methods are all about creating documents or subdocuments in the database and then returning the saved data as confirmation. In the routes for Loc8r, you have two POST requests doing different things, as listed in table 6.7.

Table 6.7   Two POST requests of the Loc8r API

Action	Method	URL path	Example
Create new location	POST	/locations	http://api.loc8r.com/locations
Create new review	POST	/locations/:locationid/reviews	http://api.loc8r.com/locations/123/reviews

POST methods work by taking form data posted to them and adding it to the database. In the same way that URL parameters are accessed via req.params and query strings are accessed via req.query, Express controllers access posted form data via req.body.

Start by looking at how to create documents.

6.4.1   Creating new documents in MongoDB

In the database for Loc8r, each location is a document, so you'll create a document in this section. Mongoose couldn't make the process of creating MongoDB documents much easier for you. You apply the create() method to your model, and send it some data and a callback function. This construct is minimal, as it would be attached to your Loc model:

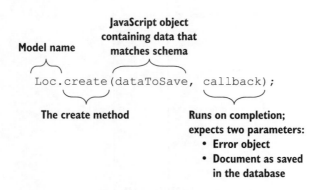

That's simple. The creation process has two main steps:

1. Use the posted form data to create a JavaScript object that matches the schema.
2. Send an appropriate response in the callback, depending on the success or failure of the create() operation.

Looking at step 1, you already know that you can get data sent to you in a form by using `req.body`, and step 2 should be familiar by now. Jump straight into the code. The following listing shows the full `locationsCreate()` controller for creating a new document.

Listing 6.5 Complete controller for creating a new location

```
const locationsCreate = (req, res) => {
  Loc.create({                              ⟵———— Applies the create method to the model
    name: req.body.name,
    address: req.body.address,
    facilities:                                    Creates an array of facilities by
     req.body.facilities.split(","),    ⟵          splitting a comma-separated list
    coords: {              ⟵
     type: "Point",
     [                            Parses coordinates from
       parseFloat(req.body.lng),  strings to numbers
       parseFloat(req.body.lat)
     ]
    }, {
      days: req.body.days2,
      opening: req.body.opening2,
      closing: req.body.closing2,
      closed: req.body.closed2,
    }]
  }, (err, location) => {       ⟵               Supplies a callback function,
    if (err) {                                  containing appropriate responses
      res                                       for success and failure
        .status(400)
        .json(err);
    } else {
      res
        .status(201)
        .json(location);
    }
  });
};
```

This listing shows how easy it can be to create a new document in MongoDB and save some data. For the sake of brevity, you've limited the `openingTimes` array to two entries, but this array could easily be extended or, better, put in a loop to check for the existence of the values.

You may also notice that no `rating` is set. Remember that in the schema, you set a default of 0, as in the following snippet:

```
rating: {
  type: Number,
  "default": 0,
  min: 0,
  max: 5
},
```

This snippet is applied when the document is created, setting the initial value to 0. Something else about this code may be shouting out at you: there's no validation!

6.4.2 *Validating the data using Mongoose*

This controller has no validation code inside it, so what's to stop somebody from entering loads of empty or partial documents? Again, you started building validations in the Mongoose schemas. In the schemas, you set a `required` flag to `true` in a few of the paths. When this flag is set, Mongoose won't send the data to MongoDB.

Given the following base schema for locations, for example, you can see that only `name` is a required field:

```
const locationSchema = new mongoose.Schema({
  name: {
    type: String,
    required: true
  },
  address: String,
  rating: {
    type: Number,
    'default': 0,
    min: 0,
    max: 5
  },
  facilities: [String],
  coords: {
    type: {type: String},
    coordinates: [Number]
  },
  openingTimes: [openingTimeSchema],
  reviews: [reviewSchema]
});
```

If this field is missing, the `create()` method raises an error and doesn't attempt to save the document to the database.

Testing this API route in Postman looks like figure 6.10. Note that the method is set to `post` and that the data type selected (above the list of names and values) is `x-www-form-urlencoded`. You'll enter the keys and values to submit with your POST request in the Postman interface, as shown in that figure. Be careful not to have any blank spaces before or after the keys you type in the Postman fields, as spaces will result in unexpected inputs.

6.4.3 *Creating new subdocuments in MongoDB*

In the context of Loc8r locations, reviews are subdocuments. Subdocuments are created and saved through their parent document. Put another way, to create and save a new subdocument, you have to

1 Find the correct parent document.
2 Add a new subdocument.
3 Save the parent document.

Finding the correct parent isn't a problem, as you've already done that and can use it as the skeleton for the next controller, `reviewsCreate()`. When you've found the parent,

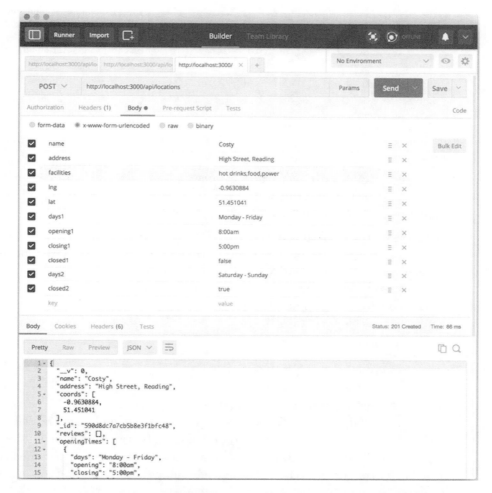

Figure 6.10 Testing a POST method in Postman, ensuring that the method and form data settings are correct

you can call an external function to do the next part (you'll write this function soon), as shown in the following listing.

Listing 6.6 Controller for creating a review

```
const reviewsCreate = (req, res) => {
  const locationId = req.params.locationid;
  if (locationId) {
    Loc
      .findById(locationId)
      .select('reviews')
      .exec((err, location) => {
        if (err) {
          res
```

```
            .status(400)
            .json(err);
      } else {
        doAddReview(req, res, location);
      }
    });
  } else {
    res
      .status(404)
      .json({"message": "Location not found"});
  }
};
```

> Successful find operation will call a new function to add a review, passing request, response, and location object

This code isn't doing anything particularly new; you've seen it all before. By putting in a call to a new function, you can keep the code neater by reducing the amount of nesting and indentation, and also make it easier to test.

ADDING AND SAVING A SUBDOCUMENT

Having found the parent document and retrieved the existing list of subdocuments, you need to add a new one. Subdocuments are arrays of objects, and the easiest way to add a new object to an array is to create the data object and use the JavaScript push() method, as the following code snippet demonstrates:

```
location.reviews.push({
  author: req.body.author,
  rating: req.body.rating,
  reviewText: req.body.reviewText
});
```

This snippet is getting posted form data; hence, it uses req.body.

When the subdocument has been added, the parent document must be saved because subdocuments can't be saved on their own. To save a document, Mongoose has a model method save(), which expects a callback with an error parameter and a returned object parameter. The following code snippet shows this method in action:

```
location.save((err, location) => {
  if (err) {
    res
      .status(400)
      .json(err);
  } else {
    let thisReview = location.reviews[location.reviews.length - 1];
    res
      .status(201)
      .json(thisReview);
  }
});
```

> **①** Finds last review in the returned array, as MongoDB returns the entire parent document, not only the new subdocument

The document returned by the save method is the full parent document, not the new subdocument alone. To return the correct data in the API response—that is, the subdocument—you need to retrieve the last subdocument from the array **①**.

When adding documents and subdocuments, you need to keep in mind any effect this action may have on other data. In Loc8r, for example, adding a review adds a new rating, and this new rating affects the overall rating for the document. On the successful save of a review, you'll call another function to update the average rating.

Putting everything you have together in the `doAddReview()` function, plus a little error trapping, gives you the following listing.

Listing 6.7 Adding and saving a subdocument

```
const doAddReview = (req, res, location) => {          When provided a
  if (!location) {                                      parent document . . .
    res
      .status(404)
      .json({"message": "Location not found"});
  } else {
    const {author, rating, reviewText} = req.body;
    location.reviews.push({                            . . . pushes new data into
      author,                                           a subdocument array . . .
      rating,
      reviewText
    });
    location.save((err, location) => {                 . . . before saving it.
      if (err) {
        res
          .status(400)
          .json(err);                                  On successful save operation,
      } else {                                         calls a function to update the
        updateAverageRating(location._id);             average rating
        const thisReview = location.reviews.slice(-1).pop();
        res
          .status(201)
          .json(thisReview);                Retrieves the  last review added
      }                                     to the array, and returns it as a
    });                                     JSON confirmation response
  }
};
```

UPDATING THE AVERAGE RATING

Calculating the average rating isn't particularly complicated, so we won't dwell on it long. The steps are

1 Find the correct document, given a provided ID.
2 Add up the ratings from all the review subdocuments.
3 Calculate the average rating value.
4 Update the rating value of the parent document.
5 Save the document.

Turning this list of steps into code gives you something along the lines of the following listing, which should be placed in the reviews.js controller file along with the review-based controllers.

Listing 6.8   Calculating and updating the average rating

Uses the location supplied data

Uses the JavaScript array reduce method to sum up the ratings of the subdocuments

```
const doSetAverageRating = (location) => {
  if (location.reviews && location.reviews.length > 0) {
    const count = location.reviews.length;
    const total = location.reviews.reduce((acc, {rating}) => {
      return acc + rating;
    }, 0);

    location.rating = parseInt(total / count, 10);
    location.save(err => {
      if (err) {
        console.log(err);
      } else {
        console.log(`Average rating updated to ${location.rating}`);
      }
    });
  }
};

const updateAverageRating = (locationId) => {
  Loc.findById(locationId)
    .select('rating reviews')
    .exec((err, location) => {
      if (!err) {
        doSetAverageRating(location);
      }
    });
};
```

Saves the parent document

Calculates the average rating value and updates the rating value of the parent document

Finds the location based on the provided locationid data

You may have noticed that you're not sending any JSON response here, because you've already sent it. This entire operation is asynchronous and doesn't need to affect sending the API response that confirms the saved review.

Adding a review isn't the only time you'll need to update the average rating, which is why it makes extra sense to make these functions accessible from the other controllers and not tightly coupled to the actions of creating a review.

What you've done here offers a sneak peek at using Mongoose to update data in MongoDB, so now you'll move on to the PUT methods of the API.

6.5   *PUT methods: Updating data in MongoDB*

PUT methods are all about updating existing documents or subdocuments in the database and returning the saved data as confirmation. In the routes for Loc8r, you have two PUT requests doing different things, as listed in table 6.8.

Table 6.8   Two PUT requests of the Loc8r API for updating locations and reviews

Action	Method	URL path	Example
Update a specific location	PUT	/locations/:locationid	http://loc8r.com/api/ locations/123

Table 6.8 Two **PUT** requests of the Loc8r API for updating locations and reviews *(continued)*

Action	Method	URL path	Example
Update a specific review	PUT	`/locations/:locationid/` `reviews/:reviewid`	http://loc8r.com/api/ locations/123/reviews/abc

PUT methods are similar to POST methods, because they work by taking form data posted to them. But instead of using the data to create new documents in the database, PUT methods use the data to update existing documents.

6.5.1 Using Mongoose to update a document in MongoDB

In Loc8r, you may want to update a location to add new facilities, change the open times, or amend any of the other data. The approach to updating data in a document is probably starting to look familiar:

1 Find the relevant document.
2 Make some changes to the instance.
3 Save the document.
4 Send a JSON response.

This approach is made possible by the way an instance of a Mongoose model maps directly to a document in MongoDB. When your query finds the document, you get a model instance. If you make changes to this instance and then save it, Mongoose updates the original document in the database with your changes.

6.5.2 Using the Mongoose save method

You saw this method in action when you updated the average rating value. The save method is applied to the model instance that the find() function returns. It expects a callback with the standard parameters of an error object and a returned data object.

A cut-down skeleton of this approach is shown in the following code snippet:

```
Loc
  .findById(req.params.locationid)          <——— Finds the document to update
  .exec((err, location) => {
    location.name = req.body.name;          <——— Makes a change to the
    location.save((err, loc) => {   <——┐          model instance, changing
      if (err) {                               a value of one path
        res
          .status(404)                  Saves the document with
          .json(err);                   Mongoose's save method
      } else {             Returns a success
        res                or failure response
          .status(200)
          .json(loc);
      }
    });
  }
);
};
```

Here, you can clearly see the separate steps of finding, updating, saving, and responding. Fleshing out this skeleton into the `locationsUpdateOne()` controller with some error trapping and the data you want to save gives you the following listing.

Listing 6.9   Making changes to an existing document in MongoDB

```
const locationsUpdateOne = (req, res) => {
  if (!req.params.locationid) {
    return res
      .status(404)
      .json({
        "message": "Not found, locationid is required"
      });
  }
  Loc
    .findById(req.params.locationid)          ◁──────  Finds the location
    .select('-reviews -rating')                        document by the
    .exec((err, location) => {                         supplied ID
      if (!location) {
        return res
          .json(404)
          .status({
            "message": "locationid not found"
          });
      } else if (err) {
        return res
          .status(400)
          .json(err);
      }
      location.name = req.body.name;
      location.address = req.body.address;
      location.facilities = req.body.facilities.split(',');
      location.coords = {
        type: "Point",
        [
          parseFloat(req.body.lng),
          parseFloat(req.body.lat)
        ]
      };                                           Updates paths with
      location.openingTimes = [{                    values from the
        days: req.body.days1,                        submitted form
        opening: req.body.opening1,
        closing: req.body.closing1,
        closed: req.body.closed1,
      }, {
        days: req.body.days2,
        opening: req.body.opening2,
        closing: req.body.closing2,
        closed: req.body.closed2,
      }];
      location.save((err, loc) => {      ◁──────  Saves the instance
        if (err) {
          res                    ◁──────
            .status(404)                  Sends an appropriate response,
                                          depending on the outcome of
                                          the save operation
```

```
          .json(err);
      } else {
        res
          .status(200)
          .json(loc);
      }
    });
  }
  );
};
```

Sends an appropriate response, depending on the outcome of the save operation

There's clearly a lot more code here, now that it's fully fleshed out, but you can still easily identify the key steps of the update process.

The eagle-eyed among you may have noticed something strange in the `select` statement:

```
.select('-reviews -rating')
```

Previously, you used the `select()` method to say which columns you *do want* to select. By adding a dash in front of a pathname, you're stating that you *don't want* to retrieve it from the database. So this `select()` statement says to retrieve everything except the `reviews` and the `rating`.

6.5.3 Updating an existing subdocument in MongoDB

Updating a subdocument is exactly the same as updating a document, with one exception: after finding the document, you have to find the correct subdocument to make your changes. Then the `save` method is applied to the document, not the subdocument. So the steps for updating an existing subdocument are

1 Find the relevant document.
2 Find the relevant subdocument.
3 Make some changes in the subdocument.
4 Save the document.
5 Send a JSON response.

For Loc8r, the subdocuments you're updating are reviews, so when a review is changed, you'll have to remember to recalculate the average rating. That's the only additional thing you'll need to add above and beyond the five steps. The following listing shows everything put into place in the `reviewsUpdateOne()` controller.

Listing 6.10 Updating a subdocument in MongoDB

```
const reviewsUpdateOne = (req, res) => {
  if (!req.params.locationid || !req.params.reviewid) {
    return res
      .status(404)
      .json({
        "message": "Not found, locationid and reviewid are both required"
      });
  }
```

```
Loc
  .findById(req.params.locationid)        ◄────── Finds the parent document
  .select('reviews')
  .exec((err, location) => {
    if (!location) {
      return res
        .status(404)
        .json({
          "message": "Location not found"
        });
    } else if (err) {
      return res
        .status(400)
        .json(err);
    }
    if (location.reviews && location.reviews.length > 0) {
      const thisReview = location.reviews.id(req.params.reviewid);
      if (!thisReview) {
        res
          .status(404)
          .json({
            "message": "Review not found"
          });
      } else {
        thisReview.author = req.body.author;
        thisReview.rating = req.body.rating;
        thisReview.reviewText = req.body.reviewText;
        location.save((err, location) => {
          if (err) {
            res
              .status(404)
              .json(err);
          } else {
            updateAverageRating(location._id);
            res
              .status(200)
              .json(thisReview);
          }
        });
      }
    } else {
      res
        .status(404)
        .json({
          "message": "No review to update"
        });
    }
  }
);
};
```

Finds the subdocument — points to `const thisReview = location.reviews.id(req.params.reviewid);`

Makes changes to the subdocument from the supplied form data

Saves the parent document — points to `location.save((err, location) => {`

Returns a JSON response, sending the subdocument object on the basis of a successful save

The five steps for updating are clear to see in this listing: find the document; find the subdocument; make changes; save; and respond. Once again, a lot of the code here is error trapping, but it's vital for creating a stable, responsive API. You don't want to save incorrect data, send the wrong responses, or delete data you don't want to delete. Speaking of deleting data, you can now move on to the final of the four API methods you're using: DELETE.

6.6 DELETE method: Deleting data from MongoDB

The DELETE method is, unsurprisingly, all about deleting existing documents or subdocuments in the database. In the routes for Loc8r, you have a DELETE request for deleting a location and another for deleting a review. The details are listed in table 6.9.

Table 6.9 Two DELETE requests of the Loc8r API for deleting locations and reviews

Action	Method	URL path	Example
Delete a specific location	DELETE	`/locations/:locationid`	http://loc8r.com/api/locations/123
Delete a specific review	DELETE	`/locations/:locationid/reviews/:reviewid`	http://loc8r.com/api/locations/123/reviews/abc

Start by taking a look at deleting documents.

6.6.1 Deleting documents in MongoDB

Mongoose makes deleting a document in MongoDB extremely simple by giving you the method `findByIdAndRemove()`. This method expects a single parameter: the ID of the document to be deleted.

The API should respond with a 404 in case of an error and a 204 in case of success. The following listing shows everything in place in the `locationsDeleteOne()` controller.

Listing 6.11 Deleting a document from MongoDB, given an ID

```
const locationsDeleteOne = (req, res) => {
  const {locationid} = req.params;
  if (locationid) {
    Loc
      .findByIdAndRemove(locationid)       ⟵  Calls findByIdAndRemove
      .exec((err, location) => {      ⟵  method, passing in locationid
        if (err) {                       Executes the method
          return res               ⟵
            .status(404)
            .json(err);              Responds with
        }                            failure or success
        res               ⟵
          .status(204)
          .json(null);
      }
    );
  } else {
    res
      .status(404)
      .json({
```

```
        "message": "No Location"
      });
   }
};
```

That's the quick and easy way to delete a document, but you can break it into a two-step process or, if you prefer, find it and then delete it. This gives you the chance to do something with the document before deleting (if you need to). This is demonstrated in the following code snippet:

```
Loc
  .findById(locationid)
  .exec((err, location) => {
    // Do something with the document
    location.remove((err, loc) => {
      // Confirm success or failure
    });
  }
);
```

This snippet has an extra level of nesting, but with it comes an extra level of flexibility, should you need it.

6.6.2   *Deleting a subdocument from MongoDB*

The process for deleting a subdocument is no different from the other work you've done with subdocuments; everything is managed through the parent document. The steps for deleting a subdocument are

1 Find the parent document.
2 Find the relevant subdocument.
3 Remove the subdocument.
4 Save the parent document.
5 Confirm success or failure of operation.

Deleting the subdocument itself is easy, as Mongoose gives you another helper method. You've already seen that you can find a subdocument by its ID with the `id` method like this:

```
location.reviews.id(reviewid)
```

Mongoose allows you to chain a `remove` method to the end of this statement like so:

```
location.reviews.id(reviewid).remove()
```

This instruction deletes the subdocument from the array. Remember to save the parent document to persist the change back to the database. Putting all the steps together—with a load of error trapping—into the `reviewsDeleteOne()` controller looks like the following listing.

```
const reviewsDeleteOne = (req, res) => {
  const {locationid, reviewid} = req.params;
  if (!locationid || !reviewid) {
    return res
      .status(404)
      .json({'message': 'Not found, locationid and reviewid are both
    required'});
  }

  Loc                                          Finds the relevant
    .findById(locationid)        ◁----------┘  parent document
    .select('reviews')
    .exec((err, location) => {
      if (!location) {
        return res
          .status(404)
          .json({'message': 'Location not found'});
      } else if (err) {
        return res
          .status(400)
          .json(err);
      }

      if (location.reviews && location.reviews.length > 0) {
        if (!location.reviews.id(reviewid)) {
          return res                                 Finds and deletes the
            .status(404)                             relevant subdocument
            .json({'message': 'Review not found'});  in one step
        } else {
          location.reviews.id(reviewid).remove();  ◁
          location.save(err => {          ◁-------- Saves the parent document
            if (err) {
              return res             ◁--------------┐
                .status(404)                        │
                .json(err);                         │ Returns the
            } else {                                │ appropriate success
              updateAverageRating(location._id);    │ or failure response
              res                       ◁-----------┘
                .status(204)
                .json(null);
            }
          });
        }
      } else {
        res
          .status(404)
          .json({'message': 'No Review to delete'});
      }
    });
};
```

Again, most of the code here is error trapping. The API could return seven possible responses, and only one is the successful one. Deleting the subdocument is easy; make absolutely sure that you're deleting the right one.

As you're deleting a review, which will have a rating associated to it, you also have to remember to call the `updateAverageRating()` function to recalculate the average rating for the location. This function should only be called if the delete operation is successful.

And that's it. You've built a REST API in Express and Node that can accept `GET`, `POST`, `PUT`, and `DELETE` HTTP requests to perform CRUD operations on a MongoDB database.

Coming up in chapter 7, you'll see how to use this API from inside the Express application, finally making the Loc8r site database-driven!

Summary

In this chapter, you learned

- The best practices for creating a REST API, including URLs, request methods, and response codes
- How the `POST`, `GET`, `PUT`, and `DELETE` HTTP request methods map to common CRUD operations
- Mongoose helper methods for creating the helper methods
- Ways to interact with the data through Mongoose models and how one instance of the model maps directly to one document in the database
- How to manage subdocuments through their parent document
- Some ways of making the API robust by checking for any possible errors you can think of so that a request is never left unanswered

Consuming a REST API: Using an API from inside Express

(chapter number 7 displayed as large decorative numeral)

This chapter covers

- Calling an API from an Express application
- Handling and using data returned by the API
- Working with API response codes
- Submitting data from the browser back to the API
- Validating and trapping errors

This chapter is an exciting one! Here's where you tie the front end to the back end for the first time. You'll remove the hardcoded data from the controllers, and eventually show data from the database in the browser instead. You'll also push data back from the browser into the database via the API, creating new subdocuments.

The technology focus for this chapter is on Node and Express. Figure 7.1 shows where this chapter fits into the overall architecture and your grand plan.

In this chapter, we'll discuss how to call an API from within Express and how to deal with the responses. You'll make calls to the API to read from the database and write to the database. Along the way, we'll look at handling errors, processing data,

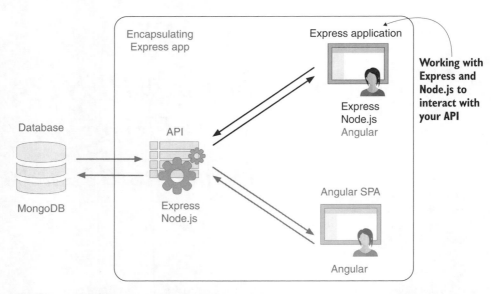

Figure 7.1   This chapter focuses on updating the Express application from chapter 4 to interact with the REST API developed in chapter 6.

and creating reusable code by separating concerns. Toward the end, we'll cover the various layers of the architecture to which you can add validation and why these different layers are useful.

Start by looking at how to call an API from an Express application.

7.1   How to call an API from Express

The first part we need to cover is how to call an API from Express. This approach isn't limited to your API; you can use it to call any API.

Your Express application needs to be able to call the API URLs that you set up in chapter 6—sending the correct request method, of course—and then be able to interpret the response. To help, you'll use a module called `request`.

7.1.1   Adding the request module to your project

The `request` module is like any of the other packages you've used so far and can be added to your project via npm. To install the latest version and add it to the package.json file, head to terminal, and type the following command:

```
$ npm install --save request
```

When npm finishes doing its thing, you can include `request` in the files that will use it. In Loc8r, you have only one file that needs to make API calls: the file with the controllers for the main server-side application. So at the top of locations.js in app_server/controllers, add the following line to require the `request` module:

```
const request = require('request');
```

Now you're good to go!

7.1.2   *Setting up default options*

Every API call with `request` must have a fully qualified URL, meaning that it must include the full address and not be a relative link. But this URL is different for development than for live environments.

To avoid having to make this check in every controller that makes an API call, you can set a default configuration option once at the top of the controllers file. To use the correct URL depending on the environment, you can use your old friend the `NODE_ENV` environment variable.

Putting this into practice, the top of the app_server/controllers/locations.js file should look something like the following listing.

> **Listing 7.1   Adding request and default API options to the locations.js controllers file**

```
const request = require('request');
const apiOptions = {
  server: 'http://localhost:3000'        Sets the default server URL
};                                       for the local development
if (process.env.NODE_ENV === 'production') {
  apiOptions.server = 'https://pure-temple-67771.herokuapp.com';
}
```

If the application is running in production mode, sets a different base URL; changes to the live address of the application

With this code in place, every call you make to the API can reference `apiOptions` `.server` and use the correct base URL.

7.1.3   *Using the request module*

The basic construct for making a request is simple, being a single command taking parameters for options and a callback like this:

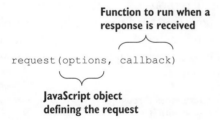

Function to run when a response is received

```
request(options, callback)
```

JavaScript object defining the request

The options specify everything for the request, including the URL, request method, request body, and query string parameters. These options, indeed, are the ones you'll be using in this chapter, and they're detailed in table 7.1.

Table 7.1   Four common request options for defining a call to an API

Option	Description	Required
url	Full URL of the request to be made, including protocol, domain, path, and URL parameters	Yes
method	Method of the request, such as GET, POST, PUT, or DELETE	No—defaults to GET if not specified
json	Body of the request as a JavaScript object; an empty object should be sent if no body data is needed	Yes—ensures that the response body is also parsed as JSON
qs	JavaScript object representing any query string parameters	No

The following code snippet shows an example of how you might put these options together for a GET request. A GET request shouldn't have a body to send but might have query string parameters:

```
const requestOptions = {
  url: 'http://yourapi.com/api/path',      ◁── Defines the URL of the API call to be made
  method: 'GET',                            ◁── Sets the request method
  json: {},                                 ◁── Defines the body of the request, even if it's an empty JSON object
  qs: {
    offset: 20
  }                                         Optionally adds any query string parameters that might be used by the API
};
```

You could specify many more options, but these four are the most common and the ones you'll use in this chapter. For more information on other possible options, take a look at the reference in the GitHub repository: https://github.com/mikeal/request.

The callback function runs when a response comes back from the API and has three parameters: an error object, the full response, and the parsed body of the response. The error object is null unless an error has been caught. Three pieces of data will be most useful in your code: the status code of the response, the body of the response, and any error thrown. The following code snippet shows how you might structure a callback for the request() function:

```
(err, response, body) => {
  if (err) {                                ◁── If an error has passed through, does something with it
    console.log(err);
  } else if (response.statusCode === 200) { ◁── If a response status code is 200 (request was successful), outputs the JSON body of the response
    console.log(body);
  } else {
    console.log(response.statusCode);       ◁── If the request returns a different status code, outputs the code
  }
}
```

The full response object contains a huge amount of information, so we won't go into it here. You can always check it out yourself by using a `console.log` statement when you start adding the API calls to your application.

Putting the parts together, the skeleton for making API calls looks like the following:

```
const requestOptions = {
  url: 'http://yourapi.com/api/path',
  method: 'GET',
  json: {},                              Defines options
  qs: {                                  for the request
    offset: 20
  }
};
request(requestOptions, (err, response, body) => {
  if (err) {                             Makes the request,
    console.log(err);                    sending through
  } else if (response.statusCode === 200) {  options and supplying
    console.log(body);                   a callback function to
  } else {                               use responses as
    console.log(response.statusCode);    needed
  }
});
```

In the next section, you'll put this theory into practice and start building the Loc8r controllers to use the API you've already built.

7.2　*Using lists of data from an API: The Loc8r homepage*

By now, the controllers file that will be doing the work should already have the `request` module required in and some default values set. Now come the fun parts: updating the controllers to call the API and pulling the data for the pages from the database.

You've got two main pages that pull data: the homepage, showing a list of locations, and a Details page, giving more information about a specific location. Start at the beginning and get the data for the homepage from the database.

The current homepage controller contains a `res.render()` function call, sending hardcoded data to the view. But the way you want it to work is to render the homepage after the API returns some data. The homepage controller will have quite a lot to do anyway, so move this rendering into its own function.

7.2.1　*Separating concerns: Moving the rendering into a named function*

There are a couple of reasons for moving the rendering into its own named function. First, you decouple the rendering from the application logic. The process of rendering doesn't care where or how it got the data; if it's given data in the right format, it uses that data. Using a separate function helps you get closer to the testable ideal that each function should do one thing. A related bonus is that the function becomes reusable, so you can call it from multiple places.

The second reason for creating a new function for the homepage rendering is that the rendering process occurs inside the callback of the API request. In addition to making the code hard to test, it makes the code hard to read. The level of nesting required makes for a rather large, heavily indented controller function. As a point of best practice, you should try to avoid deeply indenting code: it's hard to read and understand when you come back to it.

The first step is making a new function called `renderHomepage()` in the locations.js file in the app_server/controllers folder and moving the contents of the `homelist` controller into it. Remember to ensure that the new function accepts the `req` and `res` parameters too. The following listing shows a stripped-down version of what you're doing here. You can call this code from the `homelist` controller, as shown in the listing, and things will work as before.

Listing 7.2   Moving the contents of the `homelist` controller into an external function

```
const renderHomepage = (req, res) => {                    Includes all code from
  res.render('locations-list', {                          the res.render call here
    title: 'Loc8r - find a place to work with wifi',      (snipped for brevity)
    …
  });
};
const homelist = (req, res) => {          Calls a new
  renderHomepage(req, res);               renderHomepage function
};                                        from the homelist controller
```

This step is a start, but you're not there yet; you want data!

7.2.2   Building the API request

You'll get the data you want by asking the API for it, and to do this, you need to build the request. To build the request, you need to know the URL, method, JSON body, and query string to send. Looking back at chapter 6, or indeed at the API code itself, you can see that you need to supply the information shown in table 7.2.

Table 7.2   Information needed to make a request to the API for a list of locations

Parameter	Value
URL	`SERVER:PORT/api/locations`
Method	`GET`
JSON body	`null`
Query string	`lng, lat, maxDistance`

Mapping this information to a request is straightforward. As you saw earlier in the chapter, the options for a request are JavaScript objects. For the time being, you'll hardcode values for longitude and latitude into the options, which is a quicker and easier method for testing. Later in the book, you'll make the application location-aware. For now, you'll choose coordinates close to where the test data is stored. The maximum distance is set to 20 km.

When you make the request, you'll pass through a simple callback function to call the `renderHomepage()` function so that you don't leave the browser hanging. Expressing this idea as code looks like the following listing.

Listing 7.3   Updating the `homelist` controller to call the API before rendering the page

```
const homelist = (req, res) => {
  const path = '/api/locations';          ◁      Sets the path for the API
  const requestOptions = {                        request. (The server is already
    url: `${apiOptions.server}${path}`,           set at the top of the file.)
    method: 'GET',
    json: {},                                     Sets the request options,
    qs: {                                         including URL, method,
      lng: -0.7992599,                            empty JSON body, and
      lat: 51.378091,                             hardcoded query string
      maxDistance: 20                             parameters
    }
  };
  request(
    requestOptions,                        Makes request, sending
    (err, response, body) => {             through request options
      renderHomepage(req, res);              Supplies the callback to
    }                                        render the homepage
  );
};
```

If you save this code and run the application again, the homepage should display exactly as before. You might now be making a request to the API, but you're ignoring the response.

7.2.3   Using the API response data

Seeing as you're going to the effort of calling the API, the least you can do is use the data it's sending back. You can handle the response more robustly later, but you'll start with making the handler work. In order to make this happen, you're going to assume that a response body is returned to the callback, and you can pass it straight into the `renderHomepage()` function, as highlighted in the following listing.

Listing 7.4   Updating the contents of the `homelist` controller to use the API response

```
request(
  requestOptions,                            Passes the body returned by
  (err, response, body) => {                 the request to the
    renderHomepage(req, res, body);    ◁     renderHomepage() function
  }
);
```

You coded the API, so you know that the response body returned by the API should be an array of locations. The `renderHomepage()` function needs an array of locations to send to the view, so try passing it straight through, making the changes highlighted in bold in the following listing.

Listing 7.5   Updating the `renderHomepage` function to use the data from the API

```
const renderHomepage = (req, res, responseBody) => {          ◁──┐ Adds an additional
  res.render('locations-list', {                                  │ responseBody
    title: 'Loc8r - find a place to work with wifi',              │ parameter to the
    pageHeader: {                                                 │ function declaration
      title: 'Loc8r',
      strapline: 'Find places to work with wifi near you!'
    },
    sidebar: "Looking for wifi and a seat? Loc8r helps you find places
➥to work when out and about. Perhaps with coffee, cake or a pint?
➥ Let Loc8r help you find the place you're looking for.",
    locations: responseBody            ◁── Removes the hardcoded array of
  });                                      locations, and passes the
};                                         responseBody through instead
```

Can the process be that easy? Try it in the browser to see what happens. We hope that you'll get something like figure 7.2.

That looks pretty good, right? You need to do something about how the distance is displayed, but other than that, the data is coming through as you wanted. Plugging in the data was quick and easy because of the work you did up front designing the

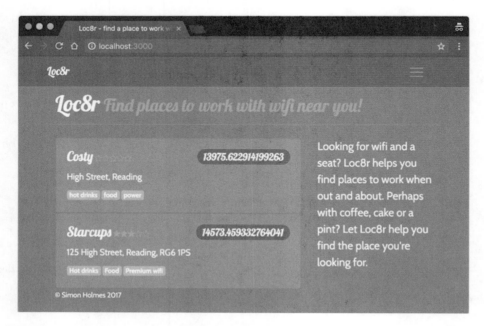

Figure 7.2   Initial result using data from the database in the browser: close to the desired result

views, building controllers based on the views, and developing the model based on the controllers.

You've made it work. Now you need to make it better. There's no error trapping yet, and the distances need some work.

7.2.4 Modifying data before displaying it: fixing the distances

At the moment, the distances in the list are displaying 15 decimal places and no unit of measurement, so they're extremely accurate and totally useless! You want to say whether each distance is in meters or kilometers and round the numbers off to a single meter or to one decimal place of a kilometer. You should do this before sending the data to the renderHomepage() function, as that function should be reserved for handling the actual rendering, not sorting out the data.

You need to loop through the array of returned locations, formatting the distance value of each one. Rather than do this inline, you'll create an external function (in the same file) called formatDistance() that accepts a distance value and returns it nicely formatted. Put the following function before renderHomepage() in the controller file.

Listing 7.6 Adding formatDistance function

```
const formatDistance = (distance) => {
  let thisDistance = 0;
  let unit = 'm';
  if (distance > 1000) {
    thisDistance = parseFloat(distance / 1000).toFixed(1);
    unit = 'km';
  } else {
    thisDistance = Math.floor(distance);
  }
  return thisDistance + unit;
};
```

If the supplied distance is more than 1000 m, converts to km, rounds to one decimal place, and adds km unit

Otherwise, rounds down to the nearest meter

Now make the change as shown in bold in the following listing. Note that the framework of the homelist controller has been left out of this code snippet. To keep things short, the request statement still sits inside the controller.

Listing 7.7 Adding and using a function to format the distance returned by the API

```
request(
  requestOptions,
  (err, response, body) => {
    let data = [];
    data = body.map( (item) => {
      item.distance = formatDistance(item.distance);
      return item;
    });
    renderHomepage(req, res, data);
  }
);
```

Creates a variable for future use

Maps the data in an array, formatting the distance value of the location

Sends the modified data to be rendered instead of the original body content

You have one small additional change to make. You added m to the API output for distances, but with the `formatDistance()` function, this addition is no longer required, so make the following change in /app_api/controllers/locations.js.

Listing 7.8   Removing the unit from the API response

```
const locations = results.map(result => {
  return {
    name: result.name,
    address: result.address,
    rating: result.rating,
    facilities: result.facilities,
    distance: `${result.distance.calculated.toFixed()}`        ⟵——  Removes m
  }                                                                   from this line
});
```

If you make these changes and refresh the page, you should see that the distances are tidied up a bit and are useful, as shown in figure 7.3.

That's better; the homepage is looking more like you want it to. For extra credit, you can add some error trapping to the `formatDistance()` function to make sure that a `distance` parameter has been passed and that it's a number.

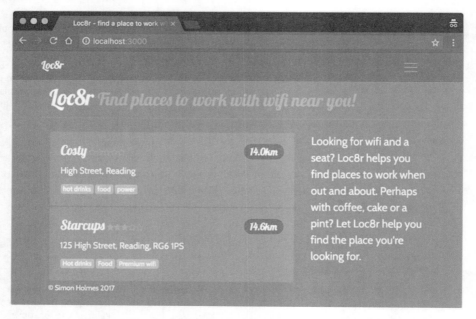

Figure 7.3   The homepage looks better after you format the distances returned by the API.

7.2.5 *Catching errors returned by the API*

So far, you've assumed that the API will always return an array of data along with a 200 success code. But this isn't necessarily the case. You coded the API to return a 200 status even if no locations are found nearby. As things stand, when this happens, the homepage will display without any content in the central area. A far better user experience would be to output a message to the user that there are no places nearby.

You also know that your API can give 404 errors, so you'll need to make sure you handle these errors appropriately. You don't want to show a 404 to the user in this case, because the error won't be due to the homepage being missing. The better option, again, is to send a message to the browser in the context of the homepage.

Handling these scenarios shouldn't be too difficult. The following sections show you how, starting with the controller.

MAKING THE REQUEST CALLBACK MORE ROBUST

One of the main reasons for catching errors is to make sure that they don't cause code to fail. The first point of weakness is in the `request` callback, where you're manipulating the response before sending the data off to be rendered. This is fine if the data is always consistent, but you don't have that luxury.

The `request` callback currently runs a `for` loop to format the distances no matter what data is returned by the API. You should run this loop only when the API returns a 200 code and some results.

The following listing shows how to achieve this result by adding a simple `if` statement (app_server/controllers/locations.js) checking the status code and the length of the returned data.

> **Listing 7.9 Validating that the API has returned some data before trying to use it**

```
request(
  requestOptions,
  (err, {statusCode}, body) =>        ◁——— Uses object destructing
    let data = [];                          to get the statusCode, as
    if (statusCode === 200 && body.length) {    that's all you need
      data = body.map( (item) => {      ◁——— Runs a loop to format
        item.distance = formatDistance(item.distance):   distances only if the API
        return item;                                     returned a 200 status
      });                                                and some data
    }
    renderHomepage(req, res, data);
  }
);
```

Updating this piece of code should prevent this callback from falling over and throwing an error if the API responds with a status code other than 200. The link in the chain is the `renderHomepage()` function.

DEFINING OUTPUT MESSAGES BASED ON THE RESPONSE DATA

As with the `request` callback, your original focus for the `renderHomepage()` function is to make it work when it's passed an array of locations to display. Now that this function might be sent different data types, you need to make it handle the possibilities appropriately.

The response body could be one of three things:

- An array of locations
- An empty array when no locations are found
- A string containing a message when the API returns an error

You already have the code in place to deal with an array of locations, so you need to address the other two possibilities. When catching these errors, you also want to set a message that can be sent to the view.

To do so, you need to update the `renderHomepage()` function to also do the following:

- Set a variable container for a message
- Check to see whether the response body is an array; if not, set an appropriate message
- If the response is an array, set a different message if it's empty (that is, no locations are returned)
- Send the message to the view

The following listing shows how this looks in code.

Listing 7.10 Outputting messages if the API doesn't return location data

```
const renderHomepage = function(req, res, responseBody){
  let message = null;
  if (!(responseBody instanceof Array)) {
    message = "API lookup error";
    responseBody = [];
  } else {
    if (!responseBody.length) {
      message = "No places found nearby";
    }
  }
  res.render('locations-list', {
    title: 'Loc8r - find a place to work with wifi',
    pageHeader: {
      title: 'Loc8r',
      strapline: 'Find places to work with wifi near you!'
    },
    sidebar: "Looking for wifi and a seat? Loc8r helps you find
➥places to work when out and about. Perhaps with coffee, cake or a
➥pint? Let Loc8r help you find the place you're looking for.",
    locations: responseBody,
    message
  });
};
```

Defines a variable to hold a message → `let message = null;`

If the response isn't an array, sets a message and sets the responseBody to be an empty array

If the response is an array with no length, sets a message

Adds a message to variables to send to the view ← `message`

The only surprise is when you set the `responseBody` to be an empty array if it was originally passed through as a string. You do this to prevent the view from throwing an error. The view expects an array to be sent in the `locations` variable; it effectively ignores it if an empty array is sent but throws an error if a string is sent.

The last link in this chain is updating the view to display a message when one is sent.

UPDATING THE VIEW TO DISPLAY THE ERROR MESSAGES

You're catching the errors from the API, and you're also working with them to pass something back to the user. The final step is letting the user see a message by adding a placeholder to the view template.

You don't need to do anything fancy here; a simple `div` with a class of `error` to contain any messages will suffice. The following listing shows the `block content` section of the homepage view `locations-list.pug` in app_server/views.

Listing 7.11 Updating the view to display an error message when needed

```
block content
  .row.banner
    .col-12
      h1= pageHeader.title
        small  #{pageHeader.strapline}
  .row
    .col-12.col-md-8
      .error= message              ◁──────  Adds a div to the main content
                                             area, and has it display a
      each location in locations            message if one is sent
        .card
          .card-block
            h4
              a(href="/location")= location.name
              small  
                +outputRating(location.rating)
              span.badge.badge-pill.badge-default.float-right=
              ↩location.distance
            p.address= location.address
            .facilities
              each facility in location.facilities
                span.badge.badge-warning= facility
    .col-12.col-md-4
      p.lead= sidebar
```

That's easy—basic, but easy. It will certainly do for now. All that's left is to test it.

TESTING THE API ERROR TRAPPING

As with any new code, you need to make sure that it works. An easy way to test this code is to change the query string values that you're sending in the `requestOptions`.

To test the `No places found nearby` trap, you can set the `maxDistance` to a small number (remembering that it's specified in kilometers) or set the `lng` and `lat` to a point where there are no locations, as shown in this example:

```
requestOptions = {
  url: `${apiOptions.server}${path}`,
  method: 'GET',
  json: {},
  qs: {
    lng: 1,                          Changes the query string values
    lat: 1,                          sent in the request to get no
    maxDistance : 0.002              results returned
  }
};
```

Fixing an interesting bug

Did you try testing the API error trapping by setting `lng` or `lat` to 0? You should have been expecting to see the `No places found nearby` message but instead saw `API lookup error`, due to a bug in the error trapping in your API code.

In the `locationsListByDistance` controller, check whether the `lng` and `lat` query string parameters were omitted by using a generic "falsey" JavaScript test. Your code has this: `if (!lng || !lat)`.

In falsey tests like this one, JavaScript looks for any of the values that it considers to be false, such as an empty string, undefined, `null`, and (important for you) 0. This introduces an unexpected bug into your code. If someone happened to be on the equator or on the Prime Meridian (that's the Greenwich Mean Time line), they'd receive an API error.

You can fix this bug by verifying the falsey test to say, "If it's false but not zero." In code, this statement looks like this: `if ((!lng && lng !== 0) || (!lat && lat !== 0))`.

Updating your controller in the API removes this bug.

You can use a similar tactic to test the 404 error. The API expects all the query string parameters to be sent and returns a 404 if one of them is missing. To test the code quickly, you can comment one of them out:

```
const requestOptions = {
  url: `${apiOptions.server}${path}`,
  method: 'GET',
  json: {},
  qs: {
    // lng: -0.7992599,        ◁————  Comment out one query string
    lat: 51.378091,                   parameter in the request to help test
    maxDistance: 20                   what happens when the API returns 404.
  }
};
```

Do these two things one at a time and refresh the homepage to see the different messages coming through. These messages are shown in figure 7.4.

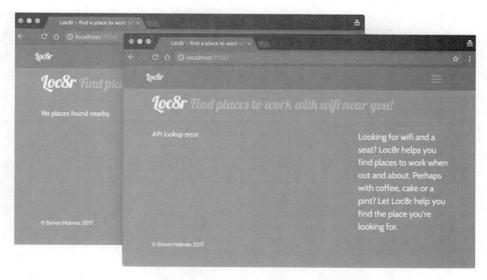

Figure 7.4 Showing error messages in the view after trapping the errors being returned

That figure shows the homepage set up nicely. Your Express application queries the API you built, which pulls data from the MongoDB database and passes it back to the application. When the application gets a response from the API, it works out what to do with it and shows either the data or an error message in the browser.

Next, you'll do the same thing for the Details page, this time working with single instances of data.

7.3 Getting single documents from an API: The Loc8r Details page

The Details page should display all the information you have about a specific location, from the name and address to ratings, reviews, facilities, and a location map. At the moment, this page is using data hardcoded into the controller and looks like figure 7.5.

In this section, you'll update the application so that it allows you to specify which location you want the details for, get the details from the API, and output them to the browser. You'll also add some error trapping, of course.

7.3.1 Setting URLs and routes to access specific MongoDB documents

The current path you have to the Details page is /location. This path doesn't offer a way to specify which location you want to look at. To address this situation, you can borrow the approach from the API routes, where you specify the ID of the location document as a URL parameter.

The API route for a single location is /api/location/:locationid. You can do the same thing for the main Express application and update the route to contain the `locationid` parameter. The main application routes for locations are in index.js in

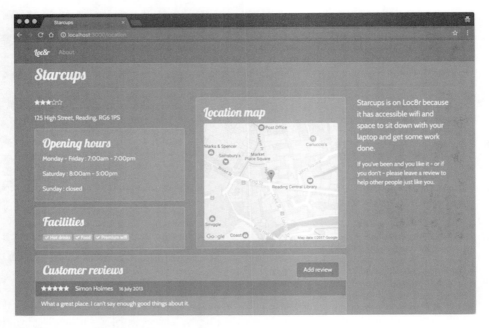

Figure 7.5   The Details page as it is now, using data hardcoded into the controller

the /routes folder. The following code snippet shows the simple change needed to update the location detail route to accept the `locationid` URL parameter (app_server/routes/index.js):

**Adds the locationid parameter
to the route for a single location**

```
router.get('/', ctrlLocations.homelist);
router.get('/location/:locationid', ctrlLocations.locationInfo);    ⟵
router.get('/location/review/new', ctrlLocations.addReview);
```

Okay, great, but where do you get the IDs of the locations from? Thinking about the application as a whole, the homepage is the best place to start, as that's where the links for the Details page come from.

When the API for the homepage returns an array of locations, each location object contains its unique ID. This entire object is already passed to the view, so it shouldn't be too difficult to update the homepage view to add this ID as a URL parameter.

It's not difficult at all, in fact! The following listing shows the little change that needs to be made in the locations-list.pug file to append the unique ID of each location to the link through to the Details page.

Listing 7.12   Updating the list view to add the location ID to the relevant links

```
block content
  .row.banner
    .col-12
      h1= pageHeader.title
```

```
              small  #{pageHeader.strapline}
    .row
      .col-12.col-md-8
        .error= message

          each location in locations
            .card
              .card-block
                h4
                  a(href=`/location/${location._id}`)= location.name
                  small  
                    +outputRating(location.rating)
                  span.badge.badge-pill.badge-default.float-right=
                  ➥location.distance
                p.address= location.address
                .facilities
                  each facility in location.facilities
                    span.badge.badge-warning= facility
```

> As each location in the array is looped through, pulls the unique ID from the object and appends it to href for a link to the Details page

If only everything in life were that easy. Now the homepage contains unique links for each of the locations, and the links all click through to the Details page. Now you need to make them show the correct data.

7.3.2 Separating concerns: Moving the rendering into a named function

As you did for the homepage, you'll move the rendering of the Details page into its own named function. Again, you do this to keep the rendering functionality separate from the API call and data processing.

The following listing shows a trimmed-down version of the new `renderDetail-Page()` function and how it's called from the `locationInfo` controller.

> **Listing 7.13 Moving contents of the `locationInfo` controller into an external function**

```
const renderDetailPage = (req, res) => {
  res.render('location-info', {
    title: 'Starcups',
    ...
  });
};
```

> Creates a new function called renderDetailPage and moves all contents of the locationInfo controller into it

```
const locationInfo = (req, res) => {
  renderDetailPage(req, res);
};
```

> Calls a new function from the controller, remembering to pass it req and res parameters

Now you're set up with a nice, clear controller, ready to query the API.

7.3.3 Querying the API using a unique ID from a URL parameter

The URL for the API call needs to contain the ID of the location. Your Details page has this ID now as the URL parameter `locationid`, so you can get the value of this by using `req.params` and add it to the `path` in the request options. The request is a GET request, so the `json` value will be an empty object.

Knowing all this, you can use the pattern you created in the homepage controller to build and make the request to the API. You'll call the `renderDetailPage()` function when the API responds. All this is shown in the following listing.

Listing 7.14   Updating the `locationInfo` controller to call the API

```
const locationInfo = (req, res) => {
  const path = `/api/locations/${req.params.locationid}`;       ◁─── Gets the locationid
  const requestOptions = {                                            parameter from the
    url: `${apiOptions.server}${path}`,          Sets all request     URL and appends it
    method: 'GET',                               options needed to    to the API path
    json: {}                                     call the API
  };
  request(
    requestOptions,
    (err, response, body) => {                   Calls the
      renderDetailPage(req, res);        ◁───    renderDetailPage()
    }                                            function when the API
  );                                             has responded
};
```

If you run this code now, you'll see the same static data as before, as you're not yet passing the data returned from the API into the view. You can add some console log statements to the `request` callback if you want to have a quick look at what's being returned.

If you're happy that everything is working as it should, it's time for you to pass the data into the view.

7.3.4   *Passing the data from the API to the view*

You're currently assuming that the API is returning the correct data; you'll get around to error trapping soon. This data needs a small amount of preprocessing: the coordinates are returned from the API as an array, but the view needs them to be named key-value pairs in an object.

The following listing shows how you can do this in the context of the `request` statement, transforming the data from the API before sending it to the `renderDetail-Page()` function.

Listing 7.15   Preprocessing data in the controller

```
request(
  requestOptions,                             Creates a copy of
  (err, response, body) => {                  the returned data
    const data = body;              ◁──────   in a new variable
    data.coords = {
      lng: body.coords[0],          Resets the coords property to be an
      lat: body.coords[1]           object, setting lng and lat using
    };                              values pulled from the API response
    renderDetailPage(req, res, data);   ◁───   Sends the transformed
  }                                            data to be rendered
);
```

The next logical step is updating the `renderDetailPage()` function to use this data rather than the hardcoded data. To make this work, you need to make sure that the function accepts the data as a parameter and then update the values passed through to the view as required. The following listing highlights the changes needed in bold.

Listing 7.16   Updating `renderDetailPage` to accept and use data from the API

```
const renderDetailPage = function (req, res, location) {        ◁── Adds a new
  res.render('location-info', {                                      parameter for
    title: location.name,                                            data in the
    pageHeader: {                                                    function definition
      title: location.name
      },
    sidebar: {
      context: 'is on Loc8r because it has accessible wifi and
      ➥space to sit down with your laptop and get some work done.',
      callToAction: "If you've been and you like it - or if you
      ➥don't - please leave a review to help other people just
      ➥like you."
    },
    location        ◁── Passes the full location data object
  });                    to the view, containing all the details
};
```

References specific items of data as needed in the function

You're able to take the approach of sending the full object through like this because you originally based the data model on what was needed by the view and the controller. If you run the application now, you should see that the page loads with the data pulled from the database, as shown in figure 7.6.

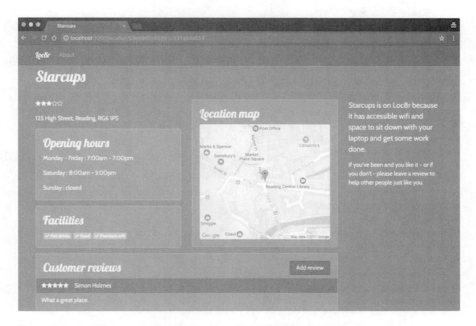

Figure 7.6   Details page pulling in data from MongoDB via the API

The eagle-eyed reader will have noticed a problem with the screenshot in figure 7.6: the review doesn't have a date associated with it.

7.3.5   Debugging and fixing the view errors

So you have a problem with the view, which isn't outputting the review date correctly. You built the data model based on the data provided by the view and controller, but now you see that you don't have enough information. In this section, you'll take a look at what's going on.

Starting with looking at the Pug file location-info.pug in app_server/views, you can isolate the line that outputs this section:

```
small.reviewTimestamp #{review.timestamp}
```

Now you need to check the schema to see whether you changed something when defining the model. The schema for reviews is in locations.js in app_api/models and looks like the following code snippet:

```
const reviewSchema = new mongoose.Schema({
  author: String,
  rating: {
    type: Number,
    required: true,
    min: 0,
    max: 5
  },
  reviewText: String,
  createdOn: {
    type: Date,
    'default': Date.now
  }
});
```

Ah, yes; here you can see that you changed the timestamp to `createdOn`, which is a more accurate name for the path.

Updating the Pug file with this value looks like the following:

```
small.reviewTimestamp #{review.createdOn}
```

Making these changes and refreshing the page gives you figure 7.7.

Success! Of sorts. The date is now showing, but not quite in the user-readable format that you'd like to see. You should be able to fix this problem by using Pug.

Figure 7.7   Pulling the name and date directly from the returned data; the format of the date isn't user friendly.

7.3.6 Formatting dates using a Pug mixin

Back when you were setting up the views, you used a Pug mixin to output the rating stars based on the rating number provided. In Pug, mixins are like functions; you can send parameters when you call them, run some JavaScript code if you want, and have them generate some output.

Formatting dates could be useful in several places, so create a mixin to do the job. Your `outputRating` mixin is in the shared HTMLfunctions.pug file in app_server/views/_includes. Add a new mixin called `formatDate` to that file.

In this mixin, you'll largely use JavaScript to convert the date from the long ISO format to the more readable format *Day Month Year* (such as *10 May 2017*). The ISO date object arrives here as a string, so the first thing to do is convert it to a JavaScript date object. When that's done, you'll be able to use various JavaScript date methods to access the various parts of the date.

The following listing shows how to do this in a mixin. Remember that lines of JavaScript in a Pug file must be prefixed by a dash.

Listing 7.17 Creating a Jade mixin to format the dates

Converts the date provided
from a string to a date object

Sets up an array of values for
the names of the months

```
mixin formatDate(dateString)
  - const date = new Date(dateString);
  - const monthNames = ['January', 'February', 'March', 'April',
  'May', 'June', 'July', 'August', 'September', 'October', 'November',
  'December'];
  - const d = date.getDate();
  - const m = monthNames[date.getMonth()];
  - const y = date.getFullYear();
  - const output = `${d} ${m}
    ${y}`;
  =output
```

Uses JavaScript data methods to extract
and convert the required parts of the date

Puts the parts back together in the
desired format and renders output

Now, that mixin takes a date and processes it to output in the format that you want. As the mixin renders the output, you simply need to call it from the correct place in the code. The following code demonstrates this call, again based on the same two isolated lines from the whole template:

```
span.reviewAuthor #{review.author.displayName}
small.reviewTimestamp
  +formatDate(review.createdOn)
```

Calls the mixin from its own line,
passing the creation date of the
review (make sure that the new
line is correctly indented)

The call to the mixin should be placed on a new line, so you'll need to remember to take care with the indentation; the date should be nested inside the <small> tag. Now the Details page is complete and looking like it should, as shown in figure 7.8.

Excellent; that's exactly what you wanted. If the URL contains an ID that's found in the database, the page displays nicely. But what happens if the ID is wrong or isn't found in the database?

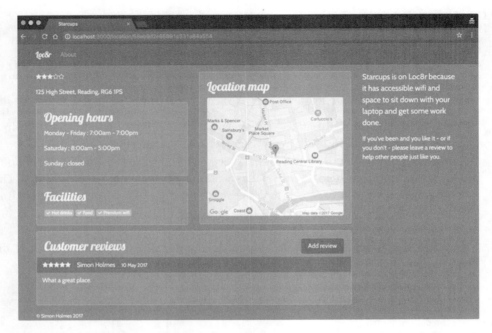

Figure 7.8   The complete Details page. The ID of the location is passed from the URL to the API, and the API retrieves the data and passes it back to the page to be formatted and rendered correctly.

7.3.7   Creating status-specific error pages

If the ID from the URL isn't found in the database, the API returns a 404 error. This error originates from the URL in the browser, so the browser should also return a 404; the data for the ID wasn't found, so in essence, the page can't be found.

Using techniques you've already seen in this chapter, you can easily catch when the API returns a 404 status by using `response.statusCode` in the `request` callback. You don't want to deal with it inside the callback, so you'll pass the flow into a new function that you can call: `showError()`.

CATCHING ALL ERROR CODES

Even better than trapping for a 404 response, you can flip it on its head and look for any response from the API that isn't a 200 success response. You can pass the status code to the `showError()` function and let it figure out what to do. To enable the `showError()` function to keep control, you'll also pass through the `req` and `res` objects.

The following listing shows how to update the `request` callback to render the Details page for successful API calls and route all other errors to the catchall function `showError()`.

Listing 7.18   Trapping any errors caused by the API not returning a 200 status

```
request(
  requestOptions,
  (err, {statusCode}, body) => {
    let data = body;
    if (statusCode === 200) {
      data.coords = {
        lng : body.coords[0],
        lat : body.coords[1]
      };
      renderDetailPage(req, res, data);
    } else {
      showError(req, res, statusCode);
    }
  }
);
```

You're interested only in the statusCode, so get only that.

Checks a for successful response from the API

Continues with rendering the page if the check was successful

If check wasn't successful, passes the error to the showError() function.

Great; now you'll try to render the Details page if you have something from the API to display. What shall you do with the errors? Well, for now you want to send a message to the users, letting them know that there's a problem.

DISPLAYING ERROR MESSAGES

You don't want to do anything fancy here—only let users know that something is going on and give them some indication of what it is. You already have a generic Pug template that's suitable for this purpose; it's called generic-text.pug and expects only a title and some content. That will do you.

If you wanted to, you could create a unique page and layout for each type of error, but for now, you're satisfied with catching it and letting the user know. As well as letting the user know, you should let the browser know by returning the appropriate status code when the page is displayed.

The following listing shows what the showError() function looks like, accepting a status parameter that, as well as being passed through as the response status code, is used to define the title and content of the page. Here, you have a specific message for a 404 page and a generic message for any other errors that are passed.

Listing 7.19   Creating an error-handling function for API status codes that aren't 200

```
const showError = (req, res, status) => {
  let title = '';
  let content = '';
  if (status === 404) {
    title = '404, page not found';
    content = 'Oh dear. Looks like you can\'t find this page. Sorry.';
  } else {
    title = `${status}, something's gone wrong`;
    content = 'Something, somewhere, has gone just a little bit wrong.';
  }
  res.status(status);
```

If the status passed through is 404, sets the title and content for the page

Otherwise, sets a generic catchall message

Uses the status parameter to set a response status

```
res.render('generic-text', {
    title,
    content
  });
};
```

Sends data to the view
to be compiled and
sent to the browser

This function can be reused from any of the controllers where you might find it useful. It's also built in such a way that you can easily add new, specific error messages for particular codes if you want to.

You can test the 404 error page by slightly changing the location ID in the URL, and you should see something like figure 7.9.

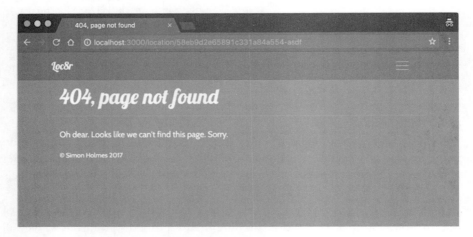

Figure 7.9   The 404 error page displayed when the location ID in the URL isn't found in the database by the API

That brings you to the end of the Details page. You can successfully display all the information from the database for a given location and also display a 404 message to the visitor if the location can't be found.

Following through the user journey, your next and final task is adding the ability to add reviews.

7.4   *Adding data to the database via the API: add Loc8r reviews*

In this section, you'll see how to take form data submitted by a user, process it, and post it to the API. Reviews are added to Loc8r by clicking the Add Review button on a location's Details page, filling in a form, and submitting it. That's the plan, anyway. You currently have the views to do this but not the underlying functionality to make it happen. You need to change that situation right now.

Here's a list of the things you'll do:

1 Make the review form aware of which location the review will be for.
2 Create a route for the form to POST to.
3 Send the new review data to the API.
4 Show the new review in place on the Details page.

Note that at this stage in development, you don't have an authentication method in place, so you have no concept of user accounts.

7.4.1 Setting up the routing and views

The first item on your list involves getting the ID of the location to the Add Review page in such a way that you can use it when the form is submitted. After all, this ID is the unique identifier that the API needs to add a review. The best approach for getting the ID to the page is to contain it in the URL, as you did for the Details page itself.

DEFINING THE TWO REVIEW ROUTES

Getting the location ID into the URL means changing the route of the Add Review page to add a locationid parameter. While you're at it, you can deal with the second item on the list and create a route for the form to POST to. Ideally, this route should have the same path as the review form and be associated with a different request method and a different controller. To do this, you'll update to the router.route syntax, making it clear that you're using a single route with two different methods.

The following code snippet shows how you can update the routes in index.js in the app_server/routes folder:

```
router.get('/', ctrlLocations.homelist);
router.get('/location/:locationid', ctrlLocations.locationInfo);
router
  .route('/location/:locationid/review/new')
  .get(ctrlLocations.addReview)
  .post(ctrlLocations.doAddReview);
```

Updates to router.route syntax, and inserts a locationid parameter into the review form route

Creates a new route on the same URL, but using the POST method and referencing a different controller

Those routes are all you'll need for this section, but restarting the application will fail because the POST route references a controller that doesn't exist. You can fix this problem by adding a placeholder function to the controller file. Add the following code snippet to locations.js in app_server/controllers, and add doAddReview to the exports list at the bottom. Then the application will fire up successfully once again:

```
const doAddReview = (req, res) => {
};
```

If you click through to the Add Review page, however, you'll get an error. Oh, yes—you need to update the link to the Add Review page from the Details page.

FIXING THE LOCATION DETAIL VIEW

You need to add the location ID to the href specified in the Add Review button on the Details page. The controller for this page passes through the full data object as returned from the API, which, along with the rest of the data, contains the _id field. This data object is called location when passed to the view.

The following code snippet shows a single line from the location-info.pug template in the app_server/views folder. This line shows how to add the location ID to the link for the Add Review button; note that you now use a JavaScript template string for the href value:

```
a.btn.btn-primary.float-right(href=`/location/${location._id}
➥/review/new`) Add review
```

With the template updated and saved, you can click through to a review form for each individual location. A couple of issues still exist, however: the form doesn't post anywhere, and the name of the location is hardcoded into the controller.

UPDATING THE REVIEW FORM VIEW

Next, you want to make sure that the form posts to the correct URL. When the form is submitted now, it makes a GET request to the /location URL:

```
form(action="/location", method="get", role="form")
```

This line is taken from the location-review-form.pug file in app_server/views. The /location path is no longer valid in your application, and you also want to use a POST request instead of a GET request. The URL you want to post the form to is the same as the URL for the Add Review: /location/:locationid/reviews/new.

An easy way to achieve this task is to set the action of the form to be an empty string and set the method to be post, as shown here:

```
form(action="", method="post", role="form")
```

Now, when the form is submitted, it makes a POST request to the URL of the current page.

CREATING A NAMED FUNCTION FOR RENDERING THE ADD REVIEW PAGE

As with the other pages, you'll move the rendering of the page to a separate named function. This step allows you the separation of concerns you're looking for when coding and prepares you for the next steps.

The following listing shows how this should look in the code. Make your changes in locations.js in app_server/controllers.

Listing 7.20 Creating a render function for the addReview controller body

```
const renderReviewForm = (req, res) => {        ⟵──┐   Creates the new function
  res.render('location-review-form', {                renderReviewForm(), and
    title: 'Review Starcups on Loc8r',               moves the contents of the
    pageHeader: { title: 'Review Starcups' }         addReview controller into it
  });
};
```

```
/* GET 'Add review' page */
const addReview = (req, res) => {
  renderReviewForm(req, res);
};
```

Calls the new function from within the addReview controller, passing the same parameters

This code might look a little odd—creating a named function and then having the call to that function be the only thing in the controller—but it will be useful in a moment.

GETTING THE LOCATION DETAIL

On the Add Review page, you want to display the name of the location to retain a sense of context for the user. You want to hit the API again, give it the ID of the location, and get the information back to the controller and into the view. You've done this for the Details page, albeit with a different controller. If you approach this task correctly, you shouldn't have to write much new code.

Rather than duplicate code and have to maintain two pieces, you'll go for a DRY (don't repeat yourself) approach. The Details page and the Add Review page both want to call the API to get the location information and then do something with it. So why not create a new function that does this? You've already got most of the code in the `locationInfo` controller; you need to change how it calls the final function. Instead of calling the `renderDetailPage()` explicitly, you'll make it a callback.

You'll have a new function called `getLocationInfo()` that makes the API request. Following a successful request, this function should invoke whatever callback function was passed. The `locationInfo` controller calls this function, passing a callback function that calls the `renderDetailPage()` function. Similarly, the `addReview` controller can call this new function, passing it the `renderReviewForm()` function in the callback.

These changes give you one function making API calls that will have different outcomes depending on the callback function sent. The following listing shows everything in place.

Listing 7.21 Creating a new reusable function to get location information

```
const getLocationInfo = (req, res, callback) => {
  const path = `/api/locations/${req.params.locationid}`;
  const requestOptions = {
    url : `${apiOptions.server}${path}`,
    method : 'GET',
    json : {}
  };
  request(
    requestOptions,
    (err, {statusCode}, body) => {
      let data = body;
      if (statusCode === 200) {
        data.coords = {
          lng : body.coords[0],
          lat : body.coords[1]
        };
```

New function getLocationInfo() accepts a callback as a third parameter and contains all code that used to be in locationInfo controller

```
            callback(req, res, data);
        } else {
            showError(req, res, statusCode);
        }
    }
  );
};

const locationInfo = (req, res) => {
  getLocationInfo(req, res,
    (req, res, responseData) => renderDetailPage(req, res, responseData)
  );
};

const addReview = (req, res) => {
  getLocationInfo(req, res,
    (req, res, responseData) => renderReviewForm(req, res, responseData)
  );
};
```

Following a successful API response, invokes callback instead of a named function

In the locationInfo controller, calls the getLocationInfo() function, passing a callback function that will call the renderDetailPage() function upon completion

Also calls getLocationInfo() from the addReview controller, but this time passes renderReviewForm() in a callback

And there you have a nice, DRY approach to the problem. It would have been easy to copy and paste the API code from one controller to another—which, if we're being honest, is absolutely fine if you're figuring out your code and what you need to do to make it work. But when you see two pieces of code doing pretty much the same thing, always ask yourself how you can make it DRY to make your code cleaner and easier to maintain.

DISPLAYING THE LOCATION DETAIL

You have one more thing to take care of. The function for rendering the form still contains hardcoded data instead of using the data from the API. A quick tweak to the function changes that situation.

Listing 7.22   Removing hardcoded data from the `renderReviewForm` function

```
const renderReviewForm = function (req, res, {name}) {
  res.render('location-review-form', {
    title: `Review ${name} on Loc8r`,
    pageHeader: { title: `Review ${name}` }
  });
};
```

Updates the renderReviewForm() function to accept a new parameter containing data, destructed to what you need

Swaps out hardcoded data for data references using template strings

The Add Review page is looking good once again, displaying the correct name based on the ID found in the URL, as shown in figure 7.10.

Figure 7.10 Add Review page pulling in the location name via the API, based on the ID contained in the URL

7.4.2 *POSTing the review data to the API*

By now, you have the Add Review page set up and ready to go, including the posting destination. You've even got the route and controller for the POST action in place. The controller, doAddReview, is an empty placeholder, though.

The plan for this controller is as follows:

1 Get the location ID from the URL to construct the API request URL.
2 Get the data posted in the form, and package it up for the API.
3 Make the API call.
4 Show the new review in place, if successful.
5 Display an error page, if not successful.

The only part of this procedure that you haven't seen yet is passing the data to the API; so far, you've passed an empty JSON object to ensure that the response is formatted as JSON. Now you'll take the form data and pass it to the API in the format it expects. You have three fields on the form and three references that the API expects. All you need to do is map one to the other. The form fields and model paths are shown in table 7.3.

Form field	API references
name	author
rating	rating
review	reviewText

Table 7.3   **Mapping the names of the form fields to the model paths expected by the API**

Turning this mapping into a JavaScript object is straightforward. Create a new object containing the variable names that the API expects, and use `req.body` to get the values from the posted form. The following code snippet shows this object in isolation, and you'll put it in the controller in just a moment:

```
const postdata = {
  author: req.body.name,
  rating: parseInt(req.body.rating, 10),
  reviewText: req.body.review
};
```

Now that you've seen how that works, you can add it to the standard pattern you've been using for these API controllers and build out the `doAddReview` controller. Remember that the status code the API returns for a successful POST operation is 201, not the 200 you've been using so far with GET requests. The following listing shows the `doAddReview` controller, using everything you've learned so far.

Listing 7.23   `doAddReview` controller used to post review data to the API

```
const doAddReview = (req, res) => {
  const locationid = req.params.locationid;              Gets location ID from
  const path = `/api/locations/${locationid}/reviews`;   the URL to construct
  const postdata = {                                     the API URL
    author: req.body.name,
    rating: parseInt(req.body.rating, 10),    Creates a data object to send to the
    reviewText: req.body.review               API, using the submitted form data
  };
  const requestOptions = {
    url: `${apiOptions.server}${path}`,       Sets the request options, including the path,
    method: 'POST',                           setting the POST method, and passing the
    json: postdata                            submitted form data into a json parameter
  };
  request(                   ◁────── Makes the request
    requestOptions,
    (err, {statusCode}, body) => {
      if (statusCode === 201) {                    Redirects to the Details page if
        res.redirect(`/location/${locationid}`);   review was added successfully,
      } else {                                     or shows an error page if the
        showError(req, res, statusCode);           API returned an error
      }
    }
  );
};
```

Figure 7.11   After filling in and submitting the review form, the review is shown in situ on the Details page.

Now you can create a review, submit it, and then see it on the Details page, as shown in figure 7.11.

Now that everything works, let's take a quick look at adding form validation.

7.5   *Protecting data integrity with data validation*

Whenever an application accepts external input and adds it to a database, you need to make sure that the data is complete and accurate—as much as you can or as much as it makes sense to. If someone adds an email address, you should check that it's a valid email format, but you can't programmatically validate that it's a *real* email address.

In this section, you'll look at the ways that you can add validation to your application to prevent people from submitting empty reviews. You can add validation in three places:

- At the schema level, using Mongoose, before the data is saved
- At the application level, before the data is posted to the API
- At the client side, before the form is submitted

You'll look at each of these places in turn and add some validation at every step.

7.5.1   *Validating at the schema level with Mongoose*

Validating the data before saving it is arguably the most important stage. This step is the final step, the one last chance to make sure that everything is as correct as it can be. This stage is particularly important when the data is exposed through an API; if you don't have control of all the applications using the API, you can't guarantee the quality of the data that you're going to get. It's important to ensure that the data is valid before saving it.

UPDATING THE SCHEMA

When you first set up the schema in chapter 5, you looked at adding some validation in Mongoose. You set the `rating` path to be required, but you also want the `author` `displayName` and `reviewText` to be required. If one of these fields is missing, a review won't make sense. Adding this to the schema is simple enough and looks like the following listing. (The schema is in locations.js in the app_api/model folder.)

Listing 7.24   Adding validation to reviews at the schema level

```
const reviewSchema = new mongoose.Schema({
  author: {
    type: String,
    required: true
  },
  rating: {
    type: Number,
    required: true,
    min: 0,
    max: 5
  },
  reviewText: {
    type: String,
    required: true
  },
  createdOn: {
    type: Date,
    'default': Date.now
  }
});
```

Makes each of these paths a required field, because if one of them is missing, a review won't make sense

createdOn doesn't need to be required, because Mongoose automatically populates it when a new review is created.

When this code is saved, you can no longer save a review without any review text. You can try, but you'll see the error page shown in figure 7.12.

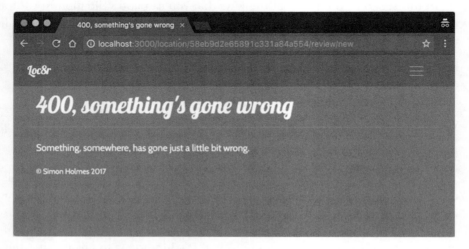

Figure 7.12   Error message shown when trying to save a review without any review text, now that the schema says it's required

On one hand, it's good that you're protecting the database, but it's not a great user experience. You should try to catch that error and let the visitor try again.

CATCHING MONGOOSE VALIDATION ERRORS

If you try to save a document with one or more required paths missing or empty, Mongoose returns an error. It does this without having to make a call to the database, because Mongoose itself holds the schema and knows what is and isn't required. The following code snippet shows an example of such an error message:

```
{
  message: 'Validation failed',
  name: 'ValidationError',
  errors: {
    'reviews.1.reviewText': {
      message: 'Path `reviewText` is required.',
      name: 'ValidatorError',
      path: 'reviewText',
      type: 'required',
      value: ''
    }
  }
}
```

In the flow of the application, this happens inside the callback from the `save` function. If you take a look at the `save` command inside the `doAddReview()` function (in app_api/controllers/reviews.js), you can see where the error bubbles up and where you set the 400 status. The following code snippet shows this, including a temporary console log statement to show the output of the error to terminal:

```
location.save((err, location) => {
  if (err) {
    console.log(err);          Mongoose validation errors are
    res                        returned through an error
      .status(400)             object following an attempted
      .json(err);             save action.
  } else {
    updateAverageRating(location._id);
    let thisReview = location.reviews[location.reviews.length - 1];
    res
      .status(201)
        .json(thisReview);
  }
});
```

Your API returns this message as the response body, alongside the 400 status. You can look for this information in your application by looking at the response body when the API returns a 400 status.

The place to do this is in the app_server—in the `doAddReview()` function in controllers/locations.js, to be precise. When you've caught a validation error, you want to let the user try again by redirecting to the Add Review page. So that the page knows that an attempt has been made, you can pass a flag in the query string.

The following listing shows this code in place, inside the request statement call-back for the `doAddReview()` function.

Listing 7.25   Trapping validation errors returned by the API

```
request(
  requestOptions,
  (err, {statusCode},{name}) => {
    if (statusCode === 201) {
      res.redirect(`/location/${locationid}`);
    } else if (statusCode === 400
         && name && name === 'ValidationError') {
      res.redirect(`/location/${locationid}/review/new?err=val`);
    } else {
      console.log(body);
      showError(req, res, statusCode);
    }
  }
);
```

> Adds a check to see whether the status is 400, the body has a name, and that name is ValidationError

> If true, redirects to the review form, passing an error flag in a query string

Now when the API returns a validation error, you can catch it and send the user back to the form to try again. Passing a value in the query string means that you can look for it in the controller that displays the review form and send a message to the view to alert the user to the problem.

DISPLAYING AN ERROR MESSAGE IN THE BROWSER

To display an error message in the view, you need to send a variable to the view if you see the `err` parameter passed in the query string. The `renderReviewForm()` function is responsible for passing variables into the view. When it's called, it's also passed the `req` object, which contains the `query` object, making it easy to pass the `err` parameter, when it exists. The following listing highlights the simple change required to make this happen.

Listing 7.26   Updating the controller to pass an error string from query object to view

```
const renderReviewForm = (req, res,{name}) => {
  res.render('location-review-form', {
    title: `Review ${name} on Loc8r`,
    pageHeader: { title: `Review ${name}` },
    error: req.query.err
  });
};
```

> Sends a new error variable to the view, passing the view any existing query parameters

The `query` object is always part of the `req` object, regardless of whether it has any content. This is why you don't need to error-trap this object to check whether it exists; if the `err` parameter isn't found, it returns `undefined`.

All that remains is to do something with this information in the view, letting the user know what the problem is. You'll show a message to the user at the top of the form, if a validation error was bubbled up. To give this message some style and presence on the page, you'll use a Bootstrap alert component: a `div` with some relevant classes and attributes. The following code snippet shows the two lines to add to the `location-review-form` view:

```
form(action="", method="post", role="form")
  - if (error == "val")
    .alert.alert-danger(role="alert") All fields required, please try again
```

Now when the API returns a validation error, you catch it and display a message to the user. Figure 7.13 shows how this message looks.

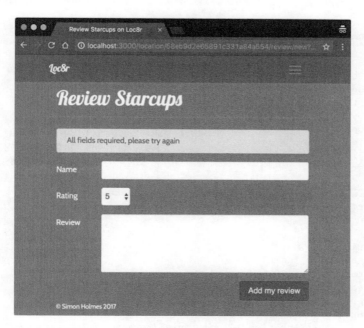

Figure 7.13   The validation error message in the browser, the result of a process kicked off by Mongoose's catching the error and returning it

This type of validation at the API level is important and generally a great place to start, because it protects a database against inconsistent or incomplete data, regardless of the origin. But the experience for end users isn't always best; they have to submit the form, and the form request makes a round trip to the API before the page reloads with an error. There's clearly room for improvement, and the first step is performing some validation at the application level before the data is passed to the API.

7.5.2 Validating at the application level with Node and Express

Validation at the schema level is the backstop, the final line of defense in front of a database. An application shouldn't rely solely on this backstop, however, and you should try to prevent unnecessary calls to the API, reducing overhead and speeding thing up for the user. One way is to add validation at the application level, checking the submitted data before sending it to the API.

In your application, the validation required for a review is simple; you can add some simple checks to ensure that each of the fields has a value. If this test fails, you redirect the user back to the form, adding the same query string error flag as before. If the validation checks are successful, you allow the controller to continue to the request method. The following listing shows the additions needed in the doAddReview controller in locations.js in the app_server/controllers folder.

Listing 7.27   Adding some simple validation to an Express controller

```
const doAddReview = (req, res) => {
  const locationid = req.params.locationid;
  const path = `/api/locations/${locationid}/reviews`;
  const postdata = {
    author: req.body.name,
    rating: parseInt(req.body.rating, 10),
    reviewText: req.body.review
  };
  const requestOptions = {
    url: apiOptions.server + path,
    method: 'POST',
    json: postdata
  };
  if (!postdata.author || !postdata.rating || !postdata.reviewText) {
    res.redirect(`/location/${locationid}/review/new?err=val`);
  } else {
    request(
      requestOptions,
      (err, {statusCode}, {name}) => {
        if (statusCode === 201) {
          res.redirect(`/location/${locationid}`);
        } else if (statusCode === 400 && name
          && name === 'ValidationError' ) {
          res.redirect(`/location/${locationid}/review/new?err=val`);
        } else {
          showError(req, res, statusCode);
        }
      }
    );
  }
};
```

> **If any of three required data fields is falsey, redirects to the Add Review page, appending the query string used to display the error message**

> **Otherwise, continues as before**

The outcome is the same as before: if the review text is missing, the user is shown the error message on the Add Review page. The user doesn't know that you're no longer posting data to the API, but it's one less round trip and so should be a faster experience. But you can make it even faster with the third tier of validation: browser-based validation.

7.5.3   *Validating in the browser with jQuery*

As application-level validation speeds things up by not requiring a call to the API, client-side validation in the browser can speed things up by catching an error before the form is submitted to the application, by removing yet another call. Catching an error at this point keeps the user on the same page.

To get JavaScript running in the browser, you need to place it in the public folder in the application. Express treats the contents of this folder as static files to be downloaded to the browser instead of run on the server. If you don't have a folder called javascripts in your public folder, create one now. Inside this folder, create a new file called validation.js.

WRITING THE JQUERY VALIDATION

Inside this new validation.js file, put a jQuery function that does the following:

- Listens for the submit event of the review form
- Checks to see that all the required fields have a value
- If one is empty, shows an error message like the ones you've used in the other types of validation and prevents the form from submitting

The following listing shows the code to do this. We won't dive into the semantics of jQuery here, assuming you have some familiarity with it or a similar library.

> **Listing 7.28 Creating a jQuery form validation function**

Listens for the submit event of the review form

```
$('#addReview').submit(function (e) {                          Checks for any
  $('.alert.alert-danger').hide();                             missing values
  if (!$('input#name').val() || !$('select#rating').val() ||
  !$('textarea#review').val()) {                    ◁────────────────
    if ($('.alert.alert-danger').length) {
      $('.alert.alert-danger').show();
    } else {
      $(this).prepend('<div role="alert" class="alert alert-danger">
      All fields required, please try again</div>');
    }
  }
  return false;   ◁──┐  Prevents the form from        Shows or injects an error
}                      submitting if a value is        message into the page if
});                    missing                         a value is missing
```

You need to ensure that the form has an ID of addReview set so that the jQuery can listen for the correct event. You also need to add this script to the page so that the browser can run it.

ADDING THE JQUERY TO THE PAGE

You'll include this jQuery file at the end of the body, along with the other client-side JavaScript files. These files are set in the layout.pug view in app_server/views, at the bottom. Add a new line below the others pointing to the new file:

```
script(src='/bootstrap/js/bootstrap.min.js')
script(src='/javascripts/validation.js')
```

That's all there is to it. Now the form validates in the browser without the data being submitted anywhere, removing a page reload and any associated calls to the server.

> **TIP**   Client-side validation may seem to be all that you need, but the other types are vital to the robustness of an application. JavaScript can be turned off in the browser, removing the ability to run this validation, or the validation could be bypassed, with data being posted directly to either the form action URL or the API endpoint.

In chapter 8, you'll introduce Angular into the mix and start playing with some interactive front-end components on top of the Express application.

Summary

In this chapter, you learned

- How to use the `request` module to make API calls from Express and how to make `POST` and `GET` requests to API endpoints
- Some ways of separating concerns by keeping rendering functions away from the API request logic
- How to apply a simple pattern to the API logic in each controller
- The application of data validation in three places in the architecture and when and why to use each

Part 3

Adding a dynamic front end with Angular

Angular is one of the most exciting technologies of our time and is a core part of the MEAN stack with proven stability and longevity. You've done a lot of work so far with Express, which is the server-side framework. Angular is the client-side framework that enables you to build entire applications that run in the browser.

You'll get to know Angular and TypeScript (like JavaScript, a bit different but *good* different) in chapter 8, seeing what all the fuss is about and getting into the particular syntax semantics and jargon associated with it. Angular can have a steep learning curve, but it doesn't have to. As you get started with Angular and TypeScript in chapter 8, you'll see how to use them to build a component for an existing web page, including calling your REST API to get data.

Chapters 9 and 10 focus on how to use Angular to build a single-page application (SPA). Building on what you learned in chapter 8, you re-create Loc8r as an SPA. You'll focus on best practices throughout, learning how to build a modular application that's easily maintainable with components that can easily be reused. By the end of part 3, you'll have a fully functioning SPA interacting with your REST API to create and read data.

Creating an Angular
application with TypeScript

This chapter covers

- Using the Angular CLI and creating an Angular application
- Understanding the basics of TypeScript
- Creating and using Angular components
- Getting data from an API and binding data to HTML templates
- Building an Angular application for production

Here it comes. It's time to take a look at the final part of the MEAN stack: Angular! When you're getting started with Angular and TypeScript, it can feel like a different language at times, but TypeScript is a superset of JavaScript, so it's JavaScript with some additional bits and pieces. TypeScript is the preferred language for creating Angular applications. We'll cover what we need to as we go, and you'll be fairly comfortable with it by the end of this chapter.

To get into it all, you'll rebuild the list of locations shown in the homepage as an Angular application. You'll embed this little application in the Express-driven homepage, replacing the list delivered by Express, to serve two purposes:

- You'll work with some of the building blocks of Angular without getting overwhelmed.
- You'll see how to use Angular to create a single component within an existing page or application.

Figure 8.1 shows where you are in the overall plan, adding Angular to the front end of the existing Express application.

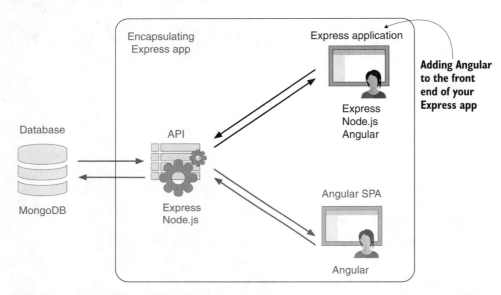

Figure 8.1   This chapter focuses on adding Angular to the front end of the existing Express application

The approach taken in this chapter is what you'd do if you wanted to enhance a page, project, or application with a bit of Angular. Building a full application entirely in Angular is coming up in chapters 9 and 10 and adds to what you'll learn in this chapter.

8.1   *Getting up and running with Angular*

In this section, you'll create a skeleton Angular application, look at how it's put together, and explore some of the tools that come with it to help development. If you haven't done so yet, you'll need to install the Angular command-line interface (CLI) as described in appendix A.

You'll start by using the CLI to create a new application.

8.1.1   *Using the command line to create a boilerplate Angular app*

The easiest way to create a new Angular application is to use the Angular CLI, which creates a fully functional small application and generates a good folder structure.

The base command is simple:

```
ng new your-app-name
```

Before you run the command to create your Angular app for Loc8r—which would create a new application called your-app-name with default settings in the current folder—you'll want to look at some options.

You can apply many options to this command, and you can see them by running `ng help` in the command line. The options you're interested in are the following:

- `--skipGit`, to skip the default Git initialization and first commit. By default, `ng new` initializes the folder as a new Git repository, but you don't need to do that, because you're going to create it inside an existing Git repo.
- `--skipTests`, to skip installation of some testing files. We don't cover unit tests in this book, so you don't need these extra files. See the sidebar "Testing Angular applications" as to why we don't cover this topic.
- `--directory`, to specify the folder where you want the application to be generated.
- `--defaults` forces default Angular settings to be used.

> ### Testing Angular applications
>
> Testing is an important, but really large, topic—so large, in fact, that there are many books written on the topic. (Several really good ones are published by Manning Publications.)
>
> We don't cover testing in this book due to space constraints. If you're interested in finding out more about testing Angular applications, then your first stop should be https://www.manning.com/books/testing-angular-applications.

Putting all this together, you'll use a command to create a boilerplate Angular application inside a new folder called app_public. This command installs a lot of stuff, so it'll take a little while to run, and you'll need to be online for it to work. Make sure that in terminal, you're in the root folder of your Loc8r application before running the following command:

```
$ ng new loc8r-public --skipGit=true --skipTests=true –defaults=true –
directory app_public
```

> **IMPROVEMENT** To those who are familiar with AngularJS (Angular 1.x), this is quite a change from the days of being able to download a single library file to start coding! The good news is that this new approach encourages better application architecture out of the box.

When everything is installed, the contents of your app_public folder should look like figure 8.2.

You may notice that this project has its own package.json file and node_modules folder, so it looks a lot like a Node application. The src folder is where you'll do most of your work.

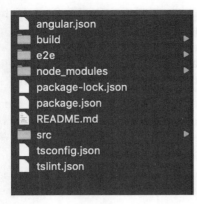

Figure 8.2   Default contents of a freshly generated Angular project

8.1.2   *Running the Angular app*

This is a fully functional Angular app, albeit a rather minimal one. Now run it, see what you've got, and take a look under the hood. To run the app, head to your app_public folder in terminal, and run the following command:

```
$ ng serve
```

When you run this command, you'll see some notifications in terminal as Angular builds the application, ending with ?wdm?: Compiled successfully. When you see this message, your app is ready to view on port 4200. To check it out, open your browser, and go to http://localhost:4200. Not much is going on here, admittedly, but if you view the source or inspect element, you should see something like figure 8.3.

Figure 8.3   The autogenerated Angular app working in the browser alongside the generated HTML

You'll see some minimal HTML and a bunch of JavaScript files being referenced. Take note of the `app-root` HTML tag, however; that's unusual and important. Remember this tag, because you'll come back to it when you look at the source files.

8.1.3 *The source code behind the application*

Angular applications are built with components, which are compiled into modules. *Component* and *module* are terms that are often used loosely to label the building blocks of an application, but in Angular, they have specific meanings. A component handles a specific piece of functionality, and a module contains one or more components working together. This default example is a simple module with one component.

Open the src folder in your editor, and you'll see several files and folders. Start at the beginning by looking at the index.html file in the src folder; it should look something like listing 8.1.

> **Listing 8.1   The default contents of the src/index.html file**

```
<!doctype html>
<html lang="en">
<head>
  <meta charset="utf-8">
  <title>Loc8rPublic</title>       ①  The title has been
  <base href="/">                        created from the
                                         application name.
  <meta name="viewport" content="width=device-width, initial-scale=1">
  <link rel="icon" type="image/x-icon" href="favicon.ico">
</head>
<body>
  <app-root></app-root>        ◁        The only tag in the
</body>                              ②  body is the app-root.
</html>
```

There's not a huge amount here aside from some basic HTML scaffolding. You can see that Angular has populated the `title` tag for you ①, taking the application name you specified in the terminal command (`loc8r-public`) and turning it into camelCase. Also, you see the `app-root` tag ② that you noticed in the source of the running application, but this time, no `<h1>` tag is inside it.

Dig a bit deeper and look inside the app folder (inside the src folder).

THE MAIN MODULE

Remember that we said *Angular applications are built with components, which are compiled into modules*? A good place to start investigating is in the module definition.

In src/app, you'll find a file called app.module.ts. This file is the central point of your Angular module, and it's where all of the components are brought together. At the moment, this file looks like listing 8.2.

We won't go deeply into the semantics of each part right now; we'll only give you a high-level view of what each section does. In essence, this file does the following things:

- Imports various pieces of Angular functionality that the app will use
- Imports the components that the app will use
- Describes the module by using a decorator
- Exports the module

> ### Decorators and dependency injection
>
> A *decorator* is a way that ES2015 and TypeScript provide metadata and annotations to functions, modules and classes. A common use case in Angular is to handle dependency injection, which is a way of saying, "This module or class depends on this piece of functionality to run."
>
> You can see in listing 8.2 that you import the module BrowserModule into your module. In this case, the decorator also declares the components it contains and which component should be used as the start point (bootstrap).

In this file, follow the journey of AppComponent, highlighted in bold in listing 8.2. First, it's imported from the file system (you may recognize the ./ syntax from require and Node.js) before being both declared and bootstrapped inside the module decorator. For more information on decorators, check out the sidebar "Decorators and dependency injection."

Listing 8.2 The default contents of the src/app/app.module.ts file

```
import { BrowserModule } from '@angular/platform-browser';
import { NgModule } from '@angular/core';

import { AppComponent } from './app.component';

@NgModule({
  declarations: [
    AppComponent
  ],
  imports: [
    BrowserModule,
  ],
  providers: [],
  bootstrap: [AppComponent]
})
export class AppModule { }
```

Imports various Angular modules that the application will use

Imports a component from the file system

Describes the module by using a decorator . . .

. . . including the entry point into the application

Exports the module

This is the main module, and you can see from the bootstrap line in the decorator that the entry point into the application itself is AppComponent. You can also see from the import statement where this component lives in the file system—in this case, in the same folder as this module definition. Check it out.

THE DEFAULT BOOTSTRAPPED COMPONENT

In the app_public/src/app folder, alongside the module file, you can see three app.component files:

- app.component.css
- app.component.html
- app.component.ts

These files are typical for any component. The CSS and HTML files define the styles and markup for the component, and the TS file defines the behavior in TypeScript.

The CSS file is empty, but the HTML file contains the following code:

```html
<!--The content below is only a placeholder and can be replaced.-->
<div style="text-align:center">
  <h1>
    Welcome to {{ title }}!
  </h1>
  <img width="300" alt="Angular Logo"
    ➥src="data:image/svg+xml;base64,PHN2ZyB4bWxucz0iaHR0cDovL3d3dy53My5vcmmcv
    ➥MjAwMC9zdmciIHZpZXdCb3g9IjAgMCAyNTAgMjUwIj4KICAgIDxwYXRoIGZpbGw9IiN
➥ERDAwMzEiIGQ9Ik0xMjUgMzBMMzEuOSA2My4ybDE0LjIgMTIzLjlMMTI1IDIzMGw3OC
➥45LTQzLjcgMTQuMi0xMjMuMXoiIC8+CiAgICA8cGF0aCBmaWwsPSIjQzMwMDJGIiBkP
➥SJNMTI1IDMwdjIyLjItLjFWMjMwbDc4LjktNDMuNyAxNC4yLTEyMy4xTDEyNSAzMHoi
➥IC8+CiAgICA8cGF0aCBmaWlsbD0iI0ZGRkZGRiIgZD0iTTEyNSA1Mi4xTDY2LjggMTg
➥yLjZoMjEuN2wxMS43LTI5LjJoNDkuNGwxMS43IDI5LjJoMjEuN0wxMjUgNTIuMS4xem0xNy
➥A4My4zaC0zNGwxNy00MC45IDE3IDQwLjl6IiAvPgogICDwvc3ZnPg==">
</div>
<h2>Here are some links to help you start: </h2>
<ul>
  <li>
    <h2><a target="_blank" rel="noopener"
href="https://angular.io/tutorial">
➥Tour of Heroes</a></h2>
  </li>
  <li>
    <h2><a target="_blank" rel="noopener"
href="https://github.com/angular/angular-
➥cli/wiki">CLI Documentation</a></h2>
  </li>
  <li>
    <h2><a target="_blank" rel="noopener"
href="https://blog.angular.io/">Angular
➥blog</a></h2>
  </li>
</ul>
```

This code makes some sense, as you think back to when you inspected the elements within the browser and saw some minimal HTML content. In Angular, double curly brackets are used to denote a binding between the data and the view. Here, the variable `title` is being bound, as are the contents of the <h1> tag. To see where this `title` variable is being defined, you need to look inside the component definition file, app.component.ts, which is shown in full in listing 8.3.

This component file does three main things:

- Imports what it needs from Angular
- Decorates the component, giving it the information that the app needs to run it
- Exports the component as a class

Listing 8.3   The default contents of app.component.ts

```
import { Component } from '@angular/core';          ◁──────  Imports the
                                                            Component from
@Component({                                                the Angular core
  selector: 'app-root',
  templateUrl: './app.component.html',      Decorates the
  styleUrls: ['./app.component.css']        component
})
export class AppComponent {          Exports the
  title = 'loc8r-public';            component
}                                    as a class
```

This file is simple, but the syntax is a bit alien if you're used to plain JavaScript. If you look inside it, though, you can see some interesting information, and you can see the pieces coming together.

Starting with the decorator, you can see the HTML and CSS files being referenced, but you can also see selector: 'app-root'. Ah-ha! That's the name of the tag you found in the index.html file! And when you inspected the elements, you saw that tag with an <h1> tag and some content inside, which matches your app.component.html file. Okay, it's coming together.

Next, you see the AppComponent class being exported, which you've already seen imported and bootstrapped in the module definition. Finally, you see the definition of title (you saw the binding in the HTML file for the component) and the value of loc8r-public (which you saw when running it in the browser). Note that no var, const, or let is associated with title because inside a class definition, you define *class members* as opposed to variables.

TYING IT ALL TOGETHER

Okay, you've seen a lot here, so we'll quickly recap how everything ties together:

- The component AppComponent comprises three files: TypeScript, HTML, and CSS.
- The TypeScript file is the key part of the component, defining the functionality referencing the other files and declaring which selector (HTML tag) it will bind to.
- The component TypeScript file exports the AppComponent class.
- The module file imports the AppComponent class from the component Type-Script file and declares it as the entry point into the application.
- The module file also imports various pieces of native Angular functionality.

Figure 8.4 illustrates all this.

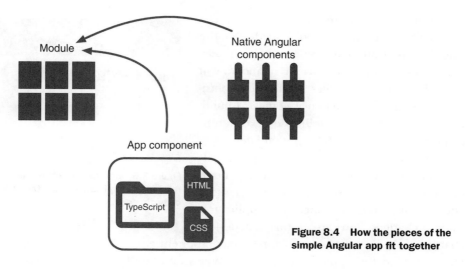

Figure 8.4   How the pieces of the simple Angular app fit together

This information gives you a good understanding of how this simple app is constructed. But when you viewed the source in the browser earlier, none of the files you looked at were referenced, and you saw a few JavaScript files. What's going on? How did the TypeScript files become JavaScript in the browser?

THE ANGULAR BUILD PROCESS

Currently, browsers don't support TypeScript—only JavaScript—and some don't fully support even ES2015 yet. But writing in TypeScript gives you more-robust code. And although this sample application is small, you can look into the future a little bit and see that if you have an application with several components, you have a lot of separate files to deal with. You don't want to have to specify all these files in your HTML source.

Angular deals with these issues by using a *build* process to take all the separate TypeScript files, convert them to vanilla JavaScript, and put them in one file called main.bundle.js. If you look at the sources in the browser, you'll be able to find `title = 'loc8r-public'` there, as shown in figure 8.5.

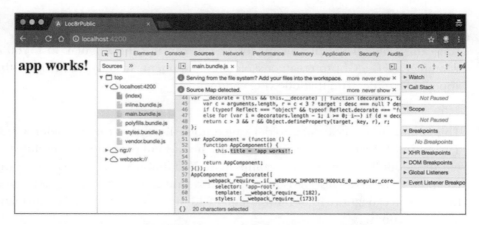

Figure 8.5   Finding the component definition inside the built JavaScript code

At the moment, you're using the `ng serve` command to compile, build, and deliver the Angular application to the browser on port 4200. This command runs in memory; you won't find these built files inside the application code anywhere. When it comes to building a final version, you'll use a different command, `ng build`. More on that later.

For development, `ng serve` is perfect. It not only gives you this browser environment, but also watches the source code for changes and rebuilds and refreshes the application when it changes. You can see this in action by

Figure 8.6 `ng serve` rebuilds and reloads the application when the source code changes.

changing `'loc8r-app'` in src/app/app.component.ts to `'I am Getting MEAN!'` Head back to the application in the browser, and you'll see that the content has changed, as shown in figure 8.6.

`ng serve` helps in the development process by eliminating the need to build and refresh manually with every change.

Now that you know enough about Angular to be dangerous, you'll make the move into building something for Loc8r. You'll uncover more about Angular and Type-Script as you go, and everything will start to become more familiar.

8.2   Working with Angular components

You'll start by building the listing section of the homepage, which you'll embed in the Express application. It's an example of how you can add some Angular functionality to an existing site, which is a common requirement on large enterprise sites where you're not likely to have complete control of everything. In the following chapters, you'll build on this foundational knowledge and see how to build a standalone single-page application (SPA) in Angular.

Begin by creating a new component.

8.2.1   Creating a new home-list component

You can create all the files manually, or you can use the Angular CLI. You'll take advantage of the CLI to create a skeleton component. In terminal, from within the app_public folder, run the following command:

```
$ ng generate component home-list
```

This command creates a new folder called home-list within the src folder. Create the TypeScript, HTML, and CSS files inside it, and also update the app.module.ts file to tell the module about the new component. You'll also see a spec.ts file in the new component folder. This file is a template for unit testing, but we're not covering it here, so you can ignore it for now. Angular CLI outputs into terminal confirmations of all these actions.

MAKING IT THE DEFAULT COMPONENT

The new home-list component will be the basis for this Angular module, so you need to make it the default component. You do this inside the app.module.ts file by changing the bootstrap value inside the module decorator from AppComponent to HomeListComponent.

AppComponent is no longer needed, so you can remove the import statement, remove it from the declarations, and even delete the files. The changes to app.module .ts are shown in the following listing.

Listing 8.4   Changing to the new component in app.module.ts

```
import { BrowserModule } from '@angular/platform-browser';
import { NgModule } from '@angular/core';

import { HomeListComponent } from './home-list/home-list.component';   ◁
                                          This line was added by the
@NgModule({                               Angular CLI; delete the
  declarations: [                         AppComponent import, as
    HomeListComponent    ◁────   Deletes  it's no longer needed.
  ],                            AppComponent from
  imports: [                    the declarations array
    BrowserModule
  ],                                      Changes AppComponent
  providers: [],                          to HomeListComponent
  bootstrap: [HomeListComponent]   ◁───   for the bootstrap value
})
```

If you run ng serve or still have it running, you'll see a blank page displayed in the browser window and several errors in the JavaScript console. These errors are a lot of red text that can seem intimidating, but the first line is helpful: it says, "The selector "app-home-list" did not match any elements."

If you think back to the original component, you'll remember that selector defines the tag on the page that the component will bind to. You've changed the component but not the tag on the page!

SETTING THE HTML TAG FOR THE COMPONENT

To ensure that you use the right tag, open the home-list.component.ts file, and check out the component decorator, which should look something like this:

```
@Component({
  selector: 'app-home-list',
  templateUrl: './home-list.component.html',
  styleUrls: ['./home-list.component.css']
})
```

Here, you can see that the selector is app-home-list, so that's what you need to use. You could change it if you want to have a different naming convention, but this will work. Open the index.html file in the src folder, and change the app-root tag to app-home-list so that it looks like this:

```
<body>
  <app-home-list></app-home-list>
</body>
```

Now check the browser—from now on, we'll assume you have ng serve running whenever you check out the browser—and see that the page has changed to say home-list works!, as shown in figure 8.7.

Now that your component is there, you can start working on making it look like it should.

8.2.2   Creating the HTML template

Using an approach similar to how you built the Express application, you'll start by creating some static HTML with hardcoded data. This way, you make sure that everything is working properly before you try to get the data from the API.

Figure 8.7   Confirmation that the new home-list component is working as the default in the application

Fortunately, you've already created the markup and the styles for this component; now, you need to transfer them to Angular.

GETTING THE HTML MARKUP

You can't copy and paste the HTML directly from the Express source code, because it's in Pug format and also is templated to use data bindings. For now, you want the full HTML, including data.

The easiest way to get the HTML is to run the Express app and go to the homepage in a browser. Different browsers have slightly different ways of getting the HTML but are similar to the following procedure in Chrome:

1 Right-click in the HTML area, and choose Inspect Element from the contextual menu.
2 Highlight the <div class="card"> element.
3 Select Copy, and then Copy Outer HTML.

Paste this into home-list.component.html, replacing the existing contents, and you should see something like the following.

Listing 8.5   Some static HTML for home-list.component.html to get started

```
<div class="card">
  <div class="card-block">
    <h4>
      <a href="/location/590d8dc7a7cb5b8e3f1bfc48">Costy</a>
      <small> 
        <i class="far fa-star"></i>
        <i class="far fa-star"></i>
        <i class="far fa-star"></i>
        <i class="far fa-star"></i>
        <i class="far fa-star"></i>
      </small>
      <span class="badge badge-pill badge-default float-
      ➥right">14.0km</span>
```

```
    </h4>
    <p class="address">High Street, Reading</p>
    <div class="facilities">
      <span class="badge badge-warning">hot drinks</span>
      <span class="badge badge-warning">food</span>
      <span class="badge badge-warning">power</span>
    </div>
  </div>
</div>
```

If you take a look in the browser when this is saved, you'll be able to see the contents, but it won't look nice. You need to add the styles.

BRINGING IN THE STYLES

Like the HTML, the CSS styles already exist in the Express application; you only need to access them. You could update the index.html file to access them directly from localhost:3000, but certain browsers give you a CORS warning if you try, because the Angular development app and the Express app are running on different ports. See the sidebar "What is CORS?" if this term is new to you.

What is CORS?

Browsers aren't allowed to access or request certain resources from a different domain, including requesting font files and making AJAX calls. This policy is known as the *same-origin policy*.

CORS (cross-origin resource sharing) is a mechanism that allows this to happen but can be set only from the server that hosts the resources. If the server denies you, there's nothing you can do from the browser side to change it.

To allow access to the resources, the server must be set to respond with a new HTTP header called `Access-Control-Allow-Origin`, with a value that matches the requesting domain.

Not all browsers give a CORS warning for a different port, but to avoid the problem altogether, grab all the styles and fonts, and drop them into the Angular app. Copy the webfonts, stylesheets, and js folders from /public folder, and paste them into the src/assets folder in app_public.

Next, reference these CSS and JS files in the index.html file (in app_public), as shown in the following listing. Notice that you're also adding the references for the bootstrap dependencies.

Listing 8.6 Adding the CSS files to index.html for the Angular app

```html
<!doctype html>
<html lang="en">
<head>
  <meta charset="utf-8">
  <title>Loc8rPublic</title>
  <base href="/">
```

```
<link rel="stylesheet" href="assets/stylesheets/bootstrap.min.css">
<link rel="stylesheet" href="assets/stylesheets/all.min.css">
<link rel="stylesheet" href="assets/stylesheets/style.css">

<meta name="viewport" content="width=device-width, initial-scale=1">
<link rel="icon" type="image/x-icon" href="favicon.ico">
</head>
<body>
  <app-home-list></app-home-list>

  <script src="https://code.jquery.com/jquery-3.3.1.slim.min.js"
➥ integrity="sha384-q8i/X+965DzO0rT7abK41JStQIAqVgRVzpbzo5smXKp4YfRv
➥ H+8abtTE1Pi6jizo" crossorigin="anonymous"></script>
  <script src="https://cdnjs.cloudflare.com/ajax/libs/popper.js/1.14.3/
➥ umd/popper.min.js" integrity="sha384-ZMP7rVo3mIykV+2+9J3UJ46
➥ jBkOWLaUAdn689aCwoqbBJiSnjAK/l8WvCWPIPm49" crossorigin="anonymous">
  </script>
  <script src="assets/javascripts/bootstrap.min.js"></script>
</body>
</html>
```

With the styles in place, you can look at the browser and see something like figure 8.8.

Figure 8.8   The Angular app displaying
static content and using the styles and fonts

NOTE   When you're building an application to sit inside another page, as you are here, the application uses the CSS of that containing page. The copies of the stylesheets you have here are for development use only, so your module looks right as you build it. When you're building an SPA, however, the final application uses the stylesheets inside the Angular app.

Now that you've got your homepage component looking about right, you're ready to move on to making the HTML smarter by moving the hardcoded data out.

8.2.3   *Moving data out of the template into the code*

As you saw earlier in this chapter, with Angular, you can define a class member inside the component code and bind it to the HTML by using curly braces. You could add this to home-list.component.ts to define the name of a location:

```
export class HomeListComponent implements OnInit {
  constructor() { }
```

```
  name = 'Costy';

  ngOnInit() { }
}
```

Then you could have this display in the HTML by replacing the location name with the binding, as shown in bold here:

```
<a href="/location/590d8dc7a7cb5b8e3f1bfc48">{{name}}</a>
```

The result would be that the browser displays the same way as before, but now part of the data is coming from the code and being bound to the template; it's no longer hardcoded HTML.

This example is good and shows you the way forward, but you need a lot more data for a location and a better way to manage it. For this purpose, you need to use a class.

DEFINING A CLASS TO GIVE STRUCTURE TO DATA

In Angular, a *class* is used to define the structure of a data object. In terms of what you've already learned, you could think of it as being similar to a simple Mongoose schema—essentially, a list of the pieces of data you expect an object to hold and the type of value.

The type is important. One thing that JavaScript doesn't have is the ability to state what type of value can be assigned to a given variable. It's easy to change the value from a string to a number to a Boolean; JavaScript doesn't care! But TypeScript does care, and it can help your code be more robust by making sure that you're always using the correct type of data for each variable. TypeScript is called *TypeScript* for a reason. See the sidebar "Types in TypeScript" for a list of available types.

Types in TypeScript

The different data types that TypeScript accepts are as follows:

- `String`—Text values.
- `number`—Any numerical value; integers and decimals are treated the same way.
- `boolean`—True or false.
- `Array`—An array of a given type of data.
- `enum`—A way of giving friendly names to a set of numeric values.
- `Any`—This data type can be anything, like how JavaScript is by default.
- `Void`—The absence of a type, typically used for functions that don't return anything.

Defining a class is a simple task, and you'll do it at the top of the home-list.component .ts file, after the initial `import` statement but before the component decorator. To define a class and make it accessible, export it; give it a name; and then list the names of the data items along with their expected data types.

Listing 8.7 Defining the `Location` class in home-list.component.ts

```
import { Component, OnInit } from '@angular/core';

export class Location {        ◁──────────────┐    Creates and exports a
  _id: string;                                 │    class called Location
  name: string;              Defines the class
  distance: number;          members and
  address: string;           their types . . .
  rating: number;
  facilities: string[];  ◁──  . . . including an array of strings
}
```

With this done, you've defined the data you expect to see in your location objects. In fact—and this is important—each object defined with the class `Location` *must* have a value for each item specified.

Now that you've defined a class, you're ready to use it.

CREATING AN INSTANCE OF THE LOCATION CLASS

When declaring variables and class members in TypeScript, you should state the type of data as well as the name, as you did when defining the properties of the `Location` class. Use the format `variableName: variableType = variableValue`.

When you added `name = 'Costy'` to the `home-list` component to try it out, for example, you should have added `name: string = 'Costy'` instead. This code would have told TypeScript that `name` should only ever be a string value.

You do the same when creating a variable or class member that's an instance of a class, but in this case stating that the type is the name of the class. Listing 8.8 shows how to add a `location` class member with the type `Location` to the `home-list` component, giving it all the values it needs. The common way to describe this is to say that *location is an instance of type Location*.

Listing 8.8 Defining a `location` with the `Location` class in home-list.component.ts

```
export class HomeListComponent implements OnInit {

  constructor() { }

  location: Location = {
    _id: '590d8dc7a7cb5b8e3f1bfc48',
    name: 'Costy',
    distance: 14.0,
    address: 'High Street, Reading',
    rating: 3,
    facilities: ['hot drinks', 'food', 'power']
  };

  ngOnInit() {
  }

}
```

A little later, you'll look at `constructor` and `ngOnInit`, seeing why they're there and what they can be used for. For now, you can ignore them and focus on the new class member you've created. That's got all the data you need for one of the homepage listings, so next, you'll use this data in the HTML.

8.2.4 *Using class member data in the HTML template*

As a quick recap, you've already seen how to bind data exposed from the component class in the HTML template by using curly braces—as in {{title}}. Now your data is a little more complex, and you need to access the properties of the class member, which you can do by using the standard JavaScript dot syntax. location.name, for example, gives you the value of the name property.

The next listing highlights some of the quick and easy changes to make to the HTML template to bring the data in.

> **Listing 8.9 Binding the first pieces of data in home-list.component.html**

```html
<div class="card">
  <div class="card-block">
    <h4>
      <a href="/location/{{location._id}}">{{location.name}}</a>
      <small> 
        <i class="far fa-star"></i>
        <i class="far fa-star"></i>
        <i class="far fa-star"></i>
        <i class="far fa-star"></i>
        <i class="far fa-star"></i>
      </small>
      <span class="badge badge-pill badge-default float-
        right">{{location.distance}}km</span>
    </h4>
    <p class="address">{{location.address}}</p>
    <div class="facilities">
      <span class="badge badge-warning">hot drinks</span>
      <span class="badge badge-warning">food</span>
      <span class="badge badge-warning">power</span>
    </div>
  </div>
</div>
```

Here, you have four single pieces of data being bound into the HTML template. The facilities and the star rating are going to take a bit more work. Start with the facilities, and loop through an array of data.

FACILITIES: LOOPING THROUGH AN ARRAY OF ITEMS IN AN HTML TEMPLATE

In the TypeScript file, you defined facilities as an array of strings, like this: ['hot drinks', 'food', 'power']. Now you'll see how Angular can help you loop through these strings and create a span tag for each facility in the array.

The secret is to use an Angular directive called *ngFor. When applied to a HTML tag and given an array of data, it loops through the array, creating an element for each entry. To access the value or properties of each item, you need to define a variable that Angular can use as it goes through the loop.

The following listing shows how to use the `*ngFor` directive to loop through the `location.facilities` array, assigning and using the variable `facility` to access the value.

> **Listing 8.10   Using `*ngFor` to loop through an array in home-list.component.html**

```
<div class="facilities">
  <span *ngFor="let facility of location.facilities" class="badge
  ➡badge-warning">{{facility}}</span>
</div>
```

The `*` is important, because without it, Angular won't perform the loop. With the `*`, it repeats the `<span>` and everything in it. Given the data facilities `['hot drinks', 'food', 'power']`, the output is

```
<span class="badge badge-warning">hot drinks</span>
<span class="badge badge-warning">food</span>
<span class="badge badge-warning">power</span>
```

Note that Angular creates some additional comments and tag attributes, which you can see in figure 8.9, along with the output in the browser.

Figure 8.9   The output of Angular looping through the array of facilities

Now that the facilities are done, you can move on to the rating stars.

RATING STARS: USING ANGULAR EXPRESSIONS TO SET CSS CLASSES

So far, the data bindings you've used have been simple: one variable name or property within the double curly braces. With Angular, you can also use simple expressions inside a binding. You could join two strings by using `{{ 'Getting ' + 'MEAN' }}` or perform a simple math operation with `{{ Math.floor(14.65) }}`.

For the rating stars, each star is defined with a Font Awesome class: `.fas.fa-star` for a solid star and `.far.fa-star` for an outline. You want to set the classes by using Angular, making sure that you have the correct number of solid and hollow stars to convey the rating.

To achieve this task, you'll use a JavaScript ternary operator, which is shorthand for a simple if / else expression. Using the first star as an example, you want to say, "If the rating is less than 1, make the star hollow; otherwise, make it solid." Example code:

```
if (location.rating < 1) {
  return 'far';
} else {
  return 'fas';
}
```

Translated into a ternary operator, the same expression looks like this:

```
{{ location.rating < 1 ? 'far' : 'fas' }}
```

Flowing this logic through into the <i> tags that make up the rating stars and putting the expressions into Angular bindings results in something that looks like the next listing. Note that each expression has a different number to show the correct stars and that you're always outputting fa-star, so you've taken it out of the expression.

Listing 8.11 Binding the ternary expressions to generate ratings-stars classes

```
<small> 
  <i class="fa{{ location.rating < 1 ? 'r' : 's' }} fa-star"></i>
  <i class="fa{{ location.rating < 2 ? 'r' : 's' }} fa-star"></i>
  <i class="fa{{ location.rating < 3 ? 'r' : 's' }} fa-star"></i>
  <i class="fa{{ location.rating < 4 ? 'r' : 's' }} fa-star"></i>
  <i class="fa{{ location.rating < 5 ? 'r' : 's' }} fa-star"></i>
</small>
```

You can validate that this code is working correctly in the browser, and you'll see something like figure 8.10.

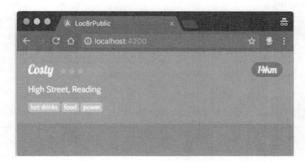

Figure 8.10 Showing the rating stars correctly, using Angular expression bindings to generate the correct class

Looking good! You have one more piece of data to deal with: the distance.

FORMATTING DATA USING PIPES

Angular gives you a way to format data within the binding, using what are known as *pipes*. For those familiar with AngularJS, pipes used to be called *filters*. Angular has several built-in pipes, including date and currency formatting, as well as uppercase, lowercase, and title-case string transformations.

You apply pipes inside a binding by adding the pipe character (|) after the variable or expression to be bound, followed by the name of the pipe. If you want to display the address of a location in uppercase, for example, you could add the uppercase binding like this:

```
<p class="address">{{location.address | uppercase}}</p>
```

You don't want to do that, but you could if you wanted to!

A pipe that can be useful for debugging is the JSON pipe, which turns a JSON object into a string so that it can be displayed in the browser. If you aren't sure what data is coming through in the `location` object, you could temporarily bind to it somewhere in the HTML and add the JSON pipe.

Some pipes can take options to define how they work. Take the currency pipe, for example. You can apply the currency pipe without any options, like this:

```
{{ 12.3485 | currency }}
```

This pipe assumes a default currency of US dollars and rounds the digit up to the nearest cent. In this example, the output would be `USD12.35`.

You can apply options to this pipe to change the currency and display the symbol instead of the currency code. Pipe options are specified directly after the pipe name, separated by colons. The order of the options is important. The first option for the currency pipe is the currency code itself, to change the currency; the second option is a Boolean to state whether to display the symbol.

If you wanted to display the currency as Euros, for example, and show the symbol instead of the code, you could use the pipe like this:

```
{{ 12.3485 | currency:'EUR':true }}
```

This pipe would output ?12.35.

That's how pipes work, and you'll work with some other default pipes as you build the Loc8r application. Now you need to format the distance into meters or kilometers, and for that purpose, you need to create a custom pipe.

DISTANCES: CREATING A CUSTOM PIPE

Before you create a new pipe to format the distance, make sure the data you're passing it reflects what you'll get from the API. In your current mocked-up data, you've got `14.0` so that the distance number displays nicely. But the API returns the distance in meters, so update the distance in home-list.component.ts to reflect this fact—`14000.1234`, for example.

To create the boilerplate files for a custom pipe, you can use the Angular CLI. In terminal, from the app_public folder, run the following command:

```
ng generate pipe distance
```

This command generates two new files—distance.pipe.ts and distance.pipe.spec.ts—in the src/app folder. The CLI adds the import to the app.module.ts file. If you want to move your pipe files somewhere else, such as into a subfolder, you'd have to update app.module.ts to say where they were moved. Leave them where they are for now.

The boilerplate pipe file, distance.pipe.ts, looks like this:

```
import { Pipe, PipeTransform } from '@angular/core';

@Pipe({
  name: 'distance'
})
export class DistancePipe implements PipeTransform {

  transform(value: any, args?: any): any {
    return null;
  }

}
```

This structure should be starting to look familiar. You've got the imports at the top, followed by the decorator, with the export class at the end. It's the contents of the class that you're interested in here—in particular, that transform function.

At first glance, this code looks a bit odd and somewhat complicated, with all the colons and any all over the place. But this code is TypeScript doing what it does: defining the types for variables. The contents of the parentheses (value: any, args?: any) is saying that the function *accepts* a parameter value of any type and other arguments of any type. The third : any, after the parentheses, is defining the type of the *return* value of the function.

You want to change these, as your distance function will accept a number and return a string. To do so, update the transform function like this:

```
transform(distance: number): string {
  return null;
}
```

Note that you've changed the name of the parameter to distance. You've already written the code to format the distance in Node, so you can copy it from /app_server/controllers/locations.js and paste it here. You want the isNumeric helper along with the contents of the formatDistance function. When that's done, the transform function looks like the following.

Listing 8.12 Creating the distance format pipe in distance.pipe.ts

```
transform(distance: number): string {
  const isNumeric = function (n) {
    return !isNaN(parseFloat(n)) && isFinite(n);
  };

  if (distance && isNumeric(distance)) {
    let thisDistance = '0';
    let unit = 'm';
    if (distance > 1000) {
      thisDistance = (distance / 1000).toFixed(1);
      unit = 'km';
    } else {
      thisDistance = Math.floor(distance).toString();
    }
```

```
    return thisDistance + unit;
  } else {
    return '?';
  }
}
```

Note that all the code, including the helper function, is inside the `transform` function. All that's left now is to update the binding to use your new pipe and remove the km from the template. The following snippet shows the updated binding from home-list.component.html:

```
<span class="badge badge-pill badge-default float-
right">{{location.distance | distance}}</span>
```

You can also check this out in the browser (see figure 8.11).

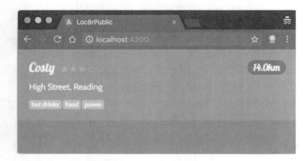

Figure 8.11   Using the Angular pipe to format the distance supplied in meters

Play around with the data in the component definition, and test that it displays as you think it should. This looks good, and you've got all the data bindings set with all the data being supplied by the component definition. This is a single item, however, and your API will return an array of multiple items; it is a list, after all! In the next section, you'll update it to work as a list.

WORKING WITH MULTIPLE INSTANCES OF A CLASS

The data for your single location is defined as `location` of type `Location`. Don't read that out loud! The construct, without data, looks like this:

```
location: Location = {};
```

When you get the data from the API, however, this will be an array, so you need to define an array of objects of type `Location`. The way to do this is to add square brackets after the class name so that it looks like this construct:

```
locations: Location[] = [{},{}];
```

If you take this approach (note that you change the member name to the plural `locations`, as you're dealing with an array) and update your `home-list` component to contain two locations, the result looks like the following.

Listing 8.13   Changing the locations instantiation to an array in home-list.component.ts

```
locations: Location[] = [{
  _id: '590d8dc7a7cb5b8e3f1bfc48',
  name: 'Costy',
  distance: 14000.1234,
  address: 'High Street, Reading',
  rating: 3,
  facilities: ['hot drinks', 'food', 'power']
}, {
  _id: '590d8dc7a7cb5b8e3f1bfc48',
  name: 'Starcups',
  distance: 120.542,
  address: 'High Street, Reading',
  rating: 5,
  facilities: ['wifi', 'food', 'hot drinks']
}];
```

Having renamed location to locations and changed the type to an array, you'll need to update the HTML template. You've already seen how to loop through an array by using *ngFor, and this process is no different. In fact, all you need to do is add an *ngFor attribute to the outermost div of a single location—the one with the class of card. It looks like this:

```
<div class="card" *ngFor="let location of locations">
```

By defining the instance name location, you don't need to change any of the data bindings inside the template, because that's what you were already using.

Now you have multiple items in your list, as shown in figure 8.12. This is looking good and working well. The next step is removing the hardcoded data entirely and calling the API instead.

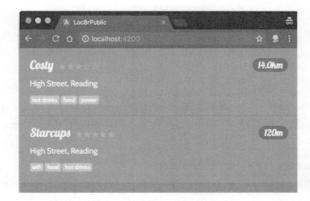

Figure 8.12   Updating the component to display multiple locations in a list

8.3 *Getting data from an API*

In this section, you'll see how to call an API from an Angular application to get data. When you've got the data, you'll display it instead of the hardcoded data you currently have.

To interact with an API, you need to use another building block of Angular applications: a *service*. A service works in the background and isn't directly connected to the user interface, like everything you've seen so far.

8.3.1 *Creating a data service*

You create a service in the same way that you've created components and pipes so far: by using the Angular CLI. You use the same `ng generate` command as before, this time followed by the options `service` and `service name`. In the app_public folder, run the following command in terminal:

```
$ ng generate service loc8r-data
```

This command generates the files for a new service called `loc8r-data` in the app/src folder. Terminal confirms the creation of the files.

Services are generated with a `providedIn` value passed to the `Injectable` decorator, which defaults to `'root'`. It takes the place of explicitly listing services in the providers array in your application root module, and is suitable for your purposes, so leave the default value as is.

Before you worry about including it, look at the boilerplate code and build it out. The code layout should look familiar by now: imports followed by a decorator followed by the exported class:

```
import { Injectable } from '@angular/core';

@Injectable({
  providedIn: 'root'
})
export class Loc8rDataService {

  constructor() { }

}
```

This boilerplate is sparse, which isn't surprising, because services can be used for many things besides requesting data from APIs. Get started by giving the service some of the things it needs.

ENABLING HTTP REQUESTS AND PROMISE HANDLING IN A SERVICE

In Angular, HTTP requests run asynchronously and return Observables, but you want to wait until the data is complete before working with it, so you'll convert them to Promises. For a quick explanation, see the sidebar "Observables and Promises."

> ## Observables and Promises
>
> Observables and Promises are great ways of handling asynchronous requests. Observables return chunks of data in a stream, whereas Promises return complete sets of data. Angular includes the RxJS library for working with observables, including converting them into Promises.
>
> There's much more to RxJS and Observables than we can cover here—enough for a whole book, in fact. Check out *RxJS in Action,* by Luis Atencio and Paul P. Daniels, to learn more (https://www.manning.com/books/rxjs-in-action).

This doesn't mean that you can't, or shouldn't, use Observables—only that you aren't in the sample application. If you want to see how to use Observables within the Loc8r application, check out appendix C.

To set up the service to make HTTP requests and return Promises, you need to inject the HTTP service into your service. You import the HTTP service by updating the top of the loc8r-data.service.ts file like this:

```
import { Injectable } from '@angular/core';
import { HttpClient, HttpHeaders } from '@angular/common/http';
```

The second step is injecting the `HTTPClient` service into your service so you can use it and call the HTTP service methods. To do this, you use the constructor part of the boilerplate code. A class constructor defines the parameters that are provided when the class is instantiated. Angular uses this to manage dependency injection, telling the class which other services or components it needs to run.

Injecting the service is simple: you define the parameter name and its type. You can also state whether the service is public or private—that is, whether it will be accessible from outside the class or kept within it. Private is the most common option.

You inject `http` of type `HttpClient`, and keep it private by updating the constructor in loc8r-data.service.ts to look like this:

```
constructor(private http: HttpClient) { }
```

Finally, you need to ensure that the `HttpClientModule` is imported and available to your application. Do this by adding the following import to your app.module.ts file:

```
import { HttpClientModule } from '@angular/common/http';
```

In the same file, add the module's name to the `imports` array in the `@NgModule` decorator, like so:

```
@NgModule({
  declarations: [
    HomeListComponent,
    DistancePipe
  ],
  imports: [
    BrowserModule,
    HttpClientModule
  ],
```

```
  providers: [],
  bootstrap: [HomeListComponent]
})
```

With those small updates, your data service can make HTTP requests and return Promises.

CREATING THE METHOD TO GET DATA

Your service needs a public method exposed so the component can call it. At this point, the method doesn't need to accept any parameters but returns a Promise containing an array of locations.

Inside the `Loc8rDataService` class, you want to define a method like this:

```
public getLocations(): Promise<Location[]> {
  // Your code will go here
}
```

This is good except that your service doesn't know what `Location` is. You defined and exported the `Location` class in your `home-list` component, so you can import that into the service by adding this line along with the other imports:

```
import { Location } from './home-list/home-list.component';
```

Now you're ready to code the meat of your service.

MAKING HTTP REQUESTS

Making the HTTP request to the API is straightforward, involving only a few steps:

1 Build the URL to call.
2 Tell the HTTP service to make a request for the URL.
3 Convert the Observable response to a Promise.
4 Convert the response to JSON.
5 Return the response.
6 Catch, handle, and return errors.

Putting these steps into code looks like the following listing, all of which is inside the `Loc8rDataService` class in loc8r-data.service.ts.

Listing 8.14   Making and returning the HTTP request to your API in loc8r-data.service.ts

```
private apiBaseUrl = 'http://localhost:3000/api';

public getLocations(): Promise<Location[]> {            Builds the URL to the API,
  const lng: number = -0.7992599;                       using parameters for
  const lat: number = 51.378091;                        future enhancements
  const maxDistance: number = 20;
  const url: string = `${this.apiBaseUrl}/locations?lng=
    ➥${lng}&lat=${lat}&maxDistance=${maxDistance}`;
  return this.http
    .get(url)        ◁
    .toPromise()     ◁
```

Returns the Promise

Converts the Observable response to a Promise

Makes the HTTP GET call to the URL you built

```
        .then(response => response as Location[])
        .catch(this.handleError);
    }

    private handleError(error: any): Promise<any> {
      console.error('Something has gone wrong', error);
      return Promise.reject(error.message || error);
    }
```

Converts the response to a JSON object of type Location

Handles and returns any errors

Note that only the method you need to call from somewhere else, getLocations, is public; everything else is defined as private so it can't be accessed externally.

That's not a lot of code, but it's doing a lot. As you'll see is quite common with Angular, after you get your head around the setting up of components, classes, and services, a lot of the actual code can be simple, because many of the common tasks have had the complexities abstracted away.

Now that your data service is created, it's time to use it from your home-list component.

8.3.2 Using a data service

You're at a point where you have an Angular component that can display an array of locations (which are currently hardcoded), an API that can return an array of locations, and a service to call that API and expose the response. The missing link is between the component and the service.

IMPORTING THE SERVICE INTO THE COMPONENT

Three steps are required to include the service in the component, all of which take place inside the home-list.component.ts file. You need to import the service, inject the service, and then provide the service.

First, import the service from the TypeScript file, which you do at the top of the component file directly below the existing import line, like this:

```
import { Component, OnInit } from '@angular/core';
import { Loc8rDataService } from '../loc8r-data.service';
```

Note that you define a relative path to the service file with ../, which means "Go up a level in the folder structure." If you move the service files to a different place, you need to remember to update the references in code.

The second step is injecting the service into the component, using the constructor as you did inside the data service itself. This time, though, you update the constructor in home-list.component.ts by injecting loc8rDataService of type Loc8rDataService and keeping it private, like this:

```
constructor(private loc8rDataService: Loc8rDataService) { }
```

By the end, the top of the home-list.component.ts file should look like the following.

Listing 8.15   Making your service available to the component in home-list.component.ts

```
import { Component, OnInit } from '@angular/core';
import { Loc8rDataService } from '../loc8r-data.service';      ◄─┐  Imports the
                                                                   service from the
export class Location {                                            source code file
  _id: string;
  name: string;
  distance: number;
  address: string;
  rating: number;
  facilities: [string];
}

@Component({
  selector: 'app-home-list',
  templateUrl: './home-list.component.html',                      Injects the
  styleUrls: ['./home-list.component.css']                        service into
})                                                                the
export class HomeListComponent implements OnInit {                component
                                                                  using the
  constructor(private loc8rDataService: Loc8rDataService) { }  ◄─┘  constructor
```

Now that the service is created and brought into the component, you can use it.

USING THE SERVICE TO GET THE DATA

Inside the class, create a private method to call your data service method and handle the Promise response. When it has the Promise response, this method can set the value of the locations array, which automatically updated in the HTML.

To show that this is working, remove all the hardcoded data from the component and declare `locations` to be of type `Location`, with no value assigned. Pop the code from the next listing into the `HomeListComponent` class definition in home-list .component.ts.

Listing 8.16   Creating a function to call the data service from home-list.component.ts

Changes the locations declaration
to have no default value

Defines a getLocations
method that accepts
no parameters and
returns nothing

```
└─► public locations: Location[];

   private getLocations(): void {   ◄──┘
     this.loc8rDataService
       .getLocations()
         .then(foundLocations => this.locations = foundLocations);  ◄─┐
   }
```

Calls your data service method

Updates the locations array with
the contents of the response

Great stuff. This code still won't work, though, because you're not calling the private `getLocations` method in the component. That step is the next and final step, but you need to make sure that you do it at the right time.

As you've seen, an Angular application is composed of many files. But you have no control of the order in which the files are put together and, therefore, no direct control of the execution order. You need to make sure that the service is called only after it's available, which is where that little empty ngOnInit() block comes into play.

ngOnInit is one of several Angular lifecycle hooks. While an Angular application is starting and running, things happen in a specific order to make sure that the application maintains integrity and always does things the same way. The lifecycle hooks allow you to listen to the process and take action at certain times.

The ngOnInit hook allows you to hook into when the component is initialized and ready. This is a good time to make that data call, because you know that it's safe to do so and that the component is ready to run. Make a call to the local getLocations method in home-list.component.ts, like so:

```
ngOnInit() {
  this.getLocations();
}
```

Now the application will compile properly, run, and make the call to the API. Great! But if you try it on certain browsers (most notably Chrome), no data comes through. If you open the browser developer tools or JavaScript console, you'll see a CORS warning, because the Angular app and Express API are running on different ports.

ALLOWING CORS REQUESTS IN EXPRESS

The CORS issue can't be fixed from the browser side; it has to be done on the server side. You need to change gears for a moment and drop back into Express.

Allowing cross-origin requests is simple, fortunately. For every request made to the API, you need to add two HTTP headers: Access-Control-Allow-Origin and Access-Control-Allow-Headers. The first of these headers can contain a specific URL from which you'll allow requests or a * as a wildcard to accept requests from any domain. You'll limit requests to your Angular development application by specifying the URL and port.

Head back to app.js in the root of the application, and add the following bold font lines before the routes are used:

```
app.use('/api', (req, res, next) => {
  res.header('Access-Control-Allow-Origin', 'http://localhost:4200');
  res.header('Access-Control-Allow-Headers', 'Origin, X-Requested-With,
  Content-Type, Accept');
  next();
});
app.use('/', indexRouter);
app.use('/api', apiRouter);
```

This code adds the two headers and their values to the responses for all requests made to the API routes. If you've still got your Express application running on port 3000 and your Angular application running on port 4200, you should see your data coming through into the browser, as in figure 8.13.

This is great! You've built a nice little self-contained Angular application without too much trouble. This isn't a bad start, especially considering that you've also been

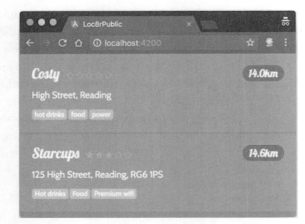

Figure 8.13   **Your Angular component is now displaying data brought in from the API.**

coming to grips with TypeScript throughout this chapter. In the next section, you'll finish this application and embed it in your Express application.

8.4   *Putting an Angular application into production*

So far, you've been working with Angular in development mode while building your little application. But as soon as you stop ng serve from running, all you're left with is a bunch of source files, nothing you could include in a website. What you need to do now is build your application for production and add it to your homepage.

8.4.1   *Building an Angular application for production*

You've been using the ng serve command throughout this chapter to rebuild your application automatically and serve the compiled files from memory. Now you'll use the ng build command to compile the files once and save them to disk.

The ng build command generates all the application files and puts them in a folder called dist. This folder is at the same level as the src folder which would be great, but if you run ng serve again afterward, it deletes the dist folder, which isn't helpful, as you can imagine. But you can change this destination folder by using the option --output-path when running the command. If you do, your destination folder won't unexpectedly be deleted the next time you decide to run ng serve.

There are far too many build options for us to go through here (you can check them out by running ng help in terminal), and the only other one you need to know right now is the one to specify that you want a production build (as opposed to a development build). You specify that by adding the --prod flag to the command.

To create a production build of your application in the folder app_public/build, run the following command in terminal from the app_public folder:

```
$ ng build --prod --output-path build
```

This command kicks off the build process. If you get an error about not being able to find where AppComponent goes, that's probably because the references were taken out of app.module.ts, but the files weren't deleted. The fix is to delete the old app.component files, because you're not using them anymore.

That's it: the application is built for production! Now you need to include it in the Express application.

8.4.2 *Using the Angular application from the Express site*

To use the Angular application in your homepage, you need to do a few small things in Express. First, you'll set the app_public folder to be a static path, meaning that you can easily reference the files in the build folder from the browser. To do the second part, update the Pug templates to include the JavaScript files in the build folder.

Easy, right? Now do it!

DEFINING A STATIC PATH FOR THE ANGULAR APPLICATION

You've already seen how Express defines folders to use for static resources, because the generator automatically defined the public folder to be static. You can do the same for the app_public folder by duplicating the line in app.js in the root of the application and setting the name to be app_public:

```
app.use(express.static(path.join(__dirname, 'public')));
app.use(express.static(path.join(__dirname, 'app_public')));
```

Now Express will serve static resources from either the public or the app_public folder. Why define the whole app_public folder and not only the build subfolder to be a static resource? Well, the build folder also contains an index.html file. If this file is included as a static resource, it shows up as the homepage, as the static resources are checked before the other Express routes. This feature will be useful in the following chapters, when you create the full Angular application, but it's not what you want right now. Right now, you want to use the Angular application *inside* your existing site, because you're replacing part of the homepage.

REFERENCING THE COMPILED ANGULAR JAVASCRIPT FILES FROM THE HTML

You want to reference the Angular files on only the homepage, not on the other pages. The problem at the moment is that you can include script files only in the layout.pug template; all the other templates extend a small nested HTML part of this. There's nowhere to put new script tags.

A simple way to address this problem is to create a new block in the layout.pug template. Then any other page that extends this layout will have an option for including page-specific scripts.

In layout.pug, include this line at the bottom to define a new block called scripts:

```
block scripts
```

Make sure that the indentation matches that of the final script tag in the file; the desired outcome is that any page-specific scripts will be added at the bottom of the HTML body.

Next, use this new `block` from within locations-list.pug, and reference all three JavaScript files from the app_public/build folder. The code should look a bit like this, but you'll have different filenames:

```
block scripts
  script(src='/build/runtime.f0178fcd0cc34a5688b1.js')
  script(src='/build/polyfills.682313b6b06f69a5089e.js')
  script(src='/build/main.ad6de91d9e2170cae9d4.js')
```

You're almost there! You only need to add a tag in the HTML for the application to bind to.

ADDING THE HTML TAG TO BIND THE ANGULAR APP

If you cast your mind back to earlier in the chapter or check the source code, you'll remember that your app was bootstrapped into an HTML tag called `app-home-list`. All you want to do now is replace the list part of the homepage with your new holding tag.

In locations-list.pug, find the `each location in locations` section, and either delete it or comment it out for reference. In its place, add `app-home-list`, ensuring that the indentation is correct. This part of the template should look something like this:

```
.row
  .col-12.col-md-8
    .error= message

    app-home-list
```

Now you're done! Head to the browser; go back on localhost:3000; and check out the homepage, now including your Angular application, which is getting data from your API.

If you've done everything properly, the page should look the same as before. To prove that the homepage is using the Angular application, inspect an element of the list; you'll see the app-home-list tag and all the Angular stuff inside (see figure 8.14).

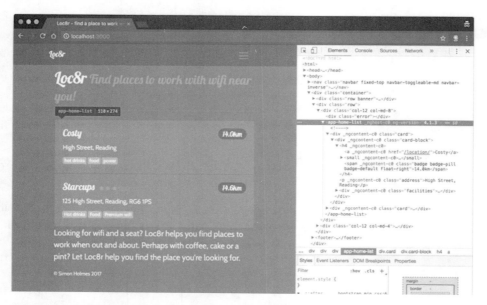

Figure 8.14   Validating that the homepage list is using the Angular module

We love this stuff! It's great how all the pieces fit together and work together. Now you're Getting MEAN. In chapter 9, you'll start work on building Loc8r as a full Angular SPA.

Summary

In this chapter, you learned

- How the Angular CLI is used to generate application boilerplate, components, and more
- How to work with TypeScript classes, importing and exporting, and using them to define types for variables
- How to control the code execution flow using Angular lifecycle hooks
- How to create and use some of the Angular building blocks to put an application together, covering modules, components, pipes, and services
- How to use the Angular CLI to target for production

Building a single-page application with Angular: Foundations

9

This chapter covers

- Working with the Angular router and navigating between pages
- Architectural best practices for an SPA
- Building up views through multiple components
- Injecting HTML into bindings
- Working with browsers' native geolocation capabilities

You saw in chapter 8 how to use Angular to add functionality to an existing page. In this chapter and chapter 10, you'll take Angular to the next level by using it to create a single-page application (SPA). Instead of running the entire application logic on the server using Express, you'll run it all in the browser using Angular. For some benefits and considerations when using an SPA instead of a traditional approach, flick through chapter 2. By the end of this chapter, you'll have the framework for an SPA in place with the first part up and running by using Angular to route to the homepage and display the content.

274

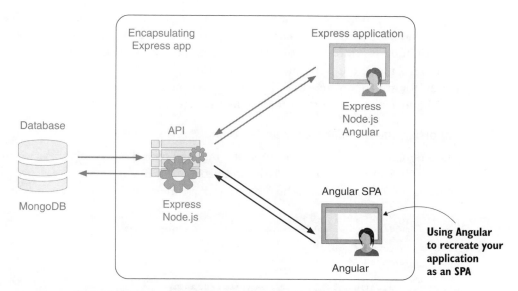

Figure 9.1 This chapter recreates the Loc8r application as an Angular SPA, moving the application logic from the back end to the front end.

Figure 9.1 shows where you are in the overall plan, recreating the main application as an Angular SPA.

In a normal development process, you probably wouldn't create an entire application on the server and recreate it as an SPA. Ideally, your early planning phases defined whether you wanted an SPA, enabling you to start in the appropriate technology. For the learning process you're going through now, it's a good approach; you're already familiar with the functionality of the site, and the layouts have already been created. This approach lets you focus on the more exciting prospect of seeing how to build a full Angular application.

In this chapter, you'll start by adding the Angular router to navigate between pages; then, you'll create the homepage and the About page and add geolocation functionality. As you add more components and functionality, you'll explore various best practices, such as making reusable components and building up a modular application.

9.1 Adding navigation in an Angular SPA

In this section, you'll add the outline of the About page and enable navigation between this new page and the homepage. The main focus of this section is the navigation; you'll complete the About page in section 9.4.

You may remember that when you configured the Express application, you defined URL paths (routes) and used the Express router to map the routes to specific pieces of functionality. In Angular, you'll do the same thing but use the Angular router instead.

One big difference in using the Angular router is that the full application is already loaded in the browser, so when you navigate between pages, the browser doesn't fully download all the HTML, CSS, and JavaScript each time. Navigating becomes a much quicker experience for the user; the only things they normally have to wait for are data from API calls and any new images.

The first step is importing the Angular router into the application.

9.1.1 Importing the Angular router and defining the first route

The Angular router needs to be imported into app.module.ts, which is also where you'll define the routes. The router is imported from `@angular/router` as `RouterModule`, which should be placed with the other Angular imports at the top of app.module.ts.

> **Listing 9.1   Adding the `RouterModule` to the list of imports in app.module.ts**

```
import { BrowserModule } from '@angular/platform-browser';
import { NgModule } from '@angular/core';
import { HttpClientModule } from '@angular/common/http';
import { RouterModule } from '@angular/router';        Imports the
                                                        Angular
                                                        RouterModule
```

In the same file, in the `@NgModule` decorator, all these modules are listed in the imports section. You need to do the same with `RouterModule`, but in this case, you also need to pass it the routing configuration you want.

9.1.2 Routing configuration

The routing configuration is an array of objects, each object specifying one route. The properties for each route are

- `path`—The URL path to match
- `component`—The name of the Angular component to use

The `path` property shouldn't contain any leading or trailing slashes, so instead of `/about/`, you'd have `about`, for example. It can also be an empty string to denote the homepage. Remember that the `base href` is set in the index.html file? You set yours to be `"/"`, as you want everything running at the top level, but even if you set it to have a value, that value wouldn't make any difference to the routing configuration. In your routing configuration, you should leave out anything set in the `base href` html tag.

You start by adding the configuration for the homepage, so `path` is an empty string, and `component` is the name of your existing component: `HomeListComponent`. The configuration is passed to a `forRoot` method on the `RouterModule`.

> **Listing 9.2   Adding the routing configuration to the decorator in app.module.ts**

```
@NgModule({
  declarations: [
    HomeListComponent,
    DistancePipe
  ],
```

```
imports: [                          Adds the RouterModule to
  BrowserModule,                    the imports, calling the
  HttpClientModule,                 forRoot method
  RouterModule.forRoot([
    {                               Defines the homepage
      path: '',                     route as an empty string
      component: HomeListComponent       Specifies the
    }                                     HomeListComponent
  ])                                      as the one to use for
],                                        this route
providers: [],
bootstrap: [HomeListComponent]
})
```

You've imported the Angular `RouterModule` into your application and told it which component to use for the homepage. You can't test it, however, because you're also specifying the same component as the default component. Note the line `bootstrap: [HomeListComponent]` in listing 9.2. What you need to do is create a new default component, which you'll use to hold the navigation.

9.1.3 *Creating a component for the framework and navigation*

To hold the navigation elements, you need to create a new component and make that the default component for the application. You'll also use this component to hold all the framework HTML, much as you did in layout.pug in Express. In reality, the framework HTML is three things: navigation, content container, and footer.

First, create a new component called `framework` by running the following in terminal from the app_public directory:

```
$ ng generate component framework
```

This command creates a new framework folder inside app_public/src/app/ and also generates all the files you need. Find the framework.component.html file, and add all the HTML shown in the following listing, which is pretty much what the HTML content of layout.pug would look like if converted to HTML

Listing 9.3 Adding the HTML for the framework in framework.component.html

```
<nav class="navbar fixed-top navbar-expand-md navbar-light">
  <div class="container">                                    Sets up the
    <a href="/" class="navbar-brand">Loc8r</a>               navigation
      <button type="button" data-toggle="collapse" data-target=  section
      ➥"#navbarMain"class="navbar-toggler">
        <span class="navbar-toggler-icon"></span>
      </button>

    <div id="navbarMain" class="navbar-collapse collapse">
      <ul class="navbar-nav mr-auto">
        <li class="nav-item">
          <a href="/about/" class="nav-link">About</a>
        </li>
      </ul>
```

```
      </div>
    </div>
  </nav>                                      Creates the
<div class="container content">    ◁────┐    main container
  <footer>                          ◁──┐
    <div class="row">                  │  Nests the footer inside the
      <div class="col-12">                main container
        <small>&copy; Getting Mean - Simon Holmes/Clive Harber 2018</small>
      </div>
    </div>
  </footer>
</div>
```

Now that you've got the component set up, you need to tell the application to use it as the default component, and tell it where to put it in the HTML.

To set the new `framework` component as the default component, update the bootstrap value in app.module.ts like so, replacing `HomeListComponent` with `Framework-Component`:

```
bootstrap: [FrameworkComponent]
```

Finally, you need to update index.html to have the correct tag for this component rather than `home-list`. Open framework.component.ts, and find the selector in the decorator, which gives you the name of the HTML tag you should use:

```
@Component({
  selector: 'app-framework',
  templateUrl: './framework.component.html',
  styleUrls: ['./framework.component.css']
})
```

So `app-framework` is the tag you need to have in index.html so Angular knows where to put the `framework` component. Update index.html to look like the following.

Listing 9.4   Updating index.html file to use the new `framework` component

```
<body>
  <app-framework></app-framework>      ◁──┐   Replaces the home-list component
</body>                                        for the app-framework
```

Now that your `framework` component is created and linked to the HTML, you can check it out in the browser, as shown in figure 9.2. If you haven't done so already, remember to run `nodemon` from the root folder of the application to get the API running, and also run `ng serve` from the app_public folder to get the development version of the Angular app running.

You can see the page header displaying, so you have success of sorts. Your new component works! But you don't see any content, even though you're on the homepage route. If you open the JavaScript console in the browser, you see an error: `Cannot find primary outlet to load 'HomeListComponent'`.

You've told the application to load `HomeListComponent` for the homepage route, but haven't specified where it should be positioned in the HTML.

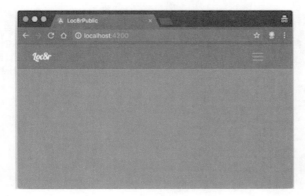

Figure 9.2 Showing the `framework` component by default instead of the listing

9.1.4 *Defining where to display the content using router-outlet*

Specifying the destination for a routed component is as simple as adding an empty tag pair in the HTML where you want it to go. This special tag is <router-outlet>. Angular adds the routed component *after* this tag, not inside it, as you might expect if you're familiar with AngularJS.

Adding this empty tag pair to the correct place in the framework HTML—where you had block content in layout.pug—looks like the following.

Listing 9.5 Adding `router-outlet` to framework.component.html

```
<div class="container">
  <router-outlet></router-outlet>        Outlet for the router; Angular uses
  <footer>                               the URL to find the component
    <div class="row">                    and injects it here.
      <div class="col-12"><small>&copy; Getting Mean - Simon Holmes/Clive
      Harber 2018</small></div>
    </div>
  </footer>
</div>
```

If you check out the browser now, you see the listing information as well as the framework. Inspecting the elements, as shown in figure 9.3, demonstrates that <router-outlet> remains empty, and that <app-home-list> was injected afterward.

You can see the framework and the listing for the homepage, but it's not the homepage you know and love. It's missing a header and sidebar. You'll come back to this page in section 9.2. First, you need to see how the navigation works.

9.1.5 *Navigating between pages*

To see the navigation in action, update the Angular application so that you can flip between the homepage and the About page. If you click the links right now, they won't work. To get the navigation working, you need to create an about component, define the about route, and change the links in the navigation to something Angular can use.

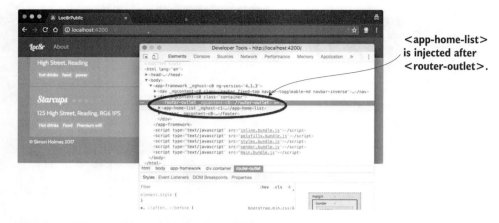

Figure 9.3   The routed component—the listing information—is now being displayed on the homepage route, with the HTML being injected after the `<router-outlet>` tag.

Creating the about component with Angular CLI should be familiar by now. In terminal, in the app_public folder, run the following generate command:

```
$ ng generate component about
```

This command creates the new component inside app_public/src/app/about. You'll leave it as it is for now, so you can focus on the navigation. In section 9.4, you'll return to the About page and build it out fully.

DEFINING A NEW ROUTE

As with the homepage route, you need to configure the route for the About page in app.module.ts. You need to specify the path for the route as well as the name of the component. The path is `'about'`. Remember that you don't need any leading or trailing slashes.

To make sure you get the name of the component correct, you can open about .component.ts to find it in the export line: export class AboutComponent implements OnInit.

Knowing the path and component name, you can add the new route in app .module.ts.

Listing 9.6   Defining the new about route in app.module.ts

```
RouterModule.forRoot([
  {
    path: '',
    component: HomeListComponent
  },
  {
    path: 'about',
    component: AboutComponent
  }
])
```

If you open the browser directly to localhost:4200/about, you get the About page, but the navigation links don't work properly yet. You'll fix them in the next section.

SETTING ANGULAR NAVIGATION LINKS

When you're using links defined in the router, Angular doesn't want to see `href` attributes in the `<a>` tags; instead, it looks for a directive called `routerLink`. Angular takes the value you give to `routerLink` to create the `href` property.

The rules that apply to defining a path in the router also apply to setting the value for a `routerLink`. You don't need to include leading or trailing slashes, and bear in mind that you don't need to duplicate anything set in the `base href`.

Following these rules, updating the navigation links in framework.component .html looks like the next listing. Replace `href` attributes with `routerLink` directives, ensuring that the values match what you have in the router definition in app.module.ts.

Listing 9.7   Defining the navigation router links in framework.component.html

```
<a routerLink="" class="navbar-brand">Loc8r</a>        ◁──  Empty routerLink path
<div id="navbarMain" class="navbar-collapse collapse">       pointing to the default
  <ul class="navbar-nav mr-auto">                           component
    <li class="nav-item">
      <a routerLink="about" class="nav-link">About</a>   ◁──  about path to cause
    </li>                                                      navigation to the
  </ul>                                                        about component
</div>
```

With this code in place and saved, you can click between the two links, as shown in figure 9.4.

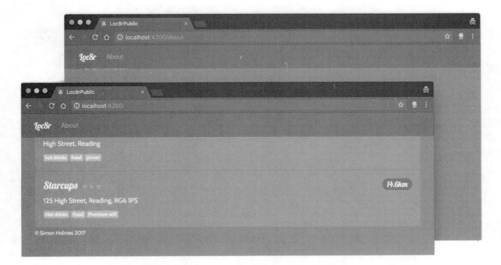

Figure 9.4   Using the navigation buttons to switch between the homepage and the About page—an Angular SPA!

Notice that the URL in the browser changes as normal, but the page doesn't reload or flicker when moving between the pages. If you check the network traffic when switching between these two pages, you'll see only calls to the API being made. You can also use the back and forward buttons in your browser, and the site will work like a traditional website. Congratulations—you've built a single-page application!

Before you move on, quickly improve the navigation by adding active styles.

9.1.6   Adding active navigation styles

It's standard practice in web design to have an `active` class on navigation items so that the link for the current page looks a bit different—a simple visual cue to tells users where they are. You've got only one link in your navigation, but the process is still worthwhile.

Twitter Bootstrap has helper classes defined to create an active navigation state; you set the class `active` on the active link. As it's such a common requirement, Angular also has a helper for this class: a directive called `routerLinkActive`.

On an `<a>` tag containing a router link, you can add the `routerLinkActive` directive and specify the name of the class you want to use for active links. You'll use the class `active` in framework.component.html:

```
<a routerLink="about" routerLinkActive="active" class="nav-link">About</a>
```

The positioning of the `routerLinkActive` attribute is important. If it doesn't seem to be working, make sure that you included it before the `class` attribute.

Now, when you visit the About page, the `<a>` tag has an extra class of `active` added to it, which Bootstrap displays as a stronger white color, as you can see in figure 9.5.

Figure 9.5   Seeing the `active` class in action; Angular adds and removes it from the link as navigation changes are made.

And with that, you've covered the basics of the Angular router, creating working navigation for your SPA. You can see that the views clearly need some work, so that's what you'll focus on in the next two sections.

9.2 Building a modular app using multiple nested components

In this section, you'll focus on building out the familiar homepage in Angular. To set yourself up for success—and to follow Angular architectural best practices—you'll do this by creating several new components and nesting them as you need to. This process gives you a modular application, so you can reuse pieces in different places in the application.

The homepage has three main sections:

- Page header
- List of locations
- Sidebar

You already have the list of locations built as a component; that's your `home-list` component. You'll need to create the header and the sidebar as two new components.

You'll also need to wrap all three of these components inside a main homepage component to ensure that everything works together, has the correct layout, and can be navigated to via the Angular router. Figure 9.6 shows an overlay of how these components fit together on top of the homepage design. You have the `framework` component on the outside, holding everything. Nested inside this component is the `homepage` component to control the content area, with the page header, listing, and sidebar components nested inside it.

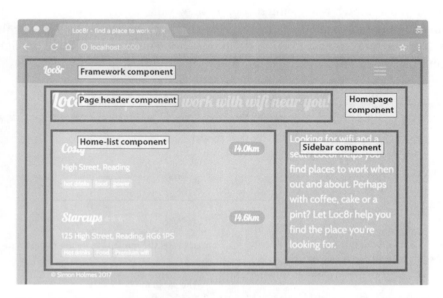

Figure 9.6   Breaking the homepage layout into components, using two levels of nesting

This is what you're going to build. You'll start with the `homepage` component.

9.2.1 Creating the main homepage component

The `homepage` component contains all the HTML and information for the homepage—everything between the header and the footer. This component is what you'll reference in the router for Angular to use whenever anybody requests the homepage.

Start by using the Angular CLI to generate the component in the now-familiar way (in terminal from the app_public folder):

```
$ ng generate component homepage
```

Next, tell the router to use this component for the default home route by updating app.module.ts like so:

```
RouterModule.forRoot([
  {
    path: '',
    component: HomepageComponent
  },
  {
    path: 'about',
    component: AboutComponent
  }
])
```

In homepage.component.html, put the selector for the `home-list` component for a moment before checking it in the browser:

```
<app-home-list></app-home-list>
```

If you look at the application in the browser, it looks the way it did before, with the navigation bar, footer, and listing section in between.

But you want to see all the content for the homepage now; that's the page header, main content, and sidebar. Taking the framework code from the Pug templates and turning it into HTML looks like the following listing. Note that you're putting the app-home-list component here to display the listing section.

> **Listing 9.8   Putting the HTML for homepage content in homepage.component.html**

```
<div class="row banner">        ⟵─── The page header
  <div class="col-12">
    <h1>Loc8r
      <small>Find places to work with wifi near you!</small>
    </h1>
  </div>
</div>
<div class="row">
  <div class="col-12 col-md-8">   ⟵─── Container for the homepage listing component
    <div class="error"></div>
    <app-home-list></app-home-list>
  </div>                                        The sidebar
  <div class="col-12 col-md-4">   ⟵─────────┘
```

```
    <p class="lead">Looking for wifi and a seat? Loc8r helps you
    ➥find places to work when out and about. Perhaps with coffee,
    ➥cake or a pint? Let Loc8r help you find the place you're
    ➥ looking for.</p>
  </div>
</div>
```

Now, when you view the page in the browser, you get something like figure 9.7—your good old familiar homepage!

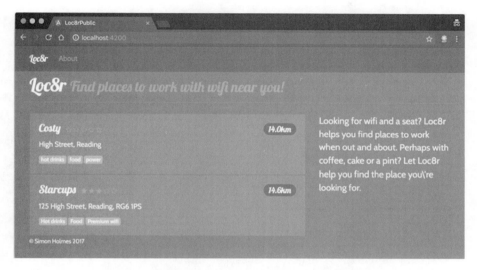

Figure 9.7 The homepage in Angular with the page header and sidebar hardcoded in the `homepage` component

Everything is there and working correctly, including the `home-list` component nested inside the `homepage` component. But you can do better. The page header and sidebar are repeated on other pages, albeit with different text content. You can follow some architectural best practices here and try to avoid repeating code by creating reusable components.

9.2.2 Creating and using reusable subcomponents

You're going to create the page header and sidebar as new components so that you never need to copy the HTML into multiple views. If the site grows to have dozens or hundreds of pages, you wouldn't want to have to repeat the same HTML in each layout. This situation gets even worse if you need to update the HTML in the future. It's much easier to update the HTML in one place, and is also much less prone to errors or omissions.

You'll make the components "smart" so that you can pass them different content to display. In your case, the reusable components are all about the HTML rather than the content. Start with the page header.

CREATING THE PAGE-HEADER COMPONENT

The first step is issuing the familiar component generation command in terminal:

```
$ ng generate component page-header
```

Following that command, copy the header content from the homepage HTML and paste it into page-header.component.html:

```
<div class="row banner">
  <div class="col-12">
    <h1>Loc8r
      <small>Find places to work with wifi near you!</small>
    </h1>
  </div>
</div>
```

Then you need to reference this content in the homepage.component.html instead of the full HTML currently there. To do so, you need the correct tag, which you can find by looking for the selector in the page-header.component.ts file. In this case, the selector is app-page-header, so that's what you'll use in the homepage component HTML.

Listing 9.9   Replacing the page header HTML in homepage.component.html

```
<app-page-header></app-page-header>
<div class="row">
  <div class="col-12 col-md-8">
    <div class="error"></div>
    <app-home-list>Loading...</app-home-list>
  </div>
  <div class="col-12 col-md-4">
    <p class="lead">Looking for wifi and a seat? Loc8r helps you find
    ➥places to work when out and about. Perhaps with coffee, cake
    ➥or a pint? Let Loc8r help you find the place you\'re looking
    ➥for.</p>
  </div>
</div>
```

Good start. You've created the new page-header component, but it still has hard-coded content. Next, you'll pass data to the page header from the homepage component.

DEFINING THE DATA FOR THE PAGE-HEADER COMPONENT ON THE HOMEPAGE

You want to set the data for the homepage instance of the page-header component from within the homepage component so you can pass it through.

Defining the data is simple. In the homepage component class definition, you create a new member to hold the data. You'll create a member called pageContent and nest the header inside it, as shown in the next listing. The class member is a simple JavaScript object with text data. Note that the strapline content is shortened in this snippet to save trees.

> **Listing 9.10　Defining the homepage page header content in homepage.component.ts**

```
export class HomepageComponent implements OnInit {
  constructor() { }

  ngOnInit() {
  }                                              Creates a new class member to
  public pageContent = {          ◁──────────    hold the page header content
    header: {
      title: 'Loc8r',
      strapline: 'Find places to work with wifi near you!'
    }
  };

}
```

The header is nested inside pageContent because, soon, you'll add the sidebar content too, and having them both within the same member will keep the code neater. Next, you pass this data to the page-header component.

PASSING DATA INTO THE PAGE-HEADER COMPONENT

The homepage class member pageContent is now available to the homepage HTML, but rather than use the data directly, you want to pass it through to the page-header component. Data is passed through to the nested component via a special binding in the HTML. The name of the binding is a property you define in the nested component, so it can be anything you want.

You'll bind the page header content to a property called content. (This property doesn't exist yet; you'll define it in the next step.) In homepage.component.html, update <app-page-header> to include the binding:

```
<app-page-header [content]="pageContent.header"></app-page-header>
```

Note that although the square brackets may not be valid HTML, that's okay here, because Angular removes them before serving the HTML to the browser. The actual HTML that the browser will receive is something like <app-page-header_ngcontent-c6="" _nghost-c2="">, which is valid HTML.

You're now passing data from the homepage component to the nested page-header component; you need to update the page header to accept and use this data.

ACCEPTING AND DISPLAYING INCOMING DATA IN A COMPONENT

You need to tell the pageHeader component that content should exist as a property and to get the value from the outside. Technically, content is an *input* to the component.

Any property of a class needs to be defined, and this one is no different. Where it differs from what you've seen before is that it needs to be defined as an input property. To do that, you need to import Input into the component from the Angular core and use it as a decorator when you define the content member.

Listing 9.11   Telling page-header.component.ts to accept content as an `Input`

```
import { Component, OnInit, Input } from '@angular/core';        ◁────────  Imports Input from
                                                                            the Angular core
@Component({
  selector: 'app-page-header',
  templateUrl: './page-header.component.html',
  styleUrls: ['./page-header.component.css']
})
export class PageHeaderComponent implements OnInit {

  @Input() content: any;        ◁────┐   Defines content as a class
                                      │   member that accepts an
  constructor() { }                   │   input of any type

  ngOnInit() {
  }

}
```

When that's done, the component will understand the data being sent to it from the homepage component, and you'll be able to display it. Replace the hardcoded text in page-header.component.html with the relevant Angular data bindings.

Listing 9.12   Putting the data bindings in page-header.component.html

```
<div class="row banner">
  <div class="col-12">
    <h1>{{ content.title }}
      <small>{{ content.strapline }}</small>
    </h1>
  </div>
</div>
```

Now you have a fully reusable component for the page header, which can display the data sent to it from a parent component. This component is an important building block of Angular application architecture. You'll cement the process by doing the same for the sidebar so that you can complete the homepage, but you'll run into a little hiccup along the way.

CREATING THE SIDEBAR COMPONENT
We won't dwell too long on the steps for setting up the sidebar component, as you completed them for the page header earlier in this chapter.

First, generate the component:

```
$ ng generate component sidebar
```

Second, grab the sidebar HTML from homepage.component.html, and paste it into sidebar.component.html. When you do, replace the text content with a binding to content:

```
<div class="col-12 col-md-4">
  <p class="lead">{{ content }}</p>
</div>
```

Third, allow the sidebar component to receive data by importing Input from Angular core and defining the content property—of type string—with the @Input decorator:

```
import { Component, OnInit, Input } from '@angular/core';

@Component({
  selector: 'app-sidebar',
  templateUrl: './sidebar.component.html',
  styleUrls: ['./sidebar.component.css']
})
export class SidebarComponent implements OnInit {

  @Input() content: string;

  constructor() { }

  ngOnInit() {
  }

}
```

Fourth, update the pageContent member in homepage.component.ts to contain the sidebar data:

```
public pageContent = {
  header : {
    title : 'Loc8r',
    strapline : 'Find places to work with wifi near you!'
  },
  sidebar : 'Looking for wifi and a seat? Loc8r helps you find places
    to work when out and about. Perhaps with coffee, cake or a pint?
    Let Loc8r help you find the place you\'re looking for.'
};
```

Fifth, update the homepage.component.html to use the new sidebar component, and pass the data through as content:

```
<app-page-header [content]="pageContent.header"></app-page-header>
<div class="row">
  <div class="col-12 col-md-8">
    <div class="error"></div>
    <app-home-list>Loading...</app-home-list>
  </div>
  <app-sidebar [content]="pageContent.sidebar"></app-sidebar>
</div>
```

All done! But is it? If you view this page in the browser, you'll notice that no matter how wide you make your browser window, the sidebar is always below the content (see figure 9.8).

The position of the sidebar is defined by the classes in the <div class="col-12 col-md-4"> element. But by putting this content inside a component, you wrapped it in a new tag, <app-sidebar>, so Bootstrap is throwing the sidebar below as a new row.

This problem is something to look out for, especially when you're nesting components. But it's easy to fix.

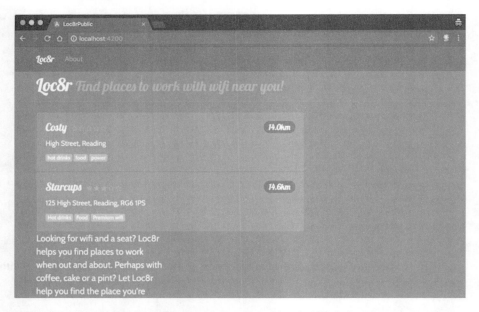

Figure 9.8   The new sidebar component is in and working, but it's below the main content instead of where it should be.

WORKING WITH ANGULAR ELEMENTS AND BOOTSTRAP LAYOUT CLASSES

The problem you have is that the browser now sees this following HTML markup generated:

```
<div class="col-12 col-md-8">
  <app-home-list>Loading...</app-home-list>
</div>
<app-sidebar [content]="pageContent.sidebar">
  <div class="col-12 col-md-4">
    <p class="lead">{{ content }}</p>
  </div>
</app-sidebar>
```

The Bootstrap `col` classes for the sidebar are in the wrong level in the hierarchy, so `<app-sidebar>` is being treated as a full-width column regardless of browser size. All you need to do is move the classes from the `<div>` in sidebar.component.html to `<app-sidebar>` in homepage.component.html, so that homepage.component.html looks like the following.

> **Listing 9.13   Moving the sidebar classes into homepage.component.html**

```
<app-page-header [content]="pageContent.header"></app-page-header>
<div class="row">
  <div class="col-12 col-md-8">
    <app-home-list>Loading...</app-home-list>
  </div>
  <app-sidebar class="col-12 col-md-4" [content]="pageContent.sidebar">
```

```
⮡</app-sidebar>
</div>
```

With that done, you no longer need the `<div>` in the sidebar markup; you can keep the `<p>` and the content. Now sidebar.component.html looks like this:

```
<p class="lead">{{ content }}</p>
```

With that fix, everything should look right with the homepage, as shown in figure 9.9.

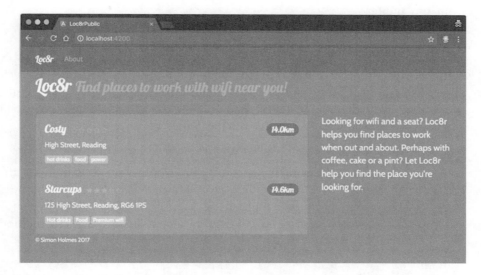

Figure 9.9 **The completed homepage rendering correctly, constructed of multiple nested components**

The homepage is looking good! Something has been missing so far, though. Wouldn't it be great if Loc8r could tell where you are and find places nearby? You'll add geolocation to the homepage in the next section.

9.3 Adding geolocation to find places near you

The main premise of Loc8r is that it's location aware and able to find places that are near the user. So far, you've been faking it by hardcoding geographic coordinates into the API requests. You're going to change that right now by adding HTML5 geolocation.

To get geolocation working, you'll need to do the following things:

- Add a call to the HTML5 location API to your Angular application.
- Query the Express API if location details are available.
- Pass the coordinates to your Angular data service, removing the hardcoded location.
- Output messages along the way so the user knows what's going on.

Starting at the top, you'll add the geolocation JavaScript function by creating a new service.

9.3.1   *Creating an Angular geolocation service*

The ability to find the location of the user feels like something that would be reusable, in this and other projects. To snap it off as a piece of standalone functionality, you'll create another service to hold it. As a rule, any code that's interacting with APIs, running logic, or performing operations should be externalized into services. Leave the component to control the services rather than perform the functions.

To create the skeleton of the geolocation service, run the following in terminal from app_public:

```
$ ng generate service geolocation
```

We won't distract you right now by diving into the details of how the HTML5/Java-Script geolocation API works. Modern browsers have a method on the `navigator` object that you can call to find the coordinates of the user. The user has to give permission for this to happen. The method accepts two parameters (a success callback and an error callback) and looks like the following:

```
navigator.geolocation.getCurrentPosition(cbSuccess, cbError);
```

You'll need to expose the standard geolocation script in a public method so that you can use it as a service. While you're here, you'll also error-trap against the possibility that the current browser doesn't support this feature. The following listing shows the full code for geolocation.service.ts, providing a public `getPosition` method that other components can call.

> **Listing 9.14   Creating a `geolocation` service using a callback to get current position**

```
import { Injectable } from '@angular/core';

@Injectable({
  providedIn: 'root'
})
export class GeolocationService {

  constructor() { }

  public getPosition(cbSuccess, cbError, cbNoGeo): void {     ⟵── Defines a public member called getPosition that accepts three callback functions for success, error, and not supported
    if (navigator.geolocation) {
      navigator.geolocation.getCurrentPosition(cbSuccess, cbError);     ⟵── If geolocation is supported, calls the native method, passing through success and error callbacks
    } else {
      cbNoGeo();     ⟵── If geolocation isn't supported, invokes the not supported callback
    }
  }
}
```

That code gives you a geolocation service, with a public method, `getPosition`, to which you can pass three callback functions. This service checks to see whether the browser supports geolocation and then attempts to get the coordinates. Then the service calls one of the three different callbacks, depending on whether geolocation is supported and whether it was able to obtain the coordinates.

The next step is adding the service to the application.

9.3.2 *Adding the geolocation service to the application*

To use your new geolocation service, you need to import it into the `home-list` component, as you did for your data service. You need to do the following:

- Import the service into the component.
- Add the service to the providers in the decorator.
- Add the service to the class constructor.

The following listing highlights in bold the additions you need to make to the `home-list` component definition to import and register the geolocation service.

Listing 9.15 Updating home-list.component.ts to bring in the geolocation service

```
import { Component, OnInit } from '@angular/core';
import { Loc8rDataService } from '../loc8r-data.service';
import { GeolocationService } from '../geolocation.service';      ← Imports the geolocation service

export class Location {
  _id: string;
  name: string;
  distance: number;
  address: string;
  rating: number;
  facilities: string[];
}

@Component({
  selector: 'app-home-list',
  templateUrl: './home-list.component.html',
  styleUrls: ['./home-list.component.css']
})
export class HomeListComponent implements OnInit {

  constructor(                                                    Passes the service into
    private loc8rDataService: Loc8rDataService,                   the class constructor
    private geolocationService: GeolocationService      ←
  ) { }
```

When you've done this, you'll be able to use the geolocation service from within your `home-list` component.

9.3.3 *Using the geolocation service from the home-list component*

The `home-list` component now has access to the geolocation service, so use it! Remember, your `getPosition` method in the service accepts three callback functions, so you'll need to create those functions before you can call the method.

As the geolocation process can take a few seconds before you even start searching the database for locations, you'll also want to provide some useful messages to users so that they know what's going on.

You already have an element for messages in your HTML, but it's currently in homepage.component.html, and you need it in home-list.component.html. Find the `<div class="error"></div>` in the homepage HTML and remove it. Then, paste it into the top of home-list.component.html, adding a binding so that you can display messages like so:

```
<div class="error">{{message}}</div>
<div class="card" *ngFor="let location of locations">
```

With this code, you'll be able to use the message binding to keep the user up to date on what's happening. Now you're ready to create the callback functions.

CREATING THE GEOLOCATION CALLBACK FUNCTIONS

Inside the component, create three new private members, one for each of the possible geolocation outcomes:

- Successful geolocation attempt
- Unsuccessful geolocation attempt
- Geolocation not supported

You'll also update the messages being displayed to users, letting them know that the system is doing something. This message is particularly important, because geolocation can take a second or two.

The success callback is the existing `getLocations` method, with some additional message-setting thrown in: the other two set error messages, as shown in the following listing. As you'll be using the message binding from within these new functions, you'll also need to define it as a property of the class with type `string`.

Listing 9.16   Setting up the geolocation callback functions in home-list.component.ts

```
export class HomeListComponent implements OnInit {

  constructor(
    private loc8rDataService: Loc8rDataService,
    private geolocationService: GeolocationService
  ) { }

  public locations: Location[];

  public message: string;                          ← Defines the message property of type string

  private getLocations(position: any): void {
    this.message = 'Searching for nearby places';   ←
    this.loc8rDataService                               Sets some messages
      .getLocations()                                   inside the existing
      .then(foundLocations => {                         getLocations member
        this.message = foundLocations.length > 0 ? '' :
        ⇨'No locations found';                      ←
        this.locations = foundLocations;
      });
  }

  private showError(error: any): void {            The function to run if
    this.message = error.message;                  geolocation is supported
  };                                               but not successful

  private noGeo(): void {
    this.message = 'Geolocation not supported by this browser.';
  };
```

The function to run if geolocation isn't supported by browser

```
ngOnInit() {
  this.getLocations();
}
```
}

You've got your three callback functions there for success, failure, and error. Now you need to use your geolocation service rather than call `getLocations()` on the `ngOnInit()` of the component.

CALLING THE GEOLOCATION SERVICE

To call the `getPosition` method of your geolocation service, you'll need to create a new member in the `home-list` component and call it on `init` instead of calling the `getLocations` method directly.

Your geolocation service accepts three callback parameters—success, error, and unsupported—so you can add a new member to home-list.component.ts called `get-Position` that calls your service, passing through your callback functions. That member should look like this:

```
private getPosition(): void {
  this.message = 'Getting your location...';
  this.geolocationService.getPosition(
    this.getLocations,
    this.showError,
    this.noGeo);
}
```

Then, you need to call this member when the component is initialized, instead of the `getLocations` method, so replace the call in `ngOnInit` to be this new member:

```
ngOnInit() {
  this.getPosition();
}
```

Save this code, and head to the browser. You should see something like figure 9.10, where the browser asks you for permission to access your location.

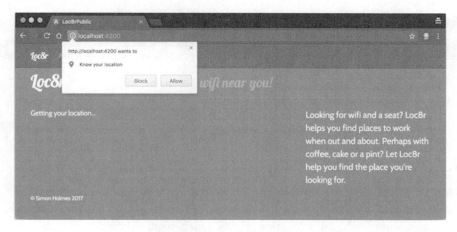

Figure 9.10 A successful call to your geolocation service is marked by a browser request to know your location.

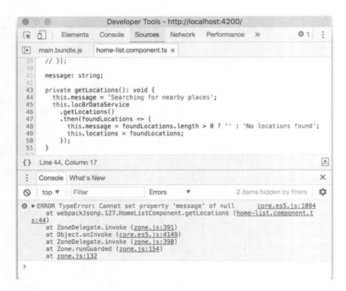

Figure 9.11   Error message shown when you're trying to set messages in the geolocation callback

Great news—until you click Allow and the screen hangs on the `Getting your location` message, quietly throwing a JavaScript error in the background. The error you're getting says `Cannot set property 'message' of null` and looks like figure 9.11.

This message tells you what the problem is and where it occurs, which helps you fix it.

WORKING WITH THIS IN CALLBACKS ACROSS COMPONENTS AND SERVICES

You can see from the error in figure 9.11 that it can't set `this.message` inside the `getLocations` callback, because `this` is null. When passing the class member through as a callback, you lose the context of `this`, which is the instance of the class itself.

Luckily, the fix is easy. You can send the context through by binding `this` to each callback as you send it. Where each callback function is passed, add `.bind(this)` to the end.

Listing 9.17   Binding `this` to geolocation callback functions in home-list.component.ts

```
private getPosition(): void {
  this.message = 'Getting your location...';
  this.geolocationService.getPosition(
    this.getLocations.bind(this),
    this.showError.bind(this),
    this.noGeo.bind(this)
  );
}
```

Now you're binding the context of `this` to the callback function so that it exists when you need it. When you visit the browser again, you have success! After displaying a few messages and getting your location, the browser displays `home-list` again.

But you're not using the location yet. You're getting it but doing nothing with it. You'll change that situation next.

USING THE GEOLOCATION COORDINATES TO QUERY THE API

In home-list.component.ts, the getPosition method calls your geolocation service to get the coordinates. When it's successful, it calls the getLocations method—again in home-list.component.ts—as a callback, passing the position as a parameter. You need to update this callback to receive the position. Then this callback calls your data service to search for locations. You need to pass the coordinates to the service, and then update the service to use these values when calling the API.

You have two things to update. Starting with getLocations() in home-list.component .ts, you need to update it to accept a position parameter, extract the coordinates from it, and pass them through to the data service, as highlighted in the following listing.

Listing 9.18   Updating home-list.component.ts to use the geolocation position

```
private getLocations(position: any): void {
    this.message = 'Searching for nearby places';
    const lat: number = position.coords.latitude;
    const lng: number = position.coords.longitude;
    this.loc8rDataService
      .getLocations(lat, lng)
      .then(foundLocations => {
        this.message = foundLocations.length > 0 ? '' : 'No locations found';
        this.locations = foundLocations;
      });
}
```

Accepts the position as a parameter

Extracts the latitude and longitude coordinates from the position

Passes the coordinates to the data service call

You're now getting the position from the geolocation service, extracting the latitude and longitude coordinates, and passing them to the data service. To get the last piece in place, you need to update the data service to accept the coordinate parameters and use them instead of the hardcoded values.

Listing 9.19   Updating loc8r-data.service.ts to use the geolocation coordinates

```
public getLocations(lat: number, lng: number): Promise<Location[]> {
    const maxDistance: number = 20000;
    const url: string = `${this.apiBaseUrl}/locations?lng=${lng}&lat=${lat}&
    maxDistance=${maxDistance}`;
    return this.http
      .get(url)
      .toPromise()
      .then(response => response.json() as Location[])
      .catch(this.handleError);
}
```

Deletes the hardcoded values you had for lat and lng before

Accepts lat and lng parameters of type number

Now the coordinates are finding their way from the geolocation service to the API call, so you're now using Loc8r to find places near you! If you check it out in the browser—if you've added some places within 20 km of where you are—you should see them listed, as shown in figure 9.12. You'll probably notice a slight change in the distance coordinates, depending on how accurate your test data was.

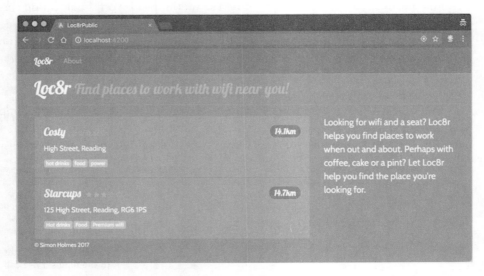

Figure 9.12   The Loc8r homepage as an Angular app, using geolocation to find places nearby from your own API

That's the last piece of the puzzle for the homepage. Loc8r now finds your current location and lists the places near you, which was the whole idea from the start. The last thing you'll do in this chapter is sort out the About page, during which you'll explore the challenges of injecting HTML through Angular bindings.

9.4   Safely binding HTML content

The current status of the About page in the Angular SPA is that it exists only as a default skeleton page, as you created it to demonstrate navigation and routing in Angular. In this section, you'll complete the page.

9.4.1   Adding the About page content to the app

The About page should be fairly straightforward. You add the content to the component definition and create the simple markup with the bindings to display it. Easy, right?

Start by adding the content to the component definition. In the following listing, you can see the class definition in about.component.ts. You're defining a `pageContent` member to hold all the text information, as you've done before. We've trimmed the text in the main content area to save ink and trees.

Listing 9.20   Creating the Angular controller for the About page

```
export class AboutComponent implements OnInit {

  constructor() { }

  ngOnInit() {
  }

  public pageContent = {
    header : {
      title : 'About Loc8r',
      strapline : ''
    },
    content : 'Loc8r was created to help people find places to sit
    ➥down and get a bit of work done.\n\nLorem ipsum dolor sit
    ➥amet, consectetur adipiscing elit.'
  };
}
```

As components go, this one is simple. No magic is going on here. Note, though, that you've still got the \n characters to denote line breaks.

Next, you need to create the HTML layout. From your original Pug templates, you know what the markup needs to be; you need a page header and then a couple of <div>s to hold the content. For the page header, you can reuse the pageHeader component that you created earlier and pass the data through as you did for the home-page. There's not much to the rest of the markup. The entire contents of about .component.html are shown in the following snippet:

```
<app-page-header [content]="pageContent.header"></app-page-header>
<div class="row">
  <div class="col-12 col-lg-8">{{ pageContent.content }}</div>
</div>
```

Again, nothing unusual here—only the page header, some HTML, and a standard Angular binding. If you look at this page in the browser, you'll see that the content is coming through, but the line breaks aren't displaying, as illustrated in figure 9.13.

This situation isn't ideal. You want your text to be readable and shown as originally intended. If you can change the way that the distances appear on the homepage by using a pipe, why not do the same thing to fix the line breaks? Give it a shot, and create a new pipe.

9.4.2   Creating a pipe to transform the line breaks

You want to create a pipe that takes the provided text and replaces each instance of \n with a <br/> tag. You've already solved this problem in Pug by using a JavaScript replace command, as shown in the following code snippet:

```
p !{(content).replace(/\n/g, '<br/>')}
```

With Angular, you can't do this inline. Instead, you need to create a pipe and apply it to the binding.

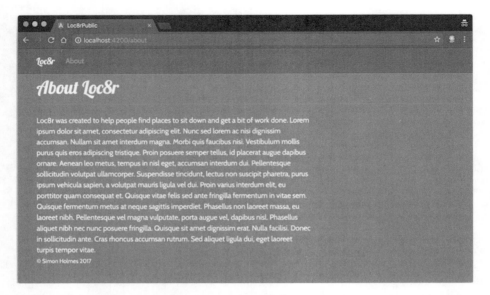

Figure 9.13   The content for the About page is coming through from the controller, but the line breaks are being ignored.

CREATING AN HTMLLINEBREAKS PIPE

As you've already seen, pipes are best created by the Angular CLI, so run the following command in terminal to generate the files and register the pipe with the application:

```
$ ng generate pipe html-line-breaks
```

The pipe itself is fairly straightforward. It needs to accept incoming text as a string value. Replace each \n with a <br/>, and then return a string value. Update the main content of html-line-breaks.html to look like the following snippet:

```
export class HtmlLineBreaksPipe implements PipeTransform {

  transform(text: string): string {
    return text.replace(/\n/g, '<br/>');
  }

}
```

When you've done that, try using it.

APPLYING THE PIPE TO THE BINDING

Applying a pipe to a binding is simple; you've already done it a few times. In the HTML, add the pipe character (|) after the data object being bound, and follow it with the name of the filter like this:

```
<div class="col-12 col-lg-8">{{ pageContent.content | htmlLineBreaks }}</div>
```

Simple, right? But if you try it in the browser, all isn't quite as you'd hoped. As you can see in figure 9.14, the line breaks are being replaced by <br/>, but they're being displayed as text instead of rendering as HTML.

Figure 9.14 The `<br/>` tags being inserted with your filter are being rendered as text rather than HTML tags.

Hmmmm, this isn't quite what you wanted, but at least the pipe seems to be working. There's a good reason for this output: security. Angular protects you and your application from malicious attacks by preventing HTML from being injected into a data binding. Think about when you let visitors write reviews for locations, for example. If they could add any HTML they wanted to, someone could easily insert a `<script>` tag and run some JavaScript, hijacking the page.

But there's a way to let a subset of HTML tags through into a binding, which you'll look at next.

9.4.3 Safely binding HTML by using a property binding

Angular lets you pass through some HTML tags if you use a property binding instead of the default bindings you normally use for content. This technique works only for a subset of HTML tags to prevent XSS hacks, attacks, and weaknesses. Think of property binding as being "one-way" binding. The component can't read the data back out and use it, but it can update it and change the data in the binding.

You used property bindings when you passed data into nested components. Remember building the About page? There, you were binding data to a property you defined in the nested component, which you called `content`. Here, you're binding to a native property of a tag—in this case, `innerHTML`.

Property bindings are denoted by wrapping square brackets around them and then passing the value. You can remove the content binding in about.component .html and use a property binding:

```
<div class="col-12 col-lg-8" [innerHTML]="pageContent.content |
    htmlLineBreaks"></div>
```

Note that you can apply pipes to this type of binding too, so you're still using your `htmlLineBreaks` pipe. Finally, when you view the About page in the browser, you'll see the line breaks in place, looking like figure 9.15.

Success! You've made a great start toward building Loc8r as an Angular SPA. You've got a couple of pages, some routing and navigation, geolocation, and a great modular application architecture. Keep on moving!

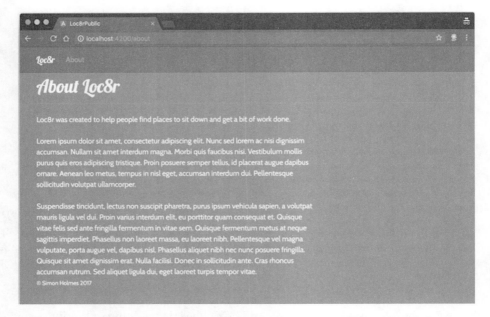

Figure 9.15   Using the `htmlLineBreaks` pipe in conjunction with the property binding, you now see the line breaks rendering as intended.

9.5   *Challenge*

Use what you've learned about Angular so far and create a new component called `rating-stars`. This component will be used in the homepage listing section and in the other places where you display rating stars, which you'll be building out in the next section.

This new component should

- Accept an incoming number value (the rating)
- Display the correct number of solid stars based on the rating
- Be reusable many times on a single page

As a clue, your elements should look something like this:

```
<app-rating-stars [rating]="location.rating"></app-rating-stars>
```

Good luck! The code (should you need it) is available in GitHub, on the chapter-09 branch.

In chapter 10, you'll continue building out the Angular SPA, encountering more-complex page layouts and modal popups, and accepting user input via forms.

Summary

In this chapter, you learned

- That Angular has a Router and how it works
- How to build a functional website and use site navigation
- That using nested components to create a modular and scalable application is best practice
- How to work with external interfaces like the browser's geolocation capabilities

Building a single-page application with Angular: The next level

10

This chapter covers

- Routing with URL parameters in Angular
- Querying the API with URL parameter data
- Building more-complex layouts and handling form submissions
- Creating a separate router configuration file
- Replacing the Express UI with the Angular app

In this chapter, you'll follow on from the work you started in chapter 9 with building a single-page application (SPA). By the end of this chapter, the Loc8r application will be a single Angular application that uses your API to get the data.

Figure 10.1 shows where you are in the overall plan, still recreating the main application as an Angular SPA.

You'll start by creating the missing pages and functionality, and see how to use URL parameters in routes, including using them when querying the API. When you've got most of the functionality in place, you'll build the form to add new

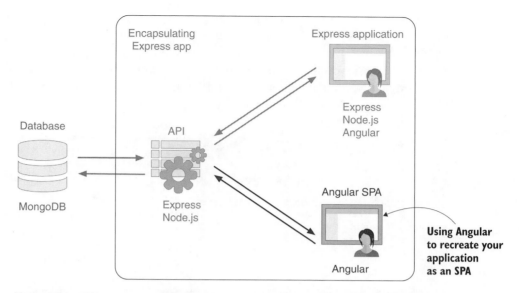

Figure 10.1   This chapter continues the work you started in chapter 9: recreating the Loc8r application as an Angular SPA, moving the application logic from the back end to the front end.

reviews, but rather than have a separate page as you had in Express, you'll include the form inline and be able to add reviews without leaving the Details page. This technique is an SPA way of doing things and eliminates extra round trips to the server. When everything's running, you'll look at a couple of ways to improve the architecture to follow some Angular and TypeScript best practices.

To finish, you'll use your Angular application as the front end for Loc8r, eliminating the need for the public-facing part of the Express application.

10.1   Working with more-complex views and routing parameters

In this section, you'll add the Details page to the Angular SPA. One crucial aspect is retrieving the location ID from the URL parameter to ensure that you get the correct data. Using URL parameters in this way is common practice and is a useful technique to know in any framework. You'll also have to update the data service to ask the API for specific location details. As you translate the Pug view into an Angular template, you'll also discover some additional functionality that Angular provides to help you create the various layouts required.

You've got a lot to do, so before you get into the fun stuff, you'd better plan it.

10.1.1   Planning the layout

The Details page has quite a bit more to it than the others you've made in Angular so far, but as you know what it looks like, you can start to plan it from a high level. When that's done, it'll be easier to add the details.

By looking at the layout and what you've done already, you can begin to see the different components you'll need and how to nest them. You'll keep the existing framework component on the outside, of course, containing the navigation and footer. In the routable area, you'll have a new details-page component containing the page header, sidebar, and main content. Figure 10.2 shows a sketch of this layout plan overlaid on a screenshot of the Details page itself.

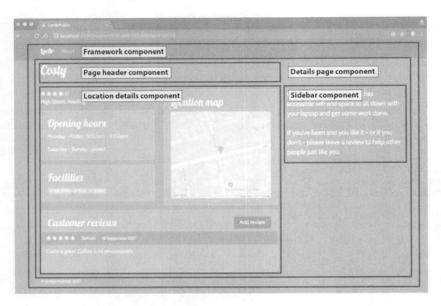

Figure 10.2   Planning the components and nesting needed for building the Details page in Angular

This plan gives you a good idea of what you need to build and what you can reuse. We hope that you're starting to see why creating reusable components is a good idea! At this point, note that you need some of the location data in three components: the page header, the location details component, and the sidebar. You'll need to take this fact into consideration when coding the page.

Of the five components in the plan, you need to create two: the Details page component to organize all the others and the location details component to display the actual details. You'll create basic versions of these components next so that you have a page to route to.

10.1.2   *Creating the required components*

You know that you want a Details page component containing the location details along with the sidebar and header. The location details component is missing, so you'll create a skeleton of that first. Then you can create the framework component ready for routing.

Use the Angular CLI to create the location details component; run the following command in terminal in the app_public folder:

```
$ ng generate component location-details
```

You can leave the default content in this new component for the time being, as you'll build it out properly soon. Next, create the Details page component, and add the skeleton layout to it. In terminal, use the Angular CLI again with the following command:

```
$ ng generate component details-page
```

You'll add some content to this component, as it's going to hold the other components for the page: the page header, location details, and sidebar. Listing 10.1 shows how you want to lay these components out in details-page.component.html. You'll also add the content bindings for the page header and sidebar so that you can pass in information from this component.

Listing 10.1   The basic layout for details-page.component.html

Page header component, including a property binding

```
<app-page-header [content]="pageContent.header"></app-page-header>
<div class="row">
  <div class="col-12 col-md-8">
    <app-location-details></app-location-details>     ⟵── Location details component
  </div>
  <app-sidebar class="col-12 col-md-4" [content]="pageContent.sidebar">
  ⮕</app-sidebar>     ⟵┐
</div>                        │ Sidebar component, including
                             │ a property binding
```

So that you'll be able to see the content in the header and sidebar, you'll create some default content. In the HTML for the Details page component, you'll use the bindings pageContent.header and pageContent.sidebar, so in the component class, you'll create a corresponding pageContent member containing header and sidebar properties. The following listing shows what this looks like in details-page.component.ts, also giving the content properties some default text.

Listing 10.2   The starting content for the Details page in details-page.component.ts

```
export class DetailsPageComponent implements OnInit {

  constructor() { }

  ngOnInit() {
  }                                    The new pageContent
  public pageContent = {     ⟵───┐    member containing . . .
    header: {               ⟵──────── header details and . . .
      title: 'Location name',
      strapline: ''
    },
    sidebar: 'is on Loc8r because it has accessible wifi and space
```

```
  ➥to sit down with your laptop and get some work done.\n\nIf
  ➥you\'ve been and you like it - or if you don\'t - please
  ➥leave a review to help other people just like you.'  ◁────────  ...sidebar
};                                                                  content
```

}

Now you've got your Details page component, containing the three nested components you need to lay out the page. You've even got some starting data being passed into two of the nested components.

You're ready to set up the routing so that you can see the page.

10.1.3 *Setting up and defining routes with URL parameters*

Defining routes with URL parameters is as easy in Angular as it is in Express. Even the syntax is the same—not something you hear often in the programming world!

Your routes for the app are defined in app.module.ts, so that's where you'll add the new one. As you want to accept a URL parameter, you'll define the route the same way you did in Express: by putting a locationId variable at the end of the path, preceded by a colon.

Listing 10.3 Adding the Details page route to app.module.ts

```
RouterModule.forRoot([
  {
    path: '',
    component: HomepageComponent
  },
  {
    path: 'about',
    component: AboutComponent           Defines a 'locationId' URL
  },                                    parameter in the route by
  {                                     prefixing it with a colon
    path: 'location/:locationId',  ◁────┘
    component: DetailsPageComponent
  }
])
```

With that in place, you can go to location/*something* in the browser, and Angular will route you to the Details page component. At the moment, this component looks like figure 10.3.

If you remember from your original layouts, the sidebar content in this page should be in two paragraphs, so your line breaks aren't coming through. Fortunately, you've already created a pipe for that purpose. You need to update the sidebar component to use it. In sidebar.component.html, change the Angular binding to an innerHTML property binding, passing in the content and the htmlLineBreaks pipe like this:

```
<p class="lead" [innerHTML]="content | htmlLineBreaks"></p>
```

Now the \n parts of the sidebar content are converted to <br/> tags and rendered as HTML, looking like figure 10.4.

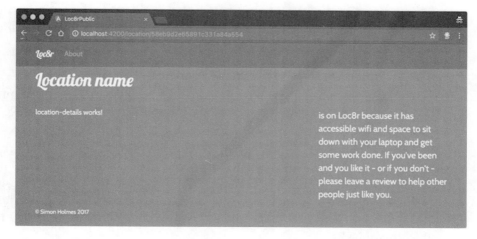

Figure 10.3   Testing the new location details route and seeing the default content you added to the components

The general page layout looks good, and you can see that it's working. Before you build it out, it would be useful to navigate to this page with real location IDs in the URL. To do so, you need to update the links in the homepage listings.

CREATING ANGULAR LINKS TO THE DETAILS PAGE

The homepage listing currently displays links to this page, and if you try them, they take you there. But you may well notice that when you do, the page flickers. This happens because the links are standard `href` attributes in an `<a>` tag, so the browser follows them like normal links. The result is that the page has a full reload and reloads the Angular application—not what you want in an SPA!

You want Angular to capture clicks of these links and to handle the navigation and routing. When you created the navigation, you used `routerLink` instead of `href` in the `<a>` tags, and you need to do the same here. In home-list.component.html, find the link to the location, and swap out the `href` attribute:

```
<a routerLink="/location/{{location._id}}">{{location.name}}</a>
```

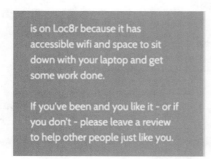

Figure 10.4   Enabling line breaks in the sidebar by using your custom pipe

The rest of the code can stay the same. With that simple change, you've made your app even more like a proper SPA. Now you're ready to start using the URL parameter in the page.

10.1.4 *Using URL parameters in components and services*

The plan is to get the location ID URL parameter and use it in a call to the API to get the details for a specific location. When the data comes back, you want to display it on the page.

Where's the best place to put this logic? Any of the components in the routable area could be configured to get the URL parameter and call the API, but you want to display data in all three nested components. So you'll go for the approach of using the "parent" Details page component to get the data and then pass it through to the three child components. First, you'll add a method to your data service to call the API to get a single location by ID.

CREATING THE DATA SERVICE TO CALL THE API

The data service that you created in chapter 8 currently has a single method: `get-Locations`. This method retrieves a list of locations when given a pair of coordinates. The new method you need has a similar construct, so make a copy of this method in loc8r-data.service.ts and call it `getLocationById`.

You need to make a few small adjustments to get this method working:

1 Change the expected input parameters to a single `locationId` of type `string`.
2 Change the return type to a single `Location` instance instead of an array.
3 Change the API URL to call, using `locationId` as a URL parameter.
4 Set the JSON response to a single `Location` instance.

The following listing shows how this method looks in code, in loc8r-data.service.ts.

> **Listing 10.4   Adding a method to get a location by ID in loc8r-data.service.ts**

```
public getLocationById(locationId: string): Promise<Location> {
  const url: string = `${this.apiBaseUrl}/locations/${locationId}`;
  return this.http
    .get(url)
    .toPromise()
    .then(response => response as Location)
    .catch(this.handleError);
}
```

Sets the correct input parameters and expected return type, both single items

Changes the API URL to use the location ID as a URL parameter

Sets the JSON response to be a single Location instance

With the data service method ready, you can import the service into the Details page component, ready to use.

IMPORTING THE DATA SERVICE INTO THE COMPONENT

You've imported a service into a component before—the data service into the home-list component—so we won't dwell on the process too much here. You'll need to import the data service into the Details page component, add it to the providers, and then make it available by declaring it in the class constructor.

While you're here, you'll also import the `Location` class from the home-list component and empty the default page content. All these updates to details-page.component are shown in the following listing.

Listing 10.5 Importing your data service in details-page.component.ts

```
import { Component, OnInit } from '@angular/core';
import { Loc8rDataService } from '../loc8r-data.service';        ← Imports your data service
import { Location } from '../home-list/home-list.component';      ←

@Component({                                                        Imports the
  selector: 'app-details-page',                                    Location class
  templateUrl: './details-page.component.html',                    definition
  styleUrls: ['./details-page.component.css'],
})
export class DetailsPageComponent implements OnInit {

  constructor(private loc8rDataService: Loc8rDataService) { }     ←

  ngOnInit(): void { }                                             Creates a private
                                                                    local instance of
  public pageContent = {            ←   Clears the default          the data service
    header : {                          page content
      title : '',
      strapline : ''
    },
    sidebar : ''
  };
}
```

The only real thing to be careful with here is the case of `loc8rDataService` in the constructor: the class type definition has an uppercase `L`, and the local instance is defined with a lowercase `l`.

Now you're ready to get the URL parameter into the component.

USING URL PARAMETERS IN A COMPONENT

Given that using URL parameters in an app is a common requirement, the process is surprisingly complicated. You need three new pieces of functionality:

- `ActivatedRoute` from the Angular router to get you the value of the current route from inside the component
- `ParamMap` from the Angular router to get you the URL parameters of the active route as an Observable
- `switchMap` from RxJS to get the values from the `ParamMap` Observable and use them to call your API, creating a second Observable

The following snippet shows in bold the additions needed in details-page.component
.ts to import these pieces of functionality:

```
import { Component, OnInit } from '@angular/core';
import { ActivatedRoute, ParamMap } from '@angular/router';
import { Loc8rDataService } from '../loc8r-data.service';
import { Location } from '../home-list/home-list.component';
import { switchMap } from 'rxjs/operators';
```

You also need to make the activated route available to the component by defining a
private member route of type ActivatedRoute in the constructor:

```
constructor(
  private loc8rDataService: Loc8rDataService,
  private route: ActivatedRoute
) { }
```

Now comes the complicated bit. Complete these steps to get a location ID from the
URL parameter and turn it into location data from the API:

1 When the component initializes, use switchMap to subscribe to the paramMap
   Observable of the activated route.
2 When the paramMap Observable returns a ParamMap object, get the value of the
   locationId URL parameter.
3 Call the getLocationsById method of your data service, passing it the ID.
4 Return the API call so that it returns an Observable.
5 Subscribe to listen for when the Observable returns the data from your API.
   The result should be a single object of type Location.
6 Set the content for the page header and sidebar, using the location name
   returned from the API.

Phew! That's a lot of steps for a seemingly simple process. All this takes place in the
ngOnInit lifecycle hook in details-page.component.ts. The next listing shows what the
code looks like.

Listing 10.6   Getting and using the URL parameter in details-page.component.ts

**Gets the paramMap Observable
of the activated route**

**Uses the pipe operator to
compose a sequence of
operations that will act
on the Observable**

**Uses switchMap to extract
the required elements
from the ParamMap and
return an Observable**

```
ngOnInit(): void {
  this.route.paramMap
    .pipe(
      switchMap((params: ParamMap) => {
        let id = params.get('locationId');
        return this.loc8rDataService.getLocationById(id);
      })
    )
```

**Uses the .get method to get the value of the
locationId URL parameter from the ParamMap**

**Makes the call to your new data service
method, returning it as an Observable**

```
    ▷  .subscribe((newLocation: Location) => {
          this.pageContent.header.title = newLocation.name;          ◁
          this.pageContent.sidebar = `${newLocation.name} is on Loc8r
          ➥[because it has accessible wifi and space to sit down with
          ➥your laptop and get some work done.\n\nIf you\'ve been and
          ➥you like it - or if you don\'t - please leave a review to
          ➥help other people just like you.`;
       });
    }
```

Sends the location name to the page header and sidebar

Subscribes to the API call Observable, expecting a Location back

That's some fairly dense code; a lot is happening in a few lines and commands. We recommend reading the plan and the annotated code a few times to piece everything together. It's powerful, a little different from what you've seen so far, and about as complex as you'll see in this book. In particular, note the two chained Observables: first, the route `paramMap` being subscribed to by the `switchMap`, which returns the second.

The good news is that when you're done, your Details page shows the location name in the page header and the sidebar, as shown in figure 10.5.

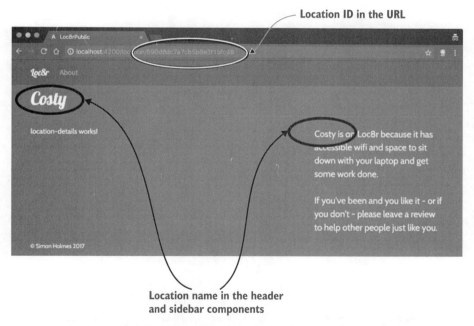

Location ID in the URL

Location name in the header and sidebar components

Figure 10.5 Displaying the location name in the header and sidebar after getting the location ID from the URL and sending it to the API

You're now using the location ID in the URL to query the database and passing a bit of the returned data to two of the components on the page. Before you build out the main part of the Details page, make sure that the final component is getting the data it needs.

10.1.5 *Passing data to the Details page component*

To pass the location data from the Details page component to the nested location details component, you need to do three things:

1 Add a class member to the Details page component to hold the location data when you get it back from the data service.
2 Pass the data into the child component, using a property binding in the HTML.
3 Update the location details component to accept this incoming data.

First, as shown in listing 10.7, define a new member `newLocation` of type `Location` in details-page.component.ts, and give it a value when you get a location back from the API call.

> **Listing 10.7 Exposing the found location details in details-page.component.ts**

```
newLocation: Location;

ngOnInit(): void {
  this.route.paramMap
    .switchMap((params: ParamMap) => {
      let id = params.get('locationId');
      return this.loc8rDataService.getLocationById(id);
    })
    .subscribe((newLocation: Location) => {
      this.newLocation = newLocation;              ⊲──  Updating the local
      this.pageContent.header.title = newLocation.name;    newLocation with
      this.pageContent.sidebar = `${newLocation.name} is on Loc8r   that received from
➥because it has accessible wifi and space to sit down with   the Observable
➥your laptop and get some work done.\n\nIf you\'ve been and
➥you like it - or if you don\'t - please leave a review to
➥help other people just like you.`;
    });
}
```

With the location details being exposed through this `newLocation` class member, you can pass this through to the nested component by adding a property binding to the element in details-page.component.html:

```
<app-location-details [location]="newLocation"></app-location-details>
```

You've seen this type of setup before. The property binding will pass the contents of `newLocation` in the Details page component to the `location` member of the location details component.

Your location details component doesn't have a location member yet, so you'll need to add it to the component definition and set it up to be an input member of type `Location`. You've performed these actions before, so the following listing serves as a handy reminder, showing everything in place in location-details.component.ts.

Listing 10.8   Accepting incoming location data in location-details.component.ts

```
import { Component, OnInit, Input } from '@angular/core';
import { Location } from '../home-list/home-list.component';

@Component({
  selector: 'app-location-details',
  templateUrl: './location-details.component.html',
  styleUrls: ['./location-details.component.css']
})
export class LocationDetailsComponent implements OnInit {

  @Input() location: Location;

  public googleAPIKey: string = '<Put your Google Maps API Key here>';

  constructor() { }

  ngOnInit() {
  }

}
```

Imports 'Input' from the Angular core

Imports your 'Location' class definition

Defines 'location' as an input member of type 'Location'

Don't forget the Google API key. (You got one in chapter 2, didn't you?)

The page is still working and looks as it did before, but now the Details page component is getting the data from the database and passing it to all three of the nested components. It's time to build out the nested view.

10.1.6   Building the Details page view

For the location details, you've already got a Pug template with Pug data bindings, and you need to transform this template into HTML with Angular bindings. You have quite a few bindings to put in place, as well as some loops, utilizing Angular's `*ngFor` construct. You'll use the `rating-stars` component that you created for the challenge at the end of chapter 9 to show the overall rating and the rating for each review. If you haven't created this component, refer to the book's code repository on GitHub. You'll also need to allow line breaks in the review text by using the `htmlLineBreaks` pipe.

GETTING THE MAIN TEMPLATE IN PLACE

Listing 10.9 shows everything in place, with the bindings in bold. This code should make up the entire contents of location-details.component.html. We've left out some pieces, such as the opening times, which you'll fill in when you've got this code in place and tested.

Listing 10.9   Angular template for location details in location-details.component.html

```
<div class="row">
  <div class="col-12 col-md-6">
    <app-rating-stars [rating]="location.rating"></app-rating-stars>
    <p>{{ location.address }}</p>
    <div class="card card-primary">
```

Use rating-stars component to show average rating for location.

```
        <div class="card-block">
          <h2 class="card-title">Opening hours</h2>
          <!-- Opening times to go here -->
        </div>
      </div>
      <div class="card card-primary">
        <div class="card-block">
          <h2 class="card-title">Facilities</h2>
          <span *ngFor="let facility of location.facilities" class="badge
          ➥badge-warning">
            <i class="fa fa-check"></i>                    Loop through facilities.
            {{facility}}
          </span>
        </div>
      </div>
    </div>
    <div class="col-12 col-md-6 location-map">
      <div class="card card-primary">              Don't forget the
        <div class="card-block">                    Google Maps API key.
          <h2 class="card-title">Location map</h2>
          <img src="https://maps.googleapis.com/maps/api/staticmap?
          ➥center={{location.coords[1]}},{{location.coords[0]}}
          ➥&zoom=17&size=400x350&sensor=false&markers={{location
          ➥coords[1]}},{{location.coords[0]}}&key=
          ➥{{googleAPIKey}}&scale=2" class="img-fluid rounded"/>  ◁
        </div>
      </div>
    </div>
  </div>
  <div class="row">
    <div class="col-12">
      <div class="card card-primary review-card">
        <div class="card-block"><a href="/location/{{location._id}}
        ➥/review/new" class="btn btn-primary float-right">Add review</a>
          <h2 class="card-title">Customer reviews</h2>
          <div *ngFor="let review of location.reviews" class="row review">
            <div class="col-12 no-gutters review-header">
              <app-rating-stars [rating]="review.rating">
              ➥</app-rating-stars>                           ◁
              <span class="reviewAuthor">{{ review.author }}</span>
              <small class="reviewTimestamp">{{ review.createdOn }}</small>
            </div>
            <div class="col-12">
              <p [innerHTML]="review.reviewText | htmlLineBreaks"></p>  ◁
            </div>
          </div>
        </div>
      </div>
    </div>
  </div>
</div>
```

Loop through reviews.

Apply htmlLineBreaks pipe to review text and bind as HTML.

Use rating-stars component to show rating for each review.

That code listing is long, but that's to be expected, as quite a lot is going on in the Details page. If you look at the page in the browser now, it looks about right. You have a few things to fix, but you know about them.

Although the page looks good, if you open the JavaScript console, you'll see that the page has thrown a lot of errors along the lines of `Cannot read property 'rating'` `of undefined`. These errors are binding errors, happening because the nested location details component is trying to bind to data as soon as the page loads, but you don't have any data until after the API call has completed.

HIDING COMPONENTS TO STOP PREMATURE-BINDING ERRORS

The binding errors are occurring because the component is trying to bind to data before the data has been provided. How do you stop this from happening? A good way is to hide the component in the HTML until the data has been received from the API and you have the location details ready to display.

Angular includes a helpful native directive called `*ngIf`, which you can add to an element in the HTML. `*ngIf` is given an expression. If the expression resolves to `true`, the element is shown; otherwise, it's hidden.

For your situation, you want to show the location details component only when the location data exists. So you can add an `*ngIf` directive to the location details element in details-page.component.html like so:

```
<div class="col-12 col-md-8">
  <app-location-details *ngIf="newLocation" [location]="newLocation">
  ➥</app-location-details>
</div>
```

With that small change, you have no more binding errors!

Now it's on to fixing the remaining page template issues. Because you're not showing opening times yet, the reviews are coming through oldest first, and the data of the reviews needs formatting.

ADDING IF-ELSE STYLE LOGIC WITH NGSWITCHCASE TO SHOW THE OPENING TIMES

It's not unusual to want some type of `if-else` logic in a template to show different chunks of HTML depending on a certain parameter. For each opening time, you want to display the days in the range and either a closed message or the opening and closing times. In your Pug template, you had a bit of logic, a simple `if` statement checking whether `closed` was `true`:

```
if time.closed
| closed
else
| #{time.opening} - #{time.closing}
```

You want to do something similar in your Angular template. You've seen how `*ngIf` can work for a one-off case, but for `if-else` logic, Angular works along the lines of JavaScript's `switch` method. With this method, you define which condition you want to check at the top, and then provide different options depending on the value of the condition.

The key parts here are an `[ngSwitch]` binding for defining the condition to switch on, an `*ngSwitchCase` directive for providing a specific value, and an `*ngSwitch-Default` directive for providing a backup option if none of the specific values matches. You can see all these parts in action in the following listing, where you add the opening times to location-details.component.html.

Listing 10.10   Using `ngSwitch` in location-details.component.html

```
<div class="card card-primary">
  <div class="card-block">
    <h2 class="card-title">Opening hours</h2>
    <p class="card-text" *ngFor="let time of location.openingTimes"
      [ngSwitch]="time.closed">
        {{ time.days }} :
        <span *ngSwitchCase="true">Closed</span>
        <span *ngSwitchDefault>{{ time.opening + " - " + time.closing}}
      </span>
    </p>
  </div>
</div>
```

Runs switch based on the value of time.closed → `[ngSwitch]="time.closed"`

When time.closed is true, outputs closed → `<span *ngSwitchCase="true">Closed</span>`

Otherwise, default action is to output opening and closing times → `</span>`

Now you have a bit of logic in the template. Note that as all the `ngSwitch` commands are property bindings and directives, they need to be added to HTML tags.

Okay, it's time to get the reviews showing most recent first.

CHANGING THE DISPLAY ORDER OF A LIST BY USING A CUSTOM PIPE

If you have experience with AngularJS, you may be expecting an update of the old `orderBy` filter, which could be used to magically reorder a repeated list in almost any way imaginable. It was flexible and powerful, but it came with a downside: with large datasets, this flexible filter became slow. For this reason, the Angular team decided not to include it in the new versions.

Without a native way to change the order of a list, the options are to write some code in the component or to create a new pipe. A pipe is often best—especially if you think you may want to reuse the functionality somewhere else—and you also know that a pipe will always be applied if the data changes.

Create a new pipe specifically to order the reviews by date, most recent first. You'll create the new pipe the normal way by running the following command in terminal, in the app_public folder:

```
$ ng generate pipe most-recent-first
```

When the pipe is generated, add it to the `*ngFor` directive looping the reviews in location-details.component.html, like so:

```
<div *ngFor="let review of location.reviews | mostRecentFirst" class="row
    review">
```

Next, you'll code the pipe itself. Remember that it comes with a `transform` hook that accepts a value and returns a value. For your purposes, you want to accept and return an array, as reviews are returned from the database as an array.

As you're working with arrays, you can use JavaScript's native array `sort` method, which accepts a function as a parameter. This function takes two items at a time from the array and can compare them however you code. The return value of the function should be a positive or negative number. A negative number means that the order stays the same; positive means that the order changes.

You're comparing dates and want the most recent first. In terms of comparison operators, a more recent date is "greater than" an older date. So if the date of the first parameter is greater than (more recent than) the date of the second, you return a negative number to keep the order the same. Otherwise, return a positive number to swap them round. That's more complicated to explain than it is to code!

The next listing shows what the pipe code looks like, creating a comparison function called `compare` and using it to sort the array of reviews before returning the updated array.

> **Listing 10.11   Creating most-recent-first.pipe.ts to change display order of reviews**

```
export class MostRecentFirstPipe implements PipeTransform {

  private compare(a, b) {                            ◁──┐ Your comparing
    const createdOnA = a.createdOn;                      │ function, taking two
    const createdOnB = b.createdOn;                      │ values from the array
                          Gets the creation date
                          of each review

    let comparison = 1;
    if (createdOnA > createdOnB)      If a is more recent than
      comparison = -1;                b, returns -1;
    }                                 otherwise, returns 1
    return comparison;
  }

  transform(reviews: any[]): any[] {          ◁──┐ The transform method, accepting
    if (reviews && reviews.length > 0) {           and returning arrays of reviews
      return reviews.sort(this.compare);    ◁──┐
    }                                           │
    return null;                                │
  }                                       Uses your compare function
}                                         to sort the array, returning
                                          the reordered version
```

If you reload the page, you should see your reviews showing in the correct order: most recent first. It's a little hard to tell, though, as the date format isn't exactly user friendly. You'll fix this problem in the next section.

FIXING THE DATE FORMAT BY USING THE DATE PIPE

Fortunately, formatting dates is much simpler than ordering by them. One of Angular's default pipes is the `date` pipe, which formats a given date in the style you want. This pipe takes one argument: the format for your date.

To apply your formatting, you send a string describing the output you want. Too many options are available to be listed here, but the format is easy to get the hang of. For the format *1 September 2017*, for example, send the string `'d MMMM yyyy'`, as shown in the following listing.

Listing 10.12   Formatting with a `date` pipe in **location-details.component.html**

```html
<div *ngFor="let review of location.reviews" class="row review">
  <div class="col-12 no-gutters review-header">
    <app-rating-stars [rating]="review.rating"></app-rating-stars>
    <span class="reviewAuthor">{{ review.author }}</span>
    <small class="reviewTimestamp">{{ review.createdOn | date : 'd MMMM
      yyyy' }}</small>
  </div>
  <div class="col-12">
    <p [innerHTML]="review.reviewText | htmlLineBreaks"></p>
  </div>
</div>
```

With that, you're done with the layout and formatting of the Details page, which should look like figure 10.6.

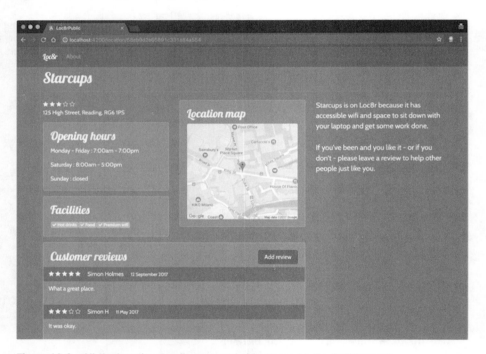

Figure 10.6   All the location details are now being shown on the Angular page.

The next and final step is enabling reviews to be added, but you're going to drop the concept of an extra page to do this, which is how you did it in Express. Instead, you'll do it inline on the page to provide a slicker experience.

10.2 Working with forms and handling submitted data

In this section, you'll create the Add Review page in Angular, and have it submit data to the API. Rather than navigate to a separate form page when the Add Review button is clicked, it'll display a form inline in the page. When the form is submitted, you'll have Angular handle the data, submit it to the API, and display the new review at the top of the list. You'll start by seeing what's involved with creating the form in Angular.

10.2.1 Creating the review form in Angular

To create the review form, you'll get the HTML in place, add data bindings to the input fields, make sure that they all work as expected, and, finally, ensure that the form is initially hidden and is displayed only if the button is clicked.

PUTTING THE FORM HTML IN PLACE

Add the inline form to the page just after the Customer reviews<h2> tag, as shown in the following listing. Much of the layout is taken from the form you used in Express, including the form input names and IDs.

> **Listing 10.13   Adding the review form to location-details.component.html**

```
<h2 class="card-title">Customer reviews</h2>
<div>                    ◁───────────
  <form action="">                      Adds the new div and the
    <hr>                                 form HTML directly after the
    <h4>Add your review</h4>             Customer reviews header
    <div class="form-group row">
      <label for="name" class="col-sm-2 col-form-label">Name</label>
      <div class="col-sm-10">
        <input id="name" name="name" required="required" class="form-
        ➥control">
      </div>
    </div>
    <div class="form-group row">
      <label for="rating" class="col-sm-2 col-form-label">Rating</label>
      <div class="col-sm-10 col-md-2">
        <select id="rating" name="rating" class="form-control">
          <option value="5">5</option>
          <option value="4">4</option>
          <option value="3">3</option>
          <option value="2">2</option>
          <option value="1">1</option>
        </select>
      </div>
    </div>
    <div class="form-group row">
      <label for="review" class="col-sm-2 col-form-label">Review</label>
      <div class="col-sm-10">
        <textarea name="review" id="review" rows="5" class="form-
        ➥control"></textarea>
      </div>
    </div>
    <div class="form-group row">
```

```
      <div class="col-12">
        <button type="submit" class="btn btn-primary float-right"
        ➥style="margin-left:15px">Submit review</button>
        <button type="button" class="btn btn-default float-
        ➥right">Cancel</button>
      </div>
    </div>
    <hr>
  </form>
</div>
```

Right now, you're not doing anything clever or asking Angular to do anything. You've put raw HTML with some Bootstrap classes in the template. In the browser, this looks like figure 10.7.

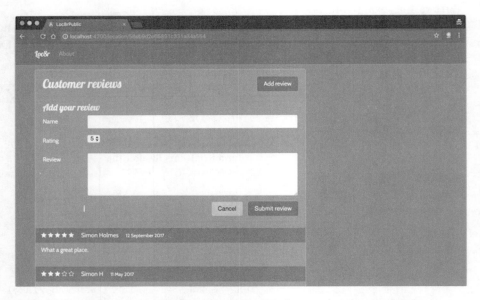

Figure 10.7   The review form displays inline in the Details page, between the Add Review button and the list of reviews.

That's the basic form in place. Next, add the data bindings.

ADDING DATA BINDINGS TO FORM INPUTS

In Express, you posted the form to another URL and handled the submitted data there, but with Angular, you don't want to change the page at all. With Angular, the approach is to add data bindings to all the fields in a form so the component can access the values.

To add a data binding to a form field, use a directive with a special syntax like this: `[(ngModel)]="bindingName"`. (Remembering the order of the brackets can be difficult, so this has become known as "banana in a boat" to help you remember!)

To use `ngModel` in your HTML, you need to have `FormsModule` and `Reactive-FormsModule` imported into the application in app.module.ts. Add the line `import { FormsModule, ReactiveFormsModule } from '@angular/forms';` to app.module.ts, and add both of those module names to the `imports` array in the same file.

In your component, you'll want to keep all the submitted form data inside a single object so you can pass it around easily. Define a new public member, `newReview`, in location-details.component.html, giving it properties for the author name, rating, and review content. Each property needs to have a default value, so the definition should look like this:

```
public newReview = {
  author: '',
  rating: 5,
  reviewText: ''
};
```

Now that this `newReview` object and its properties are defined in the component, you can use them in the HTML. The following listing shows how to add the bindings to the form in location-details.component.html.

Listing 10.14 Adding data bindings to review form in location-details.component.html

```
<form action="">
  <hr>
  <h4>Add your review</h4>
  <div class="form-group row">
    <label for="name" class="col-sm-2 col-form-label">Name</label>
    <div class="col-sm-10">
      <input [(ngModel)]="newReview.author" id="name" name="name"
      ➥required="required" class="form-control">        ◁────────────┐
    </div>                                                           │
  </div>                                                             │
  <div class="form-group row">                                      │
    <label for="rating" class="col-sm-2 col-form-label">Rating</label>
    <div class="col-sm-10">                                         │
      <select [(ngModel)]="newReview.rating" id="rating" name="rating">  ◁──┤
        <option value="5">5</option>                                │
        <option value="4">4</option>                                │
        <option value="3">3</option>                Adds the "banana │
        <option value="2">2</option>                in a boat" model│
        <option value="1">1</option>                bindings to the │
      </select>                                       form inputs   │
    </div>                                                           │
  </div>                                                             │
  <div class="form-group row">                                      │
    <label for="reviewText" class="col-sm-2 col-form-label">Review</label>
    <div class="col-sm-10">                                         │
      <textarea [(ngModel)]="newReview.reviewText" name="reviewText"│
      ➥id="reviewText" rows="5" class="form-control"></textarea>   ◁──┘
    </div>
  </div>
  <div class="form-group row">
    <div class="col-12">
```

```
      <button type="submit" class="btn btn-primary float-right"
      ➥style="margin-left:15px">Submit review</button>
      <button type="button" class="btn btn-default float-
      ➥right">Cancel</button>
    </div>
  </div>
  <hr>
</form>
```

This looks good and, on the face of it, seems to work. But you want the rating to be a number, and in a select option, `value="5"` is a string containing the character 5.

WORKING WITH SELECT VALUES THAT ARE NOT STRINGS

A select option `value` is by default a string, but your database requires a number for the rating. Angular has a way to help you get different types of data from a select field.

Instead of using `value="STRING VALUE"` inside each `<option>`, use `[ngValue]=` `"ANGULAR EXPRESSION"`. When written out, the value of `[ngValue]` looks like a string, but it's an Angular expression. This could be an object or a true Boolean, but you want a number.

In location-details.component.html, update each of the `<option>` tags to use `[ngValue]` instead of value:

```
<option [ngValue]="5">5</option>
<option [ngValue]="4">4</option>
<option [ngValue]="3">3</option>
<option [ngValue]="2">2</option>
<option [ngValue]="1">1</option>
```

Now Angular gets the value of the `<select>` as a number, not a string. This technique will be useful when you submit the data to the API. Next, you hide the form by default, as you don't want it showing all the time.

SETTING THE VISIBILITY OF THE FORM

You don't want the Add Review section of the page to be visible when the page loads; you want the Add Review button to show it, and when the form is displayed, you want the Cancel button to hide it again.

To show and hide the form, you can use your old friend `*ngIf`. `*ngIf` needs a Boolean value to decide whether to show the element it's applied to, so you'll need to define one in the component.

In location-details.component.ts, define a new public member `formVisible` of type `boolean` with a default value of `false`:

```
public formVisible: boolean = false;
```

You've set the default value to `false`, as you want the form to be hidden by default. To use this Boolean to set the visibility of the form, locate the `<div>` surrounding the `<form>` in location-details.component.html, and add the `*ngIf` directive to it like this:

```
<h2 class="card-title">Customer reviews</h2>
<div *ngIf="formVisible">
  <form action="">
```

Now the form is hidden by default when the page loads.

TOGGLING THE VISIBILITY OF THE FORM

To change the visibility of the form, you need a way to change the value of `form-Visible` when the Add Review and Cancel buttons are clicked. Not surprisingly, Angular has an on-click handler you can use to track clicks of elements and then do something.

Angular's click handler is accessed by adding `(click)` to the element and giving it an Angular expression. This expression could be one that calls a public member in the component class or any other kind of valid expression. You want to set `formVisible` to `true` when the Add Review button is clicked and `false` when the Cancel button is clicked.

In location-details.component.html, change the Add Review button from an `<a>` tag to a `<button>`, removing the `href` attribute and replacing it with a `(click)` setting `formVisible` to be `true`:

```
<button (click)="formVisible=true" class="btn btn-primary float-right">Add
    review</button>
```

In a similar way, add a `(click)` to the Cancel button, setting `formVisible` to be `false`:

```
<button type="button" (click)="formVisible=false" class="btn btn-default
    float-right">Cancel</button>
```

With those click handlers in place, you can use the two buttons to show and hide the review form, using the `formVisible` property of the component to keep track of the status. The final thing you need to do is hook up the form so that when it's submitted, a review is added.

10.2.2 *Sending submitted form data to an API*

Now is the time to make your review form work and add a review to the database when it's submitted. To get to this point, you have to complete a few steps:

1 Add a new member to your data service to `POST` new reviews to the API.
2 Have Angular handle the form when it's submitted.
3 Validate the form so that only complete data is accepted.
4 Send the review data to your service.
5 Push the review into the list in the Details page.

You'll start with step 1.

STEP 1: UPDATING THE DATA SERVICE TO ACCEPT NEW REVIEWS

To use the form to post review data, you need to add a method to your data service that talks to the correct API endpoint and can post the data. You'll call this new method `addReviewByLocationId` and have it accept two parameters: a location ID and the review data.

The contents of the method are the same as the others, except you'll use `post` instead of `get` to call the API. The following listing shows the new method to be added to loc8r-data.service.ts.

```
public addReviewByLocationId(locationId: string, formData: any): Promise<any> {
  const url: string = `${this.apiBaseUrl}/locations/${locationId}/reviews`;
  return this.http
    .post(url, formData)
    .toPromise()
    .then(response => response as any)
    .catch(this.handleError);
}
```

Brilliant; now you'll be able to use this method from your component when you've got the form handling sorted. Now move on to step 2.

STEP 2: ADDING THE ONSUBMIT FORM HANDLER

When working with a form in HTML, you typically have an action to tell the browser where to send the data and a method describing which HTTP verb to use. You may also have an `onSubmit` event handler if you want to do anything with the form data by using JavaScript before it's sent.

In an Angular SPA, you don't want the form to submit to a different URL, taking you to a new page. You want Angular to handle everything, so you'll remove the form element's `action=""` attribute and replace it with Angular's `ngSubmit` event handler to call a public member in the component. The following code snippet shows how the event handler is used, adding it to the form definition, calling a function in the component that you'll write in a moment:

```
<form (ngSubmit)="onReviewSubmit()">
```

This line calls a public method on the component called `onReviewSubmit` when the form is submitted. You need to create this method, so you'll add a simple method to location-details.component.ts to create a console log when the form is submitted:

```
public onReviewSubmit(): void {
  console.log(this.newReview);
}
```

Because you bound all the form fields to properties of `newReview`, this console log outputs all the data submitted. Now that you can capture the form data, you'll add some validation in step 3 so that only complete data is accepted.

STEP 3: VALIDATING THE SUBMITTED FORM DATA

Before you blindly send every form submission to the API to save to the database, you want to do some quick validation to ensure that all the fields are filled in. If any of them aren't filled in, you'll display an error message. Your browser may prevent forms from being submitted with empty required fields; if this is the case for you, temporarily remove the `required` attribute from the form fields to test the Angular validation.

 When a form is submitted, you'll start by removing any existing error messages before checking whether each data item in the form is truthy (that is, any form of `true` value). If any of the checks returns `false`—that is, a field has no data—you'll set a form error message in the component. If all the data exists, you'll continue to log it to the console as before.

 The following listing shows the new validation member you need to add to location-details.component.ts and how you need to change the `onReviewSubmit` function to use it.

Listing 10.16 Adding validation to the review form in location-details.component.ts

```
public formError: string;        ◁— Declares the formError variable

private formIsValid(): boolean {                        ◁
  if (this.newReview.author && this.newReview.rating
  ⟹&& this.newReview.reviewText) {
    return true;
  } else {
    return false;
  }
}

public onReviewSubmit():void {
  this.formError = '';                  ◁
  if (this.formIsValid()) {
    console.log(this.newReview);
  } else {
    this.formError = 'All fields required, please try again';
  }
}
```

Private member to check that all form fields have content

Resets any existing error messages

If form validation passes, log submits data to console

Otherwise, sets an error message

Now that you're creating an error message, you want to show it to users when it's generated. For this task, you'll add in a new Bootstrap alert `div` to the form template and bind the message as the content. You want to show the `div` only when there's an error message to display, so use the familiar `*ngIf` directive to handle this task, checking whether `formError` has a value.

 The addition you need to make to the review form template, adding the alert near the top of the form, looks like this:

```
<h4>Add your review</h4>
<div *ngIf="formError" class="alert alert-danger" role="alert">
  {{ formError }}
</div>
<div class="form-group row">
```

Now, if you click the Submit button without adding details to the form, you'll get an alert, something like figure 10.8.

 So you've got invalid data covered. Next, you'll deal with valid data, and send it to the API.

Figure 10.8   When a user tries to submit an incomplete form, an error message is displayed.

STEP 4: SENDING THE FORM DATA TO THE DATA SERVICE

Your form data is being posted, and you've got a data service ready to post it to the API. Now hook these two tasks up. You'll use the data service as you've done before; using this new method is no different.

But first, you need to import the data service into location-details.component.ts and add it to the decorator.

Listing 10.17   Importing and providing the data service to location-details.component.ts

```
import { Component, Input, OnInit } from '@angular/core';

import { Location } from '../home-list/home-list.component';
import { Loc8rDataService } from '../loc8r-data.service';

@Component({
  selector: 'app-location-details',
  templateUrl: './location-details.component.html',
  styleUrls: ['./location-details.component.css']
})
```

In the same file, you also need to add the service to the constructor so that you can use it:

```
constructor(private loc8rDataService: Loc8rDataService) { }
```

With the service now available in the component, you can call your new addReviewBy-
LocationId method. The method expects the location ID and review details, and
resolves a Promise, which returns the review record as saved in the database, as shown
in the next listing. To validate that it's working, you'll also add a console log outputting the returned review.

> **Listing 10.18 Sending new reviews to the service in location-details.component.ts**

```
public onReviewSubmit():void {
  this.formError = '';
  if (this.formIsValid()) {
    console.log(this.newReview);
    this.loc8rDataService.addReviewByLocationId(this.location._id,
    ⮡this.newReview)
    .then(review => {
      console.log('Review saved', review);
    });
  } else {
    this.formError = 'All fields required, please try again';
  }
}
```

Annotations:
- **Calls the data service method, passing the location ID and new review data**
- **The method resolves a promise, returning the saved review.**
- **Logs the saved review data**

Now you can send reviews to the database and see the console logs as demonstrated in
figure 10.9. Note the createdOn and _id in the console log that are generated by
Mongoose when the record is saved.

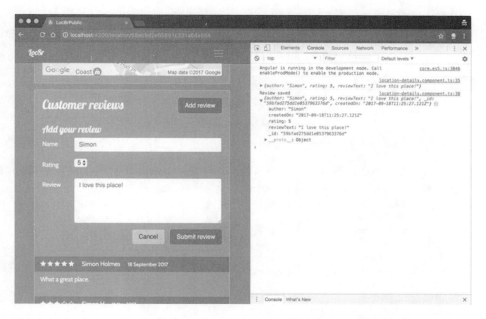

Figure 10.9   Console logs validating that reviews are being added to the database

One last thing to make it slick: push the submitted review to the list underneath the form. When the review is sent, you want to hide the form and add the review to the list that the user can see.

STEP 5: UPDATING THE LIST OF REVIEWS AND HIDING THE FORM

Displaying the new review is a simple task, fortunately. You've got the list of reviews as an array, which is already sorted most recent first. Now you'll need to use the native JavaScript `unshift` method to add the new review to the first spot in the array.

To hide the form, you can change `formVisible` to `false`, as that's what's controlling the `*ngIf` on the form. While you're at it, you can reset the values of the form so that it becomes blank again. The following listing shows all the additions you need to put in location-details.component.ts.

> **Listing 10.19   Hiding the form and showing the review in location-details.component.ts**

```
private resetAndHideReviewForm(): void {        ◁──── A new private member to
  this.formVisible = false;                            hide and reset the form
  this.newReview.author = '';
  this.newReview.rating = 5;
  this.newReview.reviewText = '';
}

public onReviewSubmit():void {
  this.formError = '';
  if (this.formIsValid()) {
    console.log(this.newReview);
    this.loc8rDataService.addReviewByLocationId(this.location._id,
    ➥this.newReview)
    .then(review => {
      console.log('Review saved', review);
      let reviews = this.location.reviews.slice(0);
      reviews.unshift(review);
      this.location.reviews = reviews;
      this.resetAndHideReviewForm();
    })
  } else {
    this.formError = 'All fields required, please try again';
  }
}
```

Calls the private member to hide and resets the form

Updates the reviews in the location object, changing the array reference, and Angular updates the page. If you manipulate the array directly, the page doesn't update.

That's it, almost. This code won't work until `reviews` is in the class definition for the `Location` type, so you'll add it as an array of type `any` in home-list.component.ts like this:

```
export class Location {
  _id: string;
  name: string;
  distance: number;
  address: string;
  rating: number;
  facilities: string[];
  reviews: any[];
}
```

That really is it. Your Angular SPA is complete and fully functional. Well done! But you can do a couple of things to improve the architecture and follow some best practices.

10.3 Improving the architecture

You've got a fully functioning SPA, which is awesome! But before you use it instead of the Express front end, you can improve the architecture by taking the routing configuration out of the app.module.ts file and the location class definition out of the home-list.component.ts file.

10.3.1 Using a separate routing-configuration file

Your first mission for improving the architecture and following an Angular best practice is moving the routing configuration into a separate file. Why is this a best practice? It largely comes down to separation of concerns. The purpose of the app.module.ts file is to tell the Angular compiler all about the app and the files it needs. If you have only a couple of routes, it's okay to keep them in the app.module.ts file, but if you add more routes, they eventually take over the file and mask the original purpose.

You've got three routes in your application at the moment, but you'll explore this best practice by moving the routing configuration into a separate file. You'll add more to this file when you look at authentication in chapter 11.

CREATING A ROUTING-CONFIGURATION FILE

You can use the Angular CLI to generate the routing-configuration file, this time using the `module` template. Run the following command in terminal in the app_public folder:

```
$ ng generate module app-routing
```

This command generates an app-routing folder (in src/app) containing an app-routing .module.ts file. You haven't seen one of these files before, so the next listing shows the default content of this file.

Listing 10.20 The default module template of app-routing.module.ts

```
import { NgModule } from '@angular/core';
import { CommonModule } from '@angular/common';

@NgModule({
  imports: [
    CommonModule
  ],
  declarations: []
})
export class AppRoutingModule { }
```

To add the application routing to this file, you need to do the following:

1 Import the router module and routes type definition from Angular router.
2 Import the components used for each of the three routes.

3 Define the paths and components for the routes.

4 Add the routes (using `routerModule.forRoot`) to the module imports.

5 Export `RouterModule` so the setup can be used.

This process seems like quite a few steps, but it doesn't use anything you haven't already seen. You've used the router module and defined routes before; now you're putting them in a different place. All the updates to the app-routing.module.ts are shown in the following listing.

Listing 10.21 Completing the routing configuration in app-routing.module.ts

```
import { NgModule } from '@angular/core';
import { CommonModule } from '@angular/common';
import { RouterModule, Routes }   from '@angular/router';   ◁────   Imports the router
                                                                    module and route
                                                                    type definition
import { AboutComponent } from '../about/about.component';
import { HomepageComponent } from '../homepage/homepage.component';
import { DetailsPageComponent } from '../details-page/details-
⮑page.component';
                                                                    Imports the
const routes: Routes = [    ◁──────                                 components
  {                                                                 for the routes
    path: '',
    component: HomepageComponent
  },                              Defines the routes
  {                               as an array of
    path: 'about',               type Routes . . .
    component: AboutComponent
  },
  {
    path: 'location/:locationId',
    component: DetailsPageComponent
  }
];

@NgModule({
  imports: [
    CommonModule,                           . . . and imports them,
    RouterModule.forRoot(routes)   ◁─────   using the router module
  ],
  exports: [RouterModule],   ◁─── Exports the router module
  declarations: []
})
export class AppRoutingModule { }
```

That's all there is to a routing configuration file. Next, you need to update the main app.module.ts file to use this file instead of the inline route definitions.

TIDYING UP THE APP.MODULE.TS FILE

You don't want or need the route definitions in two files, so you can delete them from the main module file. You also don't need to import the router from Angular router, so you can delete that line too. Your new routing-configuration file handles importing it.

Although you're deleting the routes, you do need to keep the imports for all the components. These imports are still required by app.module.ts, as this file tells the compiler what to use and where to find the source files.

Finally, you need to add an import for the new router file instead of the inline configuration. This import is normally placed between the core imports and component imports so it's easy to spot when you're looking in the file. Also, add the router file to the imports part of the decorator.

The following listing shows the final app.module.ts with all the additions and deletions having been made.

Listing 10.22 Removing inline route definitions from app.module.ts

```
import { BrowserModule } from '@angular/platform-browser';
import { NgModule } from '@angular/core';
import { FormsModule, ReactiveFormsModule } from '@angular/forms';
import { HttpClientModule } from '@angular/http';

import { AppRoutingModule } from './app-routing/app-routing.module';

import { HomeListComponent } from './home-list/home-list.component';
import { RatingStarsComponent } from './rating-stars/rating-stars.component';
import { DistancePipe } from './distance.pipe';
import { FrameworkComponent } from './framework/framework.component';
import { AboutComponent } from './about/about.component';
import { HomepageComponent } from './homepage/homepage.component';
import { PageHeaderComponent } from './page-header/page-header.component';
import { SidebarComponent } from './sidebar/sidebar.component';
import { HtmlLineBreaksPipe } from './html-line-breaks.pipe';
import { LocationDetailsComponent } from
   './location-details/location-details.component';
import { DetailsPageComponent } from './details-page/details-page.component';
import { MostRecentFirstPipe } from './most-recent-first.pipe';

@NgModule({
  declarations: [
    HomeListComponent,
    RatingStarsComponent,
    DistancePipe,
    FrameworkComponent,
    AboutComponent,
    HomepageComponent,
    PageHeaderComponent,
    SidebarComponent,
    HtmlLineBreaksPipe,
    LocationDetailsComponent,
    DetailsPageComponent,
    MostRecentFirstPipe
  ],
  imports: [
    BrowserModule,
    FormsModule,
    ReactiveFormsModule,
    HttpClientModule,
```

Imports your new routing module, containing the routing configuration for the application

```
        AppRoutingModule                           Adds it as an import
    ],                                             for the app module
    providers: [],
    bootstrap: [FrameworkComponent]
})
export class AppModule { }
```

That's all there is to it. The application will work as it did before, but we're sure you'll agree that both the routing configuration and main app module files are improved by this change. For a small application, you may not want or need to do this, but if you're planning something big, it's definitely worthwhile.

Next, you'll improve your `location` class definition.

10.3.2 *Improving the location class definition*

Your definition for the location class is currently held in home-list.component.ts. This location stems from when you created the homepage listing component in chapter 8; it was the only component doing anything in the application. Now, you're importing the location class definition in many places in the application; it's becoming a key part of the application in its own right. As such, it makes sense to separate it into its own file.

When you do, you'll also add the missing properties, as it currently defines only the properties that were used in the homepage listing; things like reviews and opening times are missing. Also, you'll create a nested class for reviews that you can use in the class definition and in the application when you're dealing directly with reviews.

When all this is done, you'll have a much better TypeScript application.

DEFINING THE LOCATION CLASS IN ITS OWN FILE

The first step is creating the file for the class definition, using the Angular CLI again:

```
$ ng generate class location
```

This command generates a file, location.ts, in the src folder of the application. And it's sparse! It should look something like this:

```
export class Location {
}
```

It's a little bit underwhelming, but at least it has nothing complex or unexpected. All you need to do is get the `Location` definition from home-list.component.ts and paste it in.

Listing 10.23   Adding the basic `Location` class definition in location.ts

```
export class Location {
  _id: string;
  name: string;
  distance: number;
  address: string;
  rating: number;
  facilities: string[];
  reviews: any[];
}
```

That's still pretty simple. The definition for the Location class is now in its own file. You'd better start using it.

USING THE NEW CLASS FILE WHERE NEEDED

The first place to use the new class definition file is home-list.component.ts, as that's where it was initially defined. To do this, delete the original inline definition from this file and replace it with a simple import command:

```
import { Component, OnInit } from '@angular/core';
import { Loc8rDataService } from '../loc8r-data.service';
import { GeolocationService } from '../geolocation.service';

import { Location } from '../location';
```

That replaces the location definition in the homepage listing, which is a good start. But if you're still running ng serve at this point, you'll get Angular compilation errors along these lines:

```
Failed to compile.
/FILE/PATH/TO/LOC8R/app_public/src/app/location-details/location-
    details.component.ts (3,10): Module
    '"/FILE/PATH/TO/LOC8R/app_public/src/app/home-list/home-list.component"'
    has no exported member 'Location'.
```

This tells you that location-details.component.ts was using the Location class exported from home-list, so you need to update that too. Change the file you're importing Location from:

```
import { Component, Input, OnInit } from '@angular/core';

import { Location } from '../location';
import { Loc8rDataService } from '../loc8r-data.service';
```

When you're done, do the same in the other places from which Location is imported: details-page.component.ts and loc8r-data.service.ts. Remember that the path to Location is preceded by one dot rather than two when you're importing it into loc8r-data.service.ts, due to the relative locations of these files.

Next, add the missing properties.

ADDING MISSING PATHS FOR THE LOCATION CLASS DEFINITION

When you use class properties in your application that you don't declare in the class definition, you run the risk of having problems at build time, even though it may work fine under ng serve.

You're currently missing coords and openingTimes from your class definition. coords is a simple addition—an array of numbers. openingTimes is a different deal, though, as that's a complex object in its own right.

Remember how with Mongoose, you can use nested schemas to define subdocuments? (See chapter 5 if you don't.) Well, you can do the same thing with classes in TypeScript. Listing 10.24 shows how to update the location.ts file to define a class called OpeningTimes, and how to define a property of the same name on the Location class to be an array of the OpeningTimes type. It also adds the coords property.

Listing 10.24   Adding missing properties and a nested class definition to location.ts

```
class OpeningTimes {                          Defines a new
  days: string;                               OpeningTimes class
  opening: string;
  closing: string;
  closed: boolean;
}

export class Location {
  _id: string;
  name: string;
  distance: number;
  address: string;                 Adds the missing coords
  rating: number;                  property to Location
  facilities: string[];
  reviews: any[];                                Adds the openingTimes property
  coords: number[];                              to the Location class to be an
  openingTimes: OpeningTimes[];                  array of the OpeningTimes class
}
```

Looking good. The class definition has all the properties you need and use. Note that the `OpeningTimes` class isn't available to be imported into other files by itself, as it isn't declared as an `export`. Although this has everything you need, you can improve the `reviews` property definition.

DEFINING A REVIEW CLASS, AVOIDING THE 'ANY' TYPE

You've got `reviews` defined as an array of type `any`. This should be a bit of a red flag, as best practice in TypeScript is to try to avoid using `any` wherever possible, as it weakens the class structure.

Here, it's possible to avoid using `any`, as you know the schema of a review, and you've seen how to define and use nested classes. Unlike with the `OpeningTimes` definition, you'll want to use the `Review` class definition elsewhere in the application, so you'll declare this one as an `export`.

The following listing shows how to define the `Review` class, export it, and use it inside the `Location` class definition. Note that the source code should also include the `OpeningTimes` definition, but we've left it out of this listing for brevity.

Listing 10.25   Defining, using, and exporting a class for reviews in locations.ts

```
export class Review {                Defines and exports the
  author: string;                    class definition for reviews
  rating: number;
  reviewText: string;
}

export class Location {
  _id: string;
  name: string;
  distance: number;
  address: string;
  rating: number;
```

```
    facilities: string[];
    reviews: Review[];                        Declares location reviews
    coords: number[];                         to be of type Review
    openingTimes: OpeningTimes[];
}
```

Now your `Location` class is complete. You've got a nested class for reviews, which is available to be used elsewhere, and another nested class for opening times, which is available only to this file. One final thing to tighten your use of the `Location` class is to use the `Review` class within the application.

EXPLICITLY IMPORTING AND USING THE REVIEW CLASS WHERE NEEDED

You have two places where you could make good use of the `Review` class: in the location details component, where you use the form to add new reviews, and in your data service, where you push the new review data to the API.

In the files for these components (location-details.component.ts and loc8r-data.service.js), update the `Location` import to also import the `Review` class, like this:

```
import { Location, Review } from '../location';
```

There are two places in the location details component where you can use the `Review` definition to add types to your variables, as shown in the next listing. The first place is when you define `newReview` and give it default values, and the second is when the saved review is returned from the API.

Listing 10.26   Updating location-details.component.ts to use the new `Review` type

```
public newReview: Review = {             Adds the Review type to
  author: '',                            the newReview definition
  rating: 5,
  reviewText: ''
};

public onReviewSubmit():void {
  this.formError = '';
  if (this.formIsValid()) {
    console.log(this.newReview);
    this.loc8rDataService.addReviewByLocationId(this.location._id,
    ➥this.newReview)
    .then((review: Review) => {                 The saved review
      console.log('Review saved', review);      returned from the
      let reviews = this.location.reviews.slice(0);   API should also be
      reviews.unshift(review);                  of type Review.
      this.location.reviews = reviews;
      this.resetAndHideReviewForm();
    })
  } else {
    console.log('Not valid');
    this.formError = 'All fields required, please try again';
  }
}
```

In a similar way, you can tighten the `addReviewByLocationId` method in your data service by specifying that the inputs and outputs should be of type `Review`, changing them from any. The three changes are shown in the following listing.

Listing 10.27   Using the `Review` type to tighten the definitions in loc8r-data.service.ts

```
public addReviewByLocationId(locationId: string, formData: Review)
  : Promise<Review> {                            ◄─────────────────────────
  const url: string = `${this.apiBaseUrl}locations/${locationId}/reviews`;
  return this.http
    .post(url, formData)
    .toPromise()
    .then(response => response.json() as Review)  ◄──
    .catch(this.handleError);         The response of the API
}                                     should also be of type
                                      Review, not any.
```

> The incoming form data should be of type Review, as should the expected return value of the method.

> The response of the API should also be of type Review, not any.

That wasn't too painful, and now you have a much tighter application following some good TypeScript and Angular best practices. Using type definitions is helpful for preventing unexpected mistakes when passing around data; it's easy to forget which parameter is supposed to be a string or an array, which properties an object should have, and so on. This approach saves you from these problems, which is especially helpful when someone else is trying to read your code or you return to it after a break and forget the finer details.

You're now in a position where you're happy with your SPA and want to use it as the front end of your Loc8r application, replacing the current Express version.

10.4   *Using the SPA instead of the server-side application*

In the final section of this chapter, you'll build your Angular app for production and update Express to deliver this app as the front end instead of the Pug templates. As you go, you'll make adjustments to ensure direct access to deep URLs in the application without compromising the API routing.

Before you do any of that, you'll prepare the application for your production environment, by updating the environments/environment files. If you take a look in the environments folder, you'll see two files: environment.ts and environment.prod.ts. Both of these files need to be updated. In environment.ts, make the following change (in bold).

Listing 10.28   Adding an environment variable to the development environment

```
export const environment = {
  apiBaseUrl: 'http://localhost:3000/api',   ◄──
  production: false
};
```

> New environment variable for development

You also need to make a similar change in environments/environment.prod.ts.

Listing 10.29   Adding an environment variable to the production environment

```
export const environment = {
  apiBaseUrl: <Heroku API URL>,
  production: true
};
```
Adds the Heroku URL to the API endpoints
(the Heroku URL with /api appended)

Instead of using the localhost address that has been used throughout development, you'll use the Heroku URL for your deployed application. Once this is done, you'll update loc8r-data.service.ts to use the newly minted environment variable.

In the `import` block at the top of loc8r-data.service.ts file, add the following:

```
import { environment } from '../environments/environment';
```

This means that you can now replace

```
private apiBaseUrl = 'http://localhost:3000/api';
```

with

```
private apiBaseUrl = environment.apiBaseUrl;
```

With this change, Angular will choose the correct environment when you build, and you're now ready build your application for deployment. As you did at the end of chapter 8, run the `ng build` command in the app_public folder in terminal, specifying options to flag it as a production build with the output folder of build:

```
$ ng build --prod --output-path build
```

When that code finishes running, you'll find a compiled version of the SPA in the folder app_public/build. This folder has everything the SPA needs to run, including the HTML page, JavaScript files, CSS, and fonts.

Next, you'll tell Express to use it.

10.4.1 *Routing Express requests to the build folder*

To get Express to serve the Angular app for the front end, you need to do two things: disable all the previous routes for the front-end application, and tell Express that your Angular build folder should serve static files.

To disable the Express-based routes for the front end, find these two lines in app.js, and delete them or comment them out:

```
const indexRouter = require('./app_server/routes/index');
```

and

```
app.use('/', indexRouter);
```

You also no longer need the /public folder for serving static files, as all the files the Angular app needs are sitting inside the Angular build folder. Don't delete that line, though, as you need Express to serve the contents of the build folder as static files. Instead, find the following line in app.js,

```
app.use(express.static(path.join(__dirname, 'public')));
```

and add a similar line below it to use the app_public/build folder, like so:

```
app.use(express.static(path.join(__dirname, 'app_public', 'build')));
```

Run the Express app, if it's not already running under `nodemon`, and head to local-host:3000 in the browser. Everything you see there now is the Angular app, which you can validate by inspecting the elements of the page, as shown in figure 10.10.

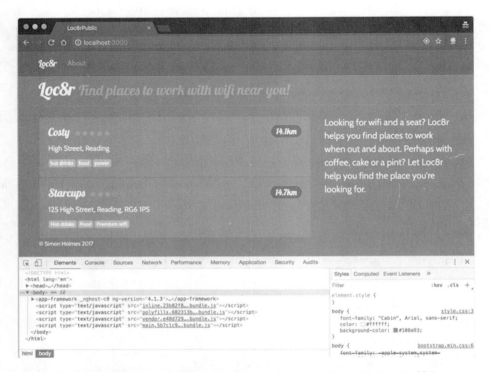

Figure 10.10 The homepage of the running Express app now delivers the Angular SPA.

With these changes, when the homepage is requested, Express serves the first matching resource, which is the index.html file in the app_public/build folder. It's no longer matching an Express route and using a Pug template.

This works great for the homepage, and you can navigate through the app fine. But if you take the URL for the About page or a Details page and paste it into the URL bar, you get a `404` error. You need to fix this inability to access deep URLs directly, as it's not a useful site if you allow people to come in only through the homepage.

10.4.2 Making sure that deep URLs work

This routing problem shouldn't be a great surprise. You've told Express to serve a static file for the homepage, but there's no about folder inside the build folder, so Express couldn't possibly know to show the Angular app.

A simple way to address this problem is to let Express try to match the routes against everything it knows to exist and then add a catchall route at the end to serve anything that hasn't matched yet. This catchall route can be defined by using a * as a wildcard for unmatched GET requests and should respond by sending the index.html file for the Angular app.

The following snippet shows how to add the catchall route after all the other route-matching statements in app.js, in this case after the definition for the API routes:

```
app.use('/api', apiRoutes);
app.get('*', function(req, res, next) {
  res.sendFile(path.join(__dirname, 'app_public', 'build', 'index.html'));
});
```

With this code in place, if any URL isn't matched by Express in the Angular build folder for the API routes, it responds with the index page for the Angular app. This is good, but you can make it a bit better.

Rather than use a * to match everything, you can use a regular expression to define a pattern to match a URL (or set of URLs) that you want to apply the routing to. The regular expression to match the /about route is simple; you need to add start and end string delimiters and escape the forward slash so that it looks like ^\/about$.

The regular expression for a Details page is a bit more complicated, due to the location ID. The location ID is a MongoDB `ObjectId` that is a 24-character, seemingly random mixture of numbers and lowercase letters. A regular expression to match these characters is `[a-z0-9]{24}`. Using the same approach as the About page's regular expression, the complete one for the location details pages is `^\/location\/[a-z0-9]{24}$`.

The following snippet shows how to update the catchall route in app.js with a combined regular expression to match either the About page or a location details page:

```
app.get(/(\/about)|(\/location\/[a-z0-9]{24})/, function(req, res, next) {
  res.sendFile(path.join(__dirname, 'app_public', 'build', 'index.html'));
});
```

That's a good change, as now Express will send the Angular app as a response only when a valid URL is entered.

With that, your SPA is now fully working, being served up by Express, and talking to the Express API, which in turn is getting data in and out of MongoDB. You've got a full MEAN stack application. Congratulations!

In chapters 11 and 12, you'll see how to manage authenticated sessions by adding the ability for users to register and log in before leaving reviews.

Summary

In this chapter, you learned

- That URL parameters can be used to pass data from routes to components and services
- That services are used to query the API

- How Angular templates have display logic in the form of `*ngIf` and `ngSwitch`
- How to create custom pipes and use them
- About best practice for placing routing configuration in a separate file to improve the architecture
- About the best practice for creating standalone class definitions, including nested classes, and for improving the use of custom type definitions through the application
- How to get Express to deliver an Angular application instead of server-side routes for certain URL requests

Part 4

Managing authentication and user sessions

The ability to identify individual users is a key piece of functionality for most web applications. Visitors should be able to register their details so that they can log back in as returning users at a later date. When users are registered and logged in, the application should be able to make use of the data.

In chapter 11, you look at how authentication works in the MEAN stack. The focus is on creating an authentication API that you'll use to power the user-centered parts of the Angular SPA.

Chapter 12 rounds things off by integrating the API you created in chapter 11 and updates the Angular application to take advantage of the new capabilities introduced. We also expand on some of the themes and patterns that we introduced to you in chapter 10.

11

Authenticating users, managing sessions, and securing APIs

This chapter covers

- Adding authentication in the MEAN stack
- Using Passport.js to manage authentication in Express
- Generating JSON Web Tokens in Express
- Registering and logging in a user
- Securing API endpoints in Express

In this chapter, you'll improve on the existing application by making users log in before they can leave reviews. This topic is an important one, as many web applications need to let users log in and manage a session.

Figure 11.1 shows where you are in the overall plan, now working with the MongoDB database, Express API, and Angular single-page application (SPA).

Your first stop is an overview of how to approach authentication in a MEAN stack application before updating Loc8r one piece at a time, working through the architecture from back end to front end. You'll update the database and data schemas before upgrading the API and finally modifying the front end. By the end of

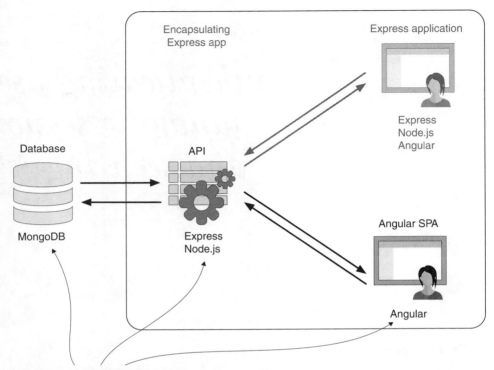

Working with the MongoDB datastore; the Node.js/Express API and the Angular SPA can be used to bring authentication to the application.

Figure 11.1   This chapter adds an authentication system to the application that touches most parts of the architecture, such as the database, API, and front-end SPA.

the chapter, you'll be able to register new users, log them in, maintain a session, and perform actions that only logged-in users can complete.

11.1   *How to approach authentication in the MEAN stack*

How to manage authentication in a MEAN application is viewed as one of the great mysteries of the stack, particularly when using an SPA, largely because the entire application code is delivered to the browser. So how do you hide some of it? How do you define who can see or do what?

11.1.1   *Traditional server-based application approach*

Much of the confusion arises because people are familiar with the traditional approach of application authentication and user session management.

In a traditional setup, the application code sits and runs on the server. To log in, a user enters their username and password in a form that gets posted to the server.

Then the server checks against a database to validate the login details. Assuming that the login is okay, the server sets a flag or session parameter in the user's session on the server to declare that the user is logged in.

The server may or may not set a cookie on a user's browser with the session information. This is common but isn't technically required to manage the authenticated session; it's the server that maintains the vital session information. This flow is illustrated in figure 11.2.

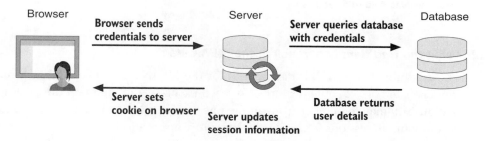

Figure 11.2 In a traditional server application, the server validates user credentials stored in the database and adds them to user's session on the server.

After this initial handshake and with an established session, when a user requests a secure resource or tries to submit some data to the database, the server validates their session and decides whether they can continue. Figure 11.3 shows how a traditional server setup manages access to secured resources by validating the user session, returning the requested resource when authorization status has been determined.

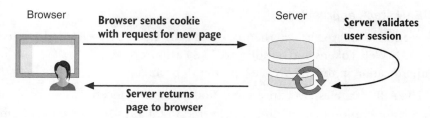

Figure 11.3 In a traditional server application, the server validates a user's session before continuing with a secure request.

Figure 11.4 continues with this theme, where the user has requested access to read/update/delete a resource contained within the application database, uses the provided data, and has a valid session.

That's what the traditional approach looks like, but does it work for the MEAN stack?

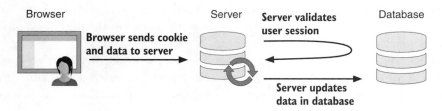

Figure 11.4   In a traditional server application, the server validates a user's session before pushing data to a database.

11.1.2 *Using the traditional approach in the MEAN stack*

This traditional approach isn't a neat fit for the MEAN stack. The approach relies on the server to reserve some resources for each user so it can maintain the session information. You may remember from all the way back in chapter 1 that Node and Express don't maintain sessions for each user; the entire application for all users runs on a single thread.

That said, you can use a version of this approach in the MEAN stack if you're using a server-side application based on Express, like the one you built in chapter 7. Rather than using server resources to maintain session information, Express can use a database to store the data. MongoDB can be used; another popular option is Redis, which is a lightning-fast key-value store.

We're not going to cover that approach in this book. Instead, we'll look at the more complicated scenario of adding authentication to an SPA hitting an API for data.

11.1.3 *Full MEAN stack approach*

In this section, you'll see how authentication fits in the MEAN stack and how easy it is to use JSON Web Tokens and middleware like Passport.js.

Authentication in the MEAN stack poses two problems:

- The API is stateless, as Express and Node have no concept of user sessions.
- The application logic is already delivered to the browser, so you can't limit the code that gets delivered.

The logical solution to these problems is to maintain some kind of session state in the browser and let the application decide what it can and can't display to the current user. This is the only fundamental change in approach. A few technical differences remain, but this is the only major shift.

A great way to securely keep user data in the browser to maintain a session is to use a JSON Web Token (JWT). In this section, we'll use *JWT* and *token* interchangeably. You'll look at these in more detail in section 11.4 when you start creating them, and further in chapter 12 when you consume them in your Angular application. In essence, a JWT is a JSON object encrypted into a string that's meaningless to the human eye but that can be decoded and understood by both the application and the server.

The next section covers how this looks at a high level, starting with the login process.

MANAGING THE LOGIN PROCESS

Figure 11.5 illustrates the flow of a login process. A user posts their credentials to the server (via an API); the server validates these credentials by using the database and returns a token to the browser. The browser saves this token to reuse it later.

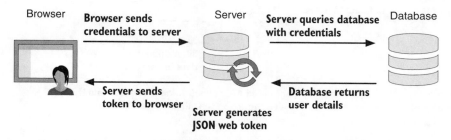

Figure 11.5   The login flow in a MEAN application, returning a JSON Web Token to the browser after the server validates user credentials

This approach is similar to the traditional approach, but instead of storing a user's session data on the server, that data is stored in the browser.

CHANGING VIEWS DURING AN AUTHENTICATED SESSION

While a user is in a session, they'll need to be able to change a page or view, and the application will need to know what they should be allowed to see. So, as illustrated in figure 11.6, the application will decode the JWT and use the information to show the appropriate data to the user.

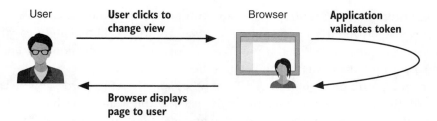

Figure 11.6   Using data inside the JWT, the SPA can determine which resources a user can use or see.

This is where the change from the traditional approach is obvious. The server is unaware that users are doing anything until they need to access the API and database.

SECURELY CALLING AN API

If parts of the application are restricted to authenticated users, it's quite likely that some database actions can be used only by authenticated users. As the API is stateless, it has no idea of who's making each call unless you tell it. The JWT comes back into play here. As figure 11.7 shows, the token is sent to the API endpoint, which decodes the token before validating whether the user is permitted to make that call.

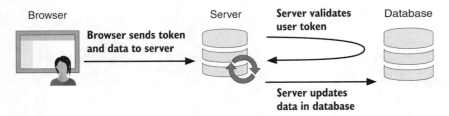

Figure 11.7   When calling an authenticated API endpoint, the browser sends the JWT along with the data; the server decodes the token to validate a user's request.

That covers the approach at a high level, and you've got a good idea of what you're aiming for. You'll make the first step toward adding an authentication mechanism into your Loc8r application by setting up MongoDB to store user details.

11.2   *Creating a user schema for MongoDB*

Usernames and passwords naturally have to be stored in the database. In your case, you'll use a User collection. To do that in the MEAN stack, you need to create a Mongoose schema. Passwords should never—absolutely never—be stored in a database as plain text, as doing so presents a massive security breach if the database is ever compromised. You'll have to do something else as you generate the schema.

11.2.1   *One-way password encryption: Hashes and salts*

The thing to do here is run a one-way encryption on the password. One-way encryption prevents anyone from decrypting the password, while still making it easy to validate a correct password. When a user tries to log in, the application can encrypt a given password and see whether it matches the stored value.

Encrypting isn't enough, though. If several people used the word *password* as their password (it happens!) the encryption for each is the same. Any hackers looking through the database could see this pattern and identify potentially weak passwords.

This is where the concept of a salt comes in. A *salt* is a random string generated by the application for each user that's combined with the password before encryption. The resulting encrypted value is called a *hash*, as illustrated in figure 11.8.

The salt and the hash are both stored in the database, rather than just a single password field. In this approach, all hashes should be unique, and passwords are well protected.

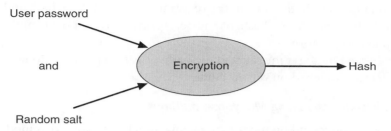

Figure 11.8   A hash is created by combining a user's password with a random salt and encrypting them.

11.2.2 Building the Mongoose schema

You'll start by creating the file that will hold the schema and require it into the application. In the folder app_api/models/, create a new file called users.js.

Next, you'll pull that file into the application by referencing it in the db.js file in the same folder. It should be required alongside the existing line that brings in the locations model, as shown in the following code snippet, at the bottom of the file:

```
// BRING IN YOUR SCHEMAS & MODELS
require('./locations');
require('./users');
```

Now you're ready to build the basic schema.

11.2.3 Basic user schema

What do you want in the user schema? You know that you need a display name to show on reviews, plus a hash and a salt for the password. In this section, you'll also add an email address and make it the unique identifier that a user logs in with.

In the new user.js file, you'll require Mongoose and define a new userSchema.

Listing 11.1   Basic Mongoose schema for users

```
const mongoose = require('mongoose');
const userSchema = new mongoose.Schema({
  email: {
    type: String,          Email should be
    unique: true,          required and unique.
    required: true
  },
  name: {                  Name is also required but
    type: String,          not necessarily unique.
    required: true
  },
  hash: String,           Hash and salt are both strings.
  salt: String
});

mongoose.model('User', userSchema);
```

The email and name are both set from the registration form, but the hash and salt are both created by the system. The hash, of course, is derived from the salt, and the password is supplied via the form.

Next, you'll see how to set the salt and the hash by using a piece of Mongoose functionality we haven't touched on yet: methods.

11.2.4   Setting encrypted paths using Mongoose methods

Mongoose allows you to add methods to a schema, which get exposed as model methods. Such methods give the code direct access to the model attributes.

The ideal outcome is to be able to do something along the lines of the following pseudocode.

> **Listing 11.2   Pseudocode for setting password using Mongoose**

```
const User = mongoose.model('User');        ⟵———— Instantiates the user model
const user = new User();      ⟵———— Creates a new user
user.name = "User's name";      ⟵———— Sets the name and email values
user.email = "test@example.com";
user.setPassword("myPassword");      ⟵┐
user.save();   ⟵┐                        │   Calls a setPassword method to set the
               │   Saves the            │   password. This method allows you to
               │   new user             │   handle the password hashing in a
                                        │   controlled and secure manner.
```

Next, you see how to add a method to Mongoose to achieve this purpose.

ADDING A METHOD TO A MONGOOSE SCHEMA

Methods can be added to a schema *after* the schema has been defined, *before* the model is compiled, because it's regular JavaScript. In the application code, methods are designed to be used after the model has been instantiated.

Adding a method to a schema is achieved by chaining onto the .methods object of the schema. It's also easy to pass in an argument. The following snippet, for example, is the outline for the actual setPassword method:

```
userSchema.methods.setPassword = function (password) {
  this.salt = SALT_VALUE;
  this.hash = HASH_VALUE;
};
```

Unusually for a snippet of JavaScript, this in a Mongoose method refers to the model itself. So, in the preceding example, setting this.salt and this.hash in the method sets them in the model.

Before you can save anything, though, you need to generate a random salt value and encrypt the hash. Fortunately, a native Node module is available for that purpose: crypto.

USING THE CRYPTO MODULE FOR ENCRYPTION

Encryption is such a common requirement that Node has a built-in module called `crypto`. This module comes with several methods for managing the encryption of data. In this section, we'll look at the following two:

- `randomBytes`—To generate a cryptographically strong string of data to use as the salt.
- `pbkdf2Sync`—To create the hash from the password and the salt. *pbkdf2* stands for *password-based key derivation function 2*, an industry standard.

You'll use these methods to create a random string for the salt and for encrypting the password and salt into the hash. The first step is to `require` crypto at the top of the users.js file:

```
const mongoose = require( 'mongoose' );
const crypto = require('crypto');
```

Second, update the `setPassword` method to set the salt and the hash for users. To set the salt, you'll use the `randomBytes` method to generate a random 16-byte string. Then, you'll use the `pbkdf2Sync` method to create the encrypted hash from the password and the salt. The following listing shows how to use these two functions in conjunction with each other.

Listing 11.3 Setting the password in the `User` model

```
userSchema.methods.setPassword = function (password) {
   this.salt = crypto.randomBytes(16).toString('hex');        ⟵┐ Creates a random
   this.hash = crypto                                            │ string for the salt
      .pbkdf2Sync(password, this.salt, 1000, 64, 'sha512')
      .toString('hex');       ⟵┐
};                                Creates an encrypted hash
```

Now, when the `setPassword` method is called and supplied a password, the salt and the hash are generated for users and added to the model instance. The password is never saved anywhere and not even stored in memory.

11.2.5 Validating a submitted password

The other aspect of storing a password is being able to retrieve it when users try to log in; you need to be able to validate their credentials. Having encrypted the password, you can't decrypt it, so what you need to do is use the same encryption on the password the user is trying to log in with and see whether it matches the stored value.

You can do the hashing and validation in a simple Mongoose method. Add the following method to users.js. It will be called from a controller when a user has been found with a given email address and return `true` or `false` depending on whether the hashes match.

Listing 11.4   Validating the submitted password

```
userSchema.methods.validPassword = function (password) {
  const hash = crypto
    .pbkdf2Sync(password, this.salt, 1000, 64, 'sha512')
    .toString('hex');
  return this.hash === hash;
};
```

Hashes the provided password

Checks the password hash against the hash

That's it. Simple, right? You'll see these methods in action when you generate the API controllers. The final thing the controller needs help to do is generate a JWT to include some of the model data.

11.2.6   *Generating a JSON Web Token*

A JWT (pronounced *jot*) is used to pass data around, in your case between the API on the server and the SPA in the browser. A JWT can also be used by the server that generated the token to authenticate a user when it's returned in a subsequent request.

The next section takes a quick look at the parts of a JWT.

THREE PARTS OF A JWT

A JWT is comprised of three random-looking, dot-separated strings. These strings can be long. Here's a real-world example:

```
eyJ0eXAiOiJKV1QiLCJhbGciOiJIUzI1NiJ9 . eyJfaWQiOiI1NTZiZWRmNDhmOTUzOTViMTlhNjc1
    ODgiLCJlbWFpbCI6InNpbW9uQGZ1bGxzdGGFja3RyYWluaW5nLmNvbSIsIm5hbWUiOiJTaW1v
    biBIb2xtZXMiLCJleHAiOjE0MzUwNDA0MTgsImlhdCI6MTQzNDQzNTYxOHO . GD7UrfnLk295
    rwvIrCikbkAKctFFoRCHotLYZwZpdlE
```

This string is meaningless to the human eye, but you should be able to spot the two dots and therefore the three separate parts. These three parts are

- *Header*—An encoded JSON object containing the type and the hashing algorithm used
- *Payload*—An encoded JSON object containing the data, the real body of the token
- *Signature*—An encrypted hash of the header and payload, using a secret that only the originating server knows

Note that the first two parts aren't encrypted; they're *encoded*, so it's easy for the browser—or indeed, other applications—to decode them. Most modern browsers have a native function called `atob()` that can decode a Base64 string. A sister function called `btoa()` can encode *to* a Base64 string.

The third part, the signature, is encrypted. To decrypt it, you need to use the secret that was set on the server. This secret should remain on the server and never be revealed in public.

The good news is that there are libraries to deal with all the complicated parts of the process. In the next section, you'll install one of these libraries into your application and create a schema method to generate a JWT.

GENERATING A JWT FROM EXPRESS

The first step in generating a JWT is including an npm module called jsonweb-token from the command line:

```
$ npm install --save jsonwebtoken
```

Then, you require it at the top of the users.js file:

```
const mongoose = require('mongoose');
const crypto = require('crypto');
const jwt = require('jsonwebtoken');
```

Finally, you create a schema method, which you'll call generateJwt. To generate a JWT, you need to provide the payload—that is, the data—and a secret value. In the payload, you'll send the user's _id, email, and name. You should also set an expiry date for the token, after which the user will have to log in again to generate a new one. You'll use a reserved field in a JWT payload, exp, which expects the expiry data as a UNIX number value.

To generate a JWT, call a sign method on the jsonwebtoken library, sending the payload as a JSON object and the secret as a string. This method returns a token, which you can return out of the method. The next listing shows everything in place.

Listing 11.5   Creating a schema method to generate a JWT

```
userSchema.methods.generateJwt = function () {
  const expiry = new Date();
  expiry.setDate(expiry.getDate() + 7);          ◁─── Creates an expiry date object,
  return jwt.sign({          ◁──                        and sets it for seven days
    _id: this._id,                             Calls the jwt.sign method,
    email: this.email,        Passes the payload  and returns what it returns
    name: this.name,          to the method
    exp: parseInt(expiry.getTime() / 1000, 10),    ◁─── Includes exp as UNIX
  }, 'thisIsSecret' );   ◁── Sends secret for hashing        time in seconds
};                           algorithm to use
```

When this generateJwt method is called, it uses the data from the current user model to create a unique JWT and return it, as illustrated in figure 11.9.

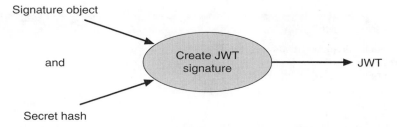

Figure 11.9   A JWT is created by combining a signature object—based on the information you want to store—and a secret hash. The signature is created and returned as a JWT.

There's one problem with this code: the secret shouldn't be visible, which creates security concerns. You'll deal with that problem next.

KEEPING THE SECRET SECRET WITH ENVIRONMENT VARIABLES

If you're going to be pushing your code around in version control (in GitHub, for example), you don't want to have the secret published. Exposing your secret dramatically weakens your security model. With your secret, anybody could issue fake tokens that your application believes to be genuine. To keep secrets secret, it's often a good idea to set them as environment variables.

Here's an easy technique that lets you keep track of environment variables in the code on your machine. First, create a file in the root of the project called .env, and set the secret as follows:

```
JWT_SECRET=thisIsSecret
```

In this case, the secret is `thisIsSecret`, but it can be whatever you want it to be so long as it's a string. Next, you need to make sure that this file isn't included in any Git commits by adding a line to the .gitignore file in the project. If you're following along with the code from GitHub, this line is already in place; if not, you need to add it. At a minimum, the .gitignore file should have the following content:

```
# Dependency directory
node_modules
# Environment variables
.env
```

To read and use this new file to set environment variables, you'll need to install and use a new npm module called `dotenv`. Use the following command in terminal:

```
$ npm install dotenv --save
```

The `dotenv` module should be `required` into the app.js file as the first line in the file, as shown here:

```
require('dotenv').load();
const express = require('express');
```

Now all that remains is to update the user schema to replace the hardcoded secret with the environment variable, highlighted in bold in the following listing.

Listing 11.6 Updating `generateJwt` with environment settings

```
userSchema.methods.generateJwt = () => {
  const expiry = new Date();
  expiry.setDate(expiry.getDate() + 7);
  return jwt.sign({
    _id: this._id,
    email: this.email,
    name: this.name,
    exp: parseInt(expiry.getTime() / 1000),      Don't keep secrets in code; use
  }, process.env.JWT_SECRET);         ⊲———        environment variables instead.
};
```

Your production environment needs to know about this environment variable too. You may remember the command from when you set the database URI on Heroku. It's the same thing here, so run the following command in terminal:

```
$ heroku config:set JWT_SECRET=thisIsSecret
```

That's the last step.

With the MongoDB and Mongoose side of things covered, next, you'll look at using Passport to manage authentication.

11.3 Creating an authentication API with Passport

Passport is a Node module by Jared Hanson that's designed to make authentication in Node easy. One of its key strengths is that it can accommodate several methods of authentication, called *strategies*. Examples of these strategies include

- Facebook
- Twitter
- OAuth
- Local username and password

You can find many more strategies by searching for *passport* on the npm website. With Passport, you can easily use one or more of these approaches to let users log in to your application. For Loc8r, you'll use the *local* strategy, as you're storing usernames and password hashes in the database. You'll start by installing the modules.

11.3.1 Installing and configuring Passport

Passport is separated out into a core module and separate modules for each of the strategies. You'll install the core module and the local strategy module via npm, using the following commands in terminal:

```
$ npm install --save passport passport-local
```

When both of those modules are installed, you can create the configuration for your local strategy.

CREATING A PASSPORT CONFIG FILE

It's the API in your application that will be using Passport, so you'll create the config inside the app_api folder. Inside app_api, create a new folder called config, and inside that folder, create a new file named passport.js.

At the top of this file, `require` Passport and the local strategy module, as well as Mongoose and the user model:

```
const passport = require('passport');
const LocalStrategy = require('passport-local').Strategy;
const mongoose = require('mongoose');
const User = mongoose.model('User');
```

Now you can configure the local strategy.

CONFIGURING A LOCAL STRATEGY

To set a Passport strategy, you use a `passport.use` method and pass it a new strategy constructor. This constructor takes an options parameter and a function that does most of the work. The skeleton for using a Passport strategy looks like the following:

```
passport.use(new LocalStrategy({},
  (username, password, done) => {
  }
));
```

By default, a Passport local strategy expects and uses the fields `username` and `password`. You have `password`, so that one's okay, but instead of `username`, you're using `email`. Passport allows you to override the username field in the options object, as shown in the following snippet:

```
passport.use(new LocalStrategy({
    usernameField: 'email'
  },
  (username, password, done) => {
  }
));
```

Next is the main function, which is a Mongoose call to find users given the username and password supplied to the function. Your Mongoose function needs to do the following:

- Find a user with the email address supplied.
- Check whether the password is valid.
- Return the user object if the user is found and the password is valid.
- Otherwise, return a message stating what's wrong.

As the email address is set to be unique in the schema, you can use the Mongoose `findOne` method. The other interesting point to note is that you'll use the `validPassword` schema method you created earlier to check whether the supplied password is correct.

The following listing shows the local strategy in its entirety.

Listing 11.7   Full Passport local strategy definition

```
passport.use(new LocalStrategy({
    usernameField: 'email'
  },
  (username, password, done) => {
    User.findOne({ email: username }, (err, user) => {    ⟵  Searches MongoDB for a user with the supplied email address
      if (err) { return done(err); }
      if (!user) {
        return done(null, false, {         ⟵  If no user is found, returns false and a message
          message: 'Incorrect username.'
        });
      }
      if (!user.validPassword(password)) {    ⟵  Calls the validPassword method, passing the supplied password
        return done(null, false, {
          message: 'Incorrect password.'     ⟵  If the password is incorrect, returns false and a message
        });
```

```
        }
        return done(null, user);  ◄
    });                                    If you've reached the end, you
}                                          can return the user object.
));
```

Now that you have Passport installed and a strategy configured, you need to register it with the application.

ADDING PASSPORT AND THE CONFIG TO THE APPLICATION

To add your Passport settings to the application, you need to do three things in app.js:

- Require Passport.
- Require the strategy config.
- Initialize Passport.

There's nothing complicated about any of these things; what's important is *where* they go in app.js.

Passport should be required *before* the database models and the configuration *after* the database models. Both should be in place before the routes are defined. If you reorganize the top of app.js slightly, you can bring in Passport and the config as shown in the following listing.

Listing 11.8   Introducing Passport to Express

```
require('dotenv').load();
const createError = require('http-errors');
const express = require('express');
const path = require('path');
const favicon = require('serve-favicon');
const logger = require('morgan');
const cookieParser = require('cookie-parser');
const bodyParser = require('body-parser');
const passport = require('passport');              Requires Passport before
require('./app_api/models/db');                    the model definition
require('./app_api/config/passport');  ◄
                                                   Requires strategy after
                                                   the model definition
```

The strategy needs to be defined after the model definition because it needs the user model to exist.

Passport should be initialized in app.js after the static routes have been defined and before the routes that are going to use authentication—in your case, the API routes—so that the authentication middleware can be applied by Express as required. The following listing shows the passport middleware in place.

Listing 11.9   Adding the passport middleware

```
app.use(express.static(path.join(__dirname, 'public')));
app.use(express.static(path.join(__dirname, 'app_public', 'build')));
app.use(passport.initialize());  ◄
...                                     Initializes passport and
app.use('/api', apiRouter);             adds it as middleware
```

One last thing you need to do is update the `Access-Control-Allow-Headers` to ensure that CORS functions correctly between these two parts of this application.

Listing 11.10   Update to CORS settings

```
app.use('/api', (req, res, next) => {
  res.header('Access-Control-Allow-Origin', 'http://localhost:4200');
  res.header('Access-Control-Allow-Headers', 'Origin, X-Requested-With,
  ➥ Content-Type, Accept, Authorization');        ⊲──────┐  Adds Authorization as
  next();                                                   an acceptable header
});
```

With that in place, Passport is installed, configured, and initialized in your application. Next, you'll create the API endpoints that let users register and log in.

11.3.2   *Creating API endpoints to return JWTs*

To enable users to log in and register via your API, you need two new endpoints. You need to add two new route definitions and two new corresponding controllers. When you've got endpoints in place, you can test them by using Postman and also validate that the registration endpoint worked by using the Mongo shell to look inside the database. First, you'll add the routes.

ADDING THE AUTHENTICATION ROUTE DEFINITIONS

The route definitions for the API are held in the index.js file in app_api/routes, so that's where you'll start. Your controllers are separated into logical collections—currently, Locations and Reviews. It makes sense to add a third collection for the authentication. The following snippet shows this collection added at the top of the file:

```
const ctrlLocations = require('../controllers/locations');
const ctrlReviews = require('../controllers/reviews');
const ctrlAuth = require('../controllers/authentication');
```

You haven't created this controllers/authentication file yet; you'll do that when you code the related controllers.

Next, add the route definitions themselves toward the end of the file (but before the `module.exports` line). You want two, one each for registration and login, which you'll create at /api/register and /api/login, respectively:

```
router.post('/register', ctrlAuth.register);
router.post('/login', ctrlAuth.login);
```

These definitions need to be `post` actions, of course, as they're accepting data. Also remember that you don't need to specify the /api part of the routes, which is added when the routes are required inside app.js.

Now you need to add the controllers before you can test.

CREATING THE REGISTER CONTROLLER

We'll look at the `register` controller first. To start, you'll create the file specified in the route definitions. In the app_api/controllers folder, create a new file called authentication.js, and enter the following to require the things you're going to need.

Listing 11.11 Importing requirements for the `register` controller

```
const passport = require('passport');
const mongoose = require('mongoose');
const User = mongoose.model('User');
```

The registration process won't use Passport at all. You can do what you need with Mongoose, as you've already set up the various helper methods on the schema.

The `register` controller needs to do the following:

1 Validate that the required fields have been sent.
2 Create a new model instance of `User`.
3 Set the name and email address of the user.
4 Use the `setPassword` method to create and add the salt and the hash.
5 Save the user.
6 Return a JWT when saved.

This list seems like a lot of things to do, but fortunately, everything is easy; you've already done the hard work by creating the Mongoose methods. Now, you need to tie everything together. The following listing shows the complete code for the `register` controller.

Listing 11.12 `register` controller for the API

```
const register = (req, res) => {
  if (!req.body.name || !req.body.email || !req.body.password) {
    return res
      .status(400)                                          Responds with an error
      .json({"message": "All fields required"});            status if not all required
  }                                                          fields are found
  const user = new User();              Creates a new user
  user.name = req.body.name;            instance, and sets the
  user.email = req.body.email;          name and email
  user.setPassword(req.body.password);        ◁──────── Uses the setPassword method
  user.save((err) => {        ◁──┐ Saves the new user    to set the salt and hash
    if (err) {                     to MongoDB
      res
        .status(404)
        .json(err);
    } else {
      const token = user.generateJwt();
      res                                             Generates a JWT, using
        .status(200)                                  the schema method, and
        .json({token});                               sends it to the browser
    }
  });
```

```
};
module.exports = {
  register
};
```

In this piece of code, there's nothing particularly new or complex, but it highlights the power of Mongoose methods. This registration controller could have been complex had everything been written inline, which would have been tempting if you'd started here instead of with Mongoose. But as it is, the controller is easy to read and understand, which is what you want from your code.

Next, you'll create the login controller.

CREATING THE LOGIN CONTROLLER

The login controller relies on Passport to do the difficult stuff. You'll start by validating that the required fields have been filled, and then hand everything to Passport. Passport does its thing—attempting to authenticate the user, using the strategy you specify—and then tells you whether it was successful. If it was successful, you can use the generateJwt schema method again to create a JWT before sending it to the browser.

All this, including the syntax required to initiate the passport.authenticate method, is shown in the next listing. This code should be added to the new authentication.js file.

Listing 11.13 login controller for the API

```
const login = (req, res) => {
  if (!req.body.email || !req.body.password) {      Validates that the
    return res                                      required fields have
      .status(400)                                  been supplied
      .json({"message": "All fields required"});
  }
  passport.authenticate('local', (err, user, info) => {    Passes the name
    let token;                                             of the strategy
    if (err) {                                             and a callback to
      return res            Returns an error if            authenticate
        .status(404)        Passport returns an error      method
        .json(err);
    }
    if (user) {
      token = user.generateJwt();      If Passport returned a
      res                              user instance, generates
        .status(200)                   and sends a JWT
        .json({token});
    } else {                 Otherwise, returns an info
      res                    message (why
        .status(401)         authentication failed)
        .json(info);
    }
  })(req, res);              Makes sure that req and res
};                          are available to Passport
```

Add the `login` function to the module exports at the bottom of the file, below the register function:

```
module.exports = {
    register,
    login
};
```

With the `login` controller, you see that once again, all the complicated work is abstracted out, this time primarily by Passport. The code is easy to read, follow, and understand, which should always be a goal when you're coding. Now that you've built these two endpoints in your API, you should test them.

TESTING THE ENDPOINTS AND CHECKING THE DATABASE

When you built the bulk of the API in chapter 6, you tested the endpoints with Postman. You can do the same here. Figure 11.10 shows testing the register endpoint and how it returns a JWT. The URL to test is http://localhost:3000/api/register, creating form fields for `name`, `email`, and `password`. Remember to select the `x-www-form-urlencoded` form type.

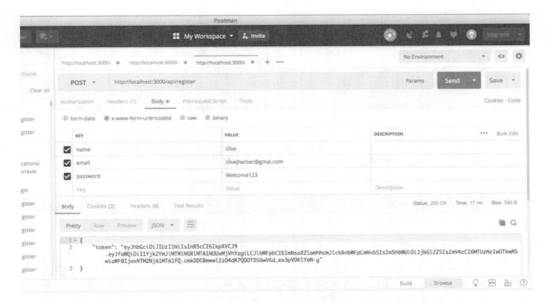

Figure 11.10 Trying out the /api/register endpoint in Postman, returning a JWT when successful

Figure 11.11 shows testing of the login endpoint, including the return of a Passport error message as well as a JWT when successful. The URL for this test is http://localhost:3000/api/login, and it requires `email` and `password` form fields.

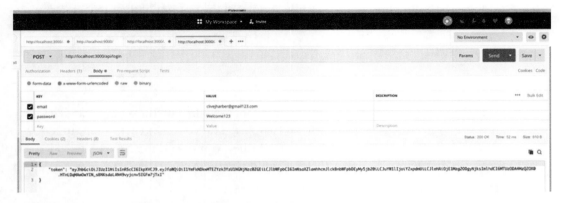

Figure 11.11   Using the api/login endpoint in Postman, testing correct credentials

As well as seeing in the browser that JWTs are returned when expected, you can take a look in the database to see whether the user has been created. You'll go back to the Mongo shell, which you haven't used for a while:

```
$ mongo
> use Loc8r
> db.users.find()
```

Or you can find a particular user by specifying the email address:

```
> db.users.find({email : "simon@fullstacktraining.com"})
```

Whichever method you use, you should see one or more user documents returned from the database, looking something like the following listing.

Listing 11.14   Possible database response

```
{ "hash" :
    "1255e9df3daa899bee8d53a42d4acf3ab8739fa758d533a84da5eb1278412f7a7bdb36e
    888aeb80a9eec4fb7bbe9bcef038f01fbbf4e6048e2f4494be44bc3d5", "salt" :
    "40368d9155ea690cf9fc08b49f328e38", "email" :
    "simon@fullstacktraining.com", "name" : "Simon Holmes", "_id" :
    ObjectId("558b95d85f0282b03a603603"), "__v" : 0 }
```

We've made the path names bold to make them easier to pick out in print, but you should be able to see all the expected data there.

Now that you've created the endpoints to enable users to register and log in, the next thing you're going to look at is how to restrict certain endpoints to authenticated users.

11.4   Securing relevant API endpoints

It's a common requirement in web applications to limit access to API endpoints to authenticated users only. In Loc8r, for example, you want to make sure that only registered users can leave reviews. This process has two parts:

- Allow only users who send a valid JWT with their request to call the new review API.
- Inside the controller, validate that the user exists and can create a review.

You'll start by adding authentication to the routes in Express.

11.4.1 *Adding authentication middleware to Express routes*

In Express, middleware can be added to routes, as you'll see in a moment. This middleware gets between the route and the controller. When a route is called, the middleware is activated before the controller and can prevent the controller from running or changing the data being sent.

You want to use middleware that validates the supplied JWT and then extracts the payload data and adds it to the req object for the controller to use. It's no surprise that an npm module is available for this purpose: express-jwt. Install it now with the following command in terminal:

```
$ npm install --save express-jwt
```

Now you can use this module in the routes file.

SETTING UP THE MIDDLEWARE

To use express-jwt, you need to require it and configure it. When included, express-jwt exposes a function that can be passed an options object, which you'll use to send the secret and also to specify the name of the property you want to add to the req object to hold the payload.

The default property added to req is user, but in your code, user is an instance of the Mongoose User model, so set it to payload to prevent confusion and maintain consistency. user is what it's called in Passport and inside the JWT, after all.

Open the API routes file, app_api/routes/index.js, and add the setup to the top of the file, highlighted in bold in the following listing.

Listing 11.15 Adding JWT to app_api/routes/locations.js

```
const express = require('express');
const router = express.Router();
const jwt = require('express-jwt');          ◁········ Requires express-
const auth = jwt({                                     jwt module
  secret: process.env.JWT_SECRET,       ◁············┐ Sets the secret using the same
  userProperty: 'payload'   ◁──┐ Defines a property on │ environment variable as before
});                             │ req to be the payload
```

Now that the middleware is configured, you can add the authentication to the routes.

ADDING AUTHENTICATION MIDDLEWARE TO SPECIFIC ROUTES

Adding middleware to the route definitions is simple. Reference it in the router commands, between the route and the controller. It does go in the middle!

The following snippet shows how to add middleware to the post, put, and delete review method, while leaving get open; the reviews are supposed to be readable by the public.

Listing 11.16 Updating routing to use the jwt module

```
router
    .route('/locations/:locationid/reviews')
    .post(auth, ctrlReviews.reviewsCreate);           ◁

router
    .route('/locations/:locationid/reviews/:reviewid')
    .get(ctrlReviews.reviewsReadOne)
    .put(auth, ctrlReviews.reviewsUpdateOne)
    .delete(auth, ctrlReviews.reviewsDeleteOne);
```

Adds auth middleware to the routing definition

So that's the middleware configured and applied. In a moment, you'll see how to use it in the controller, but first, you'll see how to deal with an invalid token that the middleware rejects.

DEALING WITH AUTHENTICATION REJECTION

When the supplied token is invalid—or perhaps doesn't exist—the middleware throws an error to prevent the code from continuing. You need to catch this error and return an unauthorized message and status (401).

The best place to add the new error handler is with the other error handlers in app.js. You'll add it as the first error handler so that generic handlers don't intercept it. The following listing shows the new error handler to be added to app.js.

Listing 11.17 Catching errors

```
// error handlers
// Catch unauthorised errors
app.use((err, req, res, next) => {
  if (err.name === 'UnauthorizedError') {           ◁
    res
      .status(401)
      .json({"message" : err.name + ": " + err.message});
  }
});
```

Makes sure that you're dealing with UnauthorizedErrors

With that in place and the app restarted, you can test that rejection occurs by using Postman again, this time submitting a review. You can use the same POST request that you used when first testing the API, the result of which is shown in figure 11.12.

As expected, trying to call the newly protected API endpoint without including a valid JWT in the request returns an unauthorized status and message, which is what you wanted. Next, you'll move on to what happens when a request is authorized by the middleware and continues to the controller.

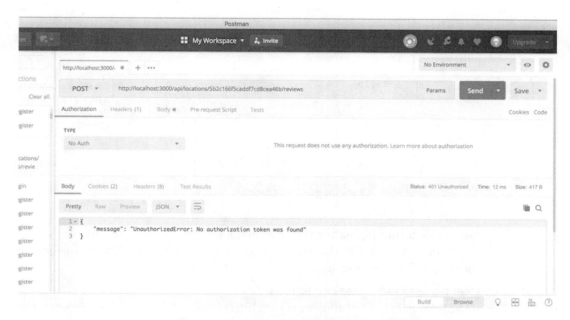

Figure 11.12   Trying to add a review without a valid JWT now results in a 401 response.

11.4.2 *Using the JWT information inside a controller*

In this section, you'll see how to use the data from the JWT that has been extracted by the middleware in Express and added to the `req` object. You'll use the email address to get the user's name from the database and add it to the review document.

RUNNING THE MAIN CONTROLLER CODE ONLY IF THE USER EXISTS

The first thing to do, as shown in listing 11.18, is take the `reviewsCreate` controller and wrap the contents in a new function that you'll call `getAuthor`. This new function should accept the `req` and `res` objects, with the existing controller code in a callback.

The whole point of the `getAuthor` function is to validate that the user exists in the database and return the user's name for use in the controller. So, you can pass this through as `userName` to the callback and, in turn, pass it through to the `doAddReview` function in app_api/controllers/review.js.

> **Listing 11.18   Update the create review controller to get the user's name first**

```
const reviewsCreate = (req, res) => {
  getAuthor(req, res, callback) => {
    (req, res, userName) => {
      const locationId = req.params.locationid;
      if (locationId) {
        Loc
          .findById(locationId)
          .select('reviews')
          .exec((err, location) => {
```

Calls the getAuthor function and passes the original controller code in as a callback; passes the user's name into the callback

```
              if (err) {
                return res
                  .status(400)
                  .json(err);
              } else {
                doAddReview(req, res, location, userName);    ◁⎯⎯⎯  Passes the user's
              }                                                      name into the
            });                                                      doAddReview
          } else {                                                   function
        res
          .status(404)
          .json({message": "Location not found"});
        }
      });           ◁⎯⎯⎯⎯⎯  Closes the getAuthor function
    };
```

Looking at this listing highlights the two things you still need to do: write the get-Author function, and update the doAddReview function. First, you'll write the getAuthor function so that you can see how to get the JWT data.

VALIDATING THE USER AND RETURNING THE NAME

The idea of the getAuthor function is to validate that the email address is associated with a user on the system and return the name to use. It needs to do the following:

- Check that there's an email address in the req object.
- Use the email address to find a user.
- Send the user's name to the callback function.
- Trap errors and send appropriate messages.

The full code for the getAuthor function is in listing 11.19. The first thing to do is check for the payload property on req and, in turn, check that it has an email property. Remember that payload is the property you specified when you added authentication to the Express routes. After that, use req.payload.email in a Mongoose query, passing the user's name through to the callback if successful.

Listing 11.19 Use data from the JWT to query the database

```
const User = mongoose.model('User');    ◁⎯⎯⎯⎯⎯⎯⎯⎯⎯⎯⎯⎯⎯⎯⎯⎯⎯  Ensures that the User
const getAuthor = (req, res, callback) => {                       model is available
  if (req.payload && req.payload.email) {    ◁⎯⎯
    User
      .findOne({ email : req.payload.email })          Validates that the JWT
      .exec((err, user) => {                           information is on the
        if (!user) {                                   request object
          return res
            .status(404)
            .json({"message": "User not found"});
        } else if (err) {
          console.log(err);
          return res
            .status(404)
            .json(err);
```

Uses the email address to find the user (annotation pointing to `.findOne({ email : req.payload.email })`)

```
      }
        callback(req, res, user.name);      ⟵┐ Runs the callback,
      });                                        passing the
    } else {                                     user's name
    return res
      .status(404)
      .json({"message": "User not found"});
  }
};
```

Now when the callback is invoked, it runs what was the original code in the controller, finding a location and passing the information to the doAddReview function. It's also now passing the username to the function, so quickly update doAddReview to use the user's name and add it to the review documents.

SETTING THE USER'S NAME ON REVIEWS

The change to the doAddReview function is simple and is shown in listing 11.20. You were already saving the author of the review, getting the data from req.body .author. Now, you have another parameter being passed to the function and can use this parameter instead. The updates are highlighted in bold.

Listing 11.20 Saving the username in the review

```
const doAddReview = (req, res, location, author) => {   ⟵┐ Adds an author
  if (!location) {                                          parameter to the
    res                                                     function definition
      .status(404)
      .json({"message": "Location not found"});
  } else {
    const {rating, reviewText} = req.body;   ⟵┐ Author is now coming from the
    location.reviews.push({                       database rather than the form
      author,                              ⟵┘
      rating,
      reviewText
    });
    location.save((err, location) => {
      if (err) {
        return res
          .status(400)
          .json(err);
      } else {
        updateAverageRating(location._id);
        const thisReview = location.reviews.slice(-1).pop();
        res
          .status(201)
          .json(thisReview);
      }
    });
  }
};
```

That simple change brings you to the end of the back-end work. You've created a new user schema, generated and consumed JWTs, created an authentication API, and secured some other API routes. That's a lot already!

In chapter 12, you'll tackle the front end and focus on integrating it into the Angular app.

Summary

In this chapter, you learned

- How to approach authentication in the MEAN stack
- Encrypting passwords with hashes and salts
- Using Mongoose model methods to add functions to schemas
- How to create a JSON Web Token with Express
- Managing authentication on the server with Passport
- Making routes in Express available to authenticated users only

Using an authentication
API in Angular applications

12

This chapter covers

- Using local storage and Angular to manage a user session
- Managing user sessions in Angular
- Using JWT in Angular Applications

In this chapter, you'll integrate the work that you completed in chapter 11 on authentication via API and use the API endpoints in your Angular application. Specifically, you'll look at how to use the Angular HTTP client library and `localStorage`.

12.1 Creating an Angular authentication service

In an Angular app, as in any other application, authentication is likely to be needed across the board. The obvious thing to do is create an authentication service that can be used anywhere it's needed. This service should be responsible for everything related to authentication, including saving and reading a JWT, returning information about the current user, and calling the login and register API endpoints.

You'll start by looking at how to manage the user session.

12.1.1 *Managing a user session in Angular*

Assume for a moment that a user has just logged in and the API has returned a JWT. What should you do with the token? Because you're running an SPA, you could keep it in the browser's memory. This approach is okay unless the user decides to refresh the page, which reloads the application, losing everything in memory—not ideal.

Next, you'll look to save the token somewhere a bit more robust, allowing the application to read it whenever it needs to. The question is whether to use cookies or local storage.

COOKIES VS. LOCAL STORAGE

The traditional approach to saving user data in a web application is to save a cookie, and that's certainly an option. But cookies are there to be used by server applications, with each request to the server sending the cookies along in the HTTP header to be read. In an SPA, you don't need cookies; the API endpoints are stateless and don't get or set cookies.

You need to look somewhere else, toward local storage, which is designed for client-side applications. With local storage, the data stays in the browser and doesn't automatically get transmitted with requests, as would happen with cookies.

Local storage is also easy to use with JavaScript. Look at the following snippet, which would set and get some data:

```
window.localStorage['my-data'] = 'Some information';
window.localStorage['my-data']; // Returns 'Some information'
```

Right, so that's settled; you'll use local storage in Loc8r to save the JWT. If `localStorage` isn't familiar territory, head to the Mozilla developer documentation at http://mng.bz/0WKz to find out more.

To facilitate the use of `localStorage` in the Angular application, you'll first create an `Injectable` called `BROWSER_STORAGE` that you can use in components. You'll hook into the `localStorage`, but you'll do so via a factory service that you inject into components that require access to the `localStorage`.

To start, generate the class file

```
$ ng generate class storage
```

and place the following code in it.

> **Listing 12.1 storage.ts**

```
import { InjectionToken } from '@angular/core';          ← Uses the InjectionToken class

export const BROWSER_STORAGE = new InjectionToken<Storage>
⮑('Browser Storage',{
  providedIn: 'root',
  factory: () => localStorage ←── factory function wrapping localStorage
});
```

Creates a new InjectionToken

CREATING A SERVICE TO SAVE AND READ A JWT IN LOCAL STORAGE

You'll start building the authentication service by creating the methods to save a JWT in local storage and read it back out again. You've seen how easy it is to work with `localStorage` in JavaScript, so now you need to wrap it in an Angular service that exposes two methods: `saveToken()` and `getToken()`. No real surprises here, but the `saveToken()` method should accept a value to be saved, and `getToken()` should return a value.

First, generate a new service called `Authentication` inside the Angular application:

```
$ ng generate service authentication
```

The following listing shows the contents of the new service, including the first two methods.

Listing 12.2   Creating the `authentication` service with the first two methods

```
import { Inject, Injectable } from '@angular/core';
import { BROWSER_STORAGE } from './storage';

@Injectable({
  providedIn: 'root'                                    Injects the importer
})                                                      BROWSER_STORAGE
export class AuthenticationService {                    wrapper

  constructor(@Inject(BROWSER_STORAGE) private storage: Storage) { }

  public getToken(): string {                    Creates the
    return this.storage.getItem('loc8r-token');  getToken function
  }

  public saveToken(token: string): void {        Creates the
    this.storage.setItem('loc8r-token', token);  saveToken function
  }
}
```

And there you have a simple service to handle saving `loc8r-token` to `localStorage` and reading it back out again. Next, you'll look at logging in and registering.

12.1.2 Allowing users to sign up, sign in, and sign out

To use the service to enable users to register, log in, and log out, you'll need to add three more methods. Start with registering and logging in.

CALLING THE API TO REGISTER AND LOG IN

You'll need two methods to register and log in, which post the form data to the `register` and `login` API endpoints you created earlier in this chapter. When successful, both these endpoints return a JWT, so you can use the `saveToken` method to save them.

To prepare, you'll generate two simple auxiliary classes to help manage the data that you need across the application—a `User` class (listing 12.3) and an `AuthResponse` class (listing 12.4):

```
$ ng generate class user
$ ng generate class authresponse
```

The following two listings show the simple classes that you'll use to maintain the given data. Listing 12.3 provides your `User` class definition, which is a simple class to hold the name and email as strings.

Listing 12.3   user.ts

```
export class User {
  email: string;              Tells typescript that you
  name: string;               require strings here
}
```

Listing 12.4 provides the definition for your `AuthResponse` object, which at this time holds the token string.

Listing 12.4   authresponse.ts

```
export class AuthResponse {
  token: string;      ◁──────  Sets the token to be a string
}
```

With these classes in place, you can add the aforementioned `register()` and `login()` methods to the authentication service, as shown in the next listing. As these methods rely on the Loc8rDataService, you'll inject that too.

Listing 12.5   authentication.service.ts

```
import { Inject, Injectable } from '@angular/core';
import { BROWSER_STORAGE } from './storage';
import { User } from './user';                            Imports the relevant
import { AuthResponse } from './authresponse';            classes and services
import { Loc8rDataService } from './loc8r-data.service';

@Injectable({
  providedIn: 'root'
})
export class AuthenticationService {

  constructor(
    @Inject(BROWSER_STORAGE) private storage: Storage,        Injects the
    private loc8rDataService: Loc8rDataService    ◁─────────  data service
  ) { }

  ...

  public login(user: User): Promise<any> {   ◁───────┐ The login
    return this.loc8rDataService.login(user)         │ function
      .then((authResp: AuthResponse) => this.saveToken(authResp.token));
  }

  public register(user: User): Promise<any> {  ◁─────── The register function
    return this.loc8rDataService.register(user)
      .then((authResp: AuthResponse) => this.saveToken(authResp.token));
  }
}
```

Take a quick look at the two methods that you've added. What you're doing is providing a wrapper for the `login()` and `register()` methods from the `Loc8rDataService` that you're about to write and ensuring that a Promise gets returned so data can be passed back to the UI. You don't necessarily care what's in the Promise—only that it's returned. Then the `token` from the `AuthResponse` object that the methods receive is saved, using the functions already in place.

Finally, you need to add the aforementioned methods to the `Loc8rDataService` that are required to communicate with the API endpoints. Changes are highlighted in bold in the next listing.

Listing 12.6 Changes to `Loc8rDataService`

```
import { Injectable } from '@angular/core';
import { HttpClient, HttpHeaders } from '@angular/common/http';
import { Location, Review } from './location';
import { User } from './user';                          Imports for User and
import { AuthResponse } from './authresponse';          AuthResponse classes

@Injectable({
  providedIn: 'root'
})
export class Loc8rDataService {                              Login method
                                                             returning the
...                                                          AuthResponse
                                                             Promise
  public login(user: User): Promise<AuthResponse> {    ◁──┘
    return this.makeAuthApiCall('login', user);
  }

  public register(user: User): Promise<AuthResponse> {  ◁───   Register method
    return this.makeAuthApiCall('register', user);             returning the
  }                                                            AuthResponse
                                                               Promise
  private makeAuthApiCall(urlPath: string, user: User):
  ➥Promise<AuthResponse> {                            ◁───
    const url: string = `${this.apiBaseUrl}/${urlPath}`;    The actual call. login
    return this.http                                        and register are
      .post(url, user)                                      similar enough to
      .toPromise()                                          make DRY.
      .then(response => response as AuthResponse)
      .catch(this.handleError);                        Uses the HttpClient POST
  }                                                    request Observable that you
                                                       convert to a Promise object
...

}
```

The call out to the API in both cases of `login` and `register` are essentially the same call; the only difference is the URL that you're required to hit to perform the action you need. In listing 12.6, you POST a payload containing the user details that you're attempting to use and returning an `AuthResponse` object on success or handling the error on failure. To that end, you have a private method (`makeAuthApiCall()`) to manage the call and public methods `login()` and `register()` to handle the specific details of which API endpoint URL you want to call.

With these methods in place, you can address signing out.

DELETING LOCALSTORAGE TO SIGN OUT

The user session in the Angular application is managed by saving the JWT in `localStorage`. If the token is there, is valid, and hasn't expired, you can say that the user is logged in. You can't change the expiry date of the token from within the Angular app; only the server can do that. What you can do is delete it.

To give users the ability to log out, you can create a new `logout` method in the authentication service to remove the Loc8r JWT.

```
public logout(): void {
  this.storage.removeItem('loc8r-token');        ⊲─┐  Deletes the token
}                                                   └  from localStorage
```

This code removes the `loc8r-token` item from the browser's `localStorage`.

Now you have methods to get a JWT from the server, save it in `localStorage`, read it from `localStorage`, and delete it. The next question is how to use it in the application to see that a user is logged in and to get data out of it.

12.1.3   *Using the JWT data in the Angular service*

The JWT saved in the browser's `localStorage` is what you use to manage a user session. The JWT is used to validate whether a user is logged in. If a user is logged in, the application can also read the user information stored inside.

First, add a method to check whether somebody is logged in.

CHECKING THE LOGGED-IN STATUS

To check whether a user is currently logged in to the application, you need to check whether the `loc8r-token` exists in `localStorage`. You can use the `getToken()` method for that task. But the existence of a token isn't enough. Remember that the JWT has expiry data embedded in it, so if a token exists, you'll need to check that too.

The expiration date and time of the JWT is part of the payload, which is the second chunk of data. Remember that this part is an encoded JSON object; it's encoded rather than encrypted, so you can decode it. In fact, we've already talked about the function to do this: `atob`.

Stitching everything together, you want to create a method that

1 Gets the stored token
2 Extracts the payload from the token
3 Decodes the payload
4 Validates that the expiry date hasn't passed

This method, added to the `AuthenticationService`, should return `true` if a user is logged in and `false` if not. The next listing shows this behavior in a method called `isLoggedIn()`.

Listing 12.8   `isLoggedIn` method for the authentication service

```
public isLoggedIn(): boolean {
  const token: string = this.getToken();          Gets the token
    if (token) {                                   from storage
      const payload = JSON.parse(atob(token.split('.')[1]));    If the token
      return payload.exp > (Date.now() / 1000);                 exists, gets the
    } else {                                                    payload, decodes
      return false;                      Validates whether      it, and parses it
    }                                     expiry is passed       to JSON
  }
}
```

That isn't much code , but it's doing a lot. After you've referenced it in the `return` statement in the service, the application can quickly check whether a user is logged in at any point.

The next and final method to add to the authentication service gets some user information from the JWT.

GETTING USER INFORMATION FROM THE JWT

You want the application to be able to get a user's email address and name from the JWT. You saw in the `isLoggedIn()` method how to extract data from the token, and your new method does exactly the same thing.

Create a new method called `getCurrentUser()`. The first thing that this method does is validate that a user is logged in by calling the `isLoggedIn()` method. If a user is logged in, it gets the token by calling the `getToken()` method before extracting and decoding the payload and returning the data you're after. The following listing shows how this looks.

Listing 12.9   `getCurrentUser()` method (authentication.service.ts)

```
public getCurrentUser(): User {          Returns the type of User
  if (this.isLoggedIn()) {               Ensures that the user is logged in
    const token: string = this.getToken();
    const { email, name } = JSON.parse(atob(token.split('.')[1]));
    return { email, name } as User;       Typecasts object
  }                                        to the User type
}
```

With that done, the Angular authentication service is complete. Looking back over the code, you can see that it's generic and easy to copy from one application to another. All you'll probably have to change are the name of the token and the API URLs, so you've got a nice, reusable Angular service.

Now that the service is in the application, you can use it. Keep moving forward by creating the Login and Register pages.

12.2 *Creating the Register and Login pages*

Everything you've done so far is great, but without a way for visitors to the website to register and log in, it would be useless. So that's what you'll address now.

In terms of functionality, you want a Register page where new users can set their details and sign up, and a Login page where users return to input their username and password. When users have gone through either of these processes and are successfully authenticated, the application should send them back to the page they were on when they started the process.

At the end of the following sections, you'd expect your Register page to look a lot like figure 12.1.

Figure 12.1   Register page

The Login page should look like figure 12.2. You'll begin with the Register page.

Figure 12.2   Login page

12.2.1 Building the Register page

To develop a working registration page, you have a few things to do:

1 Create the register component and add it to the routing.
2 Build the template.
3 Flesh out the component body, including redirection.

And, of course, you'll want to test the page when you're done.

Step 1 is creating the component. Reach for the Angular generator:

```
$ ng generate component register
```

With that done, amend the application routing by adding entries to app_routing/ app_routing.module.ts. Point the register component at the /register route, as the next listing shows.

Listing 12.10 Registration routing

```
import { NgModule } from '@angular/core';
import { CommonModule } from '@angular/common';
import { RouterModule, Routes } from '@angular/router';

import { AboutComponent } from '../about/about.component';
import { HomepageComponent } from '../homepage/homepage.component';
import { DetailsPageComponent } from '../details-page/details-page.
➥component';
import { RegisterComponent } from '../register/
➥register.component';        ◁———  Imports the newly created
                                    register component
const routes: Routes = [
...
  {                     ◁———
    path: 'register',          Adds the path
    component: RegisterComponent   information
  }
];

...
})
export class AppRoutingModule { }
```

With that done, look at the details of the component template and methods that link this template to the services that you built earlier.

BUILDING THE REGISTRATION TEMPLATE

Okay, now you'll build the template for the registration page. Aside from the normal header and footer, you'll need a few things. Primarily, you need a form to allow visitors to input their name, email address, and password. In this form, you should also have an area to display any errors. You'll also pop in a link to the Login page, in case users realize that they're already registered.

The next listing shows the template pieced together. Notice that the input fields have the credentials in the view model bound to them via ngModel.

Listing 12.11 Full template for the registration page (register/register.component.html)

Link to switch
to Login page

A **<div>** to
display errors

Input for
username

Input
for email
address

```
<app-page-header [content]="pageContent.header"></app-page-header>
<div class="row">
  <div class="col-12 col-md-8">
    <p class="lead">Already a member? Please <a routerLink="/login">
➥log in</a> instead</p>
    <form (submit)="onRegisterSubmit()">
      <div role="alert" *ngIf="formErrors" class="alert alert-danger">
➥{{ formError }}</div>
      <div class="form-group">
        <label for="name">Full Name</label>
        <input class="form-control" id="name" name="name" placeholder=
➥"Enter your name" [(ngModel)]="credentials.name">
      </div>
      <div class="form-group">
        <label for="email">Email Address</label>
        <input type="email" class="form-control" id="email" name="email"
➥placeholder="Enter email address" [(ngModel)]=
➥"credentials.email">
      </div>
      <div class="form-group">
        <label for="password">Password</label>
        <input type="pasword" class="form-control" id="password"
➥name="password" placeholder="e.g 12+ alphanumerics"
➥[(ngModel)]="credentials.password">
      </div>
      <button type="submit" role="button" class="btn
➥btn-primary">Register!</button>
    </form>
  </div>
  <app-sidebar [content]="pageContent.sidebar"  class=
➥"col-12 col-md-4"></app-sidebar>
</div>
```

Input for
password

Again, the important thing to note is that a user's name, email, and password are bound to the view model in the object `credentials`.

Next, you look at the flip side and code the component methods.

CREATING THE REGISTRATION COMPONENT SKELETON

Based on the template, you'll set up a few things in the register component. You'll need the title text for the page header and an `onRegisterSubmit()` function to handle form submission. You'll also give all the `credentials` properties a default empty string value.

The next listing shows the initial setup.

Listing 12.12 Starting the `register` component

Imports the
authentication
service

```
import { Component, OnInit } from '@angular/core';
import { Router } from '@angular/router';
import { AuthenticationService } from '../authentication.service';

@Component({
```

Imports the services
required from the Router

```
    selector: 'app-register',
    templateUrl: './register.component.html',
    styleUrls: ['./register.component.css']
})
export class RegisterComponent implements OnInit {

  public formError: string = '';        ◁——— Error string initialization

  public credentials = {        ◁———┐ credentials object
    name: '',                          │ to hold model data
    email: '',
    password: ''
  };

  public pageContent = {        ◁———┐ Page content object for
    header: {                          │ the usual page data
      title: 'Create a new account',
      strapline: ''
    },
    sidebar: ''
  };

  constructor(
    private router: Router,
    private authenticationService: AuthenticationService
  ) { }

  ngOnInit() {
  }
```

There's nothing new here—a couple of public properties to manage the component's internal data and injection of the services that you'll need to use in the component.

Add the contents of the next listing to the component that you've created.

Listing 12.13 Registration submission handler

```
public onRegisterSubmit(): void {        ◁——— Submits an event handler
  this.formError = '';
  if (
    !this.credentials.name ||        ┐ Checks that you've received
    !this.credentials.email ||        │ all the relevant information
    !this.credentials.password
  ) {
    this.formError = 'All fields are required, please try again';        ◁———┐
  } else {                                           Returns messaging │
    this.doRegister();                               in case of an error │
  }
}

private doRegister(): void {        ◁——— Performs the registration
  this.authenticationService.register(this.credentials)
    .then(() => this.router.navigateByUrl('/'))
    .catch((message) => this.formError = message);
}
```

With this code in place, you can try out the Register page and functionality by starting the application running and heading to http://localhost:4200/register.

When you've done this and successfully registered as a user, open the browser development tools, and look for the resources. As illustrated in figure 12.3, you should see a `loc8r-token` below the local storage folder.

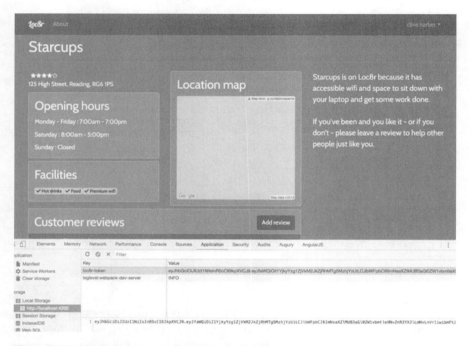

Figure 12.3   Finding the `loc8r-token` in the browser

You've added the ability for a new user to register. Next, you'll enable a returning user to log in.

12.2.2 *Building the Login page*

The approach to the Login page is similar to the approach to the Register page. Nothing here should be unfamiliar, so you'll go through it quickly.

First, generate the new component:

```
$ ng generate component login
```

Add the following to the routes object in the router (app-routing/app-routing .module.ts):

```
{
  path: 'login',
  component: LoginComponent
}
```

With this code in place, you can build up the component template file: login/login-component.html. You can see from the route where you want this file to be. It's similar to the register template, so it's probably easiest to duplicate and edit that template. All you need to do is remove the name input and change a couple of pieces of text. The following listing highlights in bold the changes you need to make in the login template.

Listing 12.14 Changes for the login template

```
<app-page-header [content]="pageContent.header"></app-page-header>
<div class="row">
  <div class="col-12 col-md-8">
    <p class="lead">Not a member? Please
      <a routerLink="/register">register</a> first
    </p>
    <form (ngSubmit)="onLoginSubmit(evt)">
      <div role="alert" *ngIf="formError" class="alert alert-danger">
        {{ formError }}
      </div>
      <div class="form-group">
        <label for="email">Email Address</label>
        <input type="email" class="form-control" id="email" name="email"
        placeholder="Enter email address" [(ngModel)]=
        "credentials.email">
      </div>
      <div class="form-group">
        <label for="password">Password</label>
        <input type="pasword" class="form-control" id="password"
         name="password" placeholder="e.g 12+ alphanumerics"
        [(ngModel)]="credentials.password">
      </div>
      <button type="submit" role="button" class="btn btn-default">
      Sign in!</button>
    </form>
  </div>
  <app-sidebar [content]="pageContent.sidebar" class="col-12 col-md-4">
  </app-sidebar>
</div>
```

Changes the link to register

Updates the submit event function call

Note that the name input is removed.

Changes the text on the button

Finally, you make changes in the login component, which is similar to the register component. The changes you need to make are these:

- Change the name of the component controller.
- Change the page title.
- Remove references to the name field.
- Rename doRegisterSubmit() to doLoginSubmit(), and doRegister to doLogin.
- Call the login() method on the AuthenticationService instead of the register() method.

Copy the main body of the component class code from register/register-component .ts, and make the following changes. The next listing shows the content of the file and highlights the changes in bold.

Listing 12.15   Changes required for the `login` component

```
import { Component, OnInit } from '@angular/core';
import { Router } from '@angular/router';
import { AuthenticationService } from '../authentication.service';

@Component({
  selector: 'app-login',                              Updates the component
  templateUrl: './login.component.html',              definition block
  styleUrls: ['./login.component.css']
})
export class LoginComponent implements OnInit {   ◁─────   Changes the
                                                           component name
  public formError: string = '';

  public credentials = {
    name: '',
    email: '',
    password: ''
  };

  public pageContent = {
    header: {
      title: 'Sign in to Loc8r',    ◁──────   Changes the page title
      strapline: ''
    },
    sidebar: ''
  };

  constructor(
    private router: Router,
    private authenticationService: AuthenticationService
  ) { }

  ngOnInit() {
  }
                                                  Changes the submit
  public onLoginSubmit(): void {    ◁────────┘    event method
    this.formError = '';
    if (!this.credentials.email || !this.credentials.password) {
      this.formError = 'All fields are required, please try again';
    } else {
      this.doLogin();
    }                                    Changes the doRegister method
  }                                      to doLogin and updates the
                                         authentication service call
  private doLogin(): void {    ◁────────┘
    this.authenticationService.login(this.credentials)
      .then( () => this.router.navigateByUrl('/'))
      .catch( (message) => {
        this.formError = message
      });
  }
}
```

That was easy! There's no need to dwell on this component as, functionally, it works like the register controller.

Now you'll move to the final stage and use the authenticated session in the Angular application.

12.3 Working with authentication in the Angular app

When you have a way to authenticate users, the next step is making use of that information. In Loc8r, you'll do two things:

- Change the navigation based on whether the visitor is logged in.
- Use the user information when creating reviews.

You'll tackle the navigation first.

12.3.1 Updating the navigation

One thing that's currently missing from the navigation is a Sign-in link, so you'll add one in the conventional place: the top-right corner of the screen. But when a user is logged in, you don't want to display a sign-in message; it would be better to display the user's name and give them an option to sign out.

That's what you'll do in this section, starting by adding a right-side section to the navigation bar.

12.3.2 Adding a right-side section to the navigation

The navigation for Loc8r is set up in the framework component that acts as a layout for every page. You may remember from chapter 9 that this is the root component that defines the router outlet; the files are in app_public/src/app/framework. The following listing highlights in bold the markup you need to add to the template (framework.component.html) to put a Sign-in link on the right side.

Listing 12.16 Changes for the framework component

```html
<div id="navbarMain" class="navbar-collapse collapse">
    <ul class="navbar-nav mr-auto">
      <li class="nav-item" routerLinkActive="active">
        <a routerLink="about" class="nav-link">About</a>
      </li>
    </ul>
    <ul class="navbar-nav justify-content-end">        ⟵──┐ Adds a navbar to the header, and pushes it to the right
      <li class="nav-item" routerLinkActive="active">
        <a routerLink="login" class="nav-link">Sign in</a>   ⟵── The Sign-in link
      </li>
      <li class="nav-item dropdown" routerLinkActive="active">
        <a class="nav-link dropdown-toggle"
data-toggle="dropdown">Username</a>   ⟵────── Area for the username when logged in
          <div class="dropdown-menu">
            <a class="dropdown-item">Logout</a> ⟵┄┄┄┄┄┐
          </div>                                       │ Link for logging out
      </li>
    </ul>
  </div>
</div>
```

The login nav option navigates to the freshly minted login component you've built.

Currently, however, an added link in the drop-down menu doesn't work, and the Logout link needs to be fleshed out.

To make this link work, you need to inject the Authentication service into the Framework component. You also need to add three methods:

- A click event to trigger the logout (doLogout())
- A method to check the current user login status
- A method to get the current user name

The following listing shows how this is done.

Listing 12.17   Changes to Framework for logout

```
import { Component, OnInit } from '@angular/core';
import { AuthenticationService } from '../authentication.service';
import { User } from '../user';

@Component({
  selector: 'app-framework',
  templateUrl: './framework.component.html',
  styleUrls: ['./framework.component.css']
})
export class FrameworkComponent implements OnInit {

  constructor(
    private authenticationService: AuthenticationService
  ) { }

  ngOnInit() {
  }

  public doLogout(): void {
    this.authenticationService.logout();
  }

  public isLoggedIn(): boolean {
    return this.authenticationService.isLoggedIn();
  }

  public getUsername(): string {
    const user: User = this.authenticationService.getCurrentUser();
    return user ? user.name : 'Guest';
  }

}
```

Imports the authentication service

Imports the User class for type checking

Injects the imported service

doLogout wrapper for the authentication service logout method

isLoggedIn wrapper

getUsername wrapper

When these functions are in place, you'll add them to the framework HTML template. You need to add an *ngIf to toggle the display of the username drop-down menu, depending on the result of isLoggedIn(). When isLoggedIn() returns true, you'll want to show the user's name in the HTML. Finally, you need to hook in the doLogout() function to the click event for the Logout link.

Listing 12.18 Changes to the framework component template

```
<ul class="navbar-nav justify-content-end">
  <li class="nav-item" routerLinkActive="active">
    <a routerLink="login" class="nav-link" *ngIf="!isLoggedIn()">
    ➡Sign in</a>                    ⟵——————— Doesn't show if logged in
  </li>
  <li class="nav-item dropdown" routerLinkActive="active"
  ➡*ngIf="isLoggedIn()">              ⟵——————— Shows if logged in
    <a class="nav-link dropdown-toggle" data-toggle="dropdown">
      {{ getUsername() }}      ⟵——┐ Shows username
    </a>                            │ if available
    <div class="dropdown-menu">
      <a class="dropdown-item" (click)="doLogout()">Logout</a>
    </div>
  </li>
</ul>
```

With the logout functionality in place, now is a good time to consider a user-experience issue. Currently, the `login` and `register` components redirect the user to the homepage on a successful response, which is not a great experience for the user. What you'll do is return the user back to the page that they were on before logging in or registering.

To do this, create a service that takes advantage of the Angular router `events` property. The events property keeps a record of the routing events that occur while the user navigates the application. To start, generate a service called `history`:

```
$ ng generate service history
```

Add this new service to the framework component so that the reference is in place before you fill in body of the `history` service.

Listing 12.19 Adding a history service to the framework component

```
import { Component, OnInit } from '@angular/core';
import { AuthenticationService } from '../authentication.service';
import { HistoryService } from '../history.service';   ⟵— Imports the service
import { User } from '../user';

@Component({
  selector: 'app-framework',
  templateUrl: './framework.component.html',
  styleUrls: ['./framework.component.css']
})
export class FrameworkComponent implements OnInit {

  constructor(
    private authenticationService: AuthenticationService,
    private historyService: HistoryService      ⟵——┐ Injects it into
  ) { }                                             │ the component
...
```

With this code in place, fill in the logic for the `HistoryService`. You need to do several things to track a user's navigation history:

- Import the Angular `Router` module.
- Subscribe to the `events` property to track each navigation event.
- Create a public method to get access to the navigation history.

The next listing shows this in action.

Listing 12.20   Adding a history service

```
import { Injectable } from '@angular/core';
import { Router, NavigationEnd } from '@angular/router';        ◁── Imports the Router
import { filter } from 'rxjs/operators';                             and NavigationEnd
                                                                     classes
@Injectable({
  providedIn: 'root'
})
export class HistoryService {
  private urls: string[] = [];

  constructor(private router: Router) {
    this.router.events        ◁── The events property subscription
      .pipe(filter(routerEvent => routerEvent instanceof NavigationEnd))
      .subscribe((routerEvent: NavigationEnd) => {
        const url = routerEvent.urlAfterRedirects;
        this.urls = [...this.urls, url];
      });
  }
  ...
}
```

Brings in the filter from rxjs

The functionality in the constructor function as given in listing 12.20 probably needs a closer look. The router `events` property returns an Observable that emits several event types, but you're interested only in the `NavigationEnd` event, which you imported from the `@angular/router`.

To get these event types from the Observable (events stream), you need to filter them out, which is where the RxJS `filter` function comes into play. This function is piped to your events stream via the Observable `pipe` method. As we're not covering RxJS in this book, we recommend *RxJS in Action* (https://www.manning.com/books/rxjs-in-action) for further detail.

The events of this pipe after you `subscribe` to them are of type `NavigationEnd`, which is exactly what you need. `NavigationEnd` events have a `urlAfterRedirects` property, which is a string that you can push to your array of `urls` that you hold in your `HistoryService`.

Last, you need to add a method that returns the previous URL from the collected URL history. Add the following method to the `HistoryService`.

Listing 12.21   `getPreviousUrl` function

```
public getPreviousUrl(): string {
  const length = this.urls.length;
  return length > 1 ? this.urls[length - 2] : '/';
}
```
⟵ Returns the default location if there's no other entry

Now that you have a history service that keeps track of where the user was before login or registration, implement it as part of your `login` and `register` components.

You'll add this to the `register` component as shown in the next listing and change the `login` component later as an exercise to be completed, as the operation is identical. The solution is available on GitHub.

Listing 12.22   Changes required in the register component

```
import { Component, OnInit } from '@angular/core';
import { Router } from '@angular/router';
import { AuthenticationService } from '../authentication.service';
import { HistoryService } from '../history.service';            ⟵ Imports the
                                                                   history service
...
  constructor(
    private router: Router,
    private authenticationService: AuthenticationService,
    private historyService: HistoryService            ⟵ Injects the history
  ) { }                                                   service into constructor

  ...

  private doRegister(): void {
    this.authenticationService.login(this.credentials)
      .then( () => {
        this.router.navigateByUrl(this.historyService.getPreviousUrl());  ⟵
      })                                                        Uses the provided
      .catch( (message) => {                                    getPreviousUrl function to
        this.formError = message;                               redirect, using the router
      });
  }
...
```

After completing this change, and maybe through a little testing, you may have noticed that the page that the `register` component returns you to is the Login page—not what you're looking for. After registering, as a user you'd like to be returned to the page before Login, because that's where you entered the login/registration loop. From a user perspective, it's not a great experience.

To avoid this experience, add a new method to the `history` service that returns the last URL encountered before either `login` or `register`. This way, it doesn't matter whether the user travels between these two pages several times before performing the desired action.

You'll achieve this by using a filter across the list of URLs already navigated, removing all the URLs that match in the exclusions list. Then, pick the last one, safe in the knowledge that you've removed all the register and login items.

Listing 12.23   `getLastNonLoginUrl()`

List of strings that you need to exclude

Filters the collected list of URLs, and returns only those not in exclude

```
public getLastNonLoginUrl(): string {
  const exclude: string[] = ['/register', '/login'];
  const filtered = this.urls.filter(url => !exclude.includes(url));
  const length = filtered.length;
  return length > 1 ? filtered[length - 1] : '/';
}
```

Returns the last element of the filtered array or a default value

Add this code the `history` service, and change the function `doLogin()` in login .component.ts and `doRegister()` in register.component.ts to use it instead, as shown in the following listing (from register.component.ts).

Listing 12.24   Updating the `doRegister` function

```
private doRegister(): void {
  this.authenticationService.register(this.credentials)
    .then( () => {
      this.router.navigateByUrl(
        this.historyService.getLastNonLoginUrl()
      );
    })
    .catch( (message) => {
      this.formError = message
    });
}
```

Changes getPreviousUrl() to getLastNonLoginUrl()

Now you can reap the benefits of being logged in. You'll inject the authentication service into location-details.component.ts so you can check to see whether a user is logged in and present functionality accordingly.

You're going to do a couple of things:

- Inject the authentication service into the component to check the user's login state.
- Modify the component to take advantage of the logged-in state.

First, do the necessary importing of the `AuthenticationService`, and then inject into the component `constructor`.

Listing 12.25   location-details.component.ts changes

```
import { Component, OnInit, Input } from '@angular/core';
import { Location, Review } from '../location';
import { Loc8rDataService } from '../loc8r-data.service';
```

```
import { AuthenticationService } from '../authentication.service';   ⟵
                                                             Imports the
...                                                    AuthenticationService
  constructor(
    private loc8rDataService: Loc8rDataService,
    private authenticationService: AuthenticationService   ⟵
  ) { }
                                                              Injects the
  ngOnInit() {}                                          AuthenticationService
                                                         into the component
...
}
```

Next, add some methods that make use of the functionality provided by the `AuthenticationService`. Add the two methods in listing 12.26 to the `location-details` component.

Listing 12.26 Methods to add to location-details.component.ts

```
public isLoggedIn(): boolean {
  return this.authenticationService.isLoggedIn();       Wrapper function for
}                                                       isLoggedIn from
                                                        AuthenticationService
public getUsername(): string {                                           ⟵
  const { name } = this.authenticationService.getCurrentUser();
  return name ? name : 'Guest';   ⟵
}                                                       Wrapper function for
              If name isn't available,                  getCurrentUser from
              returns Guest                             AuthenticationService
```

To complete this part of the exercise, you need to update the template by

- Ensuring that the user is authenticated to leave a review
- Removing the need to enter the author name when writing a review
- Providing the username as the author from the authentication service when submitting a review and preventing validation from failing

First, change the template so that, in the logged-out state, you present a button inviting the user to log in to post a review. When the user is logged in, the page presents a button to allow them to add a review.

Change the `location-details` template (location-details.component.html) as shown next.

Listing 12.27 Changes to location-details.component.html

```
<div class="row">                                          ngSwitch around the
  <div class="col-12">                                       logged-in status
    <div class="card card-primary review-card">
      <div class="card-block" [ngSwitch]="isLoggedIn()">        ⟵
        <button (click)="formVisible=true" class="btn btn-primary
        ➥float-right"*ngSwitchCase="true">Add review</button>   ⟵
        <a routerLink="/login" class="btn btn-primary float-right"
Default state  ⟶  ➥*ngSwitchDefault>Log in to add review</a>
        <h2 class="card-title">Customer reviews</h2>            Shows whether
        <div *ngIf="formVisible">                              user is logged in
```

The ngSwitch directive checks whether the user is logged in and displays the appropriate call to action. Both states are shown in figure 12.4.

Figure 12.4   The two states of the Add Review button, depending on whether the user is logged in

Now that a user needs to be logged in to post a review, you no longer need users to enter their names in the review form, as this data can now be retrieved from the JWT. As a result, you need to delete code from the location-details.component.html template. See the following listing for the elements to remove.

Listing 12.28   Code to remove from location-details.component.html

```html
<div class="form-group row">
  <label for="name" class="col-sm-2 col-form-label">Name</label>
  <div class="col-sm-10">
    <input [(ngModel)]="newReview.author" id="name" name="name"
    ➥required="required" class="form-control">
  </div>
</div>
```

Without the form field, you need to pull the author name from the getUsername() function that you conveniently created earlier. Listing 12.29 highlights in bold the pieces to be changed in onReviewSubmit() in location-details.component.ts. Figure 12.5 shows the final review form.

Listing 12.29   Removing name validation from location-details.component.ts

```
public onReviewSubmit(): void {
    this.formError = '';
    this.newReview.author = this.getUsername();        Gets the username
    if (this.formIsValid()) {                          from the component
      this.loc8rDataService.addReviewByLocationId(this.location._id,
      ➥this.newReview)
        .then((review: Review) => {
          console.log('Review saved', review);
          let reviews = this.location.reviews.slice(0);
          reviews.unshift(review);
          this.location.reviews = reviews;
          this.resetAndHideReviewForm();
        });
```

```
    } else {
      this.formError = 'All fields required, please try again';
    }
  }
  ...
}
```

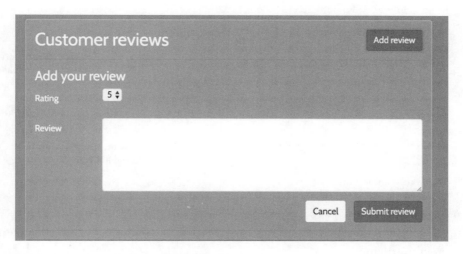

Figure 12.5   The final review form without a name field

If you try this now, you still encounter a problem. If you check the web browser's development console, you'll see that the API returns a 401 Unauthorized response, because you haven't updated the review submission API call with the JWT to allow the API to accept the request.

To make this work, you need to get access to the JWT stored in `localStorage` and pass it forward as a `Bearer` token in the `Authorization` request header.

Listing 12.30   Adding **AuthenticationService** to loc8r-data.service.ts

```
import { Injectable, Inject } from '@angular/core';
...
import { AuthResponse } from './authresponse';
import { BROWSER_STORAGE } from './storage';        ◁──── Imports the
                                                          AuthenticationService
@Injectable({
  providedIn: 'root'
})
export class Loc8rDataService {

  constructor(
    private http: HttpClient,
    @Inject(BROWSER_STORAGE) private storage: Storage    ◁──── Injects the
  ) { }                                                        imported service
                                                             into the component
```

Finally, you need to update the `addReviewByLocationId()` function to include the `Authorization` header in submissions to the API. The following listing shows the changes.

Listing 12.31 Adding `Authorization` headers to API call

```
public addReviewByLocationId(locationId: string, formData: Review):
Promise<Review> {
  const url: string = `${this.apiBaseUrl}/locations/${locationId}/
reviews`;
  const httpOptions = {                          Creates an httpOptions
    headers: new HttpHeaders({                   object for HttpHeaders
      'Authorization': `Bearer ${this.storage.getItem('loc8r-token')}`
    })
  };                                                  String Template
  return this.http                                    used here
    .post(url, formData, httpOptions)        Adds httpOptions
    .toPromise()                             to the API call
    .then(response => response as Review)
    .catch(this.handleError);
}
```

With that update, you've completed the authentication section. Users must be logged in to add a review, and through the authentication system, the review will be given the correct username.

This brings you to the end of the book. By now, you should have a good idea of the power and capabilities of the MEAN stack and be empowered to start building some cool stuff!

You have a platform to build REST APIs, server-side web applications, and browser-based single-page applications. You can create database-driven sites, APIs, and applications, and then publish them to a live URL.

When starting your next project, remember to take a little time to think about the best architecture and user experience. Spend a little time planning to make your development time more productive and enjoyable. And never be afraid to refactor and improve your code and application as you go.

You've only scratched the surface of what these amazing technologies can offer. So please dive in, build things, try stuff, keep learning, and (most important) have fun!

Summary

In this chapter, you learned

- How to use local storage to manage a user session in the browser
- How to use JWT data inside Angular
- How to pass a JWT from Angular to an API via HTTP headers

appendix A
Installing the stack

> **This appendix covers**
> - Installing Node and npm
> - Installing Express globally
> - Installing MongoDB
> - Installing Angular

Before you can build anything on the MEAN stack, you'll need to install the software to run it. This task is easy on Windows, macOS, and popular Linux distributions such as Ubuntu.

As Node underpins the stack, that's the best place to start. Node ships with npm included, which will be useful for installing some of the other software.

Installing Node and npm

The best way to install Node and npm depends on your operating system. Whenever possible, we recommend that you download an installer from the Node website at https://nodejs.org/download. This location always has the latest version as maintained by the Node core team.

LONG-TERM SUPPORT VERSIONS OF NODE

We recommend using a long-term support (LTS) version of Node. These are the ones with even major numbers, such as Node 8 and Node 10. These versions are the stable branches of Node and will be maintained and patched with nonbreaking changes for 18 months. The application in this book is built against Node 11, so the best LTS version to use is 10. No features used in this book are incompatible between versions, so feel free to use either.

INSTALLING NODE ON WINDOWS

Windows users should download an installer from the Node website.

INSTALLING NODE ON macOS

The best option for macOS users is to download an installer from the Node website. Alternatively, you can install Node and npm using the Homebrew package manager, as detailed on Joyent's Node wiki at https://github.com/joyent/node/wiki/Installing-Node.js-via-package-manager.

INSTALLING NODE ON LINUX

There aren't any installers for Linux users, but you can download binaries from the Node website if you're comfortable working with them.

Alternatively, Linux users can install Node from package managers. Package managers don't always have the latest version, so be aware of that fact. A particularly out-of-date one is the popular APT system on Ubuntu. You can find instructions for using a variety of package managers, including a fix for APT on Ubuntu, on Joyent's Node wiki on GitHub at https://github.com/joyent/node/wiki/Installing-Node.js-via-package-manager.

VERIFYING INSTALLATION BY CHECKING VERSION

After you have Node and npm installed, you can check the versions you have with a couple of terminal commands:

```
$ node --version
$ npm --version
```

These commands output the versions of Node and npm that you have on your machine. The code in this book is built with Node 11.2.0 and npm 6.4.1.

Installing Express globally

To be able to create new Express applications on the fly from the command line, you need to install the Express generator. You can do this from the command line using npm. In terminal, run the following command:

```
$ npm install -g express-generator
```

If this command fails due to a permissions error, you'll need to run it as an administrator. On Windows, right-click the command-prompt icon and choose Run As Administrator from the contextual menu. Then, try the preceding command again in the resulting window.

On macOS and Linux, you can prefix the command with `sudo`, as shown in the following code snippet; you'll be prompted for a password.

```
$ sudo npm install -g express-generator
```

When the generator finishes installing Express, you can verify it by checking the version number from terminal:

```
$ express --version
```

The version of Express used in the code samples in this book is 4.16.4.

If you run into any problems with this installation process, the documentation for Express is available on its website at http://expressjs.com.

Installing MongoDB

MongoDB is also available for Windows, macOS, and Linux. Detailed instructions about all the following options are available in the documentation at https://docs .mongodb.com/manual/administration/install-community.

INSTALLING MONGODB ON WINDOWS

Some direct downloads for Windows are available at https://docs.mongodb.org/ manual/installation, depending on which version of Windows you're running.

INSTALLING MONGODB ON MACOS

The easiest way to install MongoDB for macOS is to use the Homebrew package manager, but if you prefer, you can choose to install MongoDB manually.

INSTALLING MONGODB ON LINUX

Packages are available for all mainstream Linux distributions, as detailed at https:// docs.mongodb.org/manual/installation. If you're running a version of Linux that doesn't have MongoDB available in a package, you can choose to install it manually.

RUNNING MONGODB AS A SERVICE

After you have MongoDB installed, you'll probably want to run it as a service so that it automatically restarts whenever you reboot. Again, you can find instructions in the MongoDB installation documentation.

CHECKING THE MONGODB VERSION NUMBER

MongoDB installs not only itself, but also a Mongo shell so that you can interact with your MongoDB databases through the command line. You can check the version number of MongoDB and the Mongo shell independently. To check the shell version, run the following command in terminal:

```
$ mongo --version
```

To check the version of MongoDB, run this command:

```
$ mongod --version
```

This book uses version 4.0.4 of both MongoDB and the Mongo shell.

Installing Angular

Angular is simple to install as long as you have Node and npm already installed. What you actually install is the Angular CLI as a global npm package. To do so, run the following command in terminal:

```
$ npm install -g @angular/cli
Currently, this command installs Angular CLI version 7.0.6, which covers
Angular 7.1.0.
```

appendix B
Installing and preparing the supporting cast

This appendix covers

- Adding Twitter Bootstrap and some custom styles
- Using Font Awesome to provide a ready-made set of icons
- Installing Git
- Installing Docker and using the included container setup
- Installing a suitable command-line interface
- Signing up for Heroku
- Installing the Heroku CLI

Several technologies can help you with developing on the MEAN stack, from front-end layouts to source control and deployment tools. This appendix covers the installation and setup of the supporting technologies used throughout this book. As the actual install instructions tend to change over time, this appendix points you toward the best places to get the instructions and anything you need to look out for.

Twitter Bootstrap

Bootstrap isn't installed as such, but is added to your application. This process is as simple as downloading the library files, unzipping them, and placing them in the application.

The first step is downloading Bootstrap. This book uses version 4.1, which currently is the official release. You can get it from https://getbootstrap.com. Make sure you download the "ready to use files" and not the source. The distribution zip contains two folders: css and js.

When you have the files downloaded and unzipped, move one file from each folder into the public folder in your Express application, as follows:

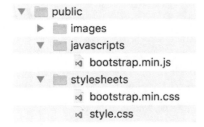

1 Copy bootstrap.min.css into your public/stylesheets folder.

2 Copy bootstrap.min.js into your public/js folder.

Figure B.1 The structure and contents of the public folder after Bootstrap has been added

Figure B.1 shows how the public folder in your application should look.

That gives you access to the default look and feel of Bootstrap, but you probably want your application to stand out from the crowd a bit. You can do so by adding a theme or some custom styles.

ADDING SOME CUSTOM STYLES

The Loc8r application in this book uses some custom styles that we created. This application is simple enough not to need a theme but was based on Bootstrap 4.1.

To add the custom styles, edit the style.css file in your public/stylesheets folder. Listing B.1 shows a good starting point and provides the CSS used throughout the book.

Listing B.1 Custom styles to give Loc8r a more distinctive look

```css
@import url("//fonts.googleapis.com/css?family=Lobster|Cabin:400,700");

h1, h2, h3, h4, h5, h6 {
  font-family: 'Lobster', cursive;
}

legend {
  font-family: 'Lobster', cursive;
}

.navbar {
  background-color: #ad1d28;
  border-color: #911821;
}

.navbar-light .navbar-brand {
  font-family: 'Lobster', cursive;
```

```
    color: #fff;
}

.navbar-light .navbar-toggler {
    color: white;
    border-color: white;
}

.navbar-light .navbar-toggler-icon {
    background-image: url("data:image/svgxml;charset=utf8,%3Csvg
    ➥viewBox='0 0 30 30'xmlns='http://www.w3.org/2000/svg'%3E%
    ➥3Cpath stroke='white' stroke-width='2'stroke-linecap='round'
    ➥stroke-miterlimit='10' d='M4 7h22M4 15h22M4 23h22'/%3E%3C/svg%3E")
}

.navbar-light .navbar-nav .nav-link,
.navbar-light .navbar-nav .nav-link:focus,
.navbar-light .navbar-nav .nav-link:hover {
    color: white;
}

.card {
    background-color: #469ea8;
    padding: 1rem;
}

.card-primary {
    border-color: #a2ced3;
    margin-bottom: 0.5rem;
}

.banner {
    margin-top: 4em;
    border-bottom: 1px solid #469ea8;
    margin-bottom: 1.5em;
    padding-bottom: 0.5em;
}

.review-header {
    background-color: #31727a;
    padding-top: 0.5em;
    padding-bottom: 0.5em;
    margin-bottom: 0.5em;
}

.review {
    margin-right: -16px;
    margin-left: -16px;
    margin-bottom: 0.5em;
}

.badge-default, .btn-primary {
    background-color: #ad1d28;
    border-color: #911821;
}

h4 a, h4 a:hover {
    color: #fff;
}
```

```
h4 small {
  font-size: 60%;
  line-height: 200%;
  color: #aaa;
}

h1 small {
  color: #aaa;
}

.address {
  margin-bottom: 0.5rem;
}

.facilities span.badge {
  margin-right: 2px;
}

p {
  margin-bottom: 0.65rem;
}

a {
  color: rgba(255, 255, 255, 0.8)
}

a:hover {
  color:#fff
}

body {
  font-family: "Cabin", Arial, sans-serif;
  color: #fff;
  background-color: #108a93;
}
```

To save you from typing all this code, you can get this file from the project repo on GitHub at https://github.com/cliveharber/gettingMean-2. It's introduced in the chapter-04 branch.

Font Awesome

Font Awesome is an awesome way to get scalable icons into your application by using fonts and CSS instead of images. As with Bootstrap, a few files need to be downloaded and put in the right places.

First, head to https://fontawesome.com/how-to-use/on-the-web/setup/hosting-font-awesome-yourself, and click the download button to download the zip file. (The button is currently a big blue one, but it may have changed when you get there.) We used version 5.2.0 in this book. The zip file contains loads of folders. The most important folders for this book are css and webfonts.

When Font Awesome is downloaded and unzipped, follow these two steps:

1 Copy the entire webfonts/ folder into the public folder in your application.
2 Copy the all.min.css file from the css folder into public/stylesheets.

When that's done, and you've got Bootstrap installed as well, your public folder should look like figure B.2.

Note that with Font Awesome, the name and position of the fonts folder relative to the all.min.css file is important. The CSS file references the fonts by using a relative path of ../webfonts/, so if this path is broken, the font icons won't work in your application.

If you don't have the patience to do all this, it's provided in the GitHub repo.

Installing Git

The source code for this book is managed with Git, so the easiest way to access it is to use Git. Also, Heroku relies on Git for managing the deployment process and pushing code from your development machine into a live environment. You need to install Git if you don't already have it.

You can verify whether you have it with a simple terminal command:

Figure B.2 The structure and contents of the public folder after Font Awesome is added

```
$ git --version
```

If this command responds with a version number, you already have it installed and can move to the next section. If not, you need to install Git.

A good starting point for macOS and Windows users who are new to Git is to download and install the GitHub user interface from https://help.github.com/articles/set-up-git.

You don't need a GUI, though, and you can install Git by itself by following the instructions on the main Git website at https://git-scm.com/downloads.

Installing Docker

With this edition, we include the capability to run the application against a local Docker environment. The eagle-eyed among you probably noticed the Docker files in the repo.

To run the Docker container, you need to have Docker locally installed. (We used Docker Desktop.) If you're on a macOS or Windows machine, head over to https://www.docker.com/products/docker-desktop, and install the version suitable to your machine.

To run the application in the container, navigate to the cloned repo, and type `make build`. Each branch has a Docker file that sets up an environment suitable to run that chapter's code in. If you need to bring the containers down, use `make destroy`.

If you want to run the code locally without Docker, that's cool too.

Installing a suitable command-line interface

You can get the most out of Git by using a CLI, even if you've downloaded and installed a GUI. Some CLIs are better than others, and you can't use the native Windows command prompt, so if you're on Windows, you definitely need to run something else. Here's what we use in a few environments:

- macOS Mavericks and later: native terminal
- macOS pre-Mavericks (10.8.5 and earlier): iTerm
- Windows: GitHub shell (this comes installed with the GitHub GUI)
- Ubuntu: native terminal

The Visual Studio Code editor comes with a nice, built-in command-line terminal, which is a good cross-platform option as well. If you have other preferences and the Git commands work, by all means use what you already have and you're used to using.

Setting up Heroku

This book uses Heroku for hosting the Loc8r application in a live production environment. You can do this too—for free—so long as you sign up, install the CLI, and log in through terminal.

SIGNING UP FOR HEROKU

To use Heroku, you need to sign up for an account. For the purposes of the application you'll be building through this book, a free account is fine. Head over to https://www .heroku.com, and follow the instructions to sign up.

INSTALLING THE HEROKU CLI

The Heroku CLI contains the Heroku command-line shell and a utility called Heroku Local. The shell is what you'll use from terminal to manage your Heroku deployment, and Local is useful for making sure that what you've built on your machine is set up to run properly on Heroku. You can download the Toolbelt for macOS, Windows, and Linux from https://devcenter.heroku.com/articles/heroku-cli.

LOGGING IN TO HEROKU USING TERMINAL

After you've signed up for an account and installed the CLI on your machine, the last step is logging in to your account from terminal. Enter the following command:

```
$ heroku login
```

This command prompts you for your Heroku login credentials. Log in, and you're all set up and ready to go with Heroku.

appendix C
Dealing with
all the views

This appendix covers

- Removing the data from all views except the homepage
- Moving the data into the controllers

Chapter 4 covers setting up the controllers and the views for the static, clickable prototype. The "how" and "why" are covered in that chapter in more detail, so this appendix focuses on the results.

Moving the data from the views to the controllers

Part of this process includes moving the data back down the MVC flow, from the views into the controllers. The example in chapter 4 deals with this task in the Loc8r homepage, but it needs to be done for the other pages too. Start with the Details page.

Details page

The Details page is the largest and most complex of the pages, with the most data requirements. The first step is setting up the controller.

SETTING UP THE CONTROLLER

The controller for this page is called `locationInfo` and is in the locations.js file in app_server/controllers. When you've analyzed the data in the view and collated it into a JavaScript object, your controller will look something like the following listing.

Listing C.1 `locationInfo` controller

```
const locationInfo = function(req, res){
  res.render('location-info', {
    title: 'Starcups',
    pageHeader: {title: 'Starcups'},
    sidebar: {
      context: 'is on Loc8r because it has accessible wifi and space to sit
      down with your laptop and get some work done.',
      callToAction: 'If you\'ve been and you like it - or if you don\'t -
      please leave a review to help other people just like you.'
    },
    location: {
      name: 'Starcups',
      address: '125 High Street, Reading, RG6 1PS',
      rating: 3,
      facilities: ['Hot drinks', 'Food', 'Premium wifi'],
      coords: {lat: 51.455041, lng: -0.9690884},          ⟵  Includes latitude and
      openingTimes: [{                    ⟵                   longitude coordinates to
        days: 'Monday - Friday',                              use in Google Map image
        opening: '7:00am',               Adds array of open
        closing: '7:00pm',               times, allowing for
        closed: false                    different data on
      },{                                 different days
        days: 'Saturday',
        opening: '8:00am',
        closing: '5:00pm',
        closed: false
      },{
        days: 'Sunday',
        closed: true
      }],                            Array for reviews
      reviews: [{          ⟵         left by other users
        author: 'Simon Holmes',
        rating: 5,
        timestamp: '16 July 2013',
        reviewText: 'What a great place. I can\'t say enough good things
        about it.'
      },{
        author: 'Charlie Chaplin',
        rating: 3,
        timestamp: '16 June 2013',
        reviewText: 'It was okay. Coffee wasn\'t great, but the wifi was
        fast.'
```

```
      }]
    }
  });
};
```

Note the latitude and longitude being sent through. You can get your current latitude and longitude from https://www.where-am-i.net. You can geocode an address—that is, get the latitude and longitude of it—from https://www.latlong.net/convert-address-to-lat-long.html. Your views will be using the `lat` and `lng` to display a Google Map image of the correct location, so it's worthwhile doing this for the prototype stage.

UPDATING THE VIEW

As this page is the most complex, data-rich page, it stands to reason that it will have the largest view template. You've already seen most of the technicalities in the home-page layout, such as looping through arrays, bringing in includes, and defining and calling mixins. You have a couple of extra things to look out for in this template, though, both of which are annotated and highlighted in bold.

First, this template uses an `if-else` conditional statement. This statement looks like JavaScript without the braces. Second, the template uses a JavaScript `replace` function to replace all line breaks in the text of reviews with `<br/>` tags. You do this by using a simple regular expression, looking for all occurrences of the characters `\n` in the text. The following listing shows the `location-info.pug` view template in full.

Listing C.2 `location-info.pug` view template in app_server/views

```
extends layout
include _includes/sharedHTMLfunctions        ◁──  Brings in sharedHTMLfunctions
block content                                      include, which contains
  .row.banner                                      outputRating mixin
    .col-12
      h1= pageHeader.title
  .row
    .col-12.col-lg-9
      .row
        .col-12.col-md-6                                Calls outputRating mixin,
          p.rating                                      sending it the rating of the
            +outputRating(location.rating)    ◁──       current location
          p 125 High Street, Reading, RG6 1PS
          .card.card-primary
            .card-block
              h2.card-title Opening hours
              each time in location.openingTimes        Loops through the
                p.card-text                             array of open times,
                  | #{time.days} :                      checking whether the
                  if time.closed                        location is closed by
                    | closed                            using an inline if-else
                  else                                  statement
                    | #{time.opening} - #{time.closing}
        .card.card-primary
          .card-block
            h2.card-title Facilities
```

```
            each facility in location.facilities
              span.badge.badge-warning
                i.fa.fa-check
                |  #{facility}
                |  
        .col-12.col-md-6.location-map
          .card.card-primary
            .card-block
              h2.card-title Location map
              img.img-fluid.rounded(src=`http://maps.googleapis.com/
              ➥maps/api/staticmap?center=${location.coords.lat},
              ➥${location.coords.lng}&zoom=17&size=400x350&sensor=
              ➥false&markers=${location.coords.lat},${location.coords.
              ➥ lng}&key={googleAPIKey}&scale=2`)
      .row
        .col-12
          .card.card-primary.review-card
            .card-block
              a.btn.btn-primary.float-right(href='/location/review/new')
              ➥Add review
              h2.card-title Customer reviews
              each review in location.reviews
                .row.review
                  .col-12.no-gutters.review-header
                    span.rating
                      +outputRating(review.rating)
                    span.reviewAuthor #{review.author}
                    small.reviewTimestamp #{review.timestamp}
                  .col-12
                    p !{(review.reviewText).replace(/\n/g, '<br/>')}
        .col-12.col-lg-3
          p.lead #{location.name} #{sidebar.context}
          p= sidebar.callToAction
```

Builds the URL for the Google Maps static image, inserting lat and lng by using an ES2015 template literal. Remember that you'll need your Google Maps API Key.

Loops through each review, calling the outputRating mixin again to generate markup for stars

Replaces any line breaks in review text with the <br/> tag so it renders as intended by the author

A question that may arise is, why replace line breaks with <br/> tags every time? Why don't you save the data with <br/> tags in? That way, you have to run the replace function only once, when the data is saved. The answer is that HTML is only one method of rendering text; it happens to be the one you're using here. Down the line, you may want to pull this information into a native mobile application. You don't want the source data tainted with HTML markup that you don't use in that environment. The way to handle that is to keep the data clean.

Add Review page

The Add Review page is simple at the moment, with only one piece of data in it: the title in the page header. Updating the controller shouldn't pose much of a problem. See the following listing for the full code of the addReview controller, in locations.js in the app_server/controllers folder.

Listing C.3 addReview controller

```
const addReview = function(req, res){
  res.render('location-review-form', {
    title: 'Review Starcups on Loc8r',
    pageHeader: { title: 'Review Starcups' }
  });
};
```

There's not much to talk about here; you've updated the text inside the titles. The following listing shows the corresponding view, location-review-form.pug, in app_server/views.

Listing C.4 location-review-form.pug template

```
extends layout
block content
  .row.banner
    .col-12
      h1= pageHeader.title
  .row
    .col-12.col-md-8
      form(action="/location", method="get", role="form")
        .form-group.row
          label.col-10.col-sm-2.col-form-label(for="name") Name
          .col-12.col-sm-10
            input#name.form-control(name="name")
        .form-group.row
          label.col-10.col-sm-2.col-form-label(for="rating") Rating
          .col-12.col-sm-2
            select#rating.form-control.input-sm(name="rating")
              option 5
              option 4
              option 3
              option 2
              option 1
        .form-group.row
          label.col-sm-2.col-form-label(for="review") Review
          .col-sm-10
            textarea#review.form-control(name="review", rows="5")
        button.btn.btn-primary.float-right Add my review
    .col-12.col-md-4
```

Again, there's nothing complicated or new here, so you can move on to the About page.

About page

The About page doesn't contain a huge amount of data, either, only a title and some content. Pull it out of the view and into the controller. Note that the content in the view currently has some <br/> tags in it, so replace each <br/> tag with \n when you put it into the controller. These tags are highlighted in bold in the following listing. The about controller is in app_server/controllers/others.js.

Listing C.5   about controller

```
const about = function(req, res){
  res.render('generic-text', {
    title: 'About Loc8r',
    content: 'Loc8r was created to help people find places to sit down
    ➥and get a bit of work done.<br/><br/>Lorem ipsum dolor sit
    ➥amet, consectetur adipiscing elit. Nunc sed lorem ac nisi digni
    ➥ssim accumsan. Nullam sit amet interdum magna. Morbi quis
    ➥faucibus nisi. Vestibulum mollis purus quis eros adipiscing
    ➥tristique. Proin posuere semper tellus, id placerat augue dapibus
    ➥ornare. Aenean leo metus, tempus in nisl eget, accumsan interdum
    ➥dui. Pellentesque sollicitudin volutpat ullamcorper.'
  });
};
```

Aside from removing the HTML from the content, not much is going on here. Take a quick look at the view, and you'll be done. The following listing shows the final generic-text view used for the About page in app_server/views. The view has to use the same piece of code as the reviews section to replace the \n line breaks with HTML <br/> tags.

Listing C.6   `generic-text.pug` template

```
extends layout
  .row.banner
    .col-12
      h1= title
  .row
    .col-12.col-lg-8
      p !{(content).replace(/\n/g, '<br/>')}
```

Replaces all line breaks with <br/> tags when rendering HTML ◁

This template is a simple, small, reusable one to use whenever you want to output some text on a page.

Switching from Promises to Observables

In chapter 8, we briefly discuss Observables and Promises and then proceed to use Promises in the application. Changing the application to use Observables isn't difficult, though, and this brief section covers the basics to give you a complete picture of how this task might be achieved. Typically, an SPA uses both Observables and Promises, depending on the problem that's being solved.

Take a look at the getLocations() method in loc8r-data.service.ts.

Listing C.7   loc8r-data.servce.ts

```
public getLocations(lat: number, lng: number): Promise<Location[]> {
    const maxDistance: number = 20000;
    const url: string =
      `${this.apiBaseUrl}/locations?lng=${lng}&lat=${lat}&maxDistance=$
➥{maxDistance}`;
    return this.http
```

```
        .get(url)
        .toPromise()                          <----------------------┐  Conversion of
        .then(response => response as Location[])                    │  Observable to Promise
        .catch(this.handleError);
    }
```

As you can see, you're taking the Observable returned by the HttpClient `get()` method and converting it to a Promise.

To switch this method to return an Observable, you first need to import Observable from rxjs, and then have the function return the result of the `get()` method directly.

Listing C.8   Changes to loc8r-data.service.ts required to return Observables

```
import { Observable } from 'rxjs'
...
public getLocations(lat: number, lng: number) : Observable<Location
➥[]> {
    const maxDistance: number = 20000;
    const url: string =
      `${this.apiBaseUrl}/locations?lng=${lng}&lat=${lat}&maxDistance=
➥${maxDistance}`;
    return this.http.get<Location[]>(url);   <-------┐  Returns a Observable
}                                                    │  type cast to Location[]
```

At this point, you're not capturing the response (Observable); to do that, you need a subscriber. This function is used in the home-list component.

Listing C.9   getLocations() from home-list.component.ts

```
private getLocations(position: any): void {
    this.message = 'Searching for nearby places';
    const lat: number = position.coords.latitude;
    const lng: number = position.coords.longitude;
    this.loc8rDataService
      .getLocations(lat, lng)                         ┌─ Responds to
        .then(foundLocations => {         <-----------┘  the Promise
          this.message = foundLocations.length > 0 ? '' :
          ➥'No locations found';
          this.locations = foundLocations;
        });
    }
```

To use the Observable, you need to alter the previous listing.

Listing C.10   Changes to subscribe to Observables

```
private getLocations(position: any): void {
    this.message = 'Searching for nearby places';
    const lat: number = position.coords.latitude;
    const lng: number = position.coords.longitude;
    this.loc8rDataService
        .getLocations(lat, lng)
```

```
        .subscribe(                    ◁──────── Observable subscriber
            (foundLocations: Location[]) => {
            this.message = foundLocations.length > 0 ? '' :
            ➥'No locations found';
            this.locations = foundLocations;
        },
        error =>
    this.handleError(error)              ◁──────── Error handler
    );
```

As you can see, switching between methods isn't difficult. The choice of method depends on the situation at hand. For reference, however, using Observables is becoming standard practice.

appendix D
Reintroducing JavaScript

This appendix covers

- Applying best practices when writing JavaScript
- Using JSON effectively to pass data
- Examining how to use callbacks and escaping callback hell
- Writing modular JavaScript with closures, patterns, and JavaScript classes
- Adopting functional programming principles

JavaScript is such a fundamental part of the MEAN stack (even if you're writing the Angular part with TypeScript) that we'll spend a little bit of time looking at it. We need to cover the bases because successful MEAN development depends on it. JavaScript is such a common language (uniquely, JavaScript has a runtime on almost every computer currently on the planet) that it seems that everybody knows some of it, partly because JavaScript is easy to start with and forgiving in the way it's written. Unfortunately, this looseness and low barrier to entry can encourage bad habits, which can cause unexpected results.

The aim of this appendix isn't to teach JavaScript from scratch; you should already know the basics. If you don't know JavaScript at all, you may struggle and find it hard going. Like all things, JavaScript has a learning curve. On the other hand, not everybody needs to read this appendix in detail, particularly experienced JavaScript developers. If you're lucky enough to count yourself as part of the experienced camp, it still may be worthwhile to skim this appendix in case you find something new here.

We don't cover TypeScript, though we hope that chapters 8 through 12 cover it in enough detail for you to be comfortable with it.

One last thing before we get started in earnest. When you look around the internet for information around JavaScript, you'll more than likely come across the appellations ES2015, ES2016, ES5, ES6, ES7, and so on.

ES5 is the version of JavaScript that has been available for the longest time, from the dim and distant past that includes the Firefox 4 web browser; the birth of Google Chrome; and the long, torturous death of the infamous Internet Explorer 6. Luckily, those days are long gone, but the specification still stands, and most browsers (mostly) adhere to it.

Officially, as of 2015, iterations of the JavaScript (or, if you prefer, ECMAScript [ES]) specification have been denoted by the year: ES2015, ES2016, and so on. Any reference to single-digit versioning post ES5, like ES6, is incorrect. Throughout this book, we've been careful to ensure that we named things correctly. Many authors across the internet haven't been so diligent and continue to perpetuate the incorrect naming scheme.

As things stand today, most browsers adhere to most of the changes made in JavaScript as part of the ES2015 spec, with some browsers also providing some functionality for later iterations (2016, 2017, and so on). The pace of adoption and implementation is sometimes slower than we, as developers, would like, so transpilers such as Babel are available. JavaScript transpilers broadly take code written utilizing more modern ideas and convert it to a form that older browsers understand. They provide a bridge between old and new and between different languages. TypeScript, CoffeeScript, Elm, and ReasonML are all transpiled to JavaScript.

Everybody knows JavaScript, right?

Not everybody knows JavaScript, but the vast majority of developers used it in one form or another at some point. Naturally, different levels of knowledge and experience exist. As a test, take a look at the following code listing. The listing contains a chunk of JavaScript code, the aim of which is to output messages to the console. If you understand the way the code is written, correctly determine what the output messages will be, and (more important) why they are what they are, you're probably good for a skim read.

Listing D.1   Example JavaScript with intentional bugs

```javascript
const myName = {
  first: 'Simon',
  last: 'Holmes'
  };
var age = 37,
  country = 'UK';
console.log("1:", myName.first, myName.last);
const changeDetails = (function () {
  console.log("2:", age, country);
  var age = 35;
  country = 'United Kingdom';
  console.log("3:", age, country);
  const reduceAge = function (step) {
    age = age - step;
    console.log("4: Age:", age);
  };
  const doAgeIncrease = function (step) {
    for (let i = 0; i <= step; i++) {
      window.age += 1;
    }
    console.log("5: Age:", window.age);
  },
  increaseAge = function (step) {
    const waitForIncrease = setTimeout(function () {
      doAgeIncrease(step);
    }, step * 200);
  };
  console.log("6:", myName.first, myName.last, age, country);
  return {
    reduceAge: reduceAge,
    increaseAge: increaseAge
  };
})();
changeDetails.increaseAge(5);
console.log("7:", age, country);
changeDetails.reduceAge(5);
console.log("8:", age, country);
```

How did you get on with that? Listing D.1 has a couple of intentional bugs that Java-Script will let you make if you're not careful. All this JavaScript is valid and legal, how-ever, and it will run without throwing an error; you can test it by running it in a browser, if you like. The bugs highlight how easy it is to get unexpected results and also how difficult it can be to spot them if you don't know what you're looking for.

Want to know what the output of that code is? If you haven't run it yourself, you can see the result in the following listing.

Listing D.2   Output of listing D.1

```
1: Simon Holmes          Age is undefined due to scope
2: undefined UK      ◁── clashes and variable hoisting.
3: 35 United Kingdom
```

```
6: Simon Holmes 35 United Kingdom
7: 37 United Kingdom
4: Age: 30
8: 37 United Kingdom
5: Age: 43
```

Country hasn't changed, but age has, due to variable scopes.

Runs when called, not when defined; uses local variables over global

Runs later due to setTimeout; age is wrong due to a mistake in the for loop

Among other things, this code snippet shows a private closure exposing public methods, issues with variable scope and side effects, variables not being defined when expected, mixing of function and lexical scope, the effects of asynchronous code execution, and an easy mistake to make in a `for` loop. There's quite a lot to take in when reading the code.

If you're not sure what some of this means or didn't get the outcome correct, read this appendix.

Good habits or bad habits

JavaScript is an easy language to learn. You can grab a snippet from the internet and pop it into your HTML page, and you've started on your journey. One reason why it's easy to learn is that in some respects, it's not as strict as it should be. It lets you do things that it possibly shouldn't, which leads to bad habits. In this section, we'll take a look at some of these bad habits and show you how to turn them into good habits.

Variables, scope, and functions

The first step is looking at *variables*, *scope*, and *functions*, which are all closely tied together. JavaScript has three types of scope: *global*, *function* (using the `var` keyword), and *lexical* (using `let` or `const` keywords). JavaScript also has *scope inheritance*. If you declare a variable in global scope, it's accessible by everything; if you declare a variable with `var` inside a function, it's accessible only to that function and everything inside it; if you declare a variable with `let` or `const` in a block, it's accessible inside the braces and everything inside that block, but unlike `var`, access doesn't bleed through to the surrounding function block.

The var keyword in ES2015 and later

Modern practice tends to frown on using the `var` keyword, which will eventually be deprecated. `var` comes with a lot of baggage, and if you're coming from other languages, its scoping can be difficult to work with and can trip up even the most experienced developer. We'll discuss it here, though, because a lot of JavaScript has been built with `var`.

With ES2015, the language specification introduced the `let` and `const` keywords, which are lexically (block) scoped. These keywords have greater similarity with other variable-definition schemes. The difference is explained in more detail in the following sections.

Working with scope and scope inheritance

Start with a simple example in which scope is used incorrectly.

Listing D.3 Scope example

```
const firstname = 'Simon';              ◁———————— Variable declared in global scope
const addSurname = function () {
  const surname = 'Holmes';          ◁———————— Variable declared in local lexical scope
  console.log(firstname + ' ' + surname);   ◁———————— Outputs "Simon Holmes"
};
addSurname();
console.log(firstname + ' ' + surname);  ◁—— Throws error because surname isn't defined
```

This piece of code throws an error because it's trying to use the variable `surname` in the global scope, but it was defined in the local scope of the function `addSurname()`. A good way to visualize the concept of scope is to draw some nested circles. In figure D.1, the outer circle depicts the global scope; the middle circle depicts the function scope; and the inner circle depicts lexical scope. You can see that the global scope has access to the variable `firstname` and that the local scope of the function `addSurname()` has access to the global variable `firstname` and the local variable `surname`. In this case, lexical scope and function scope overlap.

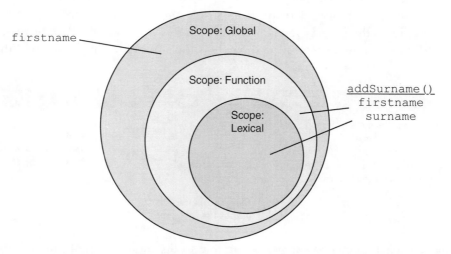

Figure D.1 Scope circles depicting global scope versus local scope and scope inheritance

If you want the global scope to output the full name while keeping the surname private in the local scope, you need a way of pushing the value into the global scope. In terms of scope circles, you're aiming for what you see in figure D.2. You want a new variable, `fullname`, that you can use in both global and local scopes.

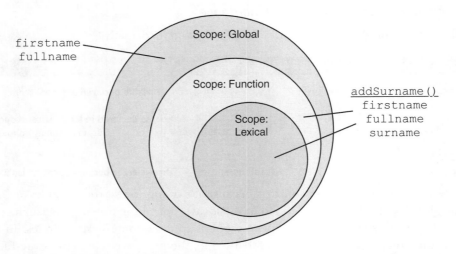

Figure D.2   Using an additional global variable to return data from the local scope

Pushing from local to global scope: The wrong way

One way you could do it—and we'll warn you now that it's bad practice—is to define a variable against the global scope from inside the local scope. In the browser, the global scope is the object window; in Node.js, it's global. Sticking with browser examples for now, the following listing shows how this would look if you updated the code to use the fullname variable.

Listing D.4   Global fullname variable

```
const firstname = 'Simon';
const addSurname = function () {
  const surname = 'Holmes';
  window.fullname = firstname + ' ' + surname;
  console.log(fullname);
};
addSurname();
console.log(fullname);
```

> The fullname variable is defined in the window object.

> Global scope can output the full name.

This approach allows you to add a variable to the global scope from inside a local scope, but it's not ideal. The problems are twofold. First, if anything goes wrong with the addSurname() function and the variable isn't defined, when the global scope tries to use it, you'll get an error thrown. The second problem becomes obvious when your code grows. Suppose that you have dozens of functions adding things to different scopes. How do you keep track of them? How do you test them? How do you explain to someone else what's going on? The answer to all these questions is *with great difficulty.*

Pushing from local to global scope: The right way

If declaring the global variable in the local scope is wrong, what's the right way? The rule of thumb is *always declare variables in the scope in which they belong*. If you need a global variable, you should define it in the global scope, as in the following listing.

Listing D.5   Declaring globally scoped variables

```
var firstname = 'Simon',
    fullname;                                          Variable declared in global
var addSurname = function () {                         scope, even if a value isn't
  var surname = 'Holmes';                              assigned to it yet
  window.fullname = firstname + ' ' + surname;
  console.log(fullname);
};
addSurname();
console.log(fullname);
```

Here, it's obvious that the global scope now contains the variable `fullname`, which makes the code easier to read when you come back to it.

Referencing global variables from local scope

You may have noticed that from within the function, the code still references the global variable by using the fully qualified `window.fullname`. It's best practice to do this whenever you reference a global variable from a local scope. Again, this practice makes your code easier to come back to and debug, because you can explicitly see which variable is being referenced. The code should look like the following listing.

Listing D.6   Using global variables in local scope

```
var firstname = 'Simon',
    fullname;
var addSurname = function () {                         When using global
  var surname = 'Holmes';                              variables in local scope,
  window.fullname = window.firstname + ' ' + surname;  always use the fully
  console.log(window.fullname);                        qualified reference.
};
addSurname();
console.log(fullname);
```

This approach might add a few more characters to your code, but it makes it obvious which variable you're referencing and where it came from. There's another reason for this approach, particularly when assigning a value to a variable.

Implied global scope

JavaScript lets you declare a variable without using `var`, which is a bad thing indeed. Worse, if you declare a variable without using `var`, JavaScript creates the variable in the global scope, as shown in the following listing.

Listing D.7 Declaring without `var`

```
var firstname = 'Simon';
var addSurname = function () {
  surname = 'Holmes';
  fullname = firstname + ' ' + surname;
  console.log(fullname);
};
addSurname();
console.log(firstname + surname);
console.log(fullname);
```

surname and fullname are both defined in the global scope by implication.

They can be used in the global scope.

We hope that you can see how this could be confusing and is a bad practice. The takeaway is *always declare variables in the scope in which they belong, using the `var` statement*.

The problem of variable hoisting

You've probably heard that with JavaScript, you should always declare your variables at the top. That's correct, and the reason is because of variable hoisting. With *variable hoisting*, JavaScript declares all variables at the top anyway without telling you, which can lead to some unexpected results.

The following code listing shows how variable hoisting might show itself. In the `addSurname()` function, you want to use the global value of `firstname` and later declare a local scope value.

Listing D.8 Shadowing example

```
var firstname = 'Simon';
var addSurname = function () {
  var surname = 'Holmes';
  var fullname = firstname + ' ' + surname;
  var firstname = 'David';
  console.log(fullname);
};
addSurname();
```

You expect this to use a global variable.

The output is actually "undefined Holmes."

Why is the output wrong? JavaScript "hoists" all variable declarations to the top of their scope. You see the code in listing D.8, but JavaScript sees the code in listing D.9.

Listing D.9 Hoisting example

```
var firstname = 'Simon';
var addSurname = function () {
  var firstname,
      surname,
      fullname;
  surname = 'Holmes';
  fullname = firstname + ' ' + surname;
  firstname = 'David';
  console.log(fullname);
};
addSurname();
```

JavaScript has moved all variable declarations to the top.

No value is assigned before it's used, so it's undefined.

When you see what JavaScript is doing, the bug is a little more obvious. JavaScript has declared the variable `firstname` at the top of the scope, but it doesn't have a value to assign to it, so JavaScript leaves the variable undefined when you first try to use it.

You should bear this fact in mind when writing your code. What JavaScript sees should be what you see. If you can see things from the same perspective, you have less room for error and unexpected problems.

Lexical scope

Lexical scope is sometimes called *block scope*. Variables defined between a set of braces are limited to the scope of those braces. Therefore, scoping can be limited to looping and flow logic constructs.

JavaScript defines two keywords that provide lexical scope: `let` and `const`. Why two? The functionality of the two is slightly different.

`let` is a bit like `var`. It sets up a variable that can be changed in the scope in which it is defined. It differs from `var` in that its scope is limited as described earlier, and variables declared this way aren't hoisted. As they're not hoisted, they're not tracked by the compiler the same way as `var`; the compiler leaves them where they are on the first pass, so if you try to reference them before they're defined, the compiler complains with a `ReferenceError`.

Listing D.10 `let` in action

```
if (true) {
    let foo = 1;          ◁───────  Initially declares variable
    console.log(foo);     ◁───────  Prints out value of 1
    foo = 2;              ◁───────  Redefines value
    console.log(foo);     ◁───────  Prints out value of 2
    console.log(bar);     ◁───────  Tries to print out a value that's
    let bar = 'something'; ◁──────    not defined yet (ReferenceError)
}
```
Definition of variable
that's not hoisted

`const` has the same caveats as `let`. `const` differs from `let` in that variables declared in such a way aren't allowed to change, either by reassignment or redeclaration; they're declared to be immutable. `const` also prevents shadowing—redefining a previously defined outer scoped variable. Suppose you have a variable defined in global scope (with `var`), and you try to define a variable with `const` with the same name in an enclosed scope. The compiler will throw an `Error`. The type of the error returned depends on what you're trying to do.

Listing D.11 Using `const`

```
var bar = 'defined';      ◁───────  Initially declares bar
if (true) {
    const foo = 1;        ◁───────  Initially declares foo variable
    console.log(foo);     ◁───────  Prints out value of 1
```

```
  foo = 2;                          ◁——— Tries to redefine foo (Error)
  const bar = 'something else';        ◁——— Tries to shadow bar variable
}
```

Because of the clarity afforded by declaring variables with `let` and `const`, this method is now the preferred way. Issues of hoisting are no longer a concern, and variables behave in a more conventional way that programmers familiar with other mainstream languages are more comfortable with.

Functions are variables

You may have noticed throughout the preceding code snippets that the `addSurname()` function has been declared as a variable. Again, this is a best practice. First, this is how JavaScript sees it anyway, and second, it makes it clear which scope the function is in.

Although you can declare a function in the format

```
function addSurname() {}
```

JavaScript interprets it as follows:

```
const addSurname = function() {}
```

As a result, it's a best practice to define functions as variables.

Limiting use of the global scope

We've talked a lot about using the global scope, but in reality, you should try to limit your use of global variables. Your aim should be to keep the global scope as clean as possible, which becomes important as applications grow. Chances are that you'll add various third-party libraries and modules. If all these libraries and modules use the same variable names in the global scope, your application will go into meltdown.

Global variables aren't the "evil" that some people would have you believe, but you must be careful when using them. When you truly need global variables, a good approach is to create a container object in the global scope and put everything there. Do this with the ongoing name example to see how it looks by creating a `nameSetup` object in the global scope and use this to hold everything else.

Listing D.12   Using const to define functions globally

```
const nameSetup = {  ◁——————┐  Declares a global
  firstname : 'Simon',        │  variable as an object
  fullname : '',
  addSurname : function () {              ┌─ Local variables are still
    const surname = 'Holmes';     ◁———————┘  okay inside functions.
    nameSetup.fullname = nameSetup.firstname + ' ' + surname;
    console.log(nameSetup.fullname);                      ┌─ Always access
  }                                                       │  values of an
};                                                        │  object by using
nameSetup.addSurname();                         ─────────┤  a fully qualified
console.log(nameSetup.fullname);                          │  reference.
```

When you code like this, all your variables are held together as properties of an object, keeping the global space nice and neat. Working like this also minimizes the risk of having conflicting global variables. You can add more properties to this object after declaration, and even add new functions. Adding to the preceding code listing, you could have the code shown next.

Listing D.13   Adding object properties

```
nameSetup.addInitial = function (initial) {
  nameSetup.fullname = nameSetup.fullname.replace(" ", " " + initial + " ");
};
nameSetup.addInitial('D');
console.log(nameSetup.fullname);
```

Defines a new function inside a global object

Invokes a function and sends a parameter

The output is "Simon D Holmes."

Working in this way gives you control of your JavaScript and reduces the chances that your code will give you unpleasant surprises. Remember to declare variables in the appropriate scope and at the correct time, and group them into objects wherever possible.

Arrow functions

So far, we've avoided discussing the JavaScript `this` variable. `this` is a fairly large topic and can be the source of much confusion. Simply put, the value of `this` changes depending on the context in which it's used. For functions defined outside an `Object` context, `this` refers to the execution context where the function was defined when in strict mode; it defaults to the current execution context if not in strict mode, so it changes depending on when it's used.

Further, `this` can be bound to a different execution context if the prototype functions `call()` or `apply()` are used.

If a function is defined as an `Object` method, `this` refers to the surrounding object context. When used in an event handler, `this` refers to the DOM object that triggered the event.

Arrow function expressions (or arrow functions) cut through some of this confusion by not defining a `this` variable on creation, as happens with the `function` keyword. Some other context-related things are also not available, but `this` is by far the most important. Instead, it binds `this` to the surrounding lexical context and makes it ideal for nonmethod functions such as event handlers, callbacks, and global functions.

The following listings provides the general form and some variations for arrow functions.

Listing D.14   Arrow function format

The most general form: arguments in parentheses (=>), function body (in braces)

With a single expression, the braces can be omitted, but you get an implicit return equivalent to => { return expression; }.

```
(param, param2, ..., paramN) => { <function body> }
(param, param2, ..., paramN) => expression     <
```

```
singleParam => { <function body> }
singleParam => expression     <
```

```
() => { <function body> }     <
```

Arrow functions with no arguments need the parentheses.

If you have a single argument, you can omit the parentheses.

If you have a single argument and a single expression, omit the parentheses and the braces; remember that implicit return.

Arrow functions provide a simpler, cleaner syntax, which in turn facilitates shorter, more compact, more expressive functions, especially combined with destructuring assignments. Plenty of examples throughout the book show how arrow functions can be used. For further information on this, see https://developer.mozilla.org/en-US/docs/Web/JavaScript/Reference/Operators/this; for more on arrow functions, see https://developer.mozilla.org/en-US/docs/Web/JavaScript/Reference/Functions/Arrow_functions.

Destructuring

Dimly reminiscent of the idea of pattern matching as used in some functional programming languages, destructuring allows for the unpacking of array values and object properties into distinct variables. If you're passing objects into functions, destructuring means that you can explicitly state which properties from the argument object you want to use.

To use destructuring, on the LHS of the assignment operator (=) place square brackets for destructuring an array or braces for an object; then, add variable names for the values that you want. For arrays, variables get assigned values based on index order. For objects, you should use the keys from the object, but that's not strictly necessary.

The following listing details how to destructure an array.

Listing D.15   Destructuring an array

```
let fst, snd, rest;
const data = ['first', 'second', 'third', 'fourth', 'fifth'];

[fst, snd, ...rest] = data;
[, fst, snd] = data;     <
```

Assigns 'first' to fst and 'second' to snd and the remaining values to rest using the rest operator (...)

Ignores the first value and pulls 'second' and 'third' into fst and snd respectively, not caring about anything else

```
const shortArr = [1];
[fst, snd = 10] = shortArr;
```
Variables in destructuring can be assigned defaults if the assignment returns undefined. Here, snd will be 10.

```
let a = 3, b = 4;
[a, b] = [b, a];
```
Swapping of variables; a becomes 4, and b becomes 3.

Destructuring objects requires a little more care; you need to know what properties the object has so that they can be unpacked.

See the following listing for examples of use.

Listing D.16   Destructuring objects

```
const obj = {a: 10, b: 100, c: 1000};

const {a, c} = obj;
const {a: ten, c: hundred} = obj;
const {a, d = 50} = obj;

const shape = {type: 'square', sides: {width: 10, height: 10}};

const areaOfSquare = ({side: {width}}) => width * width;

areaOfSquare(shape);
```

Unpacks properties a and c from the object

Unpacks a and c, and assigns values to 10 and 100

A new object with nested object structure

Unpacks a, and assigns default value to d if not in the provided object

Uses the function; prints out 100

Arrow function that destructures the provided object; ultimately gets the value of width and uses that in the function

Destructuring is an operation that can only be applied to the result of assignment, usually for function return values and regular expression matches, but can also be applied in function argument lists and in for ... of iteration. Further examples and information are available at https://developer.mozilla.org/en-US/docs/Web/JavaScript/Reference/Operators/Destructuring_assignment.

We use this technique in multiple places in the Loc8r codebase to cut down on the amount of data a function or callback is allowed to work with.

Logic flow and looping

Now we'll take a quick look at best practices for the commonly used patterns of if statements and for loops. The text assumes that you're familiar with these elements to some extent.

Conditional statements: Working with if

JavaScript is helpful with if statements. If you have one expression within an if block, you don't have to wrap it in curly braces {}. You can even follow it with an else. The code in the following listing is valid JavaScript.

Listing D.17   `if` without braces (bad practice)

```
const firstname = 'Simon';
let surname, fullname;
if (firstname === 'Simon')
  surname = 'Holmes';
else if (firstname === 'Sally')
  surname = 'Panayiotou';
fullname = `${firstname} ${surname}`;
console.log(fullname);
```

Bad practice! Omitting { } around single-expression if blocks.

Yes, you can do this in JavaScript, but no, you shouldn't! Doing this relies on the layout of the code to be readable, which isn't ideal. More important, what happens if you want to add some extra lines within the `if` blocks? Start by giving Sally a middle initial. See the following code listing for how you might logically try this.

Listing D.18   Demonstrating issue with no-brace `if`

```
const firstname = 'Simon', initial = '';
let surname, fullname;
if (firstname === 'Simon')
  surname = 'Holmes';
else if (firstname === 'Sally')
  initial = 'J';              ⟵———————— Adds line into if block
  surname = 'Panayiotou';
fullname = `${firstname} ${initial} ${surname}`;
console.log(fullname);        ⟵———————— Output is "Simon Panayiotou."
```

What went wrong here is that without the block braces, only the first expression is considered to be part of the block, and anything following is outside the block. So here, if firstname is Sally, initial becomes J, but surname always becomes Panayiotou.

The following code listing shows the correct way of writing this.

Listing D.19   Correctly formatted `if`

```
const firstname = 'Simon';
let surname, fullname, initial = '';
if (firstname === 'Simon') {
  surname = 'Holmes';
} else if (firstname === 'Sally') {
  initial = 'J';
  surname = 'Panayiotou';
}
fullname = `${firstname} ${initial} ${surname}`;
console.log(fullname);
```

Best practice! Always use { } to define if blocks.

By being prescriptive, you see what the JavaScript interpreter sees and reduce the risk of unexpected errors. It's a good aim to make your code as explicit as possible, and not leave anything open to interpretation. This practice helps both the quality of your code and your ability to understand it when you come back to it after a year of working on other things.

How many = symbols to use

In the code snippets here, you'll notice that in each of the `if` statements, `===` is used to check for a match. This is not only a best practice but also a great habit to get into.

The `===` (identity) operator is much stricter than `==` (equality). `===` provides a positive match only when the two operands are of the same type, such as number, string, and Boolean. `==` attempts type coercion to see whether the values are similar but a different type, which can lead to some interesting and unexpected results.

Look at the following code snippet for some interesting cases that could easily trip you up:

```
let number = '';
number == 0;          ◁——— True
number === 0;         ◁——— False
number = 1;
number == '1';        ◁——— True
number === '1';       ◁——— False
```

In some situations, this might appear to be useful, but it's far better to be clear and specific about what you consider to be a positive match as opposed to what Java-Script interprets as a positive match. If it doesn't matter to your code whether `number` is a string or a number type, you can match one or the other:

```
number === 0 || number === '';
```

The key is to *always use the exact operator* `===`. The same goes for the not equals operators: you should *always use the exact* `!==` instead of the loose `!=`.

Running loops: Working with for

The most common method of looping through a collection of items is the `for` loop. JavaScript handles this task fairly well, but you should be aware of a couple of pitfalls and best practices.

First, as with the `if` statement, JavaScript allows you to omit the curly braces `{}` around the block if you have only one expression in it. We hope that you know by now that this is a bad idea, as it is with the `if` statements. The following code listing shows some valid JavaScript that may not produce the results you expect.

Listing D.20 `for` loop without braces (bad practice)

```
for (let i = 0; i < 3; i++)
  console.log(i);
  console.log(i * 5);    ◁
// Output in the console
// 0
// 1
// 2
// Uncaught ReferenceError: i is not defined    ◁
```

The second statement is outside the loop, so it fires only once; and because i is defined in the for, it errors.

From the way this is written and laid out, you might expect both `console.log()` statements to run on each iteration of the loop. For clarity, the preceding snippet should be written as in the following listing.

Listing D.21 Adding braces to a `for` loop

```
for (let i = 0; i < 3; i++) {
  console.log(i);
}
console.log(i*5);
```

We know that we keep going on about this, but making sure that your code reads the same way that JavaScript interprets it helps you! Bearing in mind this fact and the best practice for declaring variables, you should never see `let` inside a `for` conditional statement. Updating the preceding code snippet to meet this best practice gives you the following listing.

Listing D.22 Extracting the variable declaration

```
let i;
for (i = 0; i < 3; i++) {      ◁——  Variables should be
  console.log(i);                    declared outside a
}                                    for statement.
console.log(i*5);
```

As the variable declaration should be at the top of the scope, there could be many lines of code between it and the variable's first use in a loop. JavaScript interpreters act as though the variable has been defined there, so that's where it should go.

A common use for the `for` loop is to iterate through the contents of an array, so next, we'll cover some best practices and issues to look out for.

Using for loops with arrays

The key to using `for` loops with arrays is remembering the arrays are zero-indexed: the first object in an array is in position 0. The knock-on effect is that the position of the last item in the array is one less than the length. This sounds more complicated than it is. A simple array breaks down like this:

```
                       Array length is the
                       number of items (three)
const myArray = [ 'one', 'two', 'three' ];
                    Position  Position  Position
                       0         1         2
```

The typical code you might see for declaring an array like this and looping through it is in the following listing.

Listing D.23 More `for` loop

```
let i;
const myArray = ["one","two","three"];
for (i = 0; i < myArray.length; i++) {
  console.log(myArray[i]);
}
```

> Starts counting at 0;
> loops through while
> count is less than length.

This code works well and loops through the array correctly, starting at position 0 and going through to the final position, 2. Some people prefer to rule out the use of i++ to autoincrement in their code because it can make code difficult to fathom. Personally, we think that for loops are the exception to this rule and in fact make the code easier to read, rather than adding a manual increment inside the loop itself.

You can do one thing to improve the performance of this code. Each time the loop goes around, JavaScript checks the length of myArray. This process would be quicker if JavaScript checked against a variable, so a better practice is to declare a variable to hold the length of the array. You can see this solution in action in the following code listing.

Listing D.24 Alternative `for` loop declaration

```
let i, arrayLength;
const myArray = ["one","two","three"];
for (i = 0, arrayLength = myArray.length; i < arrayLength; i++) {
  console.log(myArray[i]);
}
```

> Declares arrayLength
> variable with other variables

> Assigns length of array
> to arrayLength when
> setting up the loop

Now a new variable, arrayLength, is given the length of the array to be looped through when the loop is initiated. The script needs to check the length of the array only once, not on every loop.

Getting to know JSON

JavaScript Object Notation (JSON) is a JavaScript-based approach to data exchange. It's much smaller than XML, more flexible, and easier to read. JSON is based on the structure of JavaScript objects but is language independent and can be used to transfer data among all manner of programming languages.

We've used objects in our sample code in this book, and because JSON is based on JavaScript objects, we'll discuss them here briefly.

JavaScript object literals

In JavaScript, everything other than the simplest data types—string, number, Boolean, null, and undefined—is an object, including arrays and functions. Object literals are what most people think of as JavaScript objects; they're typically used to store data but can also contain functions, as you've already seen.

LOOKING AT THE CONTENTS OF A JAVASCRIPT OBJECT

A JavaScript object is a collection of key-value pairs, which are the properties of the object. Each key must have a value.

The rules for a key are simple:

- The key must be a string.
- The string must be wrapped in double quotes if it's a JavaScript reserved word or an illegal JavaScript name.

The value can be any JavaScript value, including functions, arrays, and nested objects. The following listing shows a valid JavaScript object literal based on these rules.

Listing D.25   An example of a JavaScript object literal

```
const nameSetup = {
  firstname: 'Simon',          ◁──────  A simple key-value pair
  fullname: '',
  age: 37,                                     A complex key
  married: true,                               surrounded by
  "clean-shaven": null,        ◁              double quotes
  addSurname: function () {    ◁──────  A function
    const surname = 'Holmes';
    this.fullname = `${this.firstname} ${surname}`;   ◁
  },
  children: [                  ◁
    {                                Sets up an array as a
      firstname: 'Erica'             value in the object
    },
    {
      firstname: 'Isobel'
    }
  ]
};
```

'this' in the function points to the surrounding object due to the function keyword; an arrow function here would point to the global scope.

Here, all keys in the object are strings, but the values are a mixture of types: string, number, Boolean, null, function, and array.

ACCESSING THE PROPERTIES OF AN OBJECT LITERAL

The preferred way to access properties is to use dot notation (.). Examples are

```
nameSetup.firstname
nameSetup.fullname
```

These examples can be used to get or set property values. If a property doesn't exist when you try to *get* it, JavaScript returns `undefined`. If a property doesn't exist when you try to *set* it, JavaScript adds it to the object and creates it for you.

You can't use dot notation when the key name is a reserved word or an illegal JavaScript name. To access these properties, you need to wrap the key string in square braces [ ]. A couple of examples are

```
nameSetup["clean-shaven"]
nameSetup["var"]
```

Again, these references can be used to get or set the values.

Next, we'll take a look at how JSON is related.

Differences with JSON

JSON is based on the notation of JavaScript object literals, but because it's designed to be language independent, there are a couple of important differences:

- All key names and strings must be wrapped in double quotes.
- Functions aren't a supported data type.

These two differences occur largely because you don't know what will be interpreting it. Other programming languages won't be able to process JavaScript functions and probably will have different sets of reserved names and restrictions on names. If you send all names as strings, you can bypass this issue.

ALLOWABLE DATA TYPES IN JSON

You can't send functions with JSON, but as it's a data exchange format, that's not such a bad thing. The data types you can send are

- Strings
- Numbers
- Objects
- Arrays
- Booleans
- The value `null`

Looking at this list and comparing it with the JavaScript object in listing D.25, if you remove the `function` property, you should be able to convert it to JSON.

FORMATTING JSON DATA

Unlike with the JavaScript object, we're not assigning the data to a variable; neither do we need a trailing semicolon. By wrapping all key names and strings in double quotes—and they do have to be double quotes—we can generate the following listing.

Listing D.26 An example of correctly formatted JSON

```
{                                   With JSON, you can send strings.
  "firstname": "Simon",   ←
  "fullname": "",              ←——— Empty strings
  "age": 37,            ←——— Numbers
  "married": true,         ←——— Boolean values
  "has-own-hair": null,        ←——— Null
  "children": [
    {
      "firstname": "Erica"
    },                            Arrays of other
    {                             JSON objects
      "firstname": "Isobel"
    }
  ]
}
```

This listing shows some valid JSON. This data can be exchanged between applications and programming languages without issue. It's also easy for the human eye to read and understand.

Sending strings containing double quotes

JSON specifies that all strings must be wrapped in double quotes. What if your string contains double quotes? The first double quote that an interpreter comes across will be seen as the end delimiter for the string, so it will most likely throw an error when the next item isn't valid JSON.

The following code snippet shows an example. There are two double quotes inside the string, which isn't valid JSON and will cause errors:

```
"line": "So she said "Hello Simon""
```

The answer to this problem is to escape nested double quotes with the backslash character (\). Applying this technique produces the following:

```
"line": "So she said \"Hello Simon\""
```

This escape character tells JSON interpreters that the following character shouldn't be considered to be part of the code; it's part of the value and can be ignored.

SHRINKING JSON FOR TRANSPORTING ACROSS THE INTERNET

The spacing and indentation in listing D.26 are purely to aid human readability; programming languages don't need them. You can reduce the amount of information being transmitted if you remove unnecessary whitespace before sending the code.

The following code snippet shows a minimized version of listing D.26, which is more along the lines of what you'd expect to exchange between applications:

```
{"firstname":"Simon","fullname":"","age":37,"married":true,"has-own-
    hair":null,"children":[{"firstname":"Erica"},{"firstname":"Isobel"}]}
```

The content is exactly the same as that of listing D.26, but much more compact.

Why is JSON so good?

The popularity of JSON as a data exchange format predates the development of Node by quite some time. JSON began to flourish as the ability of browsers to run complex JavaScript increased. Having a data format that was (almost) natively supported was extremely helpful and made life considerably easier for front-end developers.

The previous preferred data exchange format was XML. Compared with JSON, XML is harder to read at a glance, much more rigid, and considerably larger to send across networks. As you saw in the JSON examples, JSON doesn't waste much space on syntax. JSON uses the minimum amount of characters required to accurately hold and structure the data, not a lot more.

When it comes to the MEAN stack, JSON is the ideal format for passing data through the layers of the stack. MongoDB stores data as binary JSON (BSON). Node and Express can interpret this natively and also push it out to Angular, which also uses JSON natively. Every part of the MEAN stack, including the database, uses the same data format, so you have no data transformations to worry about.

Formatting practices

The code samples in this book use some of our personal preferences for laying out code. Some of these practices are necessary best practices; others increase readability. If you have different preferences, as long as the code remains correct, that's absolutely fine; the important thing is to be consistent.

The main reasons for being concerned about formatting are

- Ensuring syntactically correct JavaScript
- Ensuring that your code functions correctly when minified
- Improving readability for yourself and/or others on your team

Start with an easy formatting practice: indentation.

Indenting code

The only real reason to indent your code is to make it considerably easier for mere humans to read. JavaScript interpreters don't care about it and will happily run code without any indentation or line breaks.

Best practice for indentation is to use spaces, not tabs, as there's still no standard for the placement of tab stops. How many spaces you choose is up to you; we personally prefer two spaces. We find that using one space can make code difficult to follow at a glance, as the difference isn't all that big. Four spaces can make your code unnecessarily wide (again, in our opinion). We like to balance the readability gains of indentation against the benefits of maximizing the amount of code you can see onscreen at any time—well, for that reason and a dislike of horizontal scrolling.

Position of braces for functions and blocks

A best practice you should get into is placing the opening bracket of a code block at the end of the statement that starts the block. What? All the code snippets so far have been written this way. The following code listing shows the right way and the wrong way of placing braces.

Listing D.27 Brace placements

```
const firstname = 'Simon';
let surname;
if (firstname === 'Simon') {
  surname = 'Holmes';
  console.log(`${firstname} ${surname}`);
}
```

Right way: opening bracket on the same line as the statement

```
if (firstname === 'Simon')
{
  surname = 'Holmes';
  console.log(`${firstname} ${surname}`);
}
```

**Wrong way: opening
bracket on its own line**

At least 99% of the time, the second approach won't cause you a problem. The first approach won't cause you a problem 100% of the time. We'll take that over wasting time debugging; how about you?

What's the 1% of the time when the wrong approach will cause you a problem? Consider a code snippet that uses the `return` statement:

```
return
{
  name : 'name'
};
```

If you put your opening bracket on a different line, JavaScript assumes that you've missed a semicolon after the `return` command itself and adds one for you. JavaScript evaluates it like this:

```
return;
{
  name:'name'
};
```

**JavaScript inserts a semicolon
after the return statement and
so ignores the following code.**

Due to JavaScript's semicolon insertion, it doesn't return the object you intended; instead, JavaScript returns `undefined`.

Next, we'll look at semicolon use and JavaScript semicolon insertion in more detail.

Using the semicolon correctly

JavaScript uses the semicolon character to denote the end of statements. It tries to be helpful by making this character optional and injects its own semicolons at runtime if it deems it necessary to do so, which isn't a good thing at all.

When using semicolons to delimit statements, you should return to the goal of seeing in the code what the JavaScript interpreter sees and not let it make any assumptions. We treat semicolons as not optional, and we're now at a point where code looks wrong to us if they're not there.

Most lines of your JavaScript have a semicolon at the end, but not all; that would be too easy! All the statements in the following listing should end with a semicolon.

Listing D.28   Examples of semicolon use

```
const firstname = 'Simon';
let surname;
surname = 'Holmes';
console.log(`${firstname} ${surname}`);
const addSurname = function () {};
alert('Hello');
const nameSetup = { firstname : 'Simon', fullname : ''};
```

**Use a semicolon
at the end of
most statements.**

But code blocks shouldn't end with a semicolon. We're talking about blocks of code associated with `if`, `switch`, `for`, `while`, `try`, `catch`, and `function` (when not being assigned to a variable). The following listing shows a few examples.

Listing D.29   Using code blocks without semicolons

```
if (firstname === 'Simon') {
  …
}
function addSurname () {
  …
}
for (let i = 0; i < 3; i++) {
  …
}
```

No semicolon used at end of code block

The rule isn't quite so straightforward as "don't use a semicolon" after curly braces. When assigning a function or object to a variable, you *do* have a semicolon after the curly braces. You've seen a couple of examples, which we've been using throughout the book.

Listing D.30   Semicolon placement for assigned blocks

```
const addSurname = function () {
  …
};
const nameSetup = {
  firstname : 'Simon'
};
```

Semicolons after curly braces when assigning to a variable

Putting semicolons after blocks can take a little while to get used to, but it's worth the effort and eventually becomes second nature.

Placing commas in a list

When you're defining a long list of variables at the top of a scope, the most common approach is to write one variable name per line. This practice makes it easy to see at a glance what variables you've set up. The classic placement for the comma that separates variables is at the end of the line.

Listing D.31   Comma-last placement

```
let firstname = 'Simon',
  surname,
  initial = '',
  fullname;
```

Uses a comma at the end of each line, separating it from the next variable declaration

This approach is Simon's preferred approach, as he's been using it for about 15 years. Clive, on the other hand, advocates putting the comma at the front of each line.

Listing D.32   Comma-first placement

```
let firstname = 'Simon'
  , surname                    Uses a comma at start of each
  , initial = ''               line, separating it from next
  , fullname;                  variable declaration
```

This JavaScript is perfectly valid and when minified to one line, reads exactly the same as the first code snippet. Simon has tried to get used to it, but he can't; it looks wrong to him. Clive thinks that comma-first is a good idea, but he thinks Elm is great too.

There are arguments for and against both approaches. Your choice comes down to personal preference. The critical thing is to have a standard and stick to it.

Don't be afraid of whitespace

Adding a bit of whitespace between sets of braces can help readability and won't cause any problems for JavaScript. Again, you've seen this approach in all the code snippets so far. You can also add or remove whitespace from between a lot of JavaScript operators. Take a look at the following code snippet, showing the same piece of code with and without extra whitespace.

Listing D.33   Examples of whitespace formatting

```
const firstname = 'Simon';
let surname;
if (firstname === 'Simon') {        JavaScript snippet using
  surname = 'Holmes';               whitespace for readability
  console.log(`${firstname} ${surname}`);
}
const firstname='Simon';
let surname;
if(firstname==='Simon'){            Same snippet with
  surname='Holmes';                 whitespace removed
  console.log(firstname+" "+surname);   (excluding indentation)
}
```

As humans, we read by using whitespace as the delimiters for words, and the way we read code is no different. Yes, you can figure out the second part of the code snippet here, as many syntactic pointers act as delimiters, but it's quicker and easier to read and understand the first part. JavaScript interpreters don't notice the whitespace in these places, and if you're concerned about increasing the file size for browser-based code, you can always minimize it before pushing it live.

Tools to help you write good JavaScript

A couple of online code-quality checkers called JSHint and ESLint check the quality and consistency of your code. Even better, most IDEs and good text editors have plugins or extensions for one or the other, so your code can be quality-checked as you go. These tools are useful for spotting the occasional missed semicolon or a comma in the wrong place.

Of the two tools, ESLint is geared more toward linting ES2015 code. TypeScript has its own linter, TSLint, which Angular installs by default.

String formatting

ES2015 introduced an alternative way of formatting strings akin to string interpolation, as you'd find in many different languages. JavaScript calls this type of formatting *template literals.*

A template literal is denoted with backticks where you'd ordinarily use single or double quotes to define a string. To perform the interpolation, the element (variable or function call result) that you wish inserted into the string needs to be wrapped by `'${}'`. The following listing shows how this works.

Listing D.34   Using template literals

```
const value = 10;
const square = x => x * x;
console.log(`Squaring the number ${value} gives a result of          Template
➥${square(value)}`);                                                  literal
// Squaring the number 10 gives a result of 100 ←        Result of the
                                                         interpolation
```

Understanding callbacks

The next aspect of JavaScript programming that we'll look at is *callbacks*. Callbacks often seem to be confusing or complicated at first, but if you take a look under the hood, you'll find that they're fairly straightforward. Chances are that you've already used them.

Callbacks are typically used to run a piece of code after a certain event has happened. Whether this event is a link being clicked, data being written to a database, or another piece of code finishing executing isn't important, as the event could be almost anything. A callback function itself is typically an *anonymous function*—a function declared without a name—that's passed directly to the receiving function as a parameter. Don't worry if this seems like jargon right now; we'll look at code examples soon, and you'll see how easy it is.

Using setTimeout to run code later

Most of the time, you use callbacks to run code after something happens. To get accustomed to the concept, you can use a function that's built into JavaScript: `setTimeout()`. You may have already used it. In a nutshell, `setTimeout()` runs a callback function after the number of milliseconds that you declare. The basic construct for using it as follows:

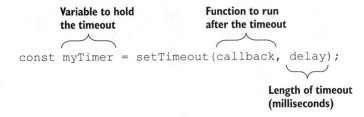

Canceling a setTimeout

If a `setTimeout` declaration has been assigned to a variable, you can use that variable to clear the timeout and stop it from completing, assuming that it hasn't already completed. You use the `clearTimeout()` function, which works like so:

```
const waitForIt = setTimeout(function () {
  console.log("My name is Simon Holmes");
}, 2000);
clearTimeout(waitForIt);
```

This code snippet wouldn't output anything to the log, as the `waitForIt` timer is cleared before it has the chance to complete.

First, `setTimeout()` is declared inside a variable so that you can access it again to cancel it, should you want to. As we mentioned earlier, a callback is typically an unnamed anonymous function. If you wanted to log your name to the JavaScript console after 2 seconds, you could use this code snippet.

Listing D.35   Capturing `setTimeout` reference

```
const waitForIt = setTimeout(function () {
  console.log("My name is Simon");
}, 2000);
```

> **NOTE**   Callbacks are asynchronous. They run when they're required, not necessarily in the order in which they appear in your code.

Keeping in mind this asynchronous nature, what would you expect the output of the following code snippet to be?

```
console.log("Hello, what's your name?");
const waitForIt = setTimeout(function () {
  console.log("My name is Simon");
}, 2000);
console.log("Nice to meet you Simon");
```

If you read the code from top to bottom, the console log statements appear to make sense. But because the `setTimeout()` callback is asynchronous, it doesn't hold up the processing of code, so you end up with this:

```
Hello, what's your name?
Nice to meet you Simon
My name is Simon
```

As a conversation, this result clearly doesn't flow properly. In code, having the correct flow is essential; otherwise, your applications quickly fall apart.

Because this asynchronous approach is so fundamental to working with Node, we'll look into it a little deeper.

Asynchronous code

Before you look at some more code, reminding yourself of the bank-teller analogy from chapter 1. Figure D.3 shows how a bank teller can deal with multiple requests by passing any time-consuming tasks to other people.

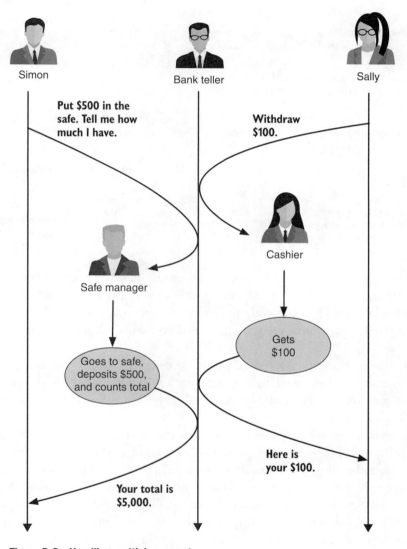

Figure D.3 Handling multiple requests

The bank teller is able to respond to Sally's request because she passed responsibility for Simon's request to the safe manager. The teller isn't interested in how the safe manager does what he does or how long it takes. This approach is asynchronous.

You can mimic this approach in JavaScript by using the `setTimeout()` function to demonstrate the asynchronous approach. All you need are some `console.log()` statements to demonstrate the bank teller's activity and a couple of timeouts to represent the delegated tasks. You can see this approach in the following code listing, where it's assumed that Simon's request will take 3 seconds (3,000 ms), and Sally's will take 1 second.

Listing D.36   Asynchronous flow

```
console.log("Taking Simon's request");         ①  Takes first request
const requestA = setTimeout(function () {
  console.log("Simon: money's in the safe, you have $5000");
}, 3000);
console.log("Taking Sally's request");         ②  Takes second request
const requestB = setTimeout(function () {
  console.log("Sally: Here's your $100");
}, 1000);
console.log("Free to take another request");   ③  Ready for another request
// ** console.log responses, in order **
// Taking Simon's request
// Taking Sally's request              Sally's response
// Free to take another request        appears after 1
// Sally: Here's your $100             second.              Simon's response
// Simon: money's in the safe, you have $5000               appears after
                                                            another 2 seconds.
```

This code has three distinct blocks: taking the first request from Simon and sending it away ①; taking the second request from Sally and sending it away ②; and ready to take another request ③. If this code were synchronous code like you'd see in PHP or .NET, you'd deal with Simon's request in its entirety before taking Sally's request 3 seconds later.

With an asynchronous approach, the code doesn't have to wait for one of the requests to complete before taking another one. You can run this code snippet in your browser to see how it works. Put it in an HTML page and run it, or enter it directly in the JavaScript console.

We hope that you see how this code mimics the scenario we talked through as we kicked off this section. Simon's request was first in, but as it took some time to complete, the response didn't come back immediately. While somebody was dealing with Simon's request, Sally's request was taken. While Sally's request was being dealt with, the bank teller became available again to take another request. As Sally's request took less time to complete, she got her response first, whereas Simon had to wait a bit longer for his response. Neither Sally nor Simon got held up by the other.

Now go one step further by looking at what might be happening *inside* the `setTimeout()` function.

Running a callback function

We're not going show you the source code of `setTimeout()` here, but a skeleton function that uses a callback. Declare a new function called `setTimeout()` that accepts the parameters `callback` and `delay`. The names aren't important; they can be anything you want. The following code listing demonstrates this function. (Note that you won't be able to run this function in a JavaScript console.)

Listing D.37 `setTimeout` skeleton

```
const setTimeout = (callback, delay) => {
  ...                          ◁──────────────────────① Delays processing for specified number of ms
  ...
  callback();       ◁────── Runs callback function
};
const requestB = setTimeout (() => {
  console.log("Sally: Here's your $100");        ② Sends anonymous
}, 1000);                                              function and delays
```

The `callback` parameter is expected to be a function, which can be invoked at a specific point in the `setTimeout()` function ①. In this case, you're passing it a simple anonymous function ② that will write a message to the console log. When the `setTimeout()` function deems it appropriate to do so, it invokes the callback, and the message is logged to the console. That's not so difficult, is it?

If JavaScript is your first programming language, you'll have no idea how weird this concept of passing anonymous functions around looks to those who are coming in from different backgrounds. But the ability to operate this way is one of JavaScript's great strengths.

Typically, you won't generally look inside the function running the callbacks, whether it's `setTimeout()`, jQuery's `ready()`, or Node's `createServer()`. The documentation for these functions tells you what the expected parameters are and what parameters may be returned.

Why setTimeout() is unusual

The `setTimeout()` function is unusual in that you specify a delay after which the callback will fire. In a more typical use case, the function itself decides when the callback should be triggered. In jQuery's `ready()` method, this is when jQuery says the DOM has loaded; in a `save()` operation in Node, this is when the data is saved to the database and a confirmation is returned.

CALLBACK SCOPE

Something to bear in mind when passing anonymous functions around this way is that the callback doesn't inherit the scope of the function it's passed into. The callback function isn't declared inside the destination function, merely invoked from it. A *callback function inherits the scope in which it's defined.*

Figure D.4 depicts scope circles. Here, you see that the callback has its own local scope inside the global scope, which is where `requestB` is defined. This is all well and good if your callback needs access only to its inherited scope, but what if you want it to be smarter? What if you want to use data from your asynchronous function in your callback?

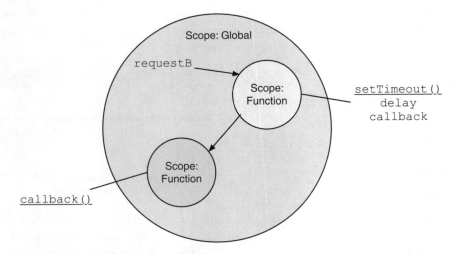

Figure D.4   A callback has its own local scope.

Currently, the example callback function has a dollar amount hardcoded into it, but what if you want that value to be dynamic—to be a variable? Assuming that this value is set in the setTimeout() function, how do you get it into the callback? You could save it to the global scope, but as you know by now, doing so would be bad. You need to pass the value as a parameter into the callback function. You should get something like the scope circles shown in figure D.5.

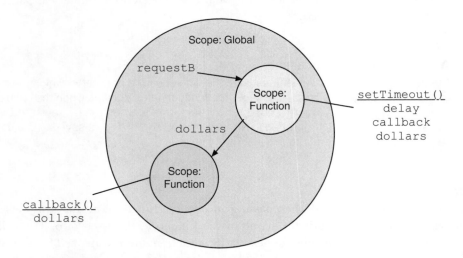

Figure D.5   Setting a variable and passing it to the callback

The same thing in code would look like the following code listing.

Listing D.38 `setTimeout` with passing data

```
const setTimeout = (callback, delay) => {      Declares a variable in
  const dollars = 100;                          the function scope
  ...                                 Passes the variable as a
  callback(dollars);                  parameter to the callback
};
const requestB = setTimeout((dollars) => {         Accepts the variable as a parameter
  console.log("Sally: Here's your $" + dollars);   in the callback and uses it
}, 1000);
```

This code snippet outputs the same message to the console that you've already seen. The big difference now is that the value of dollars is being set in the `setTimeout()` function and being passed to the callback.

It's important that you understand this approach, as the vast majority of Node code examples on the internet use asynchronous callbacks this way. But there are a couple of potential problems with this approach, particularly when your codebase gets larger and more complex. An overreliance on passing around anonymous callback functions can make the code hard to read and follow, especially when you find that you have multiple nested callbacks. It also makes running tests on the code difficult, as you can't call any of these functions by name; they're all anonymous. We don't cover unit testing in this book, but in a nutshell, the idea is that every piece of code can be tested separately with repeatable and expected results.

Let's look at a way that you can achieve this result with named callbacks.

Named callbacks

Named callbacks differ from inline callbacks in one fundamental way. Instead of putting the code you want to run directly into the callback, you put the code inside a defined function. Then, rather than passing the code directly as an anonymous function, you can pass the function name. Rather than passing the code, you're passing a *reference* to the code to run.

Sticking with the ongoing example, add a new function called `onCompletion()` that will be the callback function. Figure D.6 shows how this function looks in the scope circles.

This figure looks like the preceding example, except that the callback scope has a name. As with an anonymous callback, a named callback can be invoked without any parameters, implied in figure D.6. The following code snippet shows how to declare and invoke a named callback, putting into code what you see in figure D.6.

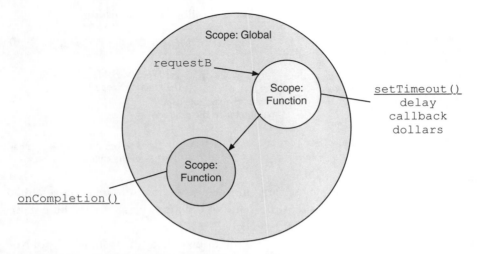

Figure D.6 Change in scope when using a named callback

Listing D.39   Named callbacks

```
const setTimeout = (callback, delay) => {
  const dollars = 100;
  ...
  callback();
};
const onCompletion = () => {
  console.log("Sally: Here's your $100");
};
const requestB = setTimeout(
  onCompletion,
  1000
);
```

❶ Declares a
named function
in distinct scope

❷ Sends the function
name as a callback

The named function ❶ now exists as an entity in its own right, creating its own scope. Notice that there's no longer an anonymous function, but the name of the function ❷ is passed as a reference.

PASSING VARIABLES

Listing D.39 uses a hardcoded dollar value in the console log again. As with anonymous callbacks, passing a variable from one scope to another is straightforward. You can pass the parameters you need into the named function. Figure D.7 shows how this looks in the scope circles.

You need to pass the variable dollars from setTimeout() to the onCompletion() callback function. You can do so without changing anything in your request, as the following code snippet shows.

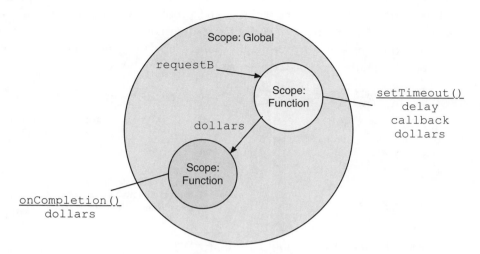

Figure D.7 Passing the required parameter into the new function scope

---

Listing D.40   `setTimeout` variable passing

```
const setTimeout = function (callback, delay) {
  const dollars = 100;
  ...
  callback(dollars);          ⟵——— Sends the dollars variable as
};                                   a parameter to the callback
const onCompletion = function (dollars) {
  console.log("Sally: Here's your $" + dollars);   Named function accepts
};                                                   and uses the parameter
const requestB = setTimeout(
  onCompletion,     ⟵———  No change is made when
  1000                     sending the callback.
);
```

Here, the setTimeout() function sends the dollars variable to the onCompletion() function as a parameter. You'll often have no control of the parameters sent to your callback, because asynchronous functions like setTimeout() are provided as is. But you'll often want to use variables from other scopes inside your callback, not what your asynchronous function provides. Next, we'll look at how to send the parameters you want to your callback.

USING VARIABLES FROM A DIFFERENT SCOPE

Suppose that you want the name in the output to come through as a parameter. The updated function looks like the following:

```
const onCompletion = function (dollars, name) {
  console.log(name + ": Here's your $" + dollars);
};
```

The problem is that the `setTimeout()` function passes only a single parameter, `dollars`, to the callback. You can address this problem by using an anonymous function as a callback again, remembering that it inherits the scope in which it's defined. To demonstrate this function outside the global scope, wrap the request in a new function, `getMoney()`, that accepts a single parameter, `name`.

Listing D.41   Variable scoping in `setTimeout`

```
const getMoney = function (name) {
  const requestB = setTimeout(function (dollars) {        Anonymous function
                                                          accepts only the
                                                          dollars parameter
    onCompletion(dollars, name);
  }, 1000);                        Named callback accepts dollars
};                                 from the anonymous function and
getMoney('Simon');                 name from the getMoney scope
```

In the scope circles, this code looks like figure D.8.

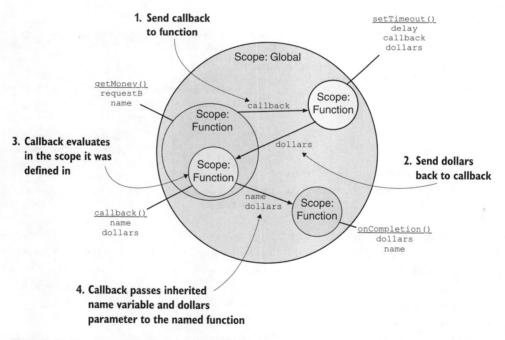

Figure D.8   The process of sending variables from different scopes to a named callback function

The next listing puts all the code together for the sake of completeness.

Listing D.42 Complete `setTimeout` example

```
const setTimeout = (callback, delay) => {
  const dollars = 100;
  ...
  callback(dollars);           <————————  Sends a callback to the
};                                          setTimeout function
const onCompletion = (dollars, name) => {
  console.log(name + ": Here's your $" + dollars);
};
const getMoney = (name) => {                        Calls a callback function
  const requestB = setTimeout((dollars) => {  <———  sending dollars variable
    onCompletion(dollars, name);     <———
  }, 1000);                                 Calls a named function
};                                          passing dollars and
getMoney('Simon');                          name parameters
```

The simple way to think of it is that calling the named function from inside the anonymous callback enables you to capture anything you need from the parent scope (get-Money(), in this case) and explicitly pass it to the named function (onCompletion()).

Seeing the flow in action

If you want to see this flow in action, you can add a debugger statement, run it in your browser, and step through the functions to see which variables and values are set where and when. Altogether, you have something like this:

```
const mySetTimeout = function (callback, delay) {
  const dollars = 100;
  callback(dollars);
};
const onCompletion = function (dollars, name) {
  console.log(name + ": Here's your $" + dollars);
};
const getMoney = function (name) {
  debugger;
  const requestB = mySetTimeout(function (dollars) {
    onCompletion(dollars,name);
  }, 1000);
};
getMoney('Simon');
```

Note that when adding a debugger statement, you'll want to change the name of the setTimeout() function so that it doesn't interfere with the native function.

Remember that you normally won't have access to the code inside the function that invokes the callback and that the callback is often invoked with a fixed set of parameters (or none, as with setTimeout()). Anything extra that you need to add must be added inside the anonymous callback.

BETTER FOR READING AND TESTING

Defining a named function in this way makes the scope and code of the function easier to comprehend at a glance, especially if you name your functions well. With a small, simple example like this one, you could think that the flow is harder to understand when you move the code into its own function, and you could well have a point. But when the code becomes more complex and you have multiple lines of code inside multiple nested callbacks, you'll definitely see the advantage of doing it this way.

Another advantage of being able to easily see what the onCompletion() function should do and what parameters it expects and requires to work is that the function becomes easier to test. Now you can say, "When the function onCompletion() is passed a number of dollars and a name, it should output a message to the console, including this number and name." This case is a simple one, but we hope that you can see its value.

That brings us to the end of discussing callbacks from a code perspective. Now that you've got a good idea of how callbacks are defined and used, look at Node to see why callbacks are so useful.

Callbacks in Node

In the browser, many events are based on user interaction, waiting for things to happen outside what the code can control. The concept of waiting for external things to happen is similar on the server side. The difference on the server side is that the events focus more on other things happening on the server or indeed on a different server. In the browser, the code waits for events such as a mouse click or form submit, whereas the server-side code waits for events such as reading a file from the file system or saving data to a database.

The big difference is that in the browser, it's generally an individual user who initiates the event, and it's only that user who's waiting for a response. On the server side, the central code generally initiates the event and waits for a response. As discussed in chapter 1, only a single thread is running in Node, so if the central code has to stop and wait for a response, every visitor to the site gets held up—not a good thing! This is why it's important to understand callbacks, because Node uses callbacks to delegate the waiting to other processes, making it asynchronous.

Next, we'll look at an example of using callbacks in Node.

A NODE CALLBACK

Using a callback in Node isn't any different from using it in the browser. If you want to save some data, you don't want the main Node process doing this, as you didn't want the bank teller going with the safe manager and waiting for the response. You want to use an asynchronous function with a callback. All database drivers for Node provide this ability. We get into the specifics about how to create and save data in the book, so for now, we'll use a simplified example. The following code snippet shows an example of asynchronously saving data using the save() method of the mySafe object and outputting a confirmation to the console when the database finishes and returns a response.

Listing D.43 Basic Node callback

```
mySafe.save(
  function (err, savedData) {
    console.log(`Data saved: ${savedData}`);
  }
);
```

Here, the save function expects a callback function that can accept two parameters, an error object (err), and the data returned from the database following the save (savedData). There's normally a bit more to functionality in the callback than this, but the basic construct is simple.

RUNNING CALLBACKS ONE AFTER ANOTHER
You get the idea of running a callback, but what do you do if you want to run another asynchronous operation when the callback is finished? Returning to the banking metaphor, suppose that you want to get a total value from all of Simon's accounts after the deposit is made to the safe. Simon doesn't need to know that multiple steps and multiple people are involved, and the bank teller doesn't need to know until everything is complete. You're looking to create a flow like the one shown in figure D.9.

Clearly, two operations will be required, with another asynchronous call to the database. You know from what we've already discussed that you can't put it in the code after the save function, as in the following code snippet.

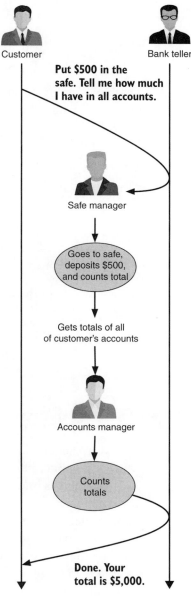

Figure D.9 Required flow when using two asynchronous operations, one after another

Listing D.44   Node callback issues

```
mySafe.save(
  function (err, savedData) {
    console.log(`Data saved: ${savedData}`);
  }
);
myAccounts.findTotal(          ◁─────────────
  function (err, accountsData) {
    console.log(`Your total: ${accountsData}`);
  }
);
// ** console.log responses, in probable order **
// Your total: 4500
// Data saved: {dataObject}
```

The second function will fire before the save function has finished, so the returned accountsData will likely be incorrect.

That's not going to work, because the `myAccounts.findTotal()` function will run immediately rather than when the `mySafe.save()` function has finished. The return value is likely to be incorrect, because it won't take into account the value being added to the safe. You need to ensure that the second operation runs when you know that the first one has finished. The solution is simple: invoke the second function from inside the first callback, a process known as *nesting* the callbacks.

Nested callbacks are used to run asynchronous functions one after another. Put the second function inside the callback from the first, as in the following listing.

Listing D.45   Nesting callbacks

```
mySafe.save(
  function (err, savedData) {
    console.log(`Data saved: ${savedData}`);
    myAccounts.findTotal(        ◁─────────────
      function (err, accountsData) {
        console.log(`Your total: ${accountsData.total}`);
      }
    );
  }
);
// ** console.log responses, in order **
// Data saved: {dataObject}
// Your total: 5000
```

Second asynchronous operation nested inside callback of first

Now you can be sure that the `myAccounts.findTotal()` function will run at the appropriate time, which in turn means that you can predict the response.

This ability is important. Node is inherently asynchronous, jumping from request to request and from site visitor to site visitor. But sometimes, you need to do things in a sequential manner. Nesting callbacks gives you a good way of doing this by using native JavaScript.

The downside of nested callbacks is the complexity. You can probably see that with one level of nesting, the code is already a bit harder to read, and following the sequential flow takes a bit more mental effort. This problem is multiplied when the code gets more complex and you end up with multiple levels of nested callbacks. The problem is so great that it has become known as *callback hell.* Callback hell is why some people think that Node (and JavaScript) is particularly hard to learn and difficult to maintain, and they use it as an argument against the technology. In fairness, many code samples you can find online do suffer from this problem, which doesn't do much to combat this opinion. It's easy to end up in callback hell when you're developing Node, but it's also easy to avoid if you start in the right way.

We've already discussed the solution to callback hell: using named callbacks. Next, we'll show you how named callbacks help with this problem.

USING NAMED CALLBACKS TO AVOID CALLBACK HELL

Named callbacks can help you avoid nested callback hell because you can use them to separate each step into a distinct piece of code or functionality. Humans tend to find this type of code easier to read and understand.

To use a named callback, you need to take the content of a callback function and declare it as a separate function. The nested callback example has two callbacks, so you're going to need two new functions: one for when the `mySafe.save()` operation has completed and one for when the `myAccounts.findTotal()` operation has completed. If these functions are called `onSave()` and `onFindTotal()`, respectively, you can create some code like the following listing.

Listing D.46   Refactor of callback code

```
mySafe.save(
  function (err, savedData) {
    onSave(err, savedData);          ⟵  Invokes the first named function
  }                                       from mySafe.save operation
);
const onSave = function (err, savedData) {          Starts the second
  console.log(`Data saved: ${savedData}`);          asynchronous operation from
  myAccounts.findTotal(          ⟵                   within the first named callback
    function (err, accountsData) {
      onFindTotal(err, accountsData);   ⟵   Invokes the second
    }                                         named function
  );
};
const onFindTotal = function (err, accountsData) {
  console.log(`Your total: ${accountsData.total}`);
};
```

Now that each piece of functionality is separated into a separate function, it's easier to look at each part in isolation and understand what it's doing. You can see what parameters it expects and what the outcomes should be. In reality, the outcomes are likely to be more complex than simple `console.log()` statements, but you get the idea. You can also follow the flow relatively easily and see the scope of each function.

By using named callbacks, you can reduce the perceived complexity of Node and also make your code easier to read and maintain. An important second advantage is that individual functions are much better suited to unit testing. Each part has defined inputs and outputs, with expected and repeatable behavior.

Promises and async/await

A Promise is like a contract: it states that a value will be available in the future when a long-running operation has completed. In essence, a Promise represents the result of an asynchronous operation. When that value has been determined, the Promise executes the given code or handles any error associated with not having received the expected value.

Promises are first-class citizens of the JavaScript specification. They have three states:

- *Pending*—The initial state of the Promise
- *Fulfilled*—The asynchronous operation successfully resolved
- *Rejected*—The asynchronous operation did not successfully resolve

Promises

When a Promise has been resolved, successfully or not, its value can't change; it becomes immutable. We'll discuss immutability in the section on functional programming later in this appendix.

To set up a Promise, you create a function that accepts two callback functions: one that executes on success and one that executes on failure. These callbacks fire when called by the Promise execution. Then, execution of the callbacks is transferred to `then()` functions (which are chainable) on success or a `catch()` function when not.

Listing D.47   Setting up/using a Promise

Creates a Promise, passing in the expected callback function

```
const promise = new Promise((resolve, reject) => {
  // set up long running, possibly asynchronous operation,
  // like an API query
  if (/* successfully resolved */) {
    resolve({data response});           On success, calls the resolve() function,
  } else {                              optionally passing data forward
    reject();         On failure, calls the reject() function, optionally
  }                   passing data or the Error object forward
});

promise
  .then((data) => {/* execute this on success */})
  .then(() => {/ * chained next function, and so on */})
  .catch((err) => {/* handle error */});
```

The then() function is called; it performs the desired operation, optionally returning a value to next then().

Catches the error. If this is at the end of a chain of then() functions, any error thrown is caught by this handler.

The next then() function in the chain, which can be as long as necessary

We use Promises in the Loc8r application, but not in a complicated way. The Promises API provides some static functions that help if you're trying to execute multiple Promises.

`Promise.all()` accepts an iterable of Promises and returns a Promise when all items in the array fulfill or reject. The `resolve()` callback receives an array of responses: a mixture of Promise-like objects and other objects in order of fulfillment. If one of the executed Promises rejects, the `reject()` callback receives a single value.

Listing D.48 `Promise.all()`

```
const promise1 = new Promise((resolve, reject) => resolve() );
const promise2 = new Promise((resolve, reject) => resolve() );
const promise3 = new Promise((resolve, reject) => reject() );
const promise4 = new Promise((resolve, reject) => resolved() );

Promise.all([
  promise1,
  promise2,
  promise3,
  promise4
])
.then(([]) => {/* process success data iterable */})
.catch(err => console.log(err));
```

Promise 3 rejects, so this is ignored (in this example).

The reject() call on Promise 3 ends up here, although all Promises are executed.

`Promise.race()` also accepts an iterable, but the output of `Promise.race()` is different. `Promise.race()` executes all provided Promises and returns the first response value that it receives whether this value is a fulfillment or a rejection.

Listing D.49 `Promise.race()`

```
const promise1 = new Promise((resolve, reject) =>
➥setTimeout(resolve, 1000, 'first') );
const promise2 = new Promise((resolve, reject) =>
➥setTimeout(reject, 200, 'second') );

Promise.race([promise1, promise2])
  .then(value => console.log(value))
  .catch(err => console.log(err));
```

The expected response here is second, because the rejection happens before the resolve of promise1 resolves.

Because Promises rely on callbacks, due to their asynchronous nature, you can get into a muddle if several callbacks are nested. Finding yourself in a deeply nested callback structure is often referred to as callback hell. Promises somewhat mitigate this problem by providing a structure and making the asynchronicity explicit.

async/await

Promises have their drawbacks. They're difficult to use in a synchronous manner, and you usually have to wade through a bunch of boilerplate code before getting to the good stuff.

`async/await` functions are there to simplify the behavior of using Promises synchronously. The `await` expression is valid only in an `async` function; if used outside an async function, the code throws a `SyntaxError`. When an `async` function is declared, the definition returns an `AsyncFunction` object. This object operates asynchronously via the JavaScript event loop and returns an implicit Promise as its result. The way the syntax is used and how it allows the code to be structured gives the impression that using `async` functions is much like using synchronous functions.

> **await**
>
> The `await` expression causes the execution of the `async` function to pause and wait until the passed Promise resolves. Then, function execution resumes.
>
> One thing to point out is that `await` is not the same as `Promise.then()`. As `await` pauses the execution, causing code to execute synchronously, it isn't chainable in the same way as `Promise.then()`.

The next listing shows async/await in use.

Listing D.50   async/await

```
function resolvePromiseAfter2s () {
  return new Promise(resolve => setTimeout(() =>
  ➥resolve('done in 2s'), 2000));
}

const resolveAnonPromise1s = () => new Promise(resolve =>
➥setTimeout(() => resolve('done in 1s'), 1000));

async function asyncCall () {
  const result1 = await resolvePromiseAfter2s();
  console.log(result1);
  const result2 = await resolveAnonPromise1s();
  console.log(result2);
}
asyncCall();
```

Defines an async function ⊳

result1 prints 'done in 2s' ⊳

Pauses execution for 2 seconds while the Promise resolves

Pauses execution for 1 second while the Promise resolves

result2 prints 'done in 1s'

Calls the async function. This function pauses the execution for a total of 3 seconds.

You can find more details on async/await at https://developer.mozilla.org/en-US/docs/Web/JavaScript/Reference/Statements/async_function.

Writing modular JavaScript

Someone anonymously tweeted a great quote:

> *The secret to writing large apps in JavaScript is not to write large apps. Write many small apps that can talk to each other.*

This quote makes great sense in a number of ways. Many applications share several features, such as user login and management, comments, reviews, and so on. The easier it is for you to take a feature from one application you've written and drop it into another, the more efficient you'll be, particularly as you'll already have (we hope) tested the feature in isolation, so you know it works.

This is where modular JavaScript comes in. JavaScript applications don't have to be in one never-ending file with functions, logic, and global variables flying loose all over the place. You can contain functionality within enclosed modules.

Closures

A *closure* essentially gives you access to the variables set in a function after the function has completed and returned. Then the closure offers you a way to avoid pushing variables into the global scope. It also offers a degree of protection to the variable and its value, because you can't overwrite it, as you could a global variable.

Sound a bit weird? Look at an example. The following listing demonstrates how you can send a value to a function and later retrieve it.

Listing D.51 Example closure

```
const user = {};
const setAge = function (myAge) {
  return {
    getAge: function () {        Returns a function that
      return myAge;             returns a parameter
    }
  };
};
user.age = setAge(30);     ◁──  Invokes the function, assigns a return
console.log(user.age);          value to the age property of user
console.log(user.age.getAge()); ◁──
                                      Retrieves a value using the
Outputs "Object {getAge: function}"  getAge() method; outputs "30"
```

Here's what's happening. The `getAge()` function is returned as a method of the `setAge()` function. The `getAge()` method has access to the scope in which it was created. So `getAge()`, and `getAge()` alone, has access to the `myAge()` parameter. As you saw earlier in this appendix, when a function is created, it also creates its own scope. Nothing outside this function has access to the scope.

`myAge()` isn't a one-off shared variable. You can call the function again—creating a second new function scope—to set (and get) the age of a second user. You could happily run the following code snippet after the preceding one, creating a second user and giving them a different age.

Listing D.52 Continuing the closure example

```
const usertwo = {};
usertwo.age = setAge(35);         ◁──  Assigns the setAge() function to
console.log(usertwo.age.getAge());      a new user with a different age
console.log(user.age.getAge());   ◁──
                                        Outputs "usertwo's age: 35"

                                        Outputs the original user's age: 30
```

Each user has a different age that isn't aware of or affected by the other. The closure protects the value from outside interference. The important takeaway here is that *the returned method has access to the scope in which it was created.*

This closure approach is a great start, but it has evolved into more useful patterns. For example, take a look at the module pattern.

Module pattern

The *module pattern* extends the closure concept, typically wrapping a collection of code, functions, and functionality into a module. The idea is that the module is self-contained, uses only data that's explicitly passed into it, and reveals only data that it's asked for directly.

Immediately Invoked Function Expression

The module pattern uses what is known as the Immediately Invoked Function Expression (IIFE). The functions we've been using in this book up until now have been function declarations, creating functions that you can call on later in the code. The IIFE creates a function expression and immediately invokes it, typically returning some values and/or methods.

The syntax for an IIFE wraps the function in parentheses and immediately invokes it by using another pair of parentheses (see the bold sections of this code snippet):

```
const myFunc = (function () {        ❶ Assigns IIFE to a variable
  return {
    myString: "a string"
  };                                 ❷ Accesses the returned
})();                                  methods as properties
console.log(myFunc.myString);          of a variable
```

This example is a typical use but not the only one. The IIFE has been assigned to a variable ❶. When you do this, the returned methods from the function become properties of the variable ❷.

This is made possible by using an IIFE. (See the sidebar in this section for a bit more information on IIFE.) Like the basic closure, the module pattern returns functions and variables as properties of the variable it's assigned to. Unlike the basic closure, the module pattern doesn't have to be manually initiated; the module immediately calls itself as soon as it has been defined.

The following listing shows a small but usable example of the module pattern.

Listing D.53   Module pattern example

```
const user = {firstname: "Simon"};        Assigns a module
const userAge = (function () {             to a variable
  let myAge;            Defines the variable
  return {             in the module scope
```

```
    setAge: function (initAge) {
      myAge = initAge;
    },
    getAge: function () {
      return myAge;
    }
  };
})();
userAge.setAge(30);
user.age = userAge.getAge();
console.log(user.age);
```

Defines a method to be returned that can take parameter and modify the module variable

Defines a method to be returned that can access the module variable

Calls the methods set and get for the module variable

Outputs "30"

In this example, the myAge variable exists within the scope of the module and is never directly exposed to the outside. You can interact with the myAge variable only in the ways defined by the exposed methods. In listing D.53, you get and set, but it's possible to modify the age property directly. You can add a happyBirthday() method to the userAge module that will increase the value of myAge by 1 and return the new value. The following listing shows the new parts in bold.

Listing D.54   Adding the happyBirthday method to the module

```
const user = {firstname: "Simon"};
const userAge = (function () {
  let myAge;
  return {
    setAge: function (initAge) {
      myAge = initAge;
    },
    getAge: function () {
      return myAge;
    },
    happyBirthday: function () {
      myAge += 1;
      return myAge;
    }
  };
})();
userAge.setAge(30);
user.age = userAge.getAge();
console.log(user.age);
user.age = userAge.happyBirthday();
console.log(user.age);
user.age = userAge.getAge();
console.log(user.age);
```

New method to increment myAge by 1 and return a new value

Calls the new method and assigns it to user.age

Outputs "31"

The new happyBirthday() method increments the myAge value by 1 and returns the new value. This result is possible because the myAge variable exists in the scope of the module function, as does the returned happyBirthday() function. The new value of myAge continues to persist inside the module scope.

Revealing module pattern

What we've looked at in the module pattern is heading close to the revealing module pattern. The *revealing module pattern* is essentially some syntax that sugarcoats the module pattern. The aim is to make obvious what is exposed as public and what remains private to the module.

TAKING DECLARATIONS OUT OF THE RETURN STATEMENT

Providing a return in the aforementioned way is also a stylistic convention but is again one that helps you and others understand your code when you come back to it after a break. When you use this approach, the return statement contains a list of the functions that you're returning without any of the actual code. The code is declared in functions above the return statement, although within the same module. The following code listing shows an example.

Listing D.55   Revealing module pattern, short example

```
const userAge = (function () {
  let myAge;
  const setAge = function (initAge) {         setAge function has
    myAge = initAge;                           been moved outside
  };                                           the return statement
  return {
    setAge            ◁──    return statement now references the
  };                        setAge function and contains no code
})();
```

You can't see the benefit of this approach in such a small example. We'll look at a longer example soon that will get you part of the way there, but you'll see the benefits when you have a module that runs to several hundred lines of code. As gathering all the variables at the top of the scope makes it obvious which variables are being used, taking the code out of the return statement makes it obvious at a glance which functions are being exposed. If you had a dozen or so functions being returned, each with a dozen or more lines of code, chances are that you wouldn't to be able to see the entire return statement on one screen of code without scrolling.

What's important in the return statement, and what you'll be looking for, is which methods are being exposed. In the context of the return statement, you aren't interested in the inner workings of each method. Separating your code like this makes sense and sets you up to have great, maintainable, and understandable code.

A FULL EXAMPLE OF THE PATTERN

In this section, we'll take a look at a larger example of the pattern, using the userAge module. The following listing shows an example of the revealing module pattern and removing code from the return statement.

Listing D.56   Revealing module pattern, full example

```
const user = {};
const userAge = (function () {
  let myAge;                                  ← ① Has an underscore, as it's
  const setAge = function (initAge) {            never directly exposed
    myAge = initAge;                             outside the module
  };
  const getAge = function () {
    return myAge;
  };
  const addYear = function () {          ② Private function
    myAge += 1;                             that isn't exposed
  };
  const happyBirthday = function () {
    addYear();                           ←
    return myAge;                           Can be called by a public
  };                                     ③ function that's exposed
  return {
    setAge,                     ④ The return statement
    getAge,                        acts as a reference for
    happyBirthday                  exposed methods.
  };
})();
userAge.setAge(30);
user.age = userAge.getAge();                    user.age and
user.age = userAge.happyBirthday();    ←        myAge are now 31.
```

This demonstrates a few interesting things. First, notice that the variable myAge ① itself is never exposed outside the module. The value of the variable is returned by various methods, but the variable itself remains private to the module.

As well as private variables, you can have private functions such as addYear() ② in the listing. Private functions can easily be called by public methods ③.

The return statement ④ is kept nice and simple and is now an at-a-glance reference to the methods being exposed by this module.

Strictly speaking, the order of the functions inside the module isn't important so long as they're above the return statement. Anything below the return statement never runs. When writing large modules, you may find it easier to group related functions. If it suits what you're doing, you could also create a nested module or even a separate module with a public method exposed to the first module so that they can talk to each other.

Remember the quote from the beginning of this section:

> *The secret to writing large apps in JavaScript is not to write large apps. Write many small apps that can talk to each other.*

This quote applies not only to large-scale applications, but also to modules and functions. If you can keep your modules and functions small and to the point, you're on your way to writing great code.

Classes

An extension to the modularity of JavaScript is the class syntax introduced with ES2015. Classes are syntactic sugar over JavaScript's prototypal inheritance model, but they work as you mostly expect classes to work, if you have object-oriented programming (OOP) experience.

Note, though, that JavaScript classes, at least up until ES2017, have public properties and public and static methods. Private and protected class visibility are due to be added to the specification at some undetermined point. They do have an inheritance hierarchy that uses the `extends` keyword, but there are no interfaces. Accessing functions from a parent involves the `super` function, and initialization uses a constructor function.

We're not going to cover the whys and wherefores of OOP, which is an exercise best left to you. (See https://developer.mozilla.org/en-US/docs/Web/JavaScript/Reference/Classes for starters.) Here, we'll cover the basics of the syntax.

Listing D.57   Class syntax examples

```
// Parent class
class Rectangle {
  width = 0;
  height = 0;

  constructor (width, height) {
    this.width = width;
    this.height = height;
  }

  get area() {
    return this.determineArea();
  }

  determineArea () {
    return this.width * this.height;
  }
    }

// Child class of Rectangle
class Square extends Rectangle {
  constructor (side) {
    super(side, side);
  }
}

const square = new Square(10);
console.log(`Square area: ${square.area()}`);
// prints Square area: 100;
```

There's plenty more to classes than this, and in this book, you'll have used them mostly in Angular as TypeScript classes to build components.

Functional programming concepts

Functional programming as a concept has been around longer than object orientation. For a long time, the concept was relegated to academia, because some of the languages used have steep learning curves, which raised the barrier to entry artificially high. Who wants to spend time learning obscure concepts only to be confused by the syntax when all you want to do is get information from the users of your site and push it into a database?

Recently, though, all mainstream object-oriented languages have been pulling in and integrating concepts of functional programming languages, because these concepts provide surety of data, reduce cognitive load, and allow for composition of functionality.

Concepts that you can apply to your JavaScript work include immutability, purity, declarative style, and function composition.

A bunch of other stuff may or may not be available, depending on which version of the language you're using. We'll cover these concepts one at a time.

IMMUTABILITY

Although immutability isn't strictly enforced at a language level, through a little bit of forward planning and some rigor, you can implement it simply and effectively. Be aware that npm packages are available to help, such as immutable.js from Facebook (https://github.com/facebook/immutable-js).

The point is that data/state that you're operating on isn't mutated. Mutation is an in-place operation and can be the cause of hard-to-track bugs.

The concept as it applies to JavaScript means that the state isn't altered; it's copied, transformed, and assigned to an alternative variable. This concept can also be applied to collections of data and objects; although slightly more rigor needs to be applied, the outcome should be the same.

For simple scalar-type variables, applying immutability is simple: declare it with `const`. That way, the JavaScript execution context can't overwrite the variable, and it throws an exception if you try by mistake. We covered this topic earlier.

For object types (`Arrays`, `Objects`, `Maps`, `Sets`), declaring with `const` isn't massively helpful. The issue is that `const` creates a reference to the object being created. As it's a reference, the data within the object can be altered. This is where the rigor comes in. Instead of using looping constructs like `for` to manipulate the collection directly, use the iterators provided by that type; they're prototype methods and should be available in both the browser and in Node.js. For functionality you want that isn't supplied, there are always libraries such as Lodash.js and Ramda.js.

Listing D.58   Examples of applying the concept of immutability

Uses the map function to iterate over the names
in the collection and assign to a new variable

Uses the filter function to remove
those items from the collection
that fail the given criteria

A simple collection of four
names assigned to const

```
const names = ['s holmes', 'c harber', 'l skywalker', 'h solo'];
const uppercasedNames = names.map(name => name.toUpperCase());
const shortNames = names.filter(name => name.length < 10);
const values = [1, 2, 3, 4, 5, 6, 7, 8, 9];
const total = values.reduce((value, acc) => acc + value, 0);
const product = values.reduceRight((value, acc) => value * acc, 1);
```

Reduces the values to a single total
value by summing them together

Reduces from the right,
creating a product of the
values in the provided list

A new array of integers

PURITY

Pure functions are functions that don't exhibit side effects or use data that hasn't been supplied. A side effect is a change to the program state that's external to the function and differs from the return value of the function. Typical side effects include changing global variables' values, sending text to the screen, and printing. Some of these side effects are unwanted and harmful, but some are unavoidable and necessary. As JavaScript programmers, we should strive to reduce side effects as much as possible. This way, program state is predictable and therefore easy to reason about if bugs occur.

Functions should operate only on the data that they've been provided. External data, such as global window state, shouldn't be changed unless absolutely necessary, and even then, only in a controlled manner by a dedicated function. If your code is reliant on global state, that's a bad code smell that you should investigate.

Pure functions are predictable, and more often than not, they exhibit a property called *idempotency*: given a set of inputs, the expected output of a function is always the same.

A simple, somewhat contrived example is a function that adds two numbers together:

```
const sum = (a, b) => a + b;
```

If you supply 1 and 2 to such a function, you always expect 3 to be returned.

What if this function also relied on a value that was maintained outside the function—such as const sumWithGlobal = (a, b) => a + b + window.c—and that this value (window.c) was generally 0 but sometimes 1 or maybe something random like a string? What would you expect in that instance when you supplied 1 and 2 as function arguments? You couldn't rely on the result to be 3; it might be 4 or something wildly different or even an exception.

This example is a simple one, but what if it involved thousands of lines of code? As you can see, this makes the size of the issue magnitudes larger. Try to keep functions pure; being able to predict outputs makes everyone's lives easier.

DECLARATIVE CODE STYLE

We don't want to speak for everybody, but we guess that most code you write is imperative in style. You set out what you want the computer to do line by line, much like a recipe. You might overlay this code with notes of object orientation, but it's still a recipe. There's nothing wrong with this approach; it works and mostly works well.

With declarative programming, you state the logic of what you're looking to achieve but leave the execution details up to the computer. In essence, you don't care how the outcome of your program is achieved so long as it's achieved.

In this style of JavaScript, code should favor the following:

- Array iterators over `for` loops
- Recursion
- Partially applicable and composable functions
- Ternary operators over `if` statements to ensure return values
- Avoiding changing state, mutating data, and side effects

We stress "should" because JavaScript doesn't support things like tail call recursion due to an internal stack frame limit. Also, partial application and function composition are things that you build into your code, not things that are natively supported.

Listing D.59 Declarative programming example

```
const compose = (...fns) => fns.reduce((f, g) => (...args) =>
➡ f(g(...args)));          ⟵————————————  Creates a compose function
const url = '...';
const parse = item => JSON.parse(item);
const fetchDataFromApi = url => data => fetch(url, data);
const convertData = item => item.toLowerCase();
const convert = (...data) => data.map(item => convertData(item));

const items = [...dataList];          ⟵———————  Creates a list of items

const getProcessableList = compose(
  parse,
  fetchDataFromApi(url),
  convert                   | Composes functions
);                   ⟵———————| together
                                              | Executes the composed
const list = getProcessableList(items);   ⟵——| functions by passing in data
```

In this code, the important part is the instruction to `getProcessableList()`. All the other elements are boilerplate required to present this contrived example. The point is that the intention is declared, but how it gets done isn't.

PARTIAL APPLICATION AND FUNCTION COMPOSITION

Pure functions provide predictable outcomes. If you can predict outcomes, you can combine your functions in innovate ways. Smaller functions can become parts of larger functions, and you don't have to worry about intermediary results. To help you understand function composition, we'll discuss partial application.

Partial application, or *currying*, means applying fewer arguments to a function than it requires, each time returning a new function and therefore holding off completing execution until all arguments are available.

Unfortunately, JavaScript has no native support for currying, but through use of syntax, you can emulate this feature. The following listing shows how.

Listing D.60   Currying example

```
const simpleSum (x, y) => x + y;          ◁──────── Simple standard noncurried function

const curriedSum x => y => x + y;          ◁──────── Curried equivalent

const simpleResult = simpleSum(2, 3);      ◁┐
                                            ├── All arguments collected
const curriedResult = curriedSum(2)(3);    ◁┘   together and applied at once

                                               Currying requires multiple
const intermediary = curriedSum(2);            function calls.
const finalCurried = intermediary(3);      ◁┐
                                            └── Applies the last required argument
                                               to return the expected value of 5
```

Here, the intermediary call applies 2 to the x argument, returning a function that requires another argument to create a result (y => 2 + y).

Currying isn't special. All you're doing is taking a multiargument function and returning a new function after the application of a single argument.

With this knowledge in place, you can look at composition. *Composition* is combining multiple functions to create complex flows. This technique allows you to avoid code that uses looping code structures that read like streams of instructions. Instead, you abstract away the complexity of the processing by combining the operations into simple, descriptive functions.

To work properly, the functions need to be small and pure, free of side effects. The functions that are being composed need the inputs and outputs to match, so applying currying is helpful but not mandatory. Having the inputs and outputs match means that a function that takes an integer shouldn't be composed with a function that takes a string. Although input mismatch is technically acceptable in JavaScript due to the language's ability to implicitly typecast, it can be a source of bugs that may be difficult to track down.

A simple way to look at this is an example. The next listing takes the `curriedSum()` function from the preceding listing.

Listing D.61   Simple composition

```
const add = x => y => x + y;                    ←——————— Add function
const multiplyFactor = fac => num => num * fac;  ←——┐
                                                     │  Simple curryable
const multiplyBy10 = multiplyFactor(10);            │  factor function

const result = multiplyBy10(add(2)(5));   ←——————┐
                                                  │  Composes the functions
                                                  │  to return a result of 100
```

This example is simple and contrived but illustrates the point.

Some libraries provide a function called `compose` that allows you to handle composition in a more elegant way, although this function isn't difficult to build by hand. The basic principle is the simple application of the mathematical formula $g(f(x))$.

Listing D.62   compose function

```
const compose = (g, f) => x => g(f(x));   ←——————— Simple compose function

const composedCompute = compose(   ←——————— Uses the composition function
  multiplyBy10,
  add(2)
);

const result = composedCompute(5);   ←——————— Obtains the result
```

Beyond these small examples, composition is a tool that can make your code cleaner and easier to understand.

Final thoughts

JavaScript is a forgiving language, which makes it easy to learn, but it's also easy to pick up bad habits. If you make a little mistake in your code, JavaScript sometimes thinks, "Well, I think you meant to do this, so that's what I'll go with." Sometimes it's right, and sometimes it's wrong. This isn't acceptable for good code, so it's important to be specific about what your code should do, and you should try to write your code in the way that the JavaScript interpreter sees it.

A key to understanding the power of JavaScript is understanding scope: global scope and function scope and lexical scope. There are no other types of scope in JavaScript. You want to avoid using the global scope as much as possible, and when you do use it, try to do it in a clean and contained way. Scope inheritance cascades down from the global scope, so it can be difficult to maintain if you're not careful.

JSON is born of JavaScript but isn't JavaScript; it's a language-independent data exchange format. JSON contains no JavaScript code and can quite happily be passed between a PHP server and a .NET server; JavaScript isn't required to interpret JSON.

Callbacks are vital to running successful Node applications, because they allow the central process to effectively delegate tasks that could hold it up. To put it another way, callbacks enable you to use sequential synchronous operations in an asynchronous environment. But callbacks aren't without their problems. It's easy to end up in callback hell, having multiple nested callbacks with overlapping inherited scopes making your code hard to read, test, debug, and maintain. Fortunately, you can use named callbacks to address this problem on all levels so long as you remember that named callbacks don't inherit scope like their inline anonymous counterparts.

Closures and module patterns provide ways to write code that's self-contained and reusable between projects. A closure enables you to define a set of functions and variables within its own distinct scope, which you can come back to and interact with through the exposed methods. This leads to the revealing module pattern, which is convention-driven to draw specific lines between what's private and what's public. Modules are perfect for writing self-contained pieces of code that can interact well with other code, not tripping up over any scope clashes.

Recent changes to the JavaScript specification, such as the addition of class syntax and greater emphasis on functional programming, flesh out the available toolkit to suit whichever style of code you want to use.

A great many other additions to the JavaScript specification aren't covered here: the rest operator, the spread operator, and generators, to name a few. It's an exciting time to be working with the JavaScript language.

index

RELATED MANNING TITLES

Angular in Action
by Jeremy Wilken

    ISBN: 9781617293313
    320 pages, $44.99
    March 2018

Angular Development with Typescript,
Second Edition
by Yakov Fain and Anton Moiseev

    ISBN: 9781617295348
    560 pages, $49.99
    December 2018

Testing Angular Applications
by Jesse Palmer, Corinna Cohn, Michael
    Giambalvo, Craig Nishina

    ISBN: 9781617293641
    240 pages, $44.99
    November 2018

MongoDB in Action, Second Edition
Covers MongoDB version 3.0
by Kyle Banker, Peter Bakkum, Shaun Verch,
    Douglas Garrett, and Tim Hawkins

    ISBN: 9781617291609
    480 pages, $44.99
    March 2016

For ordering information go to www.manning.com